McDonald's Collectibles

Illustrated Price Guide

Formerly titled: **McCOLLECTING**,
The Illustrated Price Guide to McDonald's Collectibles

by

Gary Henriques and Audre Du Vall

McDonald's Collectibles
Illustrated Price Guide

By Gary Henriques and Audre Du Vall

Formerly titled: **McCOLLECTING**, *The Illustrated Price Guide to McDonald's Collectibles.*

Published by: Piedmont Publishing
                     Post Office Box 730218
                     San Jose, CA 95173-0218

First Printing 1992
Second Printing 1993
Third Printing 1994
Printed in the United States of America

Library of Congress Cataloging in Publication Data:
Gary Henriques and Audre Du Vall
McDonald's Collectibles, Illustrated Price Guide/by
        Gary Henriques and Audre Du Vall.-First ed.
Includes Index.
1. United States-Collectors and collecting-Catalogs.
Library of Congress Catalog Number: 91-91553
ISBN 0-9631785-6-3: $24.95 Softcover

Table of Contents

FLINTSTONES, BARNEY	-	HANNA-BARBERA PROD. INC.
BOOBER, BULLDOZER, COTTERPIN, DOOZER, FOZZIE, FRAGGLE ROCK, GOBO, GONZO, KERMIT, MOKEY, MUPPET BABIES, THE GREAT MUPPET CAPER, WEMBLY, CHARACTER DESIGNS:SNOOPY, CHARLIE BROWN, LUCY, LINUS, MISS PIGGY	-	HENSON ASSOC. INC.
THE 1982 WORLD'S FAIR	-	KNOXVILLE, TENN
L.A. OLYMPIC COMMITTEE	-	L.A. OLYMPIC COMMITTEE
LEGO, LEGODUPLO	-	LEGO GROUP
MATCHBOX	-	LESNEY PROD. CORP. LTD. ENG.
RAGGEDY ANN AND ANDY	-	MACMILLAN INC
MATCHBOX	-	MATCHBOX INTERNATIONAL
BARBIE, HOT WHEELS, JUMPBUSTER	-	MATTEL INC
NASCAR TRADING CARDS	-	JR MAXX, CHARLOTTE, NC
FRANKENTYKE, VINNIE STOKER, CLEOPATRA	-	NBC
GOOMBA, KOOPA, LUIGI, SUPER MARIO BROS 3, SUPER MARIO	-	NINTENDO OF AMERICA INC
KIRK, KLINGONS, MCCOY, SPOCK, STAR TREK	-	PARAMOUNT PICTURES CORP
ARCHIES, THE NEW ARCHIES, DINO, JUGHEAD, REGGIE	-	PRIME DESIGNS LTD
PLAYMOBILE, CHARACTERS	-	SCHAPER MFG. CO.
STOMPER, BIGFOOT		DIV. KUSAN INC.
PAAS	-	SCHERING-PLOUGH HEALTHCARE PRODUCTS INC.
COMMANDRONS, DRAGONOIDS, ELEPHOIDS, OCTOPOID, POPOIDS, SCORPOID, POPPIN	-	TOMY
HOOK, CHARACTER DESIGNS: RUFIO, CAPTAIN HOOK, PETER PAN	-	TRI-STAR PICTURES INC.
TOM AND JERRY	-	TURNER ENTERTAINMENT CO.
THE FRIENDLY SKIES	-	UNITED AIRLINES
GARFIELD, ODIE, POOKY	-	UNITED FEATURE SYNDICATE INC
FIEVEL	-	UNIVERSAL CITY STUDIOS
NA, ES AND DESIGNS: ACME ACRES, TAS-FLASH, BUGS, DAFFY DUCK, DUKES OF HAZZARD, GOGO DODO, HAMPTON, LOONEY TUNES, TAS-FLASH, TINY TOON, TOONSTERS, SUPER BUGS, WONDER PIG, BAT DUCK.	-	WARNER BROS. INC

MAURICE (MAC) AND DICK McDONALD
WITH THE MULTI-MIXER MACHINE.
(FAR RIGHT: ENGINEER, IRA ROWE.)

THE   BEGINNING

RAY KROC

Customers who ordered his Multi-mixers (milkshake-making machines),frequently told Ray Kroc about a restaurant where not the usual *one*, but *eight* machines, were kept in constant service. Finally, Ray's curiosity demanded that he visit this legendary site. Ray found the McDONALD brothers, Dick and Mac, operating a remarkably efficient "Fast-Food" Drive-Up restaurant. Dazzled by the smoothness and quality of this operation, he envisioned such restaurants all over the country. The McDONALD brothers,preparing for retirement, weren't enthusiastic about expanding the business but they finally agreed to sell Ray Kroc the rights to use their food processes, the architectural design (the "Golden Arches") of the restaurant, and their name. Through diligent hard work and his unshakable adherence to " Quality, Cleanliness, Service and Value ", Ray Kroc piloted this restaurant chain to its present day prominence.
(For further reading about Ray Kroc and McDonald's see: "*Grinding It Out*" by Ray Kroc with Robert Anderson.)

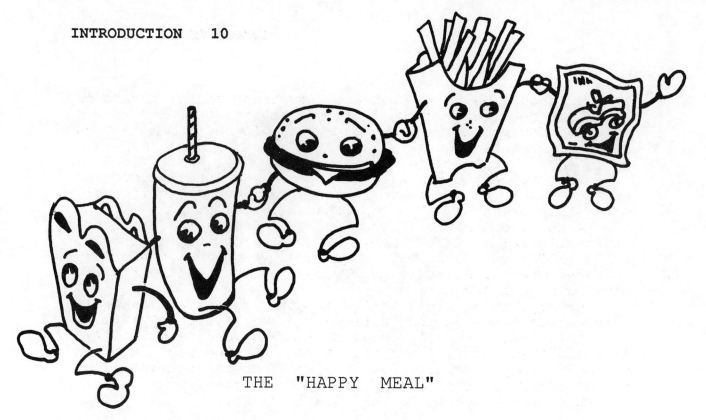

THE "HAPPY MEAL"

In 1977, Dick Brams, McDonald's regional manager in St. Louis, conceived the idea of a *special* meal for children. He contacted two local advertising agencies, Stolz in St.Louis, and Bernstein / Rein & Boasberg in Kansas City, and asked them to design the concept. Stolz offered the *"Fun To Go"* meal and BRB suggested the *"Happy Meal"*. Both programs were tested and the "Happy Meal" was selected.

The first meal cartons were round-topped, like a lunch box, but these were dropped in favor of a more "stackable" design. "CIRCUS WAGON" , introduced in June, 1979, was the first National "Happy Meal".

Children of all ages enjoy the Happy Meal and the many clever premiums which are packaged in a wide assortment of containers, such as colorful pails with lids and shovels for beach or sandbox use, pumpkin-shaped pails, to be carried by Halloween "trick- or-treaters", and snap-together, floating boat and train shapes. Colorful paper cartons, surfaced with games, puzzles and other activities, are frequently used and many of these may be punched out and reshaped to create play scenes appropriate to the premium toy.

Due to some early difficulties, close attention is paid to creating toys which are safe for all ages. Many times a special "Under 3 Yrs" version is made, which is soft with no small or moving parts. These are not offered with every Happy Meal and when available, are scarcer than the toys for older children.

It should be noted that the copyright notice marked on a premium does not always indicate the year in which it was released for promotion. Items may be offered in more than one year or promotion.

Some markets did not choose to use Nationally offered premiums and preferred to create their own "Generic" or- "Regional" premiums. ("Olympic Sports", 1988).
Also, items may be tested and then changed before being Nationally released, or they may be withdrawn entirely. ("ZOO FACE" was changed.) Occasionally, offerings on East and West coasts, differ. ("Hot Wheels", 1986, used different models on each coast.)
Rarely, items are released in other countries with only a *few* appearances in the United States. ("Airplane" 1982).
Some very "early" special meal promotions were:the "*All American Meal*" (1961), and the "Mayor McCheese Bag", a brown and gold, #6 paper sack (1975). Dubbed "*The Honorary Meal of McDONALDLAND*" , it contained the typical foods and a "McDONALDLAND Citizenship Wall Certificate".

Happy Meals are listed by the year herein, beginning with the 1977 tests to the end of 1991, and will be updated annually. A handy HAPPY MEAL CHECK LIST, located at the back of the book, will help you to keep track of your collecting progress.

THE BOOK:

Audre turned away from the computer screen as he settled his large, powerful frame into a suddenly small chair opposite her desk. He sipped his coffee; it was "break time", and they often shared a few minutes, chatting.

Gary Henriques is very knowledgeable about several categories of collecting, ranging from Daisy Air Rifles to diamonds. At one time he had his own shop, selling coins, minerals and stamps. Gary spends most of his lunch periods visiting local thrift Shops, hoping for an exciting "find". On weekends, he checks flea Markets and garage sales. As a boy of eight years, when he earned a bit of money, he bought a good coin or stamp and saved it. I guess that's how it is when you're a real Collector.

Gary lives in a house on the California ranch where he was born, with his wife, son and daughter, and several pets. His storage sheds are stuffed with his collections.

"You know," he said, "one of these days McDonald's toys and other premiums are going to be very *hot* collectibles!"

"Really? Why do you say that?" She wondered.

"Well, McDonald's items have all the right qualities: the millions of premiums are widely distributed and they're not expensive,so millions of people have a chance to collect them. They are attractive, well made, and some premiums are tied in with Coca-Cola and Disney, popular collectibles in their own right. Easy recognition, availability,inexpensive, and *fun* to collect, that's what it takes to make a good collectible. I realized this as I watched my young children playing with McDonald's toys, around 1976.

"I believe that McDonald's items will some day be as popular a collectible as stamps, coins and Coca-Cola items, and that it will surpass these and other collectibles as an investment."

"Wow!" Audre sighed, thinking she would stop for a HAPPY MEAL on her way home tonight.

A wistful expression crossed his face;

"What I'd like to do, is to make a book about all the different McDonald's items that people collect..only I don't have the least idea of how to go about it."

Audre DuVall brightened immediately. Native to New York State, she studied Commercial Art and Illustration at Rochester Institute of Technology, then later graduated with a B.A. degree in Graphic Design and Illustration, from San Jose State University, in California. Always looking for an opportunity to exercise her education, she chirped,

"I can do that! That's right in my line and I'd love to work with you on a project like that.I think that McDonald's is the "Disney" of "Fast-Foods", and I'm very much impressed with their obvious dedication to all that is happy,wholesome and good for children."

Near the Christmas Holidays in 1990, they continued to toy with the idea of collaborating on a book, and what each could contribute to the effort. At just the right moment, Audre stumbled upon a book titled "*The Self Publishing Manual*", by Dan Poynter, which outlined the step-by-step process of creating a book. With this as their guide, in February 1991, Audre bought some word-processing software and they embarked on the great adventure.

Gary was to be the "producer", bearing the publication costs and, relying on his years of experience, would locate and acquire items and estimate reasonable prices for them. He would also be in charge of Public Relations and Shows. They shared research tasks.

It was Audre's task to design the book and cover, do the "words" and photography, find a printer, and do the necessary mechanical operations to assemble it all.

After a few months into the project,they were staggered to learn of the tremendous variety of potential collectibles produced by McDonald's. What had appeared to be a small hill became a mountain as it got nearer. The task was complicated by the fact that in the "early days" of McDonald's no effort was made to document toys or premiums and it was often left to the franchiser to develop his own local premiums.

Besieged by many collectors for information,the manager of McDonald's Archives, adding to her already busy schedule, has undertaken to document the "HAPPY MEALS" premiums. This listing is available to the public. (Appendix: Resources.)

At present, it seems that the best way to learn about the "Early Days", is to contact those people who were far-sighted enough to recognize the potential and put away choice items. Any reader who is willing to share their knowledge about early items,local or international premiums, will be listed as a "Contributor" in subsequent issues. Pictures of private collections will be given credit as is done in a museum.

Gary's collector tips:
     McDonald's items are *Happy* collectibles. My spirit always lifts when I walk into a room with such displays. Collect the things *you* enjoy! If you concentrate on a few specific areas,you will find it easier to make an impressive collection, than if you try to get some of everything.

     Items may be removed from packages for mounting in interesting displays. These should be kept in dry locations, out of direct sunlight, which fades and deteriorates them, and covered with glass or plastic, if possible, to keep them dust-free and safe from accidental damage.

     Items not on display, may be stored in sealable plastic bags and labeled. I keep file cards on each item, with the quantity marked in pencil (to allow for easy changes), where I acquired it, and how much it cost. I also store my extra items in heavy duty storage boxes, safe from rain and water damage.

     Try to collect items, still in their original packages (MINT), because they have much greater value this way,and so are easier to trade. If items are not packaged, look for bright, even colors, with no chips or scratches. Acquire duplicates, especially when "Regional" premiums appear. You can then trade these scarcer items with collectors in other areas, who have their own Regional premiums.
("Regional" premiums are offered only in *certain* localities rather than- Nationally.)

     Be aware that toys offered for children: "Under 3 Yrs" are fewer and so more valuable. Many stores have four times as many "regular" toys as the "Under 3 Yrs" variety.

     Paper goods, like tray liners, bags and boxes are made to be discarded, so those in perfect condition will quickly become scarce and eventually valuable.

     Good places to find older items are "Toy Shows", "Flea-Markets", "garage sales", "thrift shops", and by trading with other collectors along the network. Read collector magazines, papers and newsletters. (We have listed some collector clubs and newsletters in the "Resources" section.)

     Prices suggested here are for use as a guide only. Good "deals" may still be found at local sales and shows.
     Enjoy the fun and nostalgia of collecting McDonald's!

    We offer you this book as an Overview of the whole
gamut of collectible McDonald's items. At the present time,
we do not have photographs of every item listed nor has our
research covered every item ever made. We are constantly
adding to our information and intend to update this book
every year, eventually including premiums from other areas
of the world also. We sincerely hope that you will enjoy
this book and find it useful and that it will add a large
measure of happiness to your life.

Gary A. Henriques

D. Audre Du Vall

Piedmont Publishing * San Jose * California

POSTCARDS:Miscellaneous

(McDonaldland Gang) (C) McDonald's System
Inc. 1978

THE CAST OF McDONALDLAND CHARACTERS

Most sets of toys and glasses feature six
main McDONALDLAND characters: RONALD McDONALD, GRIMACE,
HAMBURGLAR, CAPTAIN CROOK, BIG MAC and MAYOR McCHEESE.
In 1980, the "line-up" changed to include a feminine
influence, BIRDIE, The EARLYBIRD. Present toy sets usually
include RONALD McDONALD, GRIMACE, HAMBURGLAR and BIRDIE,
with additions of BIG MAC or FRY GUYS.Characters are listed
according to their appearance on the McDONALDLAND stage.

RONALD McDONALD

RONALD McDONALD (Also referred to as RMCD, to save space). A tall, slim, clown with a red rubber-ball nose, laughing clown mouth, and a wild mop of wooly, red hair. His costume is a golden yellow jumper with a large, red zipper, three patch pockets of different sizes,decorated with the ARCHES logo and a white collar.
The jumper is worn over a red and white striped leotard,with long sleeves and leggings.His shoes are red and very big.

RONALD first appeared in 1963,in a McDonald's restaurant,in Washington, DC. He was introduced to the nation, playing the world's largest drum, in Macy's 1966 Thanksgiving Day Parade. Accompanying him was an All-American High School Band, composed of two of the best musicians from each state.

In 1967, RONALD became the official spokesman for McDonald's company, with his appearance in a commercial on national TV. He is a very familiar figure in American and international homes,in 21 languages. In Japan (because of their difficulty with the "R" sound,he is called "DONALD McDONALD" and in China,"McDONALD Suk-Suk" (Uncle McDONALD).

Here in America and in other countries, RONALD participates in many charity and children's events at hospitals, schools, and openings of McDonald's restaurants. Hamburgers are his favorite food and children are his favorite people.

In 1984, RONALD McDONALD's Children's Charities was established in memory of Ray Kroc, dedicated to helping children in need.A cornerstone of this program is the RONALD McDONALD HOUSE, which provides living accommodations for parents near their hospitalized children. There are over 127 RONALD McDONALD HOUSES throughout the world.

RONALD McDONALD Outdoor Figure: "Miscellaneous" *by Courtesy of L. & J. Anderson "COLLECTIBLES", Morgan Hill, CA*

The first characters to join RONALD McDONALD in McDONALDLAND, were the HAMBURGLAR, GRIMACE, MAYOR McCHEESE, CAPTAIN CROOK and the PROFESSOR.

The HAMBURGLAR loves 'burgers and plots to steal them from others. His attempts are always thwarted by RONALD but his leanings have resulted in a costume of black and white, prison stripes, with long pants and sleeves. He also wears a wide-brimmed black (Spanish type) hat and a long, black cape, lined in yellow. This dark outfit is enlivened by an absurdly large necktie with yellow dots (Sometimes these dots are detailed as hamburgers).Yellow and black shoes and a black eyemask complete his costume.
This character has undergone a remarkable devolution. He began as a middle-aged man with a cartoon face,big nose and ears, prominent front teeth, and long, straggly gray hair. Through time, he has changed into a mischievous looking tyke, about five years old, with boyishly cut red hair.

GRIMACE, RONALD's best friend,is a large, fuzzy,purple, eggplant-shaped creature with flipper-like hands and feet, and a wistful expression. GRIMACE has also experienced some design changes; he was once called the "Evil GRIMACE" and an early poster shows him with *four* arms.

MAYOR McCHEESE, the Mayor of McDONALDLAND, wears yellow and purple striped trousers, a yellow vest, a formal, floor-length. red coat, and white spats on his shoes. On his lapel is a white carnation. A broad, purple sash crosses his chest and ties at his left side. He carries a "Pince-Nez" (glasses without ear-pieces) on a string. A small, purple top-hat crowns his huge cheeseburger head.

CAPTAIN CROOK is a well-dressed, kindly pirate. His costume includes a fancy, red, frock-coat with gold fringed epaulets on the shoulders, a yellow, patterned vest, white lace ruffles at his throat and cuffs, and a long, orange neck scarf.His tan trousers are tucked into brown boots with folded over cuffs. In his right hand, he holds a flat-bladed sword. His hair and long mustache are black. He wears one golden loop earring and a purple Napoleonic Tricorn hat with a large monogrammed "C" on the front.

The PROFESSOR may have been replaced by Big Mac as the sixth character, on sets of glasses. He has a large, grey mustache and beard and wears wire-rimmed glasses with a second pair of glasses perched atop his head. Over his clothes, he wears a long, white laboratory coat, its two large pockets stuffed with various gadgets. There is a scarf around his neck.

BIG MAC is a policeman, in blue pants, high black boots and a belted, knee-length, blue coat with a star badge. His huge double-cheeseburger head is topped by a tiny, blue "Bobby's" hat. A whistle hangs on a cord around his neck.

HAPPY MEAL GUYS appeared around 1979, when Happy Meals were introduced to the national menu. They represent the foods that make up a Happy Meal; soft drink, fries and a 'burger, and usually travel together.

BIRDIE, THE EARLY BIRD entered the scene in 1980, as the first feminine McDONALDLAND character. She is bright yellow, wears her hair in ribbon-tied braids and dresses as a Barnstormer Pilot, with a helmet, goggles and a long neck-scarf. Wide-eyed and energetic, she loves to rise early in the morning.

CHICKEN McNUGGETS, small, round, tan, objects with faces, arrived around 1983-1984. They wear various costumes.

FRY GUYS, FRY GIRLS, FRY KIDS. These are brightly colored, amusing, mop-headed creatures with eyes, legs and feet. As premiums, they were provided with interchangeable costume pieces. They have also been seen as passengers on a river raft, and as helicopter pilots. Their original aspect was slightly more frightening than it is now and they were called "Goblins" ("Goblin-up-fries").

COSMIC! joined the cast in 1988. He is a six-armed hybrid, space creature: part turtle, part space-vehicle, which he wears like a shell. He appeared in the Happy Meal: "COSMIC! CRAYOLA", in April 1988.

UNCLE O'GRIMACY is GRIMACE's fuzzy, green, Irish uncle. Charming but seldom seen.

McDONALD"S HISTORY LISTING

Reprinted with permission of McDONALD"S CORPORATION
Customer and Community Relations Department
Supervisor, Beth Petersohn.

1948 - Dick and Mac McDONALD opened the first McDonald's
          drive-in restaurant in December, in San Bernardino
          California.

1954 - Ray A.Kroc, a Multimixer salesman from Oak Park,
          Illinois, visited Dick and Mac's San Bernardino
          McDonald's. His curiosity was initially aroused by
          the large number of multimixers they were buying.

      - Ray Kroc became franchising agent for the McDONALD
          brothers.

1955 - April 15, Ray Kroc opened his first McDonald's in
          Des Plaines, Illinois.

      - In July,the second McDonald's was opened in Fresno
          California.

      - Total sales for the company were $235,000.

      - A little hamburger man called "Speedee" was the
          company symbol.

1956 - McDonald's added 12 restaurants in Chicago,
          Skokie, Waukegan, Joliet and Urbana, Illinois;
          Hammond, Indiana; Los Angeles, Torrance and
          Reseda, California.

      - Ray Kroc hired Fred Turner to head up operations.

1957 - McDonald's became known for the motto "QSC" for
          Quality, Service and Cleanliness.

      - Ray Kroc personally delivered free hamburgers to
          Salvation Army workers in Chicago at Christmas.
      - At year's end, sales for McDonald's 40 restaurants
          totaled $4,446,000.

1958 -   McDonald's sold its 100 millionth hamburger.

     -   Fred Turner became Vice President of the company.

     -   McDonald's annual sales skyrocketed 151% over the previous year to $11,231.059.

1959 -   100th restaurant opened in Fond Du Lac, Wisconsin

     -   In total, a record 67 restaurants opened.

     -   McDonald's began billboard advertising.

1960 -   "Look For The Golden Arches", McDonald's first jingle, played on radio.

     -   The company celebrated its 5th anniversary, opening its 200th restaurant in Knoxville, Tennessee and selling its 400 millionth hamburger.

     -   Annual sales totaled $38 million.

1961 -   Ad campaign cheered on the "All American Meal" - a hamburger, fries and a milkshake.

     -   Ray Kroc bought out the McDONALD brothers for $2.7 million.

     -   hamburger University opened in the basement of the Elk Grove Village, Illinois restaurant and granted Bachelor of Hamburgerology degrees to the first graduating class.

     -   The United States Under Secretary of Agriculture, Charles Murphy, ate the 500 millionth McDonald's hamburger.

1962 -   "Speeded" was replaced by the Golden Arches - a modernistic M, as the company's logo.

     -   "Go For Goodness at McDonald's" a new advertising slogan was introduced.

     -   McDonald's sold its 700 millionth hamburger

1962   Magazine advertising was placed nationally for
          the first time in **LIFE** magazine.

1963 -   The 500th McDonald's restaurant opened in Toledo,
          Ohio.

      -   Hamburger University graduated its 500th student.

      -   The one billionth McDonald's hamburger was served
          on the Art Linkletter Show.

      -   RONALD McDONALD made his debut in Washington, D.C.

      -   Filet-O-Fish sandwich became the first new menu
          addition since the original menu.

1964 -   At year's end there were 657 restaurants.

      -   The company's gross sales hit $130 million.

1965 -   McDonald's celebrated its 10th anniversary with
          the first public stock offering at $22.50 per
          share.

      -   Average annual sales for a McDonald's restaurant
          were $249,000.

      -   First home television network advertising began.

1966 -   RONALD McDONALD made his first national TV
          appearance in Macy's Thanksgiving Day Parade
          with the world's largest drum.

      -   In April, McDonald's stock had its first split,
          3 for 2.

      -   In May, McDonald's held its first annual public
          shareholder's meeting.

      -   On July 5, McDonald's was listed on the New York
          Stock Exchange, with the ticker symbol - MCD.

      -   McDonald's exceeded $200 million in sales and sold
          its two billionth hamburger.

1966   McDonald's in Huntsville, Alabama became the first
        restaurant with inside seating.

1967 - McDonald's All-American High School Band was
        organized.

      - Indoor seating was introduced.

      - The first McDonald's restaurants opened in Canada
        and Puerto Rico.

      - Operators' National Advertising Fund (OPNAD)
        began operation.

1968 - The Big Mac and Hot Apple Pie were added to the
        menu.

      - The 1,000th store opened in Des Plaines, Illinois.

      - McDonald's opened in Hawaii.

      - Average annual sales for McDonald's restaurants
        open at least 13 months were $333,000.

      - Class number 81 was the first to graduate from the
        new Hamburger University building.

1969 - The International division was formed.

      - McDonald's was serving 3.5 million hamburgers per
        day.

      - The "Billions Served" sign changed to "Five
        Billion".

      - A new McDonald's building design was introduced to
        replace the "red and white" design.

      - McDonald's was listed on the Midwest and Pacific
        stock exchanges.

      - Christmas gift certificates were introduced.

1970 - "You Deserve A Break Today-So Get Up And Get Away To McDonald's" was the new advertising campaign.

- The 1,500th restaurant opened in Concord, New Hampshire.

- A McDonald's in Bloomington, Minnesota, was the first to reach $1 million in annual sales.

- McDONALDLAND became the setting of a new series of commercials created for children.

- Half a million dollars was appropriated to light American flags at our restaurants.

1971 - Hamburger, GRIMACE, MAYOR McCHEESE, CAPTAIN CROOK and the PROFESSOR joined RONALD McDONALD in McDONALDLAND.

- The home office moved from Chicago to Oak Brook, Illinois.

- The first McDonald's opened in Japan, Germany, Australia, Guam and Holland.

- The first McDonald's Playland opened in Chula Vista, California.

1972 - The 10th and 11th billionth hamburgers were sold.

- McDonald's became a billion dollar corporation on December 17th.

- The 2,000th store opened in Des Plaines, Illinois

- Ray Kroc received the Horatio Alger Award.

- Stock split for the fifth time, making 100 shares of 1965 stock now equal to 1,836 shares.

- Quarter-Pounder was added to the national menu.

- Introduction of Large Fries.

1973 – McDonald's made the cover of **TIME** magazine.

     – 2,500th store opened in Hickory Hills, Illinois.

     – Egg McMuffin was introduced.

     – First McDonald's in a college facility, opened in the University of Cincinatti.

1974 – 3,000th store opened in Woolwich, England.

     – McDonald's opened its first operation in a zoo, at Toronto, Canada.

     – Fred Turner became President and Chief Executive Officer.

     – The first RONALD McDONALD House opened in Philadelphia, Pennsylvania.

     – The company sold its 15 billionth hamburger.

     – By the end of the year total sales for the company approached $2 billion.

     – McDONALDLAND Cookies were introduced.

1975 – The first drive-thru was established in Oklahoma City, Oklahoma.

     – McDonald's celebrated its 20th anniversary.

     – The 10,000th student graduated from Hamburger University.

     – The new ad campaign, " We Do it All For You ", was introduced in April.

     – " Twoallbeefpattiesspecialsaucelettucecheese-picklesonionsonasesameseedbun "promotion introduced our most famous advertising promotional jingle, advertising the Big Mac.

THE FIRST MCDONALD'S DRIVE-IN RESTAURANT
San Bernardino, CA. 1948

"ORIGINAL McDONALD'S BAR-B-Q RESTAURANT"
It became the first McDonald's Drive-In.
San Bernardino, CA. 1940-48

1976 - The 4,000th store opened in Montreal, Canada.

- McDonald's sales surpassed $3 billion.

- McDonald's directors declared the first cash dividend.

- The 20 billionth hamburger was sold.

- " You, You're The One " advertising campaign introduced.

1977 - McDonald's added a complete breakfast line to its national menu.

- President and Chief Executive Officer, Fred Turner, was named Chairman of the Board of Directors succeeding Ray Kroc, who was named Senior Chairman. Ed Schmitt was named President and Chief Administrative Officer.

- The first McDonald's All American High School Basketball Team was organized.

- Ray Kroc celebrated his 75th birthday (Oct.4)

- McDonald's announced plans to secure the land (80 acres) for its Home Office in Oak Brook,Ill.

1978 - The 5,000th restaurant opened in Fujizawa City, Japan.

- The 25 billionth hamburger was served.

- The 15,000th student graduated from Hamburger U.

- Filming store for McDonald's commercials opened in the City of Industry, California.

1979 - McDonald's introduced its new advertising campaign " Nobody Can Do It Like McDonald's Can."

- The 30 billionth hamburger was sold.

- HAPPY MEALS WERE ADDED TO THE NATIONAL MENU.

1979   The average annual sales for a restaurant in
          existence for more than 13 months exceeded
          $1 million for the first time.

     -    Four years after the domestic drive-thru concept
          was introduced, nearly half (2,884) of McDonald's
          restaurants have the facility.

1980 -   McDonald's celebrated its 25th (silver) anniver-
          sary.

     -    BIRDIE, the Early Bird, joined the McDONALDLAND
          characters.

     -    The first floating McDonald's launched on the
          historic Mississippi Riverfront in St. Louis,
          just south of the famous Gateway Arch.

     -    Mike Quinlan elected to the newly created position
          of President of McDonald's U.S.A. and Chief
          Operating Officer.

     -    The 6,000th restaurant opened in Munich, Germany.

1981 -   Leo Burnettt chosen as new national advertising
          agency.

     -    McDonald's renews its most successful campaign
          ever - " You Deserve A Break Today."

     -    5,770 stores in the United States and 1,359
          internationally, totaling 7,129 stores world-
          wide with sales at $7 billion.

     -    RONALD McDONALD Houses were opened or under
          construction in 21 markets. By the end of 1981,
          RONALD McDONALD Houses provided shelter annually
          for an estimated 33,000 families in the United
          States, Canada and Australia.

     -    First McDonald's restaurants in Spain, Denmark and
          the Phillipines were opened.

     -    Total Playlands systemwide at year end were 979.

1982 - McDonald's declared its 6th stock split (3 for 2)
         on August 31, 1981.

       - Dividend per share rose by 32% during this year.

       - American Marketing Association Achievement Award,
          the marketing profession's highest honor, was
          presented to McDonald's Corporation for excellence
          in marketing programs.

       - Ed Schmitt was elected Vice Chairman of the
          corporation and continues as Chief Administrative
          Officer.

       - Mike Quinlan was promoted to President and Chief
          Operating Officer and continues as President of
          McDonald's U.S.A.

1983 - McDonald's restaurants are located in 31 countries
         around the world.

       - The new Hamburger University opened in Oak Brook,
          Illinois.

       - McDonald's opened its 7,000th restaurant in Falls
          Church, Virginia.

       - There were 7,778 restaurants at year end.

       - Chicken McNuggets were introduced into all domes-
          tic restaurants by year end.

       - McDonald's served its 45 billionth hamburger.

1984 - Ray Kroc, Founder and Senior Chairman of the Board
         of McDonald's died, January 14.

       - McDonald's restaurants opened in 4 new countries:
          Andorra, Finland, Taiwan and Wales.

       - Chicken McNuggets were introduced in Canada, Japan,
          France and Germany, making McDonald's the second
          largest purveyor of chicken in the world.

1984   In June, McDonald's introduced a new national
        advertising campaign, "It's A Good Time For The
        Great Taste Of McDonald's."

    -   In August, McDonald's stock split for the second
        time in two years;7th split in the company's
        history.

    -   The 800th McDonald's restaurant opened in Duluth,
        Georgia.

    -   McDonald's served its 50 billionth hamburger, the
        ceremonial burger was eaten by Dick McDONALD, who
        along with his brother Mac, started the McDonald's
        system 41 years earlier.

    -   Ed Rensi was promoted to President of McDonald's
        U.S.A. while retaining his title of Chief Oper-
        ating Officer.

    -   McDonald's year-end systemwide sales surpassed
        $10 billion.

    -   McDonald's celebrated the 10th anniversary of the
        RONALD McDONALD House with a national fundraiser
        that raised more than $5 million. At year end,
        there were 73 RONALD Houses in the U.S.,Canada and
        Australia.

    -   In 1984,a new McDONALD restaurant opened somewhere
        in the world every 17 hours. (A new store has
        opened every 18 hours for the past 10 years).

    -   The average sales volume for a McDonald's restau-
        rant was $1.284 million.

1985 - McDonald's added seven new countries to its roster
        : Thailand, Luxembourg, Bermuda, Venezuela,Italy,
        Mexico and Aruba. At year end McD restaurants
        were located in 43 countries worldwide.

    -   The first European RONALD McDONALD House opened in
        Amsterdam, Holland. By December, there were more
        than 90 RMCD Houses open worldwide.

1985   On April 15, McDonald's celebrated its 30th year
            of operation, and on April 20, our 20th anniver-
            sary as a publicly owned company.

      -     Ray Kroc's first McDonald's restaurant restored
            to its original form and reopened in May as the
            McDonald's museum in Des Plaines, Illinois.

      -     In August,McDonald's "Large Fries For Small Fries"
            promotion, featuring Mary Lou Retton, helped raise
            more than $2.6 million for the Muscular Dystrophy
            Association.

      -     McBlimp. the world's largest airship, appeared in
            the skies over New York City, introducing McD's
            newest form of advertising.

      -     RONALD McDONALD Children's Charities provided an
            emergency grant to assist Mexican children suffer-
            ing from the devastating earthquake which occurred
            in September.

      -     In October, McDonald's Corporation became one of
            the 30 blue chip companies listed on the Dow Jones
            Industrial Average.

      -     McDonald's served its 55 billionth hamburger.

      -     Millions were singing "The Hot Stays Hot and The
            Cool Stays Cool" as McDonald's introduced the
            McD.L.T. sandwich on November 4.

      -     December topped off McDonald's most successful
            year to date with systemwide sales of more than
            $11 billion.

1986 -   McDonald's served one out of every four breakfasts
            eaten outside of the house in the United States.

      -     In March, McDonald's added freshly baked buttermilk
            biscuit sandwiches to the breakfast menu. McDONALD
            employees bake more than 1.5 buttermilk biscuits
            daily.

1986   McDonald's sponsored a traveling exhibit celebrating the life and message of Dr. Martin Luther King Jr. After touring 20 U.S. cities, the exhibit was donated to the King Center for Non-Violent Social Change, located in Atlanta.

-    McDonald's broke the "sound barrier" by producing "Silent Persuasion", the first-ever TV commercial featuring sign language and open captioned for the non-hearing audience.

-    The Golden Arches greeted customers for the first time in Argentina, Cuba and Turkey.

-    McDonald's Board of Directors elected President, Mike Quinlan to Chief Executive Officer,effective March 1,1987.

-    McDonald's restaurants worldwide changed their road signs to read "More Than 60 Billion Served".

-    The Long Island Jewish Medical Center hosted the opening of the 100th RONALD McDONALD House in September.

-    McDonald's common stock split 3-for-2 in June; the 8th split in the company's history

-    In July, McDonald's was added to the Tokyo Stock Exchange, and set a new volume record; 615,750 shares, for opening day trading of a non-Japanese company.

-    McDonald's became the first quick service restaurant to provide the public with a complete food product ingredient listing.

-    In honor of founder,Ray Kroc, every McDonald's office worldwide closed on October 3, and staff employees returned to the restaurants to serve customers- the people who keep McDonald's #1.

1986   On December 1, McDonald's opened the first quick service restaurant in North Pole, Alaska. The restaurant is located on Santa Clause Lane!

- Year-end systemwide sales topped $12 billion.

1987   -   Freshly tossed salads were added to the national menu on May 15.

- McDonald's announced a 3-for-1 stock split at the company's annual meeting;the 9th split in the company's history.

- On June 1, former Controller, Jim Cantalupo became President, international.

- McDonald's granted Sears Roebuck & Co. rights to carry a children's line of clothing called "McKids"

- The 30,000th student was granted a Hamburgerology Degree from McDonald's Hamburger University.

- McDonald's served its 65 billionth hamburger.

1988   -   **FORTUNE** magazine named McDonald's hamburgers among the 100 products America makes best.

- George Cohon, President, McDonald's of Canada, signed an agreement with the Soviet Union to open a McDonald's in Moscow, with a possible 19 more restaurants to follow.

- McDonald's added three countries to its roster; Hungary, Yugoslavia and Korea.

- McDonald's opened its 10,000th restaurant in Dale City, Virginia, on April 6.

- COSMIC joined the other McDonald's characters in McDONALDLAND.

- RONALD McDONALD Children's Charities has given $11 million to more than 300 charities since it was founded in 1984 in memory of Ray A. Kroc.

1988   McDonald's Corporation licensed Sears Roebuck &
        Co. to open McKids specialty stores. First one
        opened in Chicago, Illinois.

   -    McDonald's served its 70 billionth hamburger.

   -    Year end systemwide sales topped $16 billion.

1989 - McDonald's welcomed its 2.000th franchisee in the
        U.S.

   -    In May, all U.S. restaurants began serving the
        country style McChicken sandwich.

   -    McDonald's announced a 2-for-1 common stock split
        at the company's annual meeting; 10th split in the
        company's history.

   -    The Big Mac celebrated its 21st birthday.

   -    Ray Kroc, founder of McDonald's was elected to the
        Advertising Hall of Fame in recognition of his
        special contributions to the advertising industry
        and the community at large.

   -    McDonald's opened its 11,000th restaurant in Hong
        Kong on October 20.

   -    Ground breaking took place on the first McDonald's
        in Moscow. The restaurant will have five dining-
        rooms and be able to seat 700 people.

   -    McDonald's of Canada Limited brought its restaurant
        expertise to the Toronto Sky Dome. This first-of-
        a-kind stadium location has four restaurants, 20
        Skysnack locations, 48 beverage stations and a
        team of stadium vendors.

   -    McDonald's served its 75 billionth hamburger.

   -    McDonald's opened in Barbados.

   -    Year end systemwide sales topped $17 billion.

1990   -   McDonald's opened its first restaurant in the
           Soviet Union.

       -   Sales:$18,758,000,000.Hamburgers served:80 Billion

       -   Number of McDonald's Worldwide: 11,803

       -   Number of countries & Territories: 53

       -   Restaurants opened outside the United States:
           Russia   affiliate:Canada/ City of Moscow / Jan. 31
           China,Shenzhen affiliate:Hong Kong   / Oct. 8
           Chile   affiliate:Roberto Moses   / Nov. 19

       -   Restaurant closed outside the United States
           Barbados, December

       -   Chairman Fred Turner named "Adman of the Decade"
           by "AD AGE" .

       -   Nutrition: Added as permanent menu items:
           Cheerios and Wheaties, April 1st. No fat, no
           cholesterol apple-bran muffins. Low fat milk
           shakes, frozen yogurt and fruit sorbet. 91 % fat
           free, in tests, beef patty. McLean Deluxe replaced
           McDLT. McDonald's fries cooked in cholesterol-free
           100% vegetable oil. Margarine replaces butter
           US restaurants switch to 1% lowfat milk. Grilled
           chicken sandwich. "Chunky Chicken Salad" replaced
           "Chicken Salad Oriental, Jan. 15

       -   World's largest McDonald's opened January 31 at
           Gorky Street and Pushkin Square in Moscow. The
           restaurant, occupying 23,681 square feet on 4
           floors, has indoor seating for 700 with another
           200 seats outside. It is serving over 20,000
           customers daily. This represents the largest
           joint venture agreement ever made between a food
           company and the USSR.

       -   The Environment:
           McDonald's, RMCC and World Wildlife Fund join to
           produce a new environmental education booklet for
           kids called "WEcology" .

1990 - McDonald's introduces McRecycle UAD, environmental
program that sets a goal of $100 million annually
to purchase recycled materials for use in
construction, renovation and operations. This is
in addition to more than $60 million which the
company already spends on recycled paper products.

- McDonald's announced November 1st, that it would
begin phasing out plastic foam packages. Recycled
carry-out bags began testing in New York.

- McDonald's is named "Official Quick Service
Restaurant" for NASCAR.

- With the opening of the Ray Kroc Office and
3-dimensional corridor exhibits, the Visitor's
Center on the **"Plaza's"**first floor is completed.

- McDonald's "American Cup" held in Fairfax, VA,
features world's top gymnasts from more than 20
countries, including East Germany, Romania, China
and the USSR.

- 35th Anniversary celebrated in April.

- McDonald's food being served in 2 restaurant cars
on the Swiss Federal Railroad, Geneva run. This is
our first train operation.

- New advertising campaign: "Food, Folks and Fun" is
introduced.

- "Cartoon All Stars to the Rescue" a serious
comedy / adventure animation was simulcast by ABC,
CBS and NBC, April 21. The commercial free, anti-
substance-abuse special for kids was presented by
MCD, OPNAD and RMCC. Additionally, RMCC distributed
more than 350,000 video-cassettes to schools,
libraries, community groups and video stores for
free rental.

- At first quarter end, McDonald's became the only
company in the current Standard & Poor's 500 to
have publicly reported 100 consecutive quarters
of year-to-year increases in revenues, income and
earnings per share since 1965.

- McDonald's introduced Heros Anonimos, an awards program that honors unsung heroes in the Hispanic community.

- For the 19th consecutive year, McDonald's participated in the Labor Day Muscular Dystrophy Campaign.

- Ray Kroc was named one of the 100 Most Important Americans of the 20th Century by LIFE Magazine.

- McDonald's opened in Shenzhen, a special economic zone of the People's Republic of China, just across the border from Hong Kong.

- 4th "Annual McDonald's Open" held in Barcelona, Spain, featured 3 top European basketball teams and the New York "Knicks" .

- McDonald's was the sole advertising sponsor of "The World of Children". a special edition of LIFE Magazine. The issue included a 32-page "Portrait of McDonald's" featuring behind the scenes pictures of McDonald's people, all taken on October 25,1989.

- Chris Burke, star of ABC's "Life Goes On" series became McDonald's spokesperson for "McJobs" , our special program to hire and develop disabled persons as employees.

- McDonald's finally brought Downey, CA into the system by purchasing the old "Red & White" opened by Roger Williams, August 18, 1953, under a Mac Bros license. This was the only "McDonald's" which never affiliated with McDonald's Corp. after the Kroc buyout. The restaurant was closed for remodeling.

- At year end,the only "Red & White" still operating as a McDonald's was on East 152nd Street in Cleveland, Ohio. It was scheduled for relocation and remodeling in 1991.

RONALD McDONALD DOLLS

1. RMCD STUFFED CLOTH, 17", 1971   AVG:$15.00 MINT:$35.00

One-piece cloth doll lithographed details.

HEAD:features outlined in black with vertical streaks of
      "make-up" across eyes. Black lines detail the neck and
      wavy hair. Red yarn loop at top of head for hanging.
LIMBS: stiff, not poseable. Arms, are printed with red and
      white stripes. Yellow mitten-like hands, fingers are
      indicated by black lines. Pants are wide at hips. A
      short area of red and white striped legs end in large
      red shoes, heels apart and toes pointing in opposite
      directions.

CLOTHING:
JUMPER: Black outlined, white collar of jumper is narrow and
      pointed at ends. NO shirt shows at neck.
POCKETS: Three pockets, black outlined, in different sizes,
      decorated with a gold "M". Lower right pocket has "M"
      (R) .
ZIPPER: Wide white vertical band, zipper teeth suggested by
      horizontal red lines. Large tab drawn in black at top.
      Wide red border encloses three sides of the zipper.
SHOES: Large, with square tips. The shoe top and three laces
      are detailed in black line. A wide black band indicates
      the sole.
MARKS: On the back: "RONALD McDONALD " in red script /(R) .
      Front right heel : (R) .

2. RMCD STUFFED CLOTH, 16" - 17",   AVG:$15.00 MINT:$35.00
1971.
One piece cloth doll with lithographed details. Like above
doll with these differences:
    Zipper: Wide yellow vertical band, zipper teeth are
    suggested by horizontal red lines. No zipper tab.
    Ends of collar are *rounded*.

3. RMCD REMCO VINYL DOLL, 7", 1976 NP:$17.00 MIP:$37.00

REMCO set of McDONALDLAND character dolls, intended to be
accessories to a train set. Dolls were sold on hanging,
plastic covered cards, showing the characters in full color
(at left of doll). "FULLY POSEABLE / HEAD MOVES UP, DOWN AND
SIDE TO SIDE". On the back, seven dolls were shown with
train set, backdrop and accessories. REMCO's "McDONALDLAND
PLAY SET" .(C) 1976 REMCO TOYS INC. (C) 1976 McDONALD
SYSTEMS INC. **See REMCO McDONALDLAND DOLLS, Pg. 41**
HEAD: Realistically molded head, hands and feet. Hair looks
    like woman's, big bouffant style. Knob in the back
    controls head movements. Open, smiling mouth.
LIMBS: Vinyl plastic, jointed at shoulders and hips.
CLOTHING:
JUMPER: Removable, fastens at back of neck. Sewn on, white,
    vinyl patch pockets, decorated with gold "M", black
    "McDonald's"
SHOES: Clown shoes and striped leggings are painted on.
MARKS: Embossed on back: C) REMCO 1976 PAT.PEND. (C)
    1976 McDONALD SYSTEM, INC. / MADE IN HONG KONG

RONALD McDONALD (1.)

BIG MAC

HAMBURGLAR

GRIMACE

THE PROFESSOR

MAYOR McCHEESE

REMCO McDONALDLAND
DOLLS

CAPTAIN CROOK

4. RMCD STUFFED CLOTH, 13", 1977 AVG:$12.00 MINT:$27.00

One-piece cloth doll lithographed details.

HEAD: Black line details. Eyebrows raised high. Natural
      smile, showing upper row of teeth. Hair, detailed with
      black line in petal-like shapes, is narrow on top and
      wider at sides of face . Red yarn loop on top of head
      for hanging.
LIMBS: Not poseable. Arms, at sides, yellow hands are
      mitten-like, fingers indicated by short black lines.

CLOTHING:
JUMPER: Black outlined large white collar with pointed
      ends, spreads across shoulders. Red and white striped
      shirt shows at slightly pointed neckline.
POCKETS:(NOT outlined with black) Rectangular areas of
      white with black "McDonald's (R)" logos centered.
ZIPPER: Yellow zipper-teeth are detailed on wide vertical,
      red band which extends beyond end of teeth.NO TAB.
SHOES: Squared tips. Decorative rendering of laces: two
      cross laces with a bow and lacing ends, yellow,
      outlined with black
MARKS: Left heel front:(R).
      Upper back:large red outlined "M".

5. WHISTLE-BLOWING DOLL, 1978   AVG:$22.00 MINT:$42.00

20 INCHES, stuffed, cloth doll, plastic head. Mfg.Tag on
back: 1978 McDonald's CORPORATION / MADE IN TAIWAN.

HEAD: Hard plastic, red, looped yarn hair. Open mouth shows
      upper row of white teeth. Painted smile covers most of
      lower face. Eyes, painted flat black with a white
      "shine" dot. Above and below each eye is a narrow black
      arch. Brows are raised. On red cord around neck is a
      red whistle. If inserted in the open mouth it will blow
      when doll's chest is squeezed.
LIMBS: Jointed at shoulders and hips, move freely.
       Hands are realistically molded in open position.

CLOTHING:
JUMPER: Separate piece of clothing.
        Golden yellow. Very wide and
        pointed at hips. Red and white
        striped shirt shows in V-shaped
        neckline.
POCKETS: Two large patch pockets.
        Small purple, felt Grimace doll
        with hanging cord at top, is sewn
        firmly into the larger,lower left
        pocket. Below the logo,in script,
        is " Ronald McDONALD ". On seat
        is white cloth label with red
        lettering: "DO NOT MACHINE WASH".
        Other side: "RONALD McDONALD TM
        / (C) 1978 McDonald's CORPORATION
        INC / MADE IN TAIWAN / ALL NEW
        MATERIALS / FILL: POLYURETHANE
        FOAM-93% / POLYESTER FIBRE-7% /
        BODY: NYLON HAIR: ACRYLIC / 282
        REG. NO. PA PAT PENDING / HASBRO
        INDUSTRIES INC.PAWTUCKET RI 02861
        USA"
ZIPPER: Real zipper sewn with red
        stitching. Large, red pull-tab.
SHOES: Ankle-high, hard plastic with
        a knot of yellow laces at tops.

6. RMCD STUFFED CLOTH, 1981   AVG:$4.00   MINT:$8.50

4 1/2 INCHES, one-piece cloth doll with lithographed details.

HEAD: Black line detailed features. Natural smile, showing
      upper row of teeth. Hair is realistically drawn with
      black line and extends an equal amount all around head.
      Black loop cord on top of head for hanging. Narrower
      head than the 5 inch doll.
LIMBS: Not poseable. Arms held away from sides. Yellow hands
      are mitten-like. Fingers indicated by black lines.
CLOTHING:
JUMPER: Black outlined, large white collar, pointed ends.
      Red and white striped shirt shows in U-shaped neckline.
POCKETS: Black outlined, rectangular areas of white with
      centered gold "M" logo.
ZIPPER: Narrow yellow stripe on wide vertical, red band of
      same length.
SHOES: Rounded tips. Black outlined shoe with heel.
      Decorative rendering of laces: two cross laces with
      bow, yellow, outlined with black.
MARKS: On back: large "McDonald's" logo outlined in red
      covers upper back. Lower back: (C) 1981 McDonald's
      CORP. Right heel, back: KOREA.

7. RMCD STUFFED CLOTH, 1983   AVG:$14.00 MINT:$28.00

15 INCHES, One-piece cloth doll with lithographed details.

HEAD: Black line details. Natural smile, showing upper
      row of teeth. Hair: a few black lines, high on top,
      closer at sides.
LIMBS: Not poseable. Arms, wide at shoulders. Yellow mitten-
      like hands, fingers indicated with black lines.
CLOTHING:
JUMPER: Black outlined, large white collar with pointed
      ends. Red and white striped shirt shows at rounded
      neck.
POCKETS: (NOT outlined with black) Three rectangular areas,
      white with gold "M" and centered, black "McDonald's
      (R)" logo.
ZIPPER: Narrow yellow stripe on wide vertical, red band of
      same length. Yellow zipper tab with black details.
SHOES: Squared tips. Decorative rendering of laces, three
      crossed laces with a bow, yellow, outlined with black,
      as are details of heels and shoe soles.
MARKS: On back: large "M" outlined in red. Back of left
      heel:KOREA. White cloth label under right foot.
      Lettering in red "(C) 1983 McDonald's CORP / RONALD
      McDONALD (R) / CONTENTS:SYNTHETIC FIBER / PRODUCT OF
      KOREA

8. RMCD STUFFED CLOTH, 5 INCHES   AVG:$4.00 MINT:$8.00

One-piece cloth doll with lithographed details.

HEAD: Black line details. Natural smile, showing upper
      row of teeth. Hair: a few black lines, extending an
      equal amount all around head. Black loop cord on top of
      head for hanging.
LIMBS: Not poseable. Arms at sides. Yellow, mitten-like
      hands. (NO fingers indicated). Straight hips, large
      red shoes, squared toes, heels TOGETHER.

CLOTHING:
JUMPER: Black outlined, white collar with pointed ends.
      Shirt shows in U-shaped neckline
POCKETS: Outlined with black, rectangular white areas
      with centered, gold "M" logo.
ZIPPER: Detailed with black lines on white vertical band ,
      yellow tab. Wide red band on either side of zipper.
SHOES: Very large, squared tips. Decorative rendering of
      laces: three cross laces with a bow and lacing ends,
      yellow, outlined with black.
MARKS: On back: large "M" logo outlined in red. Black: "TM"
      and "MADE IN PHILIPPINES"

9. RMCD STUFFED CLOTH, 3 1/2 INCHES   AVG:$4.50   MINT:$8.50

One-piece cloth doll with lithographed details. Very like
the 5 inch doll but shorter and wider. Wider face. Eyes have
black marks at sides.

HEAD: Black line details. Natural smile, showing upper
      row of teeth. Hair: a few black lines. Short on top,
      wide at sides. Black loop cord on top of head for
      hanging.
LIMBS: Not poseable. Arms at sides. Yellow, mitten-like
      hands. Fingers indicated with black lines. Flared at
      hips, large red shoes, squared toes, heels separated.

CLOTHING:
JUMPER: Black outlined, white collar with pointed ends.
      Shirt, stripes are curved in upward arcs. Shows in
      broad neckline.
POCKETS: Outlined with black, rectangular white areas
      with centered, gold "M" logo.
ZIPPER: Wider red band on either side of vertical yellow
      stripe.
SHOES: Squared tips.Laces and shoe tops are black lines.
      Thick black "soles".
MARKS: On back: large "M" logo outlined in red. Black: "TM".

10. RMCD CLOTH & PLASTIC, 1991*   AVG:$12.00 MINT:$20.00

13 INCHES This beautiful doll is currently available
through GROUP II COMMUNICATIONS INC., produced exclusively
for McDonald's, has plastic head and stuffed cloth body.
(#49071 $13.95)

HEAD: Plastic, attractive, realistic. Nose is painted red at
      the end. Large red smile is painted over a naturally
      smiling mouth, which shows a sculpted row of white
      teeth. A mass of looped red yarn hair is nicely styled
      around the face.
LIMBS: Joints at shoulders and hips, are soft enough to be
      poseable or used with puppet strings. Hands are yellow,
      stitched to show fingers. Feet are jointed at ankles.

CLOTHING:
JUMPER: Removable. Sewn, white collar is pointed and open
      at throat, showing red and white striped shirt. side
      seams. (Leotard and shoes are all sewn on.)
POCKETS: Real patch pockets.   Small
      pocket on upper left has gold "M".
      Other pockets have gold "M" and
      black "McDonald's (R)"
ZIPPER: Real red zipper with brass tab,
      embossed "YKK".
SHOES: Red shoes, with top seam, from
      ankle to toes decorated with three
      rows of metal grommets on either
      side of the seam.
MARKS:on back: "M" outlined in red.

12. RONALD McDONALD
    INFLATABLE, 1978

13. RONALD McDONALD
    INFLATABLE, 1990

15. RONALD McDONALD
    GLOVE PUPPET, 1977

14
RONALD McDONALD
GLOVE PUPPET, 1976

11.RMCD INFLATABLE "BOP-EM" DOLL,1990 AVG:$5.00 MINT:$9.00

Currently available through GROUP II COMMUNICATIONS INC.
(#04716) 14 INCHES. Polyvinyl material with weighted base.
Bounces back when pushed. One piece, only arms extend from
body. Full color, no outlining on pockets. On back, red "M
(R)" "safety tested for children 3 and over."

12. RMCD INFLATABLE DOLL, 1978   AVG:$7.00 MINT:$12.00

37 INCHES. Full color, large head. arms and legs separate
from body. McDonald's System Inc.

13. RMCD INFLATABLE DOLL, 1990   AVG:$5.00 MINT:$10.50

Currently available through GROUP II COMMUNICATIONS INC.
(#41464) 30 INCHES. Polyvinyl material, costume detailed in
full color with no outlining on pockets. Only three stripes
instead of fully striped leggings. Arms extend outward, legs
are separated. On back, red "M (R)" "safety tested for
children three and over."

14. RMCD GLOVE PUPPET, 1976   AVG:$0.75 MINT:$1.50

9 inches. Like glove below. Differences: "Ronald McDONALD"
written in (smaller) BLACK script, under feet and "1-22".
Back side of glove shows figure from back and printing:
"(C) 1976 McDonald's System, Inc. / 2-91 / Printed in USA"

15. RMCD GLOVE PUPPET, 1977   AVG:$4.00 MINT:$8.00

11 6/8 inches. Plastic three-lobed glove with RMCD printed
on surface. Standing figure: head in top lobe. Arms extended
to sides form other two lobes. "Ronald McDONALD" written in
large, red and yellow script, under feet. MC0002 .

GRIMACE DOLLS

1. GRIMACE STUFFED-CLOTH, 11" X 11"   AVG:$4.50   MINT:$9.50

Plush purple. Wide as he is tall,(flattened front to back).
Brown, furry strips sewn on for eyebrows. Eyes are white,
felt circles with smaller black dots. Mouth is red felt
strip.

2. REMCO GRIMACE DOLL, 1976   AVG:$17.50   MINT:$37.50

Grimace is soft, stuffed, purple plush fabric, with vinyl
feet eyes., brows and smile.
REMCO set of McDONALDLAND character dolls, sold as
accessories to a train set. The dolls were sold on hanging,
plastic-covered cards which showed characters.
(to left of doll). "FULLY POSEABLE / HEAD MOVES UP,DOWN AND
SIDE TO SIDE". On back, seven dolls were shown with the
train set, backdrop and accessories. Remco's "McDONALDLAND
PLAY SET" .(C) 1976 REMCO TOYS INC. (C) 1976 McDONALD
SYSTEMS INC.

3. GRIMACE INFLATABLE DOLL, 1978   AVG:$3.50   MINT:$7.50
Violet color, with flat base.
On back: "COPYRIGHT McDonald's SYSTEMS 1978 / SAFETY
TESTED FOR CHILDREN 3 AND OVER / THIS ITEM IS NOT TO BE
USED AS A LIFE PRESERVER "

4. GRIMACE STUFFED CLOTH DOLL, 1987   AVG:$4.75   MINT:$9.00
12 INCHES.
Design of doll and clothing, printed on cloth. Colorful
outfit: white baseball suit with vertical red stripes.
Over his heart is large gold "M (R)" . Red sneakers with
white trim. On raised right hand is a brown catcher's mitt
with baseball in palm. Pleased expression. Red cap has gold
"M" printed on shade. On feet: " MADE IN CHINA (C) 1988
McDonald's".
Doll also has tag on foot: red ink on white cloth, "1988
McDonald's CORP / MB.SALES / PRODUCT OF CHINA / P.A.REG
#2515-(RC)/CONTENTS ALL NEW MATERIAL:COTTON AND POLYESTER/
FOR ALL AGES"

5. GRIMACE CLOTH, plush, 1990   AVG:$12.00   MINT:$20.00
14 INCHES.
Currently available through GROUP II COMMUNICATIONS INC.
(#49072 $13.95)
Across purple plush body, from "chin" to "hips", is a wide
band of yellow knit fabric with a large "G" in the center.
Folded at the base and sticking out are "feet" in running
shoes: white with black soles. His arms are three-lobed
flippers. On his head he wears white headband and earphones.

6. GRIMACE INFLATABLE DOLL, 1990   AVG:$4.00 MINT:$9.50
30 INCHES.
Currently available through GROUP II COMMUNICATIONS
INC.(#41465). Arms and legs are separate from body. Across
widest area, in black: "GRIMACE" . Black eyebrows, white
eyes and red mouth.

7. GRIMACE INFLATABLE "BOP-EM", 1990 AVG:$4.00 MINT:$9.00
    8 INCHES
Currently available through GROUP II COMMUNICATIONS INC.
(#00728). Polyvinyl material with a weighted base. Will
bounce back when pushed. One piece; only arms extend from
body. Across widest area, in black: "GRIMACE". Black
eyebrows, white eyes and red mouth.

8. GRIMACE GLOVE PUPPET, 1977   AVG:$0.75 MINT:$1.50

9 inches. Plastic three-lobed glove with GRIMACE printed on
surface. Standing figure: head in top lobe. Arms extended to
sides form other two lobes.

4. GRIMACE, CLOTH   1. GRIMACE, PLUSH

3. GRIMACE,   6. GRIMACE,
   INFLATABLE, 1978   INFLATABLE, 1990

2. HAMBURGLAR, 1972

1. HAMBURGLAR, 1972

4. HAMBURGLAR, 1987

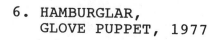
6. HAMBURGLAR,
   GLOVE PUPPET, 1977

HAMBURGLAR DOLLS

1. STUFFED CLOTH DOLL, 1972   AVG:$15.00 MINT:$25.00
15 INCHES.
Design printed on cloth. Front of suit is printed with
purple and white, horizontal stripes across arms, legs and
shoes. Vertical stripes on torso. Back and sides, purple and
black designed cape with "Hamburglar (R)" in yellow, (mid-
back). Long, yellow shoes with black trim. Yellow tie with
large, white dots. Purple tricorn hat with yellow "M" on
front and yellow hanging cord.
Feet and legs are separated, arms free, right at side, left
is raised.
FACE is grotesquely "cartooned": large misshapen nose, two
prominent teeth and narrow black mask.
Label on foot reads; "ALL NEW MATERIAL CONSISTING OF
SHREDDED CELLULOSE SHEETS AND COTTON FIBERS. License No. for
Cal. 16315, N.Y. 35495, (N.J.),Maine, Mass, Ohio,
Fla.,Texas, Penn, Il".

2. STUFFED CLOTH DOLL, 1972   AVG:$12.00 MINT:$20.00
17 INCHES.
Design printed on cloth. Suit is printed with horizontal
stripes across arms, legs and shoes. Vertical stripes on
torso. Feet are separated, arms free at sides. Curved red
tie with yellow dots.
FACE is "cartooned": large nose, three prominent teeth and
      outstanding ears.
HAT is striped on the crown, wide floppy brim extends
      out over ears.
CAPE is separate piece, black, tied on at neck, No
      lining.
MARKS: On back, in oval: "McDonald's (R) / HAMBURGLAR
      TM" IN RED SCRIPT. On back of left heel:"TM".

3. REMCO VINYL PLASTIC, 1976   AVG:$17.50   MINT:$40.00

REMCO set of McDONALDLAND character dolls, sold as
accessories to a train set. The dolls were sold on
hanging, plastic-covered cards which showed characters.
(to left of doll). "FULLY POSEABLE / HEAD MOVES UP,DOWN AND
SIDE TO SIDE". On back, seven dolls were shown with the
train set, backdrop and accessories. Remco's "McDONALDLAND
PLAY SET" .(C) 1976 REMCO TOYS INC. (C) 1976 McDONALD
SYSTEMS INC.   **See REMCO McDONALDLAND DOLLS, Pg. 41**

HEAD: Realistically molded head, hands and feet.
     Long, broad Pinnochio-like nose, large outstanding
     ears, half-lidded eyes show through his black mask
     and two prominent teeth cover his lower lip. Wide
     smile. His hair is grey-green and reaches shoulders.
     Atop his head is a black disk with yellow band, over
     which the flat, wide hat brim fits.
     A knob in the back controls head movements.
LIMBS: Vinyl plastic, jointed at shoulders and hips.
     (arms and legs are black).

CLOTHING:
SUIT: Removable, fastens at back of neck. Long sleeves
     and trousers.
TIE: Knee-length, red vinyl with yellow dots.
SHOES: Black with yellow trim.
CAPE: Calf-length, gathered at neck and tied. Gold lining.

Embossed on back: C) REMCO 1976 PAT.PEND. (C) 1976
McDONALD SYSTEM, INC. / MADE IN HONG KONG

4. HAMBURGLAR CLOTH DOLL, 1987   AVG:$4.75   MINT:$9.50

12 INCHES. MADE IN CHINA / (C) 1987 McDonald's
Design printed on cloth. This version has a cute, smiling
child's face. His left hand is raised with finger up in a
"Ssh" gesture.
Doll has tag on foot. Red ink on white cloth: "1978
McDonald's CORP / MB.SALES / PRODUCT OF CHINA / P. A. REG
#2515-(RC)/CONTENTS ALL NEW MATERIAL:COTTON AND POLYESTER/
FOR ALL AGES"

HAT: Black, wide-brimmed with a red band.
CAPE: Black, shows a glimpse of red lining.
TIE: Red, dotted with hamburgers.
SUIT: Black and white prison stripes, red gloves.
SHOES: Red and white.

5. STUFFED CLOTH & PLASTIC, 1990   AVG:$14.00 MINT:$20.00

11 INCHES (SEATED). Currently available through GROUP II
COMMUNICATIONS INC. (#49074 $15.95). Nicely molded face
with a happy smile showing two front teeth. Black mask shows
black dot eyes. Nose is realistically molded. Hair is light
red, short, curved across forehead.

HAT: Spanish style, round crown with yellow band. Wide,
        flat, black brim.
CAPE: Removable, long and black with gold lining.
TIE: Removable, long and red with designs of hamburgers.
SUIT: Black and white horizontal, "prison" stripes.
SHOES:White sneakers.

6. HAMBURGLAR GLOVE PUPPET, 1977   AVG:$0.75 MINT:$1.50

9 inches. "HAMBURGLAR" written in black script, under feet.
Back side of glove shows figure from back and printing: "(C)
1976 McDonald's System, Inc. / Printed in USA"

BIRDIE, THE EARLY BIRD DOLL

1. BIRDIE STUFFED CLOTH DOLL, 1987   AVG:$6.00 MINT:$12.00
12 INCHES
Doll has tag on foot, red ink on white cloth: "1987
McDonald's CORP / MB.SALES / PRODUCT OF CHINA / P. A.
REG #2515-(RC)/CONTENTS ALL NEW MATERIAL:COTTON AND
POLYESTER/ FOR ALL AGES"

HEAD: Orange beak and feet. Pink ribbons on braids,
      happy smile.

SUIT: Pink jumper, straps crossed in back, with gold "M"
      on chest. Pant legs are usually rolled up. Long white
      scarf hangs down on left side, in front and back.
      Right wing raised. Printed on feet "MADE IN CHINA/
      (C)1987 McDonald's".

2. BIRDIE, 1990   AVG:$12.00 MINT:$15.00

STUFFED, ACRYLIC FLEECE. 12 INCHES. Currently available
through GROUP II COMMUNICATIONS INC. (#49073 $13.95).
Typical costume: long brown yarn braids. Removable goggles
and scarf. Wings are stitched to look like large hands with
fingers and thumb.

BIG MAC DOLLS

1. REMCO VINYL PLASTIC, 1976   AVG:$17.50   MINT:$37.50

REMCO set of McDONALDLAND character dolls, sold as
accessories to a train set. The dolls were sold on
hanging, plastic-covered cards which showed characters.
(to left of doll). "FULLY POSEABLE / HEAD MOVES UP,DOWN AND
SIDE TO SIDE". On back, seven dolls were shown with the
train set, backdrop and accessories. Remco's "McDONALDLAND
PLAY SET" .(C) 1976 REMCO TOYS INC. (C) 1976_McDONALD
SYSTEMS INC. **See REMCO McDONALDLAND DOLLS, Pg. 41**

HEAD: Nicely molded plastic head. A knob in the back
      controls head movements.
LIMBS: Vinyl plastic, jointed at shoulders and hips.

CLOTHING:
SUIT: Removable, two pieces, fastens at back of neck.
BADGE: Silver.

Embossed on back: C) REMCO 1976 PAT.PEND. (C) 1976
     McDONALD SYSTEM, INC. / MADE IN HONG KONG

2. BIG MAC HAND PUPPET, 1976   AVG:$15.00   MINT:$35.00
 11 INCHES
Five inch, Vinyl, hamburger-head is split like a mouth and
can be moved. Instead of legs, body is a blue cloth-
surfaced tube, through which puppeteer's hand may be
inserted. Hem of jacket reads: "BIG MAC". Embossed on back
of neck: "(C) 1976 McD CORP / AMSCO IND. A MILTON
BRADLEY CO."

3. BIG MAC GLOVE PUPPET, 1976   AVG:$0.75   MINT:$1.00
Plastic glove, 12 INCHES
Three-lobed glove: head in top lobe, extended arms in lobe
at each side. Pictures Big Mac directing traffic: left hand
with finger pointing, whistle in right hand. Beneath feet in
large black block letters: "BIG MAC tm ". Other side of
glove shows him from the back. Bottom edge reads: "(C) 1976
McDonald's System, Inc. / 280/ Printed in U.S.A.

1. BIRDIE, THE EARLY BIRD

2. BIG MAC,
   HAND PUPPET, 1976

BIG MAC™

3. BIG MAC,
   GLOVE PUPPET, 1976

CAPTAIN CROOK

1. CAPTAIN CROOK REMCO DOLL, 1976   AVG:$17.50 MINT:$40.00
6 inches.
REMCO set of McDONALDLAND character dolls, sold as
accessories to a train set. The dolls were sold on
hanging, plastic-covered cards which showed characters.
(to left of doll). "FULLY POSEABLE / HEAD MOVES UP,DOWN AND
SIDE TO SIDE". On back, seven dolls were shown with the
train set, backdrop and accessories. Remco's "McDONALDLAND
PLAY SET" .(C) 1976 REMCO TOYS INC. (C) 1976 McDONALD
SYSTEMS INC.   **See REMCO McDONALDLAND DOLLS, Pg. 41**

HEAD: Nicely molded plastic head. A knob in the back
      controls head movements. Hair to nape of neck in
      back.
LIMBS: Vinyl plastic, jointed at shoulders and hips.
      Hands are painted to indicate white, fingerless
      gloves. Arms are white, legs are brown.

CLOTHING: Removable, three pieces.
HAT: Purple Tricorn, outlined with gold, gold "C" .
Frock COAT: Red, pieces sewn in front to simulate vest,
      yellow with red crescents. Tan plastic epaulets on
      shoulders.
SCARF: One-inch wide,knit fabric,violet.
TROUSERS: Tan, folded up at cuffs to simulate boot-tops.

Embossed on back: C) REMCO 1976 PAT.PEND. (C)1976 McDONALD
SYSTEM, INC. / MADE IN HONG KONG.

MAYOR McCHEESE

1. REMCO DOLL, 1976   AVG:$17.50   MINT:$37.50

REMCO set of McDONALDLAND character dolls, sold as
accessories to a train set. The dolls were sold on
hanging, plastic-covered cards which showed characters.
(to left of doll). "FULLY POSEABLE / HEAD MOVES UP,DOWN AND
SIDE TO SIDE". On back, seven dolls were shown with the
train set, backdrop and accessories. Remco's "McDONALDLAND
PLAY SET" .(C) 1976 REMCO TOYS INC. (C) 1976 McDONALD
SYSTEMS INC. **See REMCO McDONALDLAND DOLLS, Pg. 41**

VEST: Yellow, patterned.
SASH: Purple with gold "M".
PANTS: Striped purple and yellow.
COAT: Formal, red coat with tails reaching to the floor.
SHOES: Black with large white spats.

PROFESSOR DOLL

1. REMCO DOLL, 1976   AVG:$18.50   MINT:$40.00

REMCO set of McDONALDLAND character dolls, sold as
accessories to a train set. The dolls were sold on
hanging, plastic-covered cards which showed characters.
(to left of doll). "FULLY POSEABLE / HEAD MOVES UP,DOWN AND
SIDE TO SIDE". On back, seven dolls were shown with the
train set, backdrop and accessories. Remco's "McDONALDLAND
PLAY SET" .(C) 1976 REMCO TOYS INC. (C) 1976 McDONALD
SYSTEMS INC.

HEAD: He has a pleasant face with a generous nose, bushy
       grey eyebrows, mustache, beard and hair, balding in
       front. He wears a pair of yellow-rimmed glasses. The
       second set, atop his head, have blue lenses.

CLOTHING:
       Black trousers, a red and yellow checked shirt, and red
       ribbon tie.
SHOES: Black oxford type on black legs, jointed at hips.
HANDS: are realistic, on white arms, jointed at the
       shoulders.
COAT: White "laboratory" coat nearly covers his clothes
       and is snapped in front. Small upper pocket is drawn
       on, while two large, lower pockets are sewn on the
       coat. In the pockets (printed on a plastic sheet) are
       his tools. The right pocket holds three yellow rulers,
       the left: a pencil, pliers and a toothbrush. Attached
       to his right hand by a black string is a sort of
       crescent wrench (grey plastic).

FRY KIDS

     The Fry Guys and Girls (once called "Goblins") are
mop-headed creatures with eyes, legs and feet. They are
bright, primary colors. Girls distinguishing features are
black eyelashes and ribbons in their "hair" .

1. FRY GIRL CLOTH DOLL, 1987   AVG:$3.75 MINT:$7.75

12 INCHES. MADE IN CHINA / (C) 1987 McDonald's
Design printed on cloth. Dolls have tag on foot, red ink on
white cloth, "1978 McDonald's CORP / M B.SALES / PRODUCT OF
CHINA / P. A. REG #2515-(RC)/CONTENTS ALL NEW MATERIAL :
COTTON AND POLYESTER/ FOR ALL AGES".
The doll is printed on bright, glowing neon-red fabric.
The design is the same on front and back with the exception
that on either side, the large blue eyes look in the
opposite direction. Yellow ribbons in hair, yellow socks and
sneakers, with white soles and toes. Red pom-poms on shoe
laces. Printed on one side of shoes: "MADE IN CHINA / (C)
1987 McDonald's ".

2. FRY GIRL, cloth, 3 1/2 INCHES   AVG:$3.00 MINT:$6.50
1987 Miniature version of above doll with black cord loop.
Hanging ornament.

3. FRY GUY CLOTH DOLL, 1987   AVG:$5.50 MINT:$12.50
12 INCHES. MADE IN CHINA / (C) 1987 McDonald's
Design printed on cloth. Dolls have tag on foot, red ink on
white cloth: " 1978 McDonald's CORP / M B.SALES   / PRODUCT
OF CHINA / P. A. REG #2515-(RC)/CONTENTS ALL NEW MATERIAL :
COTTON AND POLYESTER/ FOR ALL AGES"
The doll is printed on bright, glowing, neon-blue fabric.The
design is the same on front and back, the large eyes look
downward. Long yellow knee-socks. Pink high-top sneakers,
with white soles, blue circles over ankles. Printed on one
side of shoes: "MADE IN CHINA / (C) 1987   McDonald's "

4. FRY GUY, cloth, 3 1/2 INCHES   AVG:$3.00 MINT:$6.50
1987 Miniature version of above doll with black cord loop.
Hanging ornament.

FRY GUY, FRY GIRL

GARFIELD DOLLS

The characters of Garfield and Odie derived from the syndicated comic strip. Garfield is a stout, orange striped cat and Odie is the tan dog who lives with him.

The following fleece dolls were dispensed in Mexico at Christmas,1981: three Garfield dolls in Christmas costumes, one Odie doll, dressed as a reindeer. Attached to each doll is a white cloth tag with black lettering: "GARFIELD (C)1978, 1981 UNITED FEATURE SYNDICATE, INC." / "McDonald's" / "M.B.SALES, INC. OAK BROOK, IL / All new materials / contents:100% polyester fiber / MADE IN CHINA / Surface washable only".

The dolls were packaged in plastic bags with "suffocation warnings" in both Spanish and English languages. Christmas tags affixed to dolls had outer green and orange stripes, blue center spangled with white stars and a red Christmas ornament with head of Garfield.

1. SANTA GARFIELD   12 INCHES   AVG:$4.50 MINT:$10.50

He wears a red "Santa Suit" with black belt and boots, red stocking cap with a white tassel. White beard and vinyl eyes. (no tail showing) Seated position.

2. GARFIELD ELF   12 INCHES   AVG:$4.50 MINT:$10.50

Green jumper with big yellow (cloth) buttons, red boots and a square of red (shirt) showing in front. Red peaked hat with a wide green border, edged with points. His orange striped tail escapes from seat of pants. Standing position, legs apart.

3. ANGEL GARFIELD   12 INCHES   AVG:$5.50 MINT:$11.50

Long white suit covers feet. Yellow belt with small white over-skirt.White felt wings fastened at back. Metallic gold cord "halo" circles top of his head. Tail exits at rear. Position - seated.

4. REINDEER ODIE   12 INCHES   AVG:$ 5.00 MINT:$11.00

Pale yellow fur, white eyes. Floppy brown ears, big, black vinyl nose with red tongue hanging below. Around neck is green scarf with red and white yarn fringe. Tan felt "antlers" are sewn in area between ears and eyes.Black tail.

GARFIELD DOLLS

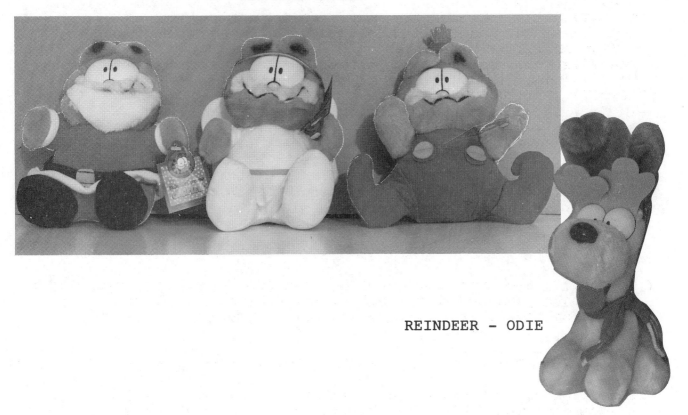

REINDEER - ODIE

MUPPET BABY DOLLS

MUPPET BABY DOLLS

Three Muppet Baby dolls were issued Christmas 1988, Miss Piggy, Kermit and Fozzie Bear (average height:12 inches).

Each toy is made of knitted fabric, has a white cloth label with black lettering, attached to seat. Label reads: "(C) 1987 Henson Associates, Inc./ (name of character) is a trademark of Henson Associates Inc./ All Rights Reserved /Simon Marketing Inc/ Los Angeles. CA / All New Materials / Contents: Polyester Fiber / Made in China / Reg. No. PA. 2621 (RC) / Surface Washable Only "

Tag reads: (C) 1988 McDonald's Corporation / MCD #88-062 FC MCDY-702 / (C) Henson Associates Inc.,1988 / MUPPET BABIES and character names are trademarks of Henson Associates, Inc. Other side reads: (to:/from:) "a portion of the proceeds from this toy will benefit Ronald McDONALD House and Ronald McDONALD Children's Charities / McDONALD'S / Made in China / Printed in Hong Kong ".

1. BABY MISS PIGGY   11 INCHES   AVG:$5.75 MINT:$8.00
Red (knit fabric) dress with cap sleeves and short full skirt, trimmed with white lace collar. Red bonnet, wide rim around face trimmed with white "fur". At forehead are two round ears and a cluster of golden curls. Eyes are large, painted plastic: blue eyes with pink lids. Nose is a short cylinder. At its base is a red tongue and lower lip. Light pink "gloves" and "boots". (skin tone-pale orange) .

2. BABY KERMIT   10 INCHES   AVG:$5.00 MINT:$7.50
Green knit fabric sewn to indicate mitten-like fingers and four-toed feet. His head is one-half of the body, a wedge of red forms the open mouth, (throat painted dark) showing a pink tongue.

Eyes are like half ping-pong balls with a black painted iris. He is in seated position with arms held out. A red-plaid vest and red stocking cap, trimmed with white fur and a white yarn tassel, complete the costume.

3. BABY FOZZIE BEAR   12 INCHES   AVG:$6.00 MINT:$8.50
Made of tan, curly fur-fabric, the bear is seated with arms out and mouth wide open. Mouth is a wedge of red fabric with pink tongue. Nose is a half-sphere covered with pink fabric. Eyes are painted vinyl with pink lids. He wears a floppy, red, wide-brimmed hat, trimmed with a green felt ribbon. Around his neck is a green knit scarf with red yarn fringed ends.

HAPPY MEALS 1977

DIRECTORY

SLAPHAPPYS

Abbreviations used to describe condition:
MINT = new, never used or unfolded.
AVG = average condition.
NP   = no original package, loose.
MIP = mint in package, in original, sealed
        container.

"FUN TO GO"   REGIONAL TEST-ST. LOUIS   OCTOBER

CARTONS (7):
1. 20,000 FILET-O-FISH   AVG:$7.00   MINT:$12.00
2. PROFESSOR IN HIS LABORATORY AVG:$7.00   MINT:$12.00
3. 2002 HAMBURGERS   AVG:$7.00   MINT:$12.00
4. McMOBILE   AVG:$7.50   MINT:$12.50
5. McDONALD'S BREAKFAST   AVG:$7.00   MINT:$12.00
6. BIG BURGER COUNTRY   AVG:$7.00   MINT:$12.00
7. MAZE CRAZE/PLANET OF PICKLES AVG:$7.50   MINT:$12.50

OTHER PREMIUMS DATED 1977 or earlier, which may have been
used by local markets:

O'GRIMACY INFLATABLES   AVG:$3.00 MINT:$5.50
12 INCHES
     Three-lobed: head in top lobe, extended flippers in
lobe at each side, with a brown walking stick held up in the
right one. His green vest, decorated with white outlined
shamrocks, is fastened in front with 2 large white buttons
and a chain. Beneath feet in large black block letters
"UNCLE O'GRIMACEY tm " . The other side shows him from the
back. At bottom edge reads "(C) 1977 McDonald's System,
Inc. / Printed in U.S.A.

PREMIUM:
STRAWS, with heads of McDONALDLAND characters:
1. RONALD McDONALD   AVG:$2.50   MINT:$4.00
2. HAMBURGLAR   AVG:$3.00   MINT:$4.50
3. BIG MAC   AVG:$2.50   MINT:$4.00
4. CAPTAIN CROOK   AVG:$3.00   MINT:$4.50

PREMIUM:
JOKE BOOKS: written by local children
        1 - 4   AVG:$4.00   MINT:$9.00

HAPPY MEAL   REGIONAL TEST -FIRST   KANSAS CITY   NOVEMBER
(Also: Phoenix, Tucson, Las Vegas & Denver)

CARTONS: " ROUND TOPS", made to look like lunch boxes

1. WHAT'S WRONG HERE?   AVG:$6.00   MINT:$12.50
2. RAINING CATS & DOGS   AVG:$6.00   MINT:$12.50
3. RONALD McD & MAYOr McCHEESE   AVG:$8.00   MINT:$15.00

PREMIUM:
WRIST WALLET: plastic, blue, red, yellow,
green. Heads of McDONALDLAND Characters on lids.

1. RONALD McDONALD   AVG:$3.50   MINT:$6.00
2. HAMBURGLAR   AVG:$5.00   MINT:$7.50
3. BIG MAC   AVG:$4.00   MINT:$6.50
4. CAPTAIN CROOK   AVG:$4.00   MINT:$6.50

PREMIUM:
RINGS: plastic, blue, red, yellow,and green,
with heads of McDONALDLAND Characters.

1. RONALD McDONALD   AVG:$3.00   MINT:$6.00
2. HAMBURGLAR   AVG:$3.00   MINT:$5.00
3. BIG MAC   AVG:$3.00   MINT:$5.00
4. CAPTAIN CROOK   AVG:$3.00   MINT:$6.00
5. GRIMACE   AVG:$3.00   MINT:$6.50

THE BURGLED HAMBURGER
A McDonaldland® Magic Trick

You can make the Hamburglar steal the hamburger—like magic!
Carefully punch out the cards. Notice that there is a secret slit half way around both the hamburger and the question mark. Carefully slide the hamburger through the slit in the front card so that it appears to be printed along with the shake and french fries on the front card. Hold the cards like this:

TO PERFORM: Ask a friend whether he thinks the Hamburglar would want to steal the shake, the hamburger or the french fries. Of course, he will say the hamburger. Then tell him to watch closely, because the Hamburglar will steal it by magic! Pass your left hand in front of the cards. As you do, your right thumb quickly slides the front card DOWN about an inch—enough to make the hamburger disappear. Then remove the front card and show that the Hamburglar really did steal the hamburger which is now in his hands! (Do not show the backs of the cards.)
PRACTICE THIS A FEW TIMES BEFORE DOING IT FOR FRIENDS. REMEMBER —A MAGICIAN NEVER REVEALS HIS SECRETS!
COLLECT ALL FOUR McDONALDLAND MAGIC TRICKS!

THE FAKE SHAKE

THE FAKE SHAKE
A McDonaldland® Magic Trick

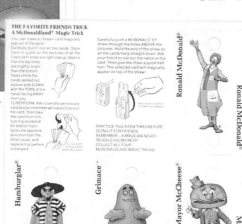

© 1977 Magic Magic Magic Unlimited

THE BURGLED HAMBURGER

THE FAVORITE FRIENDS TRICK
A McDonaldland® Magic Trick

THE VANISHING HAMBURGER

MAGIC TRICKS: Punch out cards. MCD #3233
(C) 1977 MAGIC MAGIC MAGIC UNLIMITED
(C) 1977 McDonald's System, Inc

1. "FAVORITE FRIENDS CARD TRICK"   AVG:$5.50   MINT:$10.00
2. "VANISHING HAMBURGER"   AVG:$7.00   MINT:$13.00
       Shows 14 or 15 'burgers depending on
       which way it is turned.
3. "THE FAKE SHAKE"   AVG:$7.00   MINT:$13.00
       Three cards: Grimace, Cheeseburger,
       Fries & Shake.
4. "THE BURGLED HAMBURGER"   AVG:$6.00   MINT:$11.00
       Two cards. Hamburglar makes burger
       disappear.

PAPER STENCIL: to draw faces.
1. Ronald McDONALD   AVG:$4.00   MINT:$7.50
2 Hamburglar   AVG:$4.00   MINT:$7.50

MAKE FUNNY FACES: paper punch-out.   AVG:$4.00   MINT:$7.00
pull strips through face area to see
expression change

STICKERS: 3 1/4 X 2 1/4 inches: AVG:$4.00   MINT:$7.00
1. RMCD: "Ride Safely"
2. HAMBURGLAR: "Lights On For Safety"
3. BIG MAC: "Obey All Rules Of The Road"
4. CAPTAIN CROOK: "Don't Tailgate"

"FORTUNE BURGER": rub-off game   AVG:$5.50   MINT:$9.00
  (C) 1976 McDonald's System, Inc.

COLOR CARD, 1977   AVG:$5.00   MINT:$8.00
Folded size: 3 1/2" X 3 1/2", open:5" X 7".
Provides six colors to be applied with dampened swab.
Figures, head to waist. (C)1977 McDonald's Systems Inc.
1. RONALD McDONALD
2. CAPTAIN CROOK

COMICS, MCDLAND, 1976   AVG:$45.00   MINT:$45.00
No.101. 'THE 200 YEAR TRIP".
6 5/8" x 10" .

PUNKIN' MAKINS: punch-out parts to stick on Halloween
pumpkins. (C) 1976 McDonald's System, Inc. MCD #1755-P
12" X 17 3/4" sheets with picture of finished design -
McDONALDLAND characters.   AF900-289

1. GRIMACE   AVG:$3.00   MINT:$8.00
2. HAMBURGLAR   AVG:$3.00   MINT:$8.00
3. GOBLIN   AVG:$3.00   MINT:$8.00

PAPER, MAZE & PUZZLE CARDS:
(C) 1976 McDonald's System, Inc. MCD #1755-P
(C) 1977 McDonald's System, Inc MCD #2323
3 X 9 inches:

1. "McDonald's Maze & Puzzle"   AVG:$7.00   MINT:$12.00
2. "Race to McDONALDLAND"   AVG:$6.00   MINT:$10.00
3. "Pour-Um Game"   AVG:$8.00   MINT:$13.00
4. "Match Game"   AVG:$8.00   MINT:$13.00

STENCIL, HAMBURGLAR, 1973   AVG:$4.50   MINT:$7.00
Cardboard   punch-out.   Standing   figure.
4" X 6 1/2".

McDONALDLAND "SLAPHAPPYS". 5 1/2 x 8 1/4 INCHES.
      Paper punch-out puppets.
1. RMCD   AVG:$8.00   MINT:$10.00
   "Ronald McDonald and the French Fry Thatch".
   PRINTED IN U.S.A. (C) 1973.
2. HAMBURGLAR   AVG:$8.00   MINT:$10.00
   ".Hamburglar and the Hamburger Patch."
   PRINTED IN U.S.A.
3. MAYOR McCHEESE   AVG:$8.00   MINT:$10.00
   "Mayor McCheese & The Gobblins".
   PRINTED IN U.S.A.
4. BIG MAC & GRIMACE   AVG:$10.00 MINT:$15.00
   "Big Mac & The Evil Grimace."
   NOTE: Grimace has four arms.
   PRINTED IN U.S.A.

Fortune Burger

Rub off cover from meat area of hamburger with wet cloth. See your fortune appear.

©1977 McDonald's System, Inc.

WRIST WALLET

MAKE FUNNY FACES

Ronald McDonald® Faces

Punch out perforated areas. Place stencil down on plain paper and draw outline of head using both sides of stencil. Then place eyes, nose and mouth in position. You can draw different expressions by using different sets of features.

©1977 McDonald's System, Inc.

Separate eye and mouth strips carefully along perforation. Insert them into slots in face to make funny faces.

MAYOR McCHEESE®

Separate eye and mouth strips carefully along perforation. Insert them into slots in face to make funny faces.

RONALD McDONALD®

GAME CARDS

McDonald's® Maze and Puzzle

Instructions: Separate all pieces. Game consists of 9 pieces.

1. Mix pieces and begin assembly of puzzle.
2. Puzzle pieces should be laid out in rows of 3 vertically and horizontally as shown.
3. After puzzle is complete, follow the maze to see if you can go from "Enter Here" to "Exit Here."

© 1977 McDonald's System Inc. The figures are trademarks of McDonald's Corporation. McD #2323.

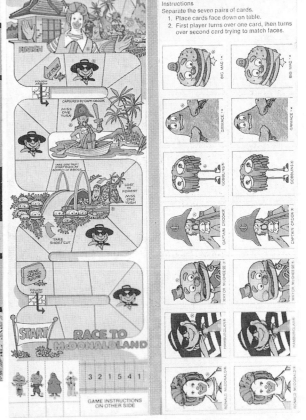

McDonald's® Pair-um Game

Instructions
Separate the seven pairs of cards.

1. Place cards face down on table.
2. First player turns over one card, then turns over second card trying to match faces.

BIKE STICKERS

Hamburglar® Says
"Lights On For Safety"
®1977 McDonald's System, Inc.

Captain Crook® says
"Don't Tailgate"
©1977 McDonald's System, Inc.

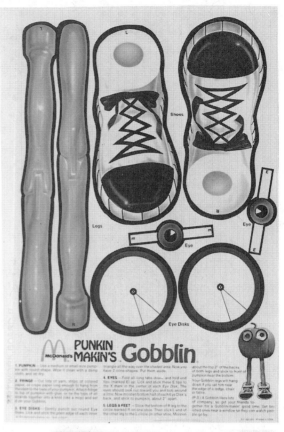

Big Mac™ says
"Obey All Rules Of The Road"
®1977 McDonald's System, Inc.

Ronald McDonald® says
"Ride Safely"
®1977 McDonald's System, Inc.

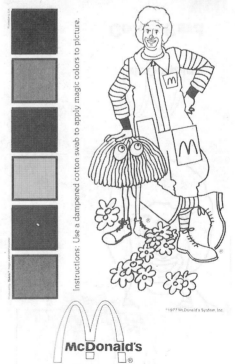

RINGS

Color-Card

HAPPY MEALS 1978

DIRECTORY

```
┌─────────────────────────────────────────────────────────┐
│        Abbreviations used to describe condition:         │
│        MINT = new, never used or unfolded.               │
│        AVG  = average condition.                         │
│        NP   = no original package, loose.                │
│        MIP  = mint in package, in original, sealed       │
│                   container.                             │
└─────────────────────────────────────────────────────────┘
```

HAPPY MEAL   REGIONAL TEST - 2ND, KANSAS CITY   FEBRUARY

PREMIUM:
    SPACE RAIDERS:(SEE DESCRIPTION "HAPPY MEALS 1979".)

PREMIUM:
    McDONALDLAND PENCIL PUPPETS   AVG:$3.50 MINT:$5.25

PREMIUM:
    McDONALDLAND PRESS-ONS   AVG:$3.00 MINT:$5.00

PREMIUM:
    UNCLE O'GRIMACY RINGS   AVG:$3.50 MINT:$6.00

PREMIUM:
    RONALD MAGIC PADS   AVG:$2.50 MINT:$4.75

PREMIUM: AVG:$3.25 MINT:$5.25
    SUNDAE SMILE SKIMMER

CARTONS (3):
    1. MAKE A FACE   AVG:$2.25 MINT:$5.50
    2. JINGLE JAMBOREE   AVG:$2.25 MINT:$5.50
    3. WEIRD CREATURES   AVG:$3.00 MINT:$6.00
```
```

HAPPY MEAL   REGIONAL TEST 3RD – KANSAS CITY   JUNE

PREMIUM:
FOUR JOKE BOOKS   AVG:$3.25   MINT:$5.25

PREMIUM:
JIGSAW PUZZLES, McDonald's System Inc.
manufactured by A/D Enterprises, Faifield, CT

1. PUZZLE   AVG:$4.00   MINT:$6.00
Professor and Grimace painting fence.
Text: "The Professor has hung up his
signs a bit late. The Grimace has
already opened the gate."

2. PUZZLE   AVG:$4.00   MINT:$6.00
Captain Crook and Big Mac. Text:
" Captain Crook needed help 'cause
his boat had a crack, so he borrowed
a board but got caught in the act."

PREMIUM:
        McDONALDLAND RUB-OFFS   AVG:$3.00   MINT:$5.50

PREMIUM:
        RING-AROUND-RONALD   AVG:$3.00   MINT:$5.00

PREMIUM:
        COLOR YOUR OWN XMAS ORNAMENT   AVG:$2.50   MINT:$4.50

PREMIUM:
        BIKE REFLECTORS, 3 X 1 inches   AVG:$6.00 MINT:$6.50
        McDONALDLAND characters holding
        spectra strip reflector with
        adhesive backing.

        1. RONALD McDONALD
        2. HAMBURGLAR
        3. BIG MAC
        4. CAPTAIN CROOK

BAG: plastic, Halloween   AVG:$4.50 MINT:$6.00
        "Trick or Treat", 1978, with safety rules.

JIGSAW PUZZLES

LIFT-PADS

BIKE REFLECTORS

PREMIUM:
SPINNING TOPS,plastic   AVG:$3.50   MINT:$5.75
Red, green, blue. Finger twist type.
Spiral of golden arches when moving.

OTHER PREMIUMS DATED 1978, which may
have been used by local markets:

STICKER, "KIDS DAY"   AVG:$3.00   MINT:$4.00

FAMILY FUN FOR ALL: paper,   AVG:$3.00   MINT:$4.75
5 1/2 X 8 1/2 inches,puzzles
and games. Four different designs.

MYSTERY PUZZLE: white cardboard   AVG:$3.50   MINT:$5.50

COMIC BOOKS: 6 1/2 X 3 1/2 inches.
(C) McDonald's System Inc. 1978.
1.   AVG:$3.00   MINT:$4.00
RONALD McDONALD AND THE FRIES FARMERS.
2.   AVG:$3.50   MINT:$5.00
RONALD McDONALD in the DISAPPEARING ACT.

FINGER PUPPETS: punch out, fold and put
on finger.(C) McDonald's System Inc. 1978

1. HAMBURGLAR   AVG:$2.50   MINT:$3.50
2. BIG MAC   AVG:$2.50   MINT:$3.50

McDONALDLAND PAINT-WITH-WATER   AVG:$3.75   MINT:$6.00
3 7/8 X 2 6/8 inches. cardboard,
with its own punch-out frame and
easel.(C) McDonald's System Inc. 1978

McDONALDLAND COLORING STAND-UPS   AVG:$3.50   MINT:$5.00
Color, and punch out.Fold to stand up.
(C) McDonald's System Inc. 1978

COLORING STAND-UPS

COMIC BOOKS

MYSTERY   PUZZLE

GAME CARDS: 3 X 9 inches:
(C) McDonald's System inc. 1978

SILLY METRICS TRADING CARD	AVG:$3.10	MINT:$4.25
RACE TO McDONALDLAND	AVG:$3.00	MINT:$4.00
McDONALDLAND PAIR-UM GAME	AVG:$3.50	MINT:$5.00
McDONALDLAND MATCH GAME	AVG:$3.00	MINT:$4.00
PUNCH OUT CARD	AVG:$3.10	MINT:$4.50
MAKE-A-SCULPTURE		

FAVORITE FRIENDS MAGIC TRICK   AVG:$3.00   MINT:$4.00
Seven punch-out cards picturing
McDONALDLAND characters. (See 1977
for photograph.)

PICTURE   AVG:$3.25 MINT:$6.00
Transparent. To be applied to a window, picturing the
Professor, Grimace and a Goblin.
(C) McDonald's System Inc. 1978

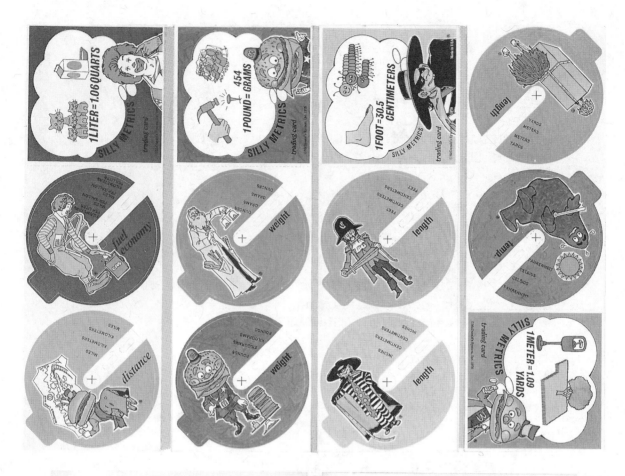

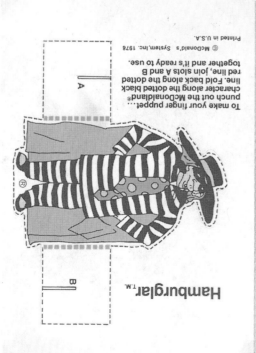

FINGER PUPPETS

HAPPY MEALS 1979

DIRECTORY

```
┌─────────────────────────────────────────────────────────┐
│        Abbreviations used to describe condition:          │
│        MINT = new, never used or unfolded.                │
│        AVG  = average condition.                          │
│        NP   = no original package, loose.                 │
│        MIP  = mint in package, in original, sealed        │
│               container.                                  │
└─────────────────────────────────────────────────────────┘
```

GENERIC HAPPY MEALS & PREMIUMS:

"LION CIRCUS"   HAPPY MEAL   1979
Rubber toys made by Diener Ind. Inc. All figurines are
marked with "DIENER IND INC (C)". Toys average 1 1/2 inches
in height. Animals are in sitting positions.
Colors: yellow, pink, green and orange.

1. LION   NP:$8.00   MINT:$12.00
2. ELEPHANT   NP:$7.00   MINT:$10.00
3. HIPPOPOTAMUS   NP:$8.25   MINT:$13.00
4. BEAR   NP:$8.25   MINT:$13.00

CARTON:
"WHAT'S THIS ?"   AVG:$4.00   MINT:$9.50
        Circus Scenes

"WHAT IS IT ?"   HAPPY MEAL   1979
Premiums were rubber toys made by Diener Ind. ENG. and were
produced in blue, green, pink, orange and yellow.
1.4 to 1.8 inches. Diener rubber figures are still being
sold.

1. OWL   AVG:$1.00   MINT:$1.75
2. BEAR   AVG:$1.00   MINT:$1.75
3. BABOON   AVG:$1.50   MINT:$2.00
4. HORNED SNAKE   AVG:$1.25   MINT:$2.00
5. SKUNK   AVG:$1.00   MINT:$1.75
6. SQUIRREL   AVG:$1.25   MINT:$1.75

CARTON:
"WHAT IS IT ?"   AVG:$4.00   MINT:$9.00
        16 Quizzes.
```
```

LION CIRCUS

WHAT IS IT?

ANIMAL RIDDLES

"ANIMAL RIDDLES"   HAPPY   MEAL   1979
Premiums were rubber toys made by Diener Ind. ENG. and were
produced in blue, green, pink, orange and yellow. 2 to 2 1/2
inches. The Diener rubber figures are still being sold.

No identifying marks on these:
1. CONDOR   AVG:$2.00   MINT:$2.50
    Baby buzzard with large head.

2. SNAIL, orange   AVG:$1.00   MINT:$1.75
    Wearing a vest, bow tie and cap.

3. TURTLE   AVG:$1.00   MINT:$1.50
    Playing a guitar and singing.

4. MOUSE   AVG:$1.50   MINT:$2.50
    Large ears. wearing jacket, hands
    clasped behind back.
    Marked: DIENER IND. ENG.

5. ANTEATER   AVG:$1.50   MINT:$2.50
    Wears long jacket, collar, tie and
    bowler hat.

6. ALLIGATOR   AVG:$1.00   MINT:$1.50
    Left hand is raised with finger
    pointing up as if speaking or singing.
    Left leg crossed in front of body.
    Wears jacket, bow-tie and handkerchief in
    breast pocket.

7. COW, pink   AVG:$1.00   MINT:$1.75

8. DINOSAUR   AVG:$1.50   MINT:$2.50
    Sitting up, short front legs.

CARTON: AVG:$5.00   MINT:$11.00

"SMART DUCK"   HAPPY MEAL   1979
CARTON: AVG:$5.00   MINT:$11.00

HAPPY MEAL TEST

MINI-FLEXI. Ten rubber futuristic matchbox cars, with
no moving parts. MATCHBOX (R) LESNEY PROD. CORP. LTD. ENG.
Names are incised on sides of cars. 1.8 To 2.3 inches.
Colors: green, pink, blue, yellow and orange. Still being
sold by Diener Ind..

1. COSMOBIL   AVG:$1.50   MINT:$2.50
   Armored type vehicle.
   Two pipes on roof.

2. FANDANGO   AVG:$1.00   MINT:$1.75
   Sleek. fan on back.

3. PLANET SCOUT   AVG:$1.00   MINT:$2.00
   Rocket car.

4. HAIRY HUSTLER   AVG:$1.25   MINT:$2.25
   Air scoop on back.

5. DATSUN   AVG:$1.00   MINT:$1.75
   Design of flames over top.

6. HI-TAILER   AVG:$1.00   MINT:$2.00
   High spoiler, rocket-like engine.

7. BAJA BUGGY   AVG:$1.00   MINT:$1.75
   Dune buggy with roof, raised
   back engine.

8. BEACH HOPPER   AVG:$1.00   MINT:$2.00
   Open dune buggy. Driver wearing
   cap.

9. (unknown)
10. (unknown)

McDONALDLAND COMIC BOOKS   AVG:$3.50   MINT:$5.75
Regions: BUFFALO, KANSAS CITY, DENVER, ST.LOUIS.

McDONALDLAND Lift-ups, Mystery Games:
   MAYOR WORD GUESS   AVG:$3.00   MINT:$7.00
   RONALD MAZE   AVG:$3.50   MINT:$7.50
   PROFESSOR DOT GAME   AVG:$3.50   MINT:$7.50
   BIG MAC TIC-TAC-TOE   AVG:$4.00   MINT:$8.00

MINI-FLEXI

"CIRCUS WAGON'   HAPPY MEAL   JUNE
Rubber toys made by Diener Ind. Inc. Except for Ape,
all figurines are marked with "DIENER IND INC (C)".
Colors: yellow, pink, blue and orange.

1. CLOWN   NP:$6.00   MINT:$10.00
Huge shoes. Holds a ball in both hands,
above right shoulder. 2 3/8 inches high.

2. HORSE   NP:$5.00   MINT:$10.00
Rearing, front feet off ground.
Decorative harness and head ornament.
2 1/2 inches high.

3. APE   NP:$6.25   MINT:$10.50
Chimpansee-like. Seated, scratching
thigh with left hand. Wears a bowler hat.
1 5/8 inches.

4. POODLE DOG   NP:$6.25   MINT:$10.50
Sitting up, front feet held in front
of body. 1 1/2 inches high.

CARTONS (6):
In St. Louis, 6 types were used. (Only one national carton.)
1.WHEN DOES A MONKEY CHASE A BANANA ? AVG:$3.00   MINT:$5.00
2.WHAT KIND OF CAT IN LIBRARY ?   AVG:$3.00   MINT:$5.00
3.WHAT DO ZEBRAS HAVE ?   AVG:$2.50   MINT:$5.50
4.WHY DO ELEPHANTS HAVE
     WRINKLED KNEES ?   AVG:$4.00   MINT:$6.00
5.WHEN DO LIONS HAVE 8 FEET   AVG:$4.00   MINT:$6.00
6.WHY ISN'T A SEAL'S NOSE 12" LONG ?   AVG:$3.75   MINT:$5.50

"SPACE"   HAPPY MEAL   JULY
SPACE ALIENS & SPACE RAIDERS. All areas did not use the same
premiums.

SPACE ALIENS: (hard rubber,marked DIENER (C) IND.)
Colors: orange, pink, lavender, yellow, green and blue.
The Diener rubber figures are still being sold.

1.GILL FACE   NP:$1.50 MIP:$2.25
Wears scaly armor shirt, armored all
over, pads on left shoulder, knees,
elbows and chest. Right arm is raised
from elbow. Large head with pointed ears.
Gills fill in face area below eyes.

2.TREE TRUNK MONSTER   NP:$1.50 MIP:$2.25
Ape-like creature with long dangling
arms ending in three fingers each. Legs
end in flat circular roots. Body is
grooved all over like hair or bark.
Tendrils cross face area and torso.
The mouth is a toothy circle.

3.LIZARD MAN   NP:$1.00 MIP:$2.50
Scaly texture all over, four lobed feet,
finned wrists and a lizard head.
A raised ridge runs from top of head
to end of spine.

4.VAMPIRE BAT   NP:$1.25 MIP:$2.50
Male humanoid creature in bikini suit.
Hands and feet have three digits each.
Large bat wings fall from upraised arms.
Furred bat head with big pointed ears. Open mouth.

5.WINGED AMPHIBIAN   NP:$1.25 MIP:$2.00
Humanoid creature, pebbled-textured
surface. The feet end in three claws
and the hands end in pincer-claws. At
sides of arms are wide spread fins; a
smaller set adorn either side of its head.
Fish-like face with open mouth showing teeth.

6.HORNED CYCLOPS   NP:$1.50   MIP:$2.00
Hairy and built like a gorilla, it
sports two horns on its ape head.
One central eye and an open mouth.

7.INSECTMAN   NP:$1.00   MIP:$1.75
Humanoid creature of mixed parentage:
large fly head, sow bug abdomen, upper
arms, chest and back are lizard-like.
Lower furred arms end in pincers.
Furred legs with cloven hooves.

8.VEINED CRANIUM   NP:$1.75   MIP:$2.50
Body has child-like proportions, huge
head. Area above face embossed with veins.
Large pointed ears. It wears a scaly-
textured shirt and smooth boots. The
long arms are held at sides.

SPACE RAIDERS: rubber, marked DIENER IND. on back,
name of character embossed on front.
Colors:orange, pink, lavender, yellow, green & blue.
The Diener rubber figures are still being sold.

1.POINTED EARS, DARD   NP:$1.00   MIP:$1.50
Wears space suit with square boots,
finned gloves, armored upper body,
small cannister on back. Helmet has big,
pointed, ear-like projections on both sides.

2.ALIEN, ZAMA   NP:$1.00   MIP:$1.75
Robot. Wears diving type helmet with a
single viewer plate on front. Instrument
plate over armored chest. Gloves with
pincers, boots are blocked. Circular
grooves suggest arms and legs in flexible armor.

3.ALIEN, HORTA   NP:$1.00   MIP:$1.50
Belted space suit has wide shoulder
cover, two ports on front. Gloves on
upraised hands, rounded boots. Triangular
helmet has face plate with areas designed
for eyes, nose and mouth.

4.ROUND HEAD, DRAK   NP:$1.00   MIP:$1.90
Robot head has large, rounded top which
is patterned to suggest electronic parts
and circuitry. Below this are two,round
eye-lenses and a smaller round speaker.
Space suit: short sleeved shirt with
instrument panel on chest, brief pants
over armored legs and arms. Big rounded
boots. Arms differ: left arm has four fingers,
right arm has six fingers.(may have been
an occasional manufacturing error).

5.FLYING SAUCER, LYRA 4   NP:$1.00   MIP:$1.50
Two inches in diameter. Top patterned
with circles and grooves. On outer edge
marks: "LYRA 4", on the underside is a
cluster of eight rockets. "DIENER IND".

6.ROCKET, KRYOO 5   NP:$1.00   MIP:$1.50
Two-inch rocket ship, wide V-shaped
wings. The top surface is patterned
with pods. Thruster area is lettered:
"KRYOO 5". Underside: rockets, landing
gear and "(C) DIENER IND".

7.ROCKET, CETI-3   NP:$1.00   MIP:$1.75
Space ship booster-nozzle. First two
inches are cylindrical with cone on
front end, patterned to suggest appropriate
hardware. Small rocket on one side and
"(C) DIENER IND". On the other side is
an exhaust nozzle and "CETI-3". Below the
cylinder is a wider, half-inch long, rocket
pod holding eight rockets.

8.ROCKET, ALTAIR 2   NP:$1.50   MIP:$1.75
Rocket ship. 3 1/4 inches long. Sharply
pointed nose has small V-shaped fins.
Body is a narrow, tapering cylinder with
a central pair of larger V-shaped fins
and a larger pair of fins on the tail
section (which also has a rudder fin).
The tail section contains a pod of eight
rockets. By the pilot's area is: "ALTAIR",
on the rudder is: "2". The underside shows
two small rockets and "DIENER IND" .

CARTONS (6):
1.GRIMACE MAKING SHAKES   AVG:$14.00   MINT:$20.00
2.SPACE ZOO   AVG:$10.00   MINT:$17.50
3.McDONALDLAND CHARACTERS   AVG:$18.00   MINT:$24.00
4.RMCD AND SPACE CREATURE   AVG:$12.00   MINT:$18.00
5.BIG MAC AND MARTIANS   AVG:$17.00   MINT:$22.00
6.RMCD AND MAYOR McCHEESE   AVG:$14.00   MINT:$20.00

"STAR TREK"   HAPPY MEAL   DECEMBER
Set of five toys based on the popular Movie and TV show.
(C) Paramount Pictures Corp.

VIDEO COMMUNICATOR
Black, silver or blue plastic " walkie-talkie" toy with a
handle-crank, displays 12-frame "mini-movies". At least five
different movies versions are available.

STRIP:
1. "STAR TREK STARS"   AVG:$15.00 MINT:$28.00
2. "A PILL SWALLOWS THE ENTERPRISE"   AVG:$17.00 MINT:$30.00
3. "TIME AND TIME AND TIME AGAIN"   AVG:$18.00 MINT:$35.00
4. "VOTEC'S FREEDOM"   AVG:$17.00 MINT:$30.00
5. "STARLIGHT STAR FRIGHT"   AVG:$17.00 MINT:$30.00

STARFLEET GAME   AVG:$15.00 MINT:$22.00
Board game for as many as five players.
(paper) MCD#5986

DECALS   AVG:$12.00 MINT:$20.00
DOUBLE GLITTER IRON-ON decals.
Show: figure, name, Startrek insignia
and text: "Startrek" . Two per box.
Four *STAR TREK* characters in different colors.
(C) 1979 Paramount Pictures Corp.
     1. MR. SPOCK   3. DR. McCOY
     2. LT. ILIA   4. CAPTAIN KIRK

BRACELET: NAVIGATION   AVG:$9.50 MINT:$15.00
Dark blue plastic with scene of galaxy
or navigational charts. Six decals.

RING: SPACE
Ring with square case. Lid opens on
inner compartment. Lids embossed with:
1. Captain Kirk   AVG:$7.00 MINT:$11.00
2. Spock   AVG:$7.00 MINT:$11.00
3. Startrek insignia   AVG:$7.00 MINT:$11.00
4. Enterprise   AVG:$7.00 MINT:$11.00

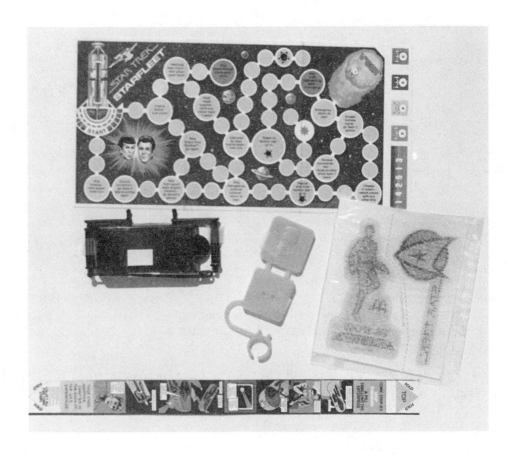

CARTONS (6):" McDonald's STAR TREK MEAL"
McD #5937-P   AF 920-0110

1.TRANSPORTER ROOM   AVG:$10.00 MINT:$13.00
"The transporter moves objects or
people from one place to another."

2.KLINGONS   AVG:$ 8.00 MINT:$12.00
"These are the aliens that live
outside the Federation boundaries..."

3.THE BRIDGE, planets   AVG:$ 8.00 MINT:$12.00
"Captain Kirk runs the ship from the
control room. The Bridge is the "brain"
of the ship" (Find the faces in the planets)

4.UNITED FEDERATION OF PLANETS   AVG:$ 8.00 MINT:$12.00
"The Federation oversees the universe
and keeps peace. The Earth is a member
of the Federation".

5.SPACESUIT   AVG:$10.00 MINT:$14.00
"The suit worn by Enterprise crew
members has a rocket on the back that
moves them through space..."

6.BRIDGE, alien   AVG:$ 9.00 MINT:$12.00
"Captain Kirk runs the ship from the
control room. The Bridge is the "brain"
of the ship" (Draw the Alien.)

Other miscellaneous items which may have been premiums:

O'GRIMACY INFLATABLES	AVG:$3.00	MINT:$5.50

(Becomes a puppet by cutting off bottom.)

McDONALDLAND YOYO ,red ,yellow	AVG:$3.00	MINT:$5.00
SKIMMER RINGS, SUNDAE SMILE SAUCER	AVG:$2.50	MINT:$3.75
FRENCH FRY RINGS	AVG:$8.00	MINT:$12.00

    XOGraph picture of fries.

RONALD STYRO-GLIDER: punch-out plane	AVG:$4.00	MINT:$6.00
FRENCH FRY FLUTES, SPINNING TOPS	AVG:$3.00	MINT:$5.00
"SILLY SIDE SHOW": punch out card	AVG:$5.00	MINT:$9.00
"FISHIN' FUN WITH CAPTAIN CROOK" :	AVG:$5.00	MINT:$9.00

paper punch out game

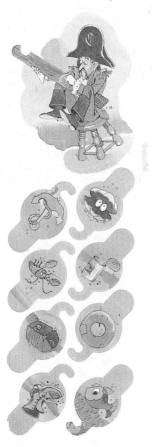

FISHIN' FUN WITH
CAPTAIN CROOK

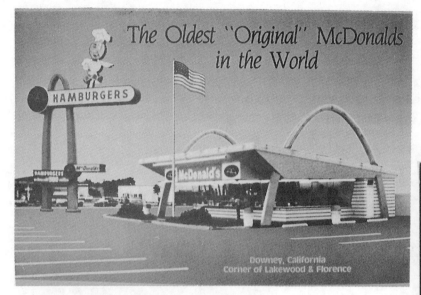

McDONALD'S RIVERBOAT
RESTAURANT. The only
floating McDonald's.
St. Louis, MO.

ILLINOIS TOLLWAY
SYSTEM. McDONALD'S
"OASIS" RESTAURANTS
Belvidere, Ill

"THE WORLD'S LARGEST
MCDONALD'S" (was)
Vinita, Oklahoma.
29,135 square feet.

McDONALD'S DES PLAINES MUSEUM
Illinois.

POSTCARDS:Miscellaneous

HAPPY MEALS 1980

DIRECTORY

Abbreviations used to describe condition:
MINT = new, never used or unfolded.
AVG = average condition.
NP   = no original package, loose.
MIP = mint in package, in original, sealed
         container.

"DALLAS COWBOYS SUPER BOX"   HAPPY MEAL (REGIONAL*)   1980
(regional - Texas)
Set of three Cartons only, from which Baseball Trading Cards
could be cut.

1.CHUCK HOWLEY/DON PERKINS   AVG:$8.00 MINT:$15.00
2.DON MEREDITH/BOB LILLY   AVG:$9.00 MINT:$17.00
3.ROGER STAUGACH/W.GARRISON   AVG:$9.00 MINT:$17.00

"LOOK-LOOK BOOKS"   HAPPY MEAL (REGIONAL*)   1980
(regional - St. Louis) Set of four books published by
Western Publishing Co.

1."ANIMALS THAT FLY"   AVG:$3.00 MINT:$7.50
2."ANIMALS OF THE SEA"   AVG:$3.00 MINT:$7.50
3."CATS IN THE WILD"   AVG:$4.00 MINT:$8.50
4."THE BIGGEST ANIMALS"   AVG:$2.50 MINT:$7.00

"UNDERSEA"   HAPPY MEAL (OPTIONAL)   SPRING
Set of six cartons. Some regions also offered Diener, soft &
hard rubber figures in colors: lt. green, lt. blue, yellow,
pink and orange. Some of the figures have "DIENER IND"
or the name of the animal incised.
The Diener rubber figures are still being sold.

DIENER FIGURES:
1. SEAL   NP:$1.00   MIP:$1.75
2. DOLPHIN   NP:$1.10   MIP:$2.25
       Stands on tail in curl of wave.
       Marked: "DIENER".
3. TIGER SHARK   NP:$1.00   MIP:$1.75
4. HAMMERHEAD SHARK   NP:$1.00   MIP:$1.75
       Marked: "HAMMERHEAD".
5. SEA TURTLE   NP:$1.00   MIP:$1.75
6. PENGUIN   NP:$1.00   MIP:$1.75
7. WHALE   NP:$1.10   MIP:$2.25
       Tail and head raised, mouth
       open.Marked: "DIENER".
8. WHALE SHARK   NP:$1.00   MIP:$2.00
       Marked: "WHALESHARK".
9. WALRUS   NP:$1.00   MIP:$2.25
       Marked: "DIENER INC (C)1966".
10. CROCODILE   NP:$1.00   MIP:$2.00
       Marked: "DIENER INC (C)1977".
11. GREAT WHITE SHARK   NP:$1.00   MIP:$2.25

CARTONS (6):
1. RONALD IN SUB   AVG:$5.00 MINT:$9.00
2. GRIMACE SQUID & SCUBA DIVER   AVG:$7.00 MINT:$12.00
3. EEL & SCUBA DIVER   AVG:$7.00 MINT:$12.00
4. RONALD,CAPT' IN FISH MOUTH   AVG:$7.00 MINT:$12.00
5. GRIMACE ON PORPOISE,SQUID   AVG:$5.00 MINT:$9.00
6. (unknown)

"SAFARI ADVENTURE"   HAPPY MEAL   (OPTIONS)   SUMMER
Some regions offered Diener, soft & hard rubber figures in
colors: blue, yellow, pink, lavender and orange. Figures
have "DIENER IND" incised on bodies. Average height is two
inches. The Diener rubber figures are still being sold.

ANIMAL FIGURINES:
1. ELEPHANT   NP:$1.00 MINT:$2.25
          Trunk raised
2. TIGER   NP:$1.00 MINT:$2.00
          Lying on stomach, head raised.
3. HIPPOPOTAMUS   NP:$1.25 MINT:$1.75
              Standing
4. RHINOCEROS   NP:$1.00 MINT:$1.75
              Standing
5. LION   NP:$1.00 MINT:$2.00
     Seated, head turned over right shoulder
6. ALLIGATOR   NP:$1.00 MINT:$1.75
     (No teeth showing, may be a crocodile.)
7. GORILLA   NP:$1.25 MINT:$2.25
     Thumps chest with left hand, right
     hand raised.
8. MONKEY   NP:$1.25 MINT:$2.25
     Holds banana in upraised hand.

CARTONS (4):
1.RONALD AND GRIMACE   AVG:$9.00   MINT:$16.00
2.RONALD AND MONKEYS/GOBLIN   AVG:$12.00 MINT:$20.00
3.RONALD AND HYENA   AVG:$12.00 MINT:$20.00
4.RONALD AND MONKEYS/HIPPO   AVG:$9.00   MINT:$16.00

HAPPY MEALS 1981

DIRECTORY

```
+--------------------------------------------------------------+
|         Abbreviations used to describe condition:            |
|         MINT = new, never used or unfolded.                  |
|         AVG  = average condition.                            |
|         NP   = no original package, loose.                   |
|         MIP  = mint in package, in original, sealed          |
|                container.                                    |
+--------------------------------------------------------------+
```

"OLD WEST"   HAPPY MEAL (OPTIONAL)   SPRING
(Optional use of generic premiums. Some areas used Diener
Ind. rubber figures. Color: yellow, no markings.)

FIGURINES:
1.FRONTIERSMAN, with knife   AVG:$8.00   MINT:$12.00
2.LADY, with gun   AVG:$10.00 MINT:$15.00
3.INDIAN   AVG:$10.00 MINT:$15.00
      Looking over right shoulder,
      right hand out from side.
4.INDIAN WOMAN   AVG:$10.00 MINT:$15.00
      Arms crossed. Long dress.
5.SHERIFF   AVG:$8.00   MINT:$12.00
      Hands on hips.
6.MAN, with hands up   AVG:$9.00   MINT:$11.00
      Dressed as cowboy.
      Gun holsters on each side.
      hands raised even with hat brim.

CARTONS (6):
1.BLACKSMITH SHOP   AVG:$8.00   MINT:$13.00
2.HOTEL   AVG:$7.00   MINT:$12.00
3.SHERIFF'S OFFICE   AVG:$7.00   MINT:$12.00
4.GENERAL STORE   AVG:$9.00   MINT:$15.00
5.MUSIC HALL   AVG:$8.00   MINT:$13.00
6.TRAIN DEPOT   AVG:$9.00   MINT:$15.00

"GOING PLACES"   HAPPY MEAL   1981
(Optional; re-run in 1983) Cartons only.

CARTONS (6):
1.AIRPLANE   AVG:$4.00   MINT:$6.25
2.GREY ELEPHANT   AVG:$4.00   MINT:$6.25
3.PADDLE WHEELER   AVG:$6.00   MINT:$9.20
4.DUNE BUGGY   AVG:$4.50   MINT:$7.00
5.FIRE ENGINE   AVG:$6.00   MINT:$9.00
6.STEAM ENGINE   AVG:$4.50   MINT:$7.00

"3-D HAPPY MEAL"   HAPPY MEAL   1981
Designs were done in "3-D" on cartons which included "3-D
glasses".

CARTONS (4):
1.BUGSVILLE/HUNGRY FUNNIES   AVG:$8.00   MINT:$11.50
2.CLOWNISH CAPERS/HIGH JINX   AVG:$7.50   MINT:$10.75
3.LAUGHING STOCK/LOCO MOTION   AVG:$8.00   MINT:$11.50
4.SPACE FOLLIES/GURGLE GAGS   AVG:$7.00   MINT:$10.00
```
```

"THE ADVENTURES OF RONALD McDONALD"   HAPPY MEAL   MAY
Premiums are McDONALDLAND figures, made in both hard and
soft rubber. Backs of Hard rubber toys incised with "(C)
McDONALD'S CORP. 1981".   Colors: yellow, orange, blue, pink
and green.

FIGURES:
1. RONALD McDONALD,	AVG:$4.50	MINT:$6.00
2. GRIMACE	AVG:$4.00	MINT:$5.50
3. BIRDIE	AVG:$4.00	MINT:$5.50
4. BIG MAC	AVG:$4.25	MINT:$5.25
5. MAYOR McCHEESE	AVG:$4.25	MINT:$5.25
6. CAPTAIN CROOK	AVG:$4.50	MINT:$6.00
7. HAMBURGLAR	AVG:$4.00	MINT:$5.50

CARTONS (6):
1.MIDNIGHT AT McDonald's	AVG:$6.00	MINT:$10.25
2.END OF RAINBOW	AVG:$7.00	MINT:$11.25
3.WHO'S GOBLIN UP THE FRIES	AVG:$6.00	MINT:$10.00
4.THE BIG HUNT	AVG:$8.00	MINT:$12.00
5.CHEESEBURGER EXPRESS	AVG:$7.50	MINT:$12.75
6.RODEO COWBOY	AVG:$8.00	MINT:$13.00

"DINOSAUR DAYS"   HAPPY MEAL   WINTER
Optional: some areas used rubber dinosaurs figures, marked
with "(C) DIENER IND " and the dinosaur's name.
Colors: brown, red, green, lt. blue and dark blue.
The Diener rubber figures are still being sold.
Option: XOgraphs of dinosaurs.

DINOSAUR FIGURES:
1.DIMETRODON   AVG:$1.75 MINT:$2.50
      Large headed "lizard":
      standing on all four feet, huge vertical fin on back
      (Name on tail, logo on underbelly).

2.STEGOSAURUS   AVG:$1.00 MINT:$1.75
      Standing on all four feet,
      the body raises high in the hip area. The back ridge
      is lined with large, separate, bony plates and a
      spiked tail.(name and logo on tail)

3.TYRANNOSAURUS   AVG:$2.00 MINT:$2.75
      Stands on powerful back legs,
      balanced by its thick tail. Tiny front legs are held
      closely to its chest. The enormous head is open-
      mouthed. (name and logo on tail)

4.TRICERATOPS   AVG:$1.75 MINT:$2.50
      The rhino-shaped body
      stands on all four feet, raising higher over the back
      legs. Its huge head ends in a parrot-like beak, has a
      short horn over the nose and a longer horn above the
      eyes. A flared mantle of bone stands out around the
      back of the head. (name on tail, logo on underbelly)

5.ANKYLOSAURUS   AVG:$1.00 MINT:$1.75
      Turtle-like creature;
      its upper shell is heavily plated and narrows into a
      knob at the tail end. Crouched on all four feet, its
      head is crowned by a raised ridge of scales.
      (underside: logo on feet, name on tail)

6.PTERANODON   AVG:$1.00 MINT:$1.75
      The bird-like, furry body
      stands on taloned back legs, with its great wings,
      (which are attached to long front legs) spread wide.
      The head is wedge-shaped with a huge beak. A bony
      projection at the back of the head creates a hammer-
      like profile.

DINOSAUR DAYS - XOGRAPHS

XOGRAPHS: "WONDERS OF THE PREHISTORIC WORLD" This series of six cards shows two different pictures, revealed alternately as card is tilted. On the back is a description of the animals pictured. 1981 McDonald's CORPORATION.TEXT BY EDITORS OF THE WORLD BOOK ENCYCLOPEDIA.

1.MASTODONS   AVG:$6.00 MINT:$12.00
scene 1: mother and baby
      in grassy area mountains in background.
scene 2: herd of three animals in grassy area.

2.STEGOSAURUS   AVG:$5.00 MINT:$10.00
scene 1: single animal in desert setting
scene 2: two animals eating by a pond.

3.TRICERATOPS   AVG:$5.00 MINT:$10.00
scene 1: single animal on plains.
scene 2: skeleton of animal.

4.BRONTOSAURUS   AVG:$6.50 MINT:$12.50
scene 1: close-up of head.
      In background another feeds, standing in water.
scene 2: pair of animals at edge of lake.

5.SABER-TOOTHED TIGER   AVG:$5.00 MINT:$10.00
scene 1: close-up view of head.
scene 2: animal standing at edge of grassy cliff.

6.TYRANNOSAURUS REX   AVG:$6.00 MINT:$12.00
scene 1: animal standing on plains,
          volcano in background.
scene 2: head, close-up. Pteranodon in sky.

CARTONS (6):
1.BRONTOSAURUS   AVG:$12.00 MINT:$16.00
2.ANKYLOSAURUS   AVG:$12.00 MINT:$16.00
3.BRONTOSAURUS, skeletons   AVG:$18.00 MINT:$24.00
4.BRACHIOSAURUS   AVG:$14.50 MINT:$19.50
5.ANATOSAURUS   AVG:$18.00 MINT:$22.00
6.WOOLY MAMMOTH   AVG:$12.00 MINT:$16.00

HAPPY MEALS 1982

DIRECTORY

```
Abbreviations used to describe condition:
MINT = new, never used or unfolded.
AVG  = average condition.
NP   = no original package, loose.
MIP  = mint in package, in original, sealed
       container.
```

"SPACESHIP"   HAPPY MEAL   JANUARY
Set of sixteen, two-piece, plastic spaceships plus sheet
of decals. Four styles made in four different colors.
(previously tested in Kansas City & St. Louis)
SPACESHIPS   AVG:$6.00 MINT:$14.00

"GOING PLACES"   HAPPY MEAL   FEBRUARY
Consisted of cartons only. Some areas may have used their
own premiums, "Happy Cups", or may not have participated.
Intended to be re-run nationally in 1983.

CARTONS (6):
1. DUNE BUGGY   AVG:$6.00 MINT:$10.00
2. STEAM ENGINE   AVG:$8.00 MINT:$12.00
3. AIRPLANE   AVG:$5.50 MINT:$9.00
4. GREY ELEPHANT   AVG:$6.00 MINT:$10.00
5. PADDLE WHEELER   AVG:$7.00 MINT:$11.00
6. FIRE ENGINE   AVG:$6.00 MINT:$10.00

GIGGLES AND GAMES"   HAPPY MEALS   1982
Cartons with games etc. used for optional generic premiums.

CARTONS:
1.CHASE
2.MONSTER   AVG:$8.00   MINT:$12.00
3.OUTER SPACE   AVG:$7.00   MINT:$10.00
4.BUMPER CAR   AVG:$10.00 MINT:$14.00
5.SUNKEN TREASURE   AVG:$7.00   MINT:$10.00
6.ROAD RALLY   AVG:$11.00 MINT:$15.00
                            AVG:$9.00   MINT:$13.00

"AIRPLANE: HAPPY MEAL   1982
This was a set of six cartons distributed internationally,
and in only a few national areas. The cartons could be
punched out to form funny airplanes.
CARTONS   AVG:$18.00 MINT:$27.00

"SKYBUSTERS""   HAPPY MEAL   1982
Set of six soft or hard, rubber airplanes. Colors: yellow,
orange, blue, green and brown. Average: 2.8 inches.
Markings: "MATCHBOX LESNEY PROD. CORP. LTF. ENG".

1.UNITED DC-10   AVG:$1.50 MINT:$4.00
2.MIG-21   AVG:$1.25 MINT:$3.50
3.MIRAGE F1   AVG:$1.00 MINT:$3.00
  "target" design on each wing.
4.TORNADO   AVG:$1.50 MINT:$4.00
  Cross design on each wing.
5.PHANTOM F4E   AVG:$1.25 MINT:$3.50
  "target" design on each wing.
6.SKYHAWK AAF   AVG:$1.75 MINT:$4.50
  Star in circle design on wings.

"DUKES OF HAZZARD"   HAPPY MEAL (*REGIONAL)   1982
(* regional: St. Louis) Set of five plastic cars, used as
containers. Also: HAPPY CUPS with pictures of characters
from the TV show.

CARS:
1.CADILLAC, white	AVG:$6.00	MINT:$13.00
2.GENERAL LEE CAR, orange	AVG:$6.75	MINT:$16.00
3.JEEP, white	AVG:$6.00	MINT:$15.00
4.SHERIFF CAR,white	AVG:$6.00	MINT:$15.00
5.PICKUP, white	AVG:$6.50	MINT:$16.00

HAPPY CUPS:
Set of six, white, 16oz, plastic cups, 4.8 inches high. The
design shows the head and shoulders of character with name
in black text. Above head is "THE DUKES OF HAZZARD" ; below
design: "TM & (C) Warner Bros Inc 1982". Alternates twice
around cup with golden ARCHES logo,and "McDonald's (R)" in
black. Colors used: blue, red, yellow and black.

1.LUKE   AVG:$4.00 MINT:$7.50
    Smiling young man, blue and
    black plaid shirt.

2.BOSS HOGG   AVG:$4.00 MINT:$7.00
    Middle-aged man in white bow-tie,
    shirt,jacket and cowboy hat.

3.SHERIFF ROSCOE   AVG:$4.00 MINT:$7.00
    Man in black cowboy hat and tie,
    blue shirt. Beagle dog.

4.DAISY   AVG:$5.00 MINT:$8.00
    Girl with long brown hair and
    red dress.

5.UNCLE JESSE   AVG:$4.00 MINT:$7.00
    Elderly man with white hair,
    beard and mustache. Blue shirt.

6.BO DUKE   AVG:$4.00 MINT:$7.50
    Blonde young man in white jacket
    over blue shirt.

McDONALDLAND EXPRESS

"McDONALDLAND EXPRESS"   HAPPY MEAL   JUNE
Set of four plastic train cars used as containers, with
decals of McDONALDLAND characters. (Tested in St. Louis)
MCD#8931   (C) 1982 McDonald's Corporation

1.RONALD McDONALD ENGINE   AVG:$6.00   MINT:$12.00
   Red or blue.
2.COACH, blue   AVG:$5.00   MINT:$10.00

3.FREIGHT CAR   AVG:$5.00   MINT:$10.00
   orange or yellow

4.CABOOSE, green   AVG:$5.00   MINT:$10.00

LITTLE GOLDEN BOOKS"   HAPPY MEAL   JULY
Set of five books:

1."MONSTER AT THE END OF THE BOOK" AVG:$4.00   MINT:$7.00
   (C) Muppets Inc 109-31.

2."COUNTRY MOUSE AND CITY MOUSE" AVG:$3.00   MINT:$6.00
   (C) Western Publishing Co.Inc.
   #426.

3.MGM's "TOM AND JERRY'S PARTY"   AVG:$4.00   MINT:$7.00
   (C) Western Publishing Co.Inc.

4."POKY LITTLE PUPPY"   AVG:$3.50   MINT:$6.50
   (C) Western Publishing Co.Inc.
   #301-32.

5."BENJI,FASTEST DOG IN THE WEST" AVG:$3.50   MINT:$6.50
   (C) 1978 Mulberry Square
   Products Inc. 111-36.

CARTON   AVG:$3.00   MINT:$5.50

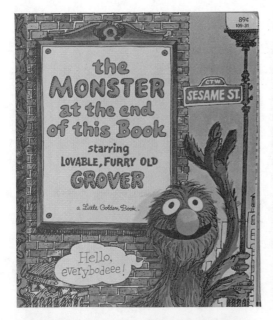

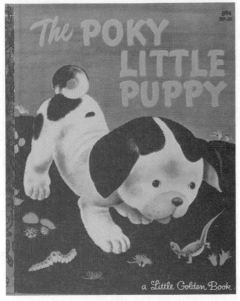

LITTLE GOLDEN BOOKS

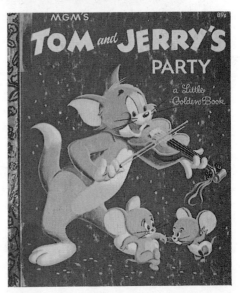

" PLAYMOBIL "   HAPPY MEAL   OCTOBER
The Playmobil people were designed by Schaper Manufacturing
Co., a division of Kusan Inc., in 1982. Set of five plastic
toys with accessories. An additional accessory kit could be
purchased for $1.89 with coupons found in the Happy Meal.
(these premiums were recalled due to problems. As a result,
McDonald's began to make and offer "under 3 yrs" toys)

1.SHERIFF   AVG:$10.00 MINT:$15.00
Possible figure:
Legs and body are black. Silver six-pointed star on chest.
White arms & hands. Pink face, features in brown. Yellow
hair.
(bag stamped "made in MALTA")
Accessories, four pieces: brown rocking chair, tan rifle,
black hat, white cape.

2.INDIAN   AVG:$12.00 MINT:$22.00
     Accessories: decals, shield,
       head-dress, rifle and spear

3.HORSE & SADDLE   AVG:$10.00 MINT:$15.00
     Accessory: water trough

4.UMBRELLA GIRL   AVG:$10.00 MINT:$18.00
     Accessories: umbrella, purse and hat

5.FARMER   AVG:$12.00 MINT:$20.00
     Accessories: dog, scythe, rake and hat

CARTONS (4): (C)1982 McDonald's CORPORATION MCD #9469
FC 930-736.

1.BARN   AVG:$5.00   MINT:$9.00
2.LOG CABIN   AVG:$6.00   MINT:$10.00
3.SCHOOLHOUSE   AVG:$5.00   MINT:$9.00
4.TRADING POST   AVG:$6.00   MINT:$10.00

"HOT WHEELS"   HAPPY MEAL   1983
Tested on West and East coasts in 1982, and ran
nationally in 1983. Packaged on cards with no McDonald's
logo. Marks: "(C) Mattel Inc. 1981" "THE HOT ONES"

COMMON TO BOTH COASTS:

3250	FIREBIRD FUNNY CAR, red	AVG:$7.00	MINT:$13.00
3259	JEEP CJ7, brown	AVG:$8.00	MINT:$13.50
2019	SHERIFF PATROL,"Sheriff 701"	AVG:$6.50	MINT:$9.00
2022	BAJA BREAKER, camper,orange	AVG:$5.00	MINT:$9.00
3260	LAND LORD, orange	AVG:$5.00	MINT:$9.00
9241	CORVETTE STINGRAY, red	AVG:$8.00	MINT:$13.50

WEST COAST:

1132	3 WINDOW '34, "HI RAKERS"	AVG:$5.00	MINT:$10.50
1136	SPLIT WINDOW '63, gold	AVG:$6.00	MINT:$12.50
1694	TURISMO, red	AVG:$4.00	MINT:$7.50
1697	MINITREK, camper, white	AVG:$6.50	MINT:$9.00
3261	MERCEDES 380 SEL, silver	AVG:$6.00	MINT:$10.50
3362	CHEVY CITATION, brown	AVG:$5.00	MINT:$10.00
5180	PORSCHE 928, Turbo,	AVG:$4.00	MINT:$8.00
9037	MALIBU GRAND PRIX, black	AVG:$5.00	MINT:$9.00

EAST COAST:

1130	TRICAR X-8	AVG:$6.00	MINT:$12.50
3257	FRONT RUNNING FAIRMONT	AVG:$5.00	MINT:$10.00
3364	DIXIE CHALLENGER	AVG:$7.00	MINT:$13.00
3255	DATSUN 200 SX	AVG:$5.00	MINT:$10.50
9647	'56 HI-TAIL HAULER	AVG:$7.00	MINT:$13.00

OR:

1126	STUTZ BLACKHAWK	AVG:$8.00	MINT:$12.00
1698	CADILLAC SEVILLE	AVG:$6.00	MINT:$10.50
2013	'57 T-BIRD	AVG:$7.00	MINT:$13.00
2021	RACE BAIT 308	AVG:$5.00	MINT:$9.00

PLAYMOBIL

HOT WHEELS

HAPPY MEALS 1983

DIRECTORY

```
+-----------------------------------------------------------+
|            Abbreviations used to describe condition:      |
|            MINT = new, never used or unfolded.            |
|            AVG  = average condition.                      |
|            NP   = no original package, loose.             |
|            MIP  = mint in package, in original, sealed    |
|                     container.                            |
+-----------------------------------------------------------+
```

"McDONALDLAND JUNCTION"   HAPPY MEAL   JANUARY
Set of four plastic, snap-together train cars (with wheels)
which may be connected to form a train. Instructions for
assembling are embossed on each toy. "(C) 1982 McDonald's
CORPORATION / MADE IN USA "M" LOGO on both sides".
(Optional: instead of train, premium could be *Fun Times
Magazine*, with transportation themed stories and games)

1.RMCD ENGINE   AVG:$3.00   MINT:$6.00
Four pieces: red or blue.
RMCD drives engine and bobs up and down.

2.HAMBURGER PATCH FLAT CAR   AVG:$3.00   MINT:$6.00
Four pieces: green or white.
Hamburger "passengers" bob up and down.

3.BIRDIE PARLOR CAR   AVG:$3.00   MINT:$6.00
Four pieces: yellow or pink.
Birdie rocks back and forth.

4.GRIMACE CABOOSE   AVG:$3.00   MINT:$6.00
Four pieces: purple or orange.
Grimace bobs up through the roof.

CARTONS (6)   AVG:$3.00   MINT:$4.75
May be assembled to make a town.
1.TOWN HALL
2.STATION
3.TRAIN TUNNEL
4.POST OFFICE
5.ENGINE BARN
6.SIGNAL TOWER

McDONALDLAND JUNCTION

ASTROSNIKS I

"ASTROSNIKS I"   HAPPY MEAL   1983
This is a set of eight, hard-rubber, green-skinned space-
creatures, which average 3 inches in height. Shared
characteristics are: pointed ears, a pair of short antennae
with knobbed ends, big noses, white eyes, and two large,
prominent, front teeth. Marks:" (C) Bully-Figuren TM /
Astrosnik (R) / McDonald's / HONG KONG".

1.SPORT, WITH FOOTBALL   NP:$4.75 MIP:$7.25
Purple jogging suit and hat,(yellow band,
shade), yellow sneakers, red football with gold "M".

2.ROBO THE ROBOT   NP:$4.75 MIP:$7.25
Gold robot with gold "M" in
red rectangle, on chest. Large head, arms and legs

3.SCOUT WITH FLAG   NP:$4.00 MIP:$7.00
Purple suit with red harness and yellow
flag holster. In left hand he carries a yellow-staffed,
triangular red flag with a gold "M".

4.THIRSTY WITH DRINK   NP:$4.75 MIP:$7.25
Purple suit. Red shoulder harness
holds a large red cup with white straw and gold "M".

5.ICE SKATER   NP:$4.75 MIP:$7.25
Purple suit, red skater's helmet with "M"
Red ice skates with white blades, green gloves.

6.ASTRALIA, WITH CONE   NP:$4.00 MIP:$7.00
Blonde-haired girl
in sleeveless purple suit, yellow laced shoes.
In left hand she holds ice cream cone (red "M").

7.LASER   NP:$4.75 MIP:$7.25
Purple suit with wide red belt,
gold "M" on buckle. He holds a red laser gun.

8.SNIKAPOTAMUS   NP:$4.75 MIP:$7.25
Green dragon-like creature
with a pink underbelly, purple back and tail fin, a red
tongue and one antenna. He wears a red saddle and collar,
each decorated with a gold "M".

CARTONS (4):   AVG:$5.00 MINT:$9.00

1."WHAT HAPPENS WHEN THE MAN IN THE MOON
   EATS AT McDONALD'S?"
2."WHAT'S BLACK & YELLOW ON THE OUTSIDE ?"
3."TWINKLE,TWINKLE,LITTLE STAR"
4."OUR MOTTO:SMALL IS NICER"

"MYSTERY"   HAPPY MEAL   MARCH
(Optional : could offer *Fun Times Magazine* instead)

1.UNPREDICT-A-BALL   **AVG:$7.00   MINT:$14.00**
Ball rolls crooked or straight
depending on how started. McDONALDLAND characters as
decoration. Colors: red,blue & yellow

2.RONALD DETECTIVE KIT   **AVG:$8.00   MINT:$12.00**
Secret message and code,
tweezers and finger paint. Colors: red & blue.

3.MAGIC BALL   **AVG:$17.00 MINT:$30.00**
RMCD, Big Mac and Mayor McCheese
appear in ball. Colors: yellow or clear

4.MAGNI FINDER   AVG:$7.00   MINT:$14.50
Hidden case trick with RMCD,
Birdie & Fry Guy. Color: clear.

CARTONS (6):   AVG:$4.00   MINT:$6.50
1.DOGGONE MYSTERY
2.THUMP! BLAM!
3.CASE OF THE GOLDEN KEY
4.MYSTERIOUS MAP
5.OCEANS AWAY
6.CASE OF THE MISSING SHOE

SHIP SHAPE I"   HAPPY MEAL   JUNE
Set of four plastic boats plus decals, which served as two-
piece meal containers. Same as set offered in 1985.

1.HAMBURGLAR JET SPLASHDASHER   AVG:$7.00   MINT:$9.50
     Colors: white & red

2.GRIMACE TUBBY TUBBER   AVG:$8.00   MINT:$11.00
     Colors: green & magenta

3.CAPTAIN CROOK RUB-A-DUB SUB   AVG:$8.00   MINT:$11.00
     Colors: blue & green

4.RMCD RIVERBOAT   AVG:$7.50   MINT:$10.00
     Colors: yellow & red

"CIRCUS"   HAPPY MEAL   SEPTEMBER
Set of eight premiums based on a circus theme.
(optional : could use generic theme or *Fun Times Magazine*)

1.STRONG GONG   NP:$5.00   MIP:$7.50
Three pieces: plastic mallet, seat & Grimace.
Hitting the target knocks Grimace off his seat.
Colors: yellow, purple & green.

2.ACROBATIC RONALD   NP:$5.25   MIP:$8.00
Ronald spins on his trapeze.
Colors: red & blue

3.RMCD FUN HOUSE MIRROR   NP:$4.00   MIP:$7.00
Mirror creates odd reflections
with three different positions. Colors: blue, red & yellow.

4.FRENCH FRY FALLER   NP:$4.00   MIP:$7.00
Colors: yellow,orange & blue.

PUNCH-OUT SHEETS:
5.CIRCUS BACKDROP I   AVG:$13.00   MINT:$20.50
circus scenes and animals.

6.CIRCUS BACKDROP II   AVG:$11.00   MINT:$15.50
circus scenes and animals.
(different from #5 above.)

7.PUPPET SHOW BACKDROP   AVG:$12.50   MINT:$18.25
Intended to accompany circus backdrop II

8.FUN HOUSE BACKDROP   AVG:$10.00   MINT:$15.50
Circus Midway scene

CARTONS (6)
Cut-outs to add to circus scenes:
1.TUMBLERS AND JUGGLERS   AVG:$9.00   MINT:$16.00
2.HIGH WIRE SHOW   AVG:$7.00   MINT:$12.00
3.CLOWN CAR   AVG:$8.00   MINT:$14.00
4.MONKEY CAGE   AVG:$6.00   MINT:$10.00
5.AMAZING ANIMAL ACTS   AVG:$7.00   MINT:$12.00
6.CIRCUS BAND   AVG:$9.00   MINT:$16.00

"WINTER WORLDS"   HAPPY MEALS (OPTIONAL)   NOVEMBER
Set of five flat, vinyl McDONALDLAND characters with average
height of 3 5/8 inches. Back of object reads: "(C) 1983
McDonald's CORP. / SAFETY TESTED FOR CHILDREN 3 AND OLDER /
TAIWAN / (name of character)". Personalities are in their
usual costumes, full color on front and back, top is pierced
for hanging.
(Option: to use these premiums or generic themes)

1.RMCD	AVG:$3.00	MINT:$5.50
2.GRIMACE	AVG:$3.00	MINT:$5.50
3.HAMBURGLAR	AVG:$4.00	MINT:$6.00
4.BIRDIE	AVG:$3.00	MINT:$5.50
5.MAYOR McCHEESE	AVG:$4.00	MINT:$6.00

CARTONS (5):   AVG:$3.00 MINT:$5.50
1.LANDS OF ICE & SNOW
2.LAND OF MIDNIGHT SUN
3.MAMMALS
4.BIRDS

"HOT WHEELS"   HAPPY MEAL   1983
Tested on West and East coasts in 1982, and ran
nationally in 1983. Packaged on cards with no McDonald's
logo. Marks: "(C) Mattel Inc. 1981" "THE HOT ONES"

COMMON TO BOTH COASTS:

3250	FIREBIRD FUNNY CAR, red	AVG:$7.00	MINT:$13.00
3259	JEEP CJ7, brown	AVG:$8.00	MINT:$13.50
2019	SHERIFF PATROL,"Sheriff 701"	AVG:$6.50	MINT:$9.00
2022	BAJA BREAKER, camper,orange	AVG:$5.00	MINT:$9.00
3260	LAND LORD, orange	AVG:$5.00	MINT:$9.00
9241	CORVETTE STINGRAY, red	AVG:$8.00	MINT:$13.50

WEST COAST:

1132	3 WINDOW '34, "HI RAKERS"	AVG:$5.00	MINT:$10.50
1136	SPLIT WINDOW '63, gold	AVG:$6.00	MINT:$12.50
1694	TURISMO, red	AVG:$4.00	MINT:$7.50
1697	MINITREK, camper, white	AVG:$6.50	MINT:$9.00
3261	MERCEDES 380 SEL, silver	AVG:$6.00	MINT:$10.50
3362	CHEVY CITATION, brown	AVG:$5.00	MINT:$10.00
5180	PORSCHE 928, Turbo,	AVG:$4.00	MINT:$8.00
9037	MALIBU GRAND PRIX, black	AVG:$5.00	MINT:$9.00

EAST COAST:

1130	TRICAR X-8	AVG:$6.00	MINT:$12.50
3257	FRONT RUNNING FAIRMONT	AVG:$5.00	MINT:$10.00
3364	DIXIE CHALLENGER	AVG:$7.00	MINT:$13.00
3255	DATSUN 200 SX	AVG:$5.00	MINT:$10.50
9647	'56 HI-TAIL HAULER	AVG:$7.00	MINT:$13.00

OR:

1126	STUTZ BLACKHAWK	AVG:$8.00	MINT:$12.00
1698	CADILLAC SEVILLE	AVG:$6.00	MINT:$10.50
2013	'57 T-BIRD	AVG:$7.00	MINT:$13.00
2021	RACE BAIT 308	AVG:$5.00	MINT:$9.00

HAPPY MEALS 1984

DIRECTORY

```
+-----------------------------------------------------------+
|           Abbreviations used to describe condition:       |
|           MINT = new, never used or unfolded.             |
|           AVG  = average condition.                       |
|           NP   = no original package, loose.              |
|           NIP  = mint in package, in original, sealed     |
|                  container.                               |
+-----------------------------------------------------------+
```

"GOOD SPORTS"   HAPPY MEAL   FEBRUARY
Set of six stickers, 2 1/2 inches high, optional: "puffy" or
generic. Theme:Winter Olympics. (C) 1984 McDonald's Corp. By
the foot: "(R)"

1.RMCD   NP:$5.00 MIP:$8.00
     Ice skating.
2.BIRDIE   NP:$4.00 MIP:$7.50
     Soccer.
3.GRIMACE   NP:$4.00 MIP:$7.50
     Sledding.
4.MAYOR McCHEESE   NP:$4.00 MIP:$7.50
     Skiing.
5.SAM OLYMPIC EAGLE   NP:$5.00 MIP:$8.00
     Basketball.
6. HAMBURGLAR   NP:$4.00 MIP:$7.50
     Hockey. Hamburglar on skates
     with hockey stick and puck.

CARTONS (4):   AVG:$3.50 MINT:$6.00
1.SKI JUMP
2.SLED RUN
3.GYMNASTICS
4.BASKETBALL

"OLYMPIC SPORTS"   HAPPY MEAL   JUNE
Set of five puzzles depicting Olympic Sports.

1."WINNING GOAL"   AVG:$5.00 MINT:$7.50
2."BIGGEST SPLASH"   AVG:$4.00 MINT:$7.50
3."HELP THEM ROW"   AVG:$3.50 MINT:$7.00
4."SMILES AHEAD"   AVG:$4.00 MINT:$7.50
5."UNDER THE WIRE"   AVG:$3.50 MINT:$7.00

CARTONS (5):   AVG:$2.00 MINT:$4.50
1."BOATS AFLOAT"
2."IN THE SWIM"
3."MAKING TRACKS"
4."JUST FOR KICKS"
5."PEDAL POWER"

"HAPPY PAIL-OLYMPICS"   HAPPY MEAL   SUMMER
Set of four plastic pails with shovels and lids, celebrating
the Olympic Games. Served as containers for meals.
MCD#11761 FC 931-252.

1.CYCLING   AVG:$4.00 MINT:$8.00

2.TRACK & FIELD   AVG:$3.75 MINT:$7.00
     Design: medal with pin, ribbon
and disk. Pin reads: "ATHLETICS / An
Official 1984 Olympic Games". RMCD,and
BIRDIE jumping hurdles. Medal shows SAM
jumping hurdle.

3.OLYMPIC GAMES   AVG:$3.75 MINT:$7.00
     Design: medal with pin, ribbon
and disk. Pin reads: "OFFICIAL MASCOT /
1984 OLYMPIC GAMES". Medal shows Sam
standing, left hand out.

4.SWIMMING   AVG:$4.00 MINT:$8.00

HAPPY PAILS - OLYMPICS

"ASTROSNIKS II"   HAPPY MEAL   1984
Set of six, hard-rubber, green-skinned space creatures,
averaging 3 inches in height. Characteristics shared are:
pointed ears, a pair of short antennae with knobbed ends,
big noses, white eyes and two large, prominent front
teeth.On back: (C) Bully-Figuren TM / Astrosnik (R) /
McDonald's / HONG KONG.

1.DRILL   NP:$4.75 MIP:$7.50
In purple, segmented suit and miner's
helmet with a red lamp (Gold "M" on lens),
yellow boots. Holds a large red and silver
drill with both hands.

2.COMMANDER   NP:$4.00 MIP:$6.50
Wears purple helmet, shorts and halter
decorated with a red shield with a gold
"M". Purple high-boots, helmet, mask and
long gloves. One antenna, and a horn on
each side of his head.Yellow eyes.

3.RACING   NP:$4.00 MIP:$6.50
Purple shirt and helmet (green striped)
with yellow goggles. He sits in a small
red and green sled, ("M" on the front)
held on by red straps over his shoulders.

4.COPTER   NP:$4.75 MIP:$7.50
In a purple suit, arms held out from his
sides. His eyes are closed in a blissful
expression. A gold halter and harness hold
the Copter Unit. "M" on belt buckle.
Embossed on back is "HELIKS".

5.SKI   NP:$4.75 MIP:$7.50
Purple ski-suit, green striped helmet
with a gold "M", boots with yellow straps,
silver goggles and ski poles, green skis.

6.PERFIDO   NP:$4.00 MIP:$6.50
He has only 1 antenna on his bald
green head. Orange beard. Wears a short
yellow gown with purple straps across
the chest. Red cape, embossed on the back
with a gold "M".

CARTONS (2):   AVG:$2.75 MINT:$3.90
1.Drill,Perfido and Racing
2.Copter,Ski and Commander

ASTROSNIKS II

LEGO BUILDING SET

"BEACH BALL"   HAPPY MEAL   SUMMER
Beach balls with designs celebrating the Olympic Games.

1. BIRDIE   AVG:$4.00 MINT:$8.00
Blue, Birdie on sailboat
2. RMCD   AVG:$4.00 MINT:$8.00
Red, in Olympic event
3. GRIMACE   AVG:$4.00 MINT:$8.00
Purple, in kayak

"SCHOOL DAYS"   HAPPY MEALS   AUGUST
Set of five types of school tools.

  1.PENCILS: AVG:$1.00 MINT:$3.00
        RMCD
        HAMBURGLAR
        GRIMACE

  2.ERASERS: AVG:$1.00 MINT:$3.00
        RMCD
        HAMBURGLAR
        GRIMACE
        BIRDIE
        CAPTAIN CROOK

3.RULER   AVG:$3.00 MINT:$5.00

4.PENCIL SHARPENERS: AVG:$2.50 MINT:$4.50
        RMCD
        GRIMACE

5.PENCIL CASE   AVG:$4.00 MINT:$7.50

CARTONS (4):   AVG:$2.00 MINT:$3.75
1."ABC'S"
2.HISTORY
3.NUMBERS
4.SCIENCE

"LEGO BUILDING SET"   HAPPY MEAL (TEST)   OCTOBER
(Tested in 1983 - Salt Lake City) Four LEGO DUPLO (R)
Building Sets made in Switzerland.

1.TRUCK   NP:$3.00   MIP:$4.75
          17 pieces

2.SHIP   NP:$3.00   MIP:$5.75
          27 pieces

3.HELICOPTER   NP:$3.00   MIP:$5.75
          19 pieces

4.AIRPLANE   NP:$3.00   MIP:$5.75
          18 pieces

UNDER 3 YRS:
1.ANIMAL   NP:$3.50   MIP:$6.00
          figure, red pkg.

2.BUILDING   NP:$3.50   MIP:$6.00
          Character, blue pkg.

CARTONS (4):   AVG:$1.75   MINT:$3.00
          1.AIRPLANE
          2.MASTER MAZE
          3.FRY GUY
          4.SHIP-SHAPE

"HAPPY HOLIDAYS"   HAPPY MEAL (OPTIONAL)   NOVEMBER
(optional - not all areas used this) Christmas theme Sticker
sheets, two types.

1.STICKER SHEET, HOUSE   AVG:$3.50   MINT:$5.00
   Gingerbread Holiday House card.

2.STICKER SHEET, TRAIN   AVG:$4.00   MINT:$6.00
   Toy Train set card.

CARTONS (2):
1.GIFT TAG   AVG:$2.75   MINT:$4.00
   Green box.

2.ORNAMENTS   AVG:$2.75   MINT:$4.00
   Red box.

HAPPY MEALS 1985

DIRECTORY

HALLOWEEN

```
Abbreviations used to describe condition:
MINT = new, never used or unfolded.
AVG  = average condition.
NP   = no original package, loose.
MIP  = mint in package, in original, sealed
         container.
```

"PLA DOH"   HAPPY MEAL (TEST)   FEBRUARY
(National test: Kansas, Kentucky,Missouri, Oklahoma,
Southern Illinois) Two-ounce cans of Pla-Doh.

Set of eight colors: AVG:$3.00   MINT:$4.25
1.RED
2.ORANGE
3.YELLOW
4.GREEN
5.BLUE
6.PURPLE
7.WHITE
8.PINK

CARTON   AVG:$2.00   MINT:$3.00

"DAY AND NIGHT"   HAPPY MEAL-CARTONS   1985
Set of two cartons to be used for generic offerings or
backup cartons.   MCD#85-008   FC#MCDY-932-258

CARTONS (2):
1.WHO'S AFRAID OF THE DARK?   AVG:$3.00   MINT:$4.50
2.ALL STAR SUNDAY   AVG:$5.00   MINT:$6.00

"ON THE GO"   HAPPY MEAL   1985
Set of five games. (C) 1985 McDonald's CORPORATION

1.DECAL TRANSFER   AVG:$3.00 MINT:$4.75
2."STOP AND GO" BEAD GAME   AVG:$3.00 MINT:$4.75
3."STOP LIGHT" SHAPE BEAD GAME   AVG:$3.00 MINT:$4.75
4."SLATE-BOARD RONALD" LIFT-PAD   AVG:$3.50 MINT:$5.00
5."SLATE-BOARD HAMBURGLAR"   AVG:$3.50 MINT:$5.00
        LIFT-PAD

CARTONS (4):   AVG:$1.35 MINT:$2.00
MCD$13092 FC#MCDY-932-254

1."McDONALDLAND BRIDGE"
     The carton may be made into a covered bridge.
2.TUNNEL
3."McDONALDLAND GARAGE"
     The carton may be made into a 2-car garage.
4."McDONALDLAND DRIVE THROUGH"
     The carton may be made into a Drive-Thru restaurant

"CRAZY CREATURES"   HAPPY MEAL   1985
Set of four "Popoids". Each comes with two bellows
(Not the same as August 1985, or 1984 test.)

POPOIDS: NP:$4.00 MIP:$8.50
1. CUBE, 6 holes
2. BALL, 6 holes
3. FLAT CIRCLE, 10 holes
4. PENTA JOINT

CARTONS (4):   AVG:$1.50 MINT:$3.00
1.SCORPOID
2.DRAGONPOID
3.ELEPHOID
4.OCTOPOID

"STICKER CLUB"   HAPPY MEALS   MARCH
Set of five different types of stickers.

STICKERS: NP:$2.00 MIP:$3.75
1. COLOR PAPER DESIGN,
   Twelve stickers picturing McDONALDLAND characters.

2. SCRATCH & SNIFF STICKERS
   Five stickers: RMCD,Grimace,Hamburglar,Birdie & Fry Guy.

3. REFLECTOR STICKERS
   Six stickers: RMCD,Grimace,Birdie,Mayor McCheese,
   Lg. Fries & MCD sign.

4. ACTION STICKERS
   Four stickers: RMCD, Hamburglar,Birdie & Professor.

5. PUFFY STICKERS
   Two stickers: RMCD & Grimace.

CARTONS (4):   AVG:$1.50 MINT:$2.50
1."CLUB MEETING"
2."PICNIC"
3."PARTY"
4."TRADING DAYS"

"SHIP SHAPE"   HAPPY MEAL   MAY
Set of four plastic boats with decals which served as meal
containers. Same as set offered in 1983. (See photo 1983)

BOATS:
1. HAMBURGLAR JET SPLASHDASHER   AVG:$7.00 MINT:$9.50
     White & red.

2. GRIMACE TUBBY TUBBER   AVG:$8.00 MINT:$11.00
     Green & magenta.

3. CAPTAIN CROOK RUB-A-DUB SUB   AVG:$8.00 MINT:$11.00
     Blue & green.

4. RMCD RIVERBOAT   AVG:$7.50 MINT:$10.00
     Yellow & red.

UNDER 3 YRS:
1. GRIMACE TUB TOY, purple   AVG:$3.50 MINT:$5.50
2. FRY GUY & FRIENDS TUB TOY   AVG:$3.50 MINT:$5.50

SHIP SHAPE - DECALS

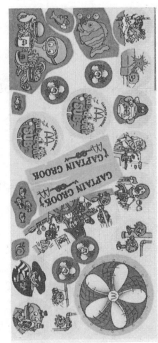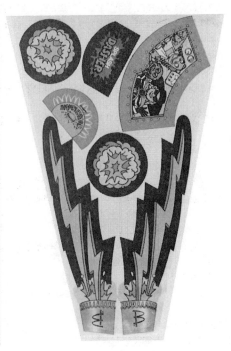

SHIP SHAPE

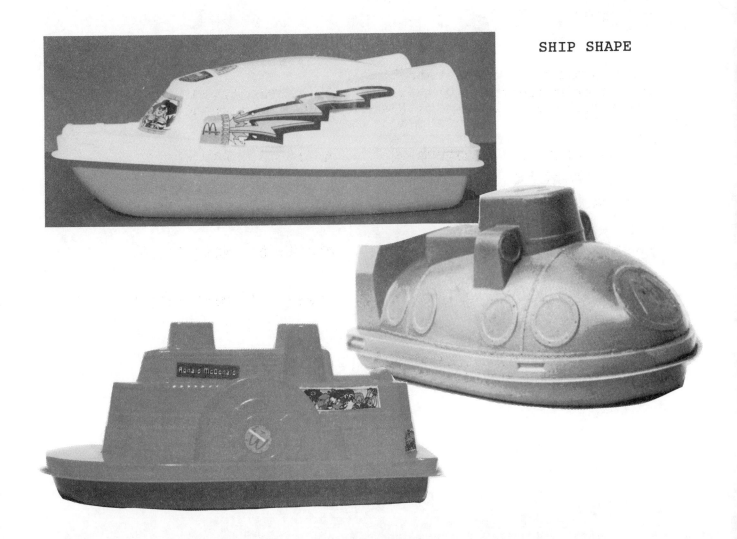

"COMMANDRONS"   HAPPY MEAL (TEST)   1985
Set of four, true transformers. These pull-back action,
robot- vehicles are in a colorful blister package with a
mini-comic book. Back of package pictures the four toys
available with instructions for using them as a vehicle or a
robot.
The comic books text: "COMMANDRONS" / (book title) /
ARCHES logo / "DC"
(C) 1985 McDonald's Corporation / (C) 1985 TOMY CORP.

1.VELOCITOR (TM)   AVG:$8.00 MINT:$12.00
     Space Shuttle:
White body with red & blue trim.
Panels on back with red & blue
chevrons on silver.
     Robot: blue body, red arms,
white hands like pliers.
Comic book: *"Dawn of the Commandrons"*

2.MOTRON (TM)   AVG:$10.00 MINT:$15.00
     Sports Car:
Silver decal with red and blue
chevrons on hood and spoiler.
White body. Red fenders.
     Robot: long red arms, white
pincer hands, blue body.
Comic Book: *"Robo-Mania"*

3.SOLARDYN (TM)   AVG:$8.00 MINT:$12.00
     Space Ship, Interstellar:
Red & white ship with blue
undercarriage, small decals.
     Robot: long, curved red arms,
tall blue body with faceplate.
Comic Book: *"The Copy-bots"*

4.COMMANDER MAGNA (TM)   AVG:$9.00 MINT:$14.00
     Jet Fighter:
White body, red wings, blue cabin
and undercarriage, black wheels,
decals on dual tail fins.
     Robot: conical "face", red
arms with pincer hands.
Comic Book: *"Airborne!"*

COMMANDRONS

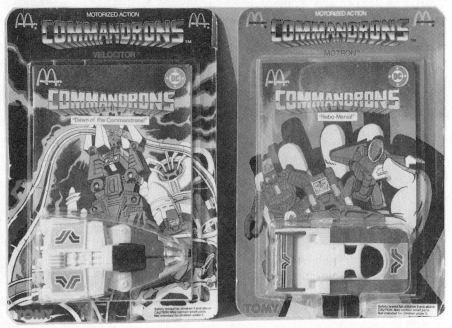

"MY LITTLE PONY / TRANSFORMERS" HAPPY MEAL (*TEST)   1985
(tested in St. Louis) A choice for boys and girls between
four different transformers, or six pony charms.
TRANSFORMERS: NP:$5.00 MIP:$9.75
These were available in six color sets.
    1.BUMBLEBEE
    2.GEARS
    3.CLIFF JUMPER
    4.BRAWN

PONY CHARMS: NP:$3.75 MIP:$5.50
Each pony has a different design on body.
    1.MINTY, green. Clover design.
    2.COTTON CANDY, pink. Paw shaped design.
    3.BLUE BELLE, blue. Star design.
    4.BUTTERSCOTCH, yellow. Butterfly design.
    5.BLOSSOM, purple. Flower design.
    6.SNUZZLE, gray. Heart design.

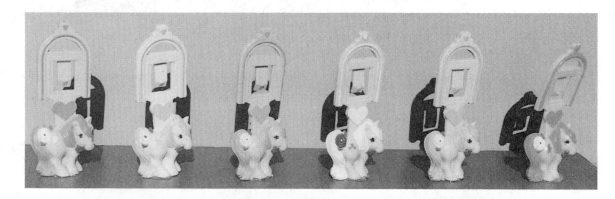

TRANSFORMERS

"PICTURE PERFECT"   HAPPY MEAL (TEST)   JUNE
(Tested in Evansville ,Indiana) Crayola products.
(NO FURTHER INFORMATION AVAILABLE AT THIS TIME)

CARTON:
1. "RONALD QUICK DRAW"   AVG:$3.00 MINT:$4.75

```
"E.T."                  HAPPY MEAL                         JULY
Set of four, posters (17 x 24 inches) with "E.T." Movie
scenes.
POSTER:
1. Boy and ET on flying bike     AVG:$6.00   MINT:$10.00
2. Boy and ET touching fingers   AVG:$4.75   MINT:$7.50
3. ET with radio                 AVG:$5.00   MINT:$8.00
4. ET raising hand               AVG:$6.50   MINT:$9.00

CARTONS (2):                     AVG:$3.00   MINT:$5.00
1."THE GREAT ADVENTURE"
2."E.T. MAKES FRIENDS"
```

```
"MUSIC"          HAPPY MEAL   (*REGIONAL)              1985
(* Regional - St. Louis )Four different records: 45 rpm type
with songs on both sides and a story. MCD#85-017 /FC 932-140
(C)1985 FISHER-PRICE, (C) & (P)1985 McDONALD'S CORP.

1.GREEN LABEL                        AVG:$4.00   MINT:$8.50
Songs:"HEAD,SHOULDERS,KNEES AND TOES.."
      "SHE'LL BE COMIN' ROUND THE MOUNTAIN.."
Story:"THE OBJECT IS MUSIC"

2.YELLOW LABEL                       AVG:$4.00   MINT:$8.50
Songs: "DO THE HOKEY-POKEY.."
       "EENSY,WEENSY SPIDER.."
Story: "RMCD ORCHESTRA"

3.PURPLE LABEL                       AVG:$4.00   MINT:$6.50
Songs: "DOES YOUR EAR HANG LOW?"
       "BOOM BOOM,AIN'T IT GREAT TO BE CRAZY?"
Story: "MUSIC MACHINE"

4.BLUE LABEL                         AVG:$4.00   MINT:$7.50
Songs: "IF YOU'RE HAPPY."
       "LITTLE BUNNY FOO FOO"
Story: "RMCD ONE-MAN BAND"

CARTONS (4):                         AVG:$3.00   MINT:$4.75
    1."JAM SESSION"
    2."CAN YOU FIND?"
    3."WHO'S NOT PLAYING?"
    4. AUDIENCE CLAPPING
```

"POPOIDS"   HAPPY MEAL   AUGUST
This was tested in St. Louis in 1984 with two different
cartons and six packets. Set of four. Each set has two
bellows and a connecting part. Mark: "TOMY"

POPOIDS: NP:$4.00   MIP:$6.26
SET 1: CYLINDER.
     Three pieces: two bellows , red and
     blue. One flat orange cylinder with
     eight holes around sides, plus two holes
     at top and bottom.
SET 2: CUBE .
     Three pieces: two bellows , red and
     yellow. One white cube with one hole
     on each of six sides.
SET 3: SPHERE.
     Three pieces: two bellows , yellow and
     blue. One white sphere, six holes,
     one on each side.
SET 4: TRIANGLE.
     Three pieces: two bellows , red and
     yellow. One triangular, orange, with
     seven planes, five holes.

CARTONS (4):   AVG:$4.00   MINT:$6.25
     1.OCTOPOID
     2.ELEPHOID
     3.DRAGONOID
     4.SCORPOID

"MAGIC SHOW"   HAPPY MEAL   SEPTEMBER
Set of four magic tricks:
1.Disappearing Hamburger Patch   NP:$3.00 MIP:$4.95
Three pieces. (MINT= on plastic tree)
Two covers, plate with burger. Blue

2.Magic String Pull   NP:$3.00 MIP:$4.95
One piece.
Slowly pull string in either direction
and watch it change color. Top side
embossed with design of Birdie. ARCHES logo,
"Birdie the Early Bird",(C) 1985 McDonald's".
Colors: orange, green.

3.Magic Tablet   NP:$3.00 MIP:$4.95
4.Magic Picture   NP:$3.00 MIP:$4.95

CARTONS (4):   MCD#12247   AVG:$1.50 MINT:$3.00
     1."EGGS WITH LEGGS"
     2."GHOST WRITER"
     3."TUG-O-WAR"
     4."A STICKY CARD TRICK"

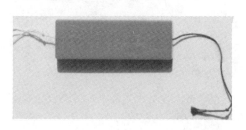 

"STOMPER MINI I"   HAPPY MEAL (REGIONAL)   SEPTEMBER
Region-St. Louis. Push type cars, rubber tires.

1. JEEP RENEGADE, white & maroon   NP:$8.00 MIP:$12.00
2. CHEVY S-10, yellow   NP:$8.00 MIP:$12.00
3. CHEVY S-10, silver & black   NP:$8.00 MIP:$12.00
4. DODGE RAMPAGE maroon & blue   NP:$8.00 MIP:$12.00

CARTON: AVG:$4.00 MINT:$8.50

"HALLOWEEN"   HAPPY MEAL   OCTOBER
(Tested in the New York area in 1985 when most markets had
one pumpkin only) Set of three pumpkin-shaped containers
with handles and perforated lids with round, half-inch
holes. Name and McDonald's logo on back. Some had different
names in different areas of the country.

1.McBOO   AVG:$3.00 MINT:$5.75
2.McGOBLIN / McJACK   AVG:$3.50 MINT:$7.00
3.McPUNK'N / McPUNKY   AVG:$3.00 MINT:$5.50

E.T. POSTER

MUSIC

ASTROSNIKS III

"ASTROSNIKS III"   HAPPY MEAL (*REGIONAL)   1985
(* regional - Oklahoma) Same as earlier Astrosniks but these
do not have the "M" logo. Other characters were added to
those pictured on cartons. Hard-rubber, happy little green-
skinned space creatures, averaging three inches in height.
These cheery creatures, so the story goes, are menaced by
the evil brothers: Perfido and Galaxo. Characteristics
shared are: pointed ears, a pair of short antennae with
knobbed ends, big noses and white eyes, and two large,
prominent front teeth.(on back:(C) '83 Bully-Figuren TM /
Astrosnik (R) / HONG KONG./ '83 SCHAPEN.

1. COMMANDER   NP:$4.00 MIP:$6.50
Wears purple helmet, shorts and halter
with a red shield. Purple high boots,
helmet, mask and long gloves. In addition
to his antennae, he has yellow and green horns
where each ear would normally be. Yellow eyes.

2. ROBO THE ROBOT   NP:$4.75 MIP:$6.00
Gold robot large head, arms and legs.

3. SCOUT WITH FLAG   NP:$4.00 MIP:$7.00
Purple suit with red harness and yellow
flag holster. In left hand he carries
a yellow-staffed red flag with
"ASTROSNIKS", in gold lettering.

4. PERFIDO   NP:$4.00 MIP:$6.50
He has one antenna on his bald green head.
Orange beard. Wears a short yellow gown
with purple straps across the chest
and a red cape.

5. ASTRALIA   NP:$4.00 MIP:$7.00
Blonde-haired girl in sleeveless purple
suit. Yellow laced shoes.

6. LASER   NP:$4.75 MIP:$7.25
Purple suit with wide gold belt,
He holds a gold laser gun. One eye closed.

7. SNIKAPOTAMUS   NP:$4.75 MIP:$7.25
Green dragon-like creature with a pink
underbelly, purple back and tail fin,
red tongue and one antenna.
He wears a red saddle (no collar).

8. BOY WITH CONE   NP:$4.50   MIP:$6.75
Wears a purple hat and suit
(long sleeves, shoes). Rubs stomach
with left hand, holds pink cone in
right hand. Red tongue sticks out.

9. PYRAMIDO   NP:$4.00   MIP:$7.00
Green pyramid-shaped creature with purple
antennae, purple arms and legs,
green hands,yellow shoes. Happy smile

10. ASTROSNIK WITH RADIO   NP:$4.00   MIP:$7.00
He wears yellow headphones and holds a
yellow radio in his left hand. Red
belt and shoulder strap, purple suit.

11. ASTROSNIK ON ROCKET   NP:$6.00   MIP:$12.50

Also found with the same marks as above:
" '83 SCHAPEN / '83 BULLY FIGUREN":

12. RACING   NP:$4.00   MIP:$6.50
Purple shirt and green striped helmet
with yellow goggles. He sits in a small
red and green sled held to him by red straps
over his shoulders.

13.COPTER   NP:$4.75   MIP:$7.50
In a purple suit with his arms held out
from his sides. His eyes are closed in a blissful
expression. A gold halter and harness hold the Copter Unit.
Embossed on back is "HELIKS".

14. GALAXO   NP:$4.25   MIP:$7.50
Perfido's evil brother. Green skin with
ragged orange hair and one central antenna.
His right hand is clutched on the belt
of his short yellow suit. A purple cape
is wrapped around his left arm. The black
patch over his left eye gives him a
"pirate" look. A large "G" is embossed on his back.

"SANTA CLAUSE, THE MOVIE"   HAPPY MEAL   NOVEMBER
Two storybooks published by Gosset & Dunlap, (8 X 8 inches)
and two "activity" books.

BOOKS:
1.*"THE LEGEND OF SANTA CLAUSE"*   AVG:$3.00   MINT:$5.00
        ISBN# 0-448-18975-5, 24 pages
2.*"THE ELVES AT THE TOP OF THE WORLD"*   AVG:$3.00   MINT:$5.00
        ISBN# 0-448-18976-3, 24 pages

ACTIVITY BOOKS:
1."*SLEIGHFULL OF SURPRISES*"   AVG:$3.50   MINT:$5.50
        activity type book
2."*WORKSHOP OF ACTIVITIES*"   AVG:$3.50   MINT:$5.50
     coloring book

CARTONS (2)   AVG:$3.00   MINT:$5.00
May be fastened together with cutouts
to create Santa's Village.
        1.COTTAGE
        2.WORKSHOP

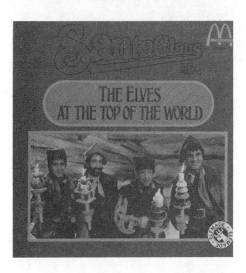

"FEELING GOOD"   HAPPY MEAL   DECEMBER
Set of five types of children's grooming aids.

1. TOOTHBRUSH, RMCD   AVG:$1.25   MINT:$3.00
        Yellow brush,full color figure of RMCD
        modeled in handle.
1a.TOOTHBRUSH, HAMBURGLAR   AVG:$2.00   MINT:$3.50
        Yellow brush, full color figure of
        HAMBURGLAR sculpted in handle.
2. SOAP DISH, GRIMACE   AVG:$3.00   MINT:$5.00
        Purple
3. SPONGE, FRY GUY   AVG:$3.00   MINT:$5.00
4. MIRROR, BIRDIE   AVG:$3.00   MINT:$5.00
        Handle design: BIRDIE in pink jumper.
5. COMB, CAPTAIN CROOK   AVG:$2.50   MINT:$3.25

UNDER 3 YRS:
1.GRIMACE TUB TOY, purple   AVG:$2.50   MINT:$4.00
2.FRY GUY TUB TOY, yellow   AVG:$2.50   MINT:$4.00
        Fry Guy on back of duck

CARTONS (4):   AVG:$1.90   MINT:$2.75
        1."SNOOZE BLUES"
        2."BIRDIE BATH"
        3."GUESS WHO"
        4."FIND THE PAIN"

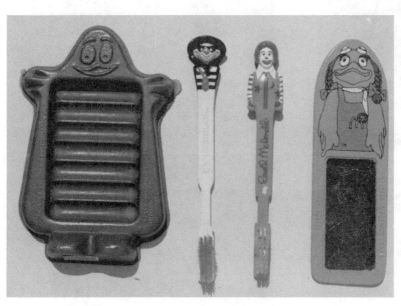

HAPPY MEALS 1986

DIRECTORY

```
Abbreviations used to describe condition:
MINT = new, never used or unfolded.
AVG  = average condition.
NP   = no original package, loose.
MIP  = mint in package, in original, sealed
       container.
```

(NOTE:THE HAPPY MEAL"FEELING GOOD" RAN FROM DECEMBER 1985 THROUGH MARCH 1986.)

"AIRPORT"   HAPPY MEAL   MARCH
Set of five plastic snap-together airplanes with McDONALDLAND characters. Underside of wing reads:(C) 1986 McDONALD'S MADE IN USA / SAFETY TESTED FOR CHILDREN 3 AND OVER / PUSH TOP WING ONTO BOTTOM WING / SNAP ON WHEELS AND PROPELLER".

1.FRY GUY FLYER   AVG:$3.50   MINT:$6.00
Three pieces,blue single wing airplane

2.BIG MAC 'COPTER   AVG:$3.50   MINT:$6.00
Three pieces, green helicopter

2a.FRY GUY "HELLO'COPTER"   AVG:$3.50   MINT:$6.00
Three peices, green

3.RMCD SEA PLANE   AVG:$3.50   MINT:$6.00
Three pieces, red sea-plane

4.GRIMACE ACE   AVG:$4.00   MINT:$6.50
Four pieces, purple Biplane

5.BIRDIE BLAZER   AVG:$4.00   MINT:$6.50
Four pieces, pink, bent-wing airplane

UNDER 3 YRS; one-piece, soft plastic
1.GRIMACE SMILING SHUTTLE   AVG:$5.00   MINT:$8.00
    Blue rocket ship
2.FRY GUY FRIENDLY FLYER   AVG:$5.00   MINT:$8.00
    Blue. Single wing plane

CARTONS (4):   AVG:$1.50   MINT:$2.50
    1.TERMINAL
    2.CONTROL TOWER
    3.LUGGAGE CLAIM
    4.HANGAR

AIRPORT

OLD McDONALD'S FARM

"OLD McDONALD'S FARM" HAPPY MEAL   (*REGIONAL)   1986
(* Regional: St. Louis) Set of six simple plastic figures
with movable parts. Minimal detail.

1.FARMER   NP:$3.00 MIP:$6.00
     Brown hat and mustache,green and
     white body movable head and arms.

2.WIFE   NP:$3.00 MIP:$6.00
     Yellow hair in braids,blue smock,
     white skirt movable head and arms.

3.COW   NP:$3.00 MIP:$6.00
     White and brown. Movable head, legs and tail

4.ROOSTER   NP:$4.00 MIP:$7.00
     White, movable head

5.PIG   NP:$4.00 MIP:$7.00
     Pink, movable head and legs

6.SHEEP   NP:$4.00 MIP:$7.00
     White, movable head and legs

CARTONS (2):   AVG:$5.00 MINT:$12.00
May be made into an attractive farm setting.
          1.BARN
          2.HOUSE

"THE STORY OF TEXAS" HAPPY MEAL (*REGIONAL)   1986
(* Regional: Austin, Texas) set of three story books with
map of Texas.

     SET:
     1.TEXAS I   AVG:$2.00 MINT:$4.00
     2.TEXAS II   AVG:$3.00 MINT:$5.00
     3.TEXAS III   AVG:$3.00 MINT:$5.00

     CARTON   AVG:$6.00 MINT:$12.00

"BEACH BALL"   HAPPY MEAL   1986
Set of three inflatable beach balls. "(C) 1986 McDonald's
Corporation. Safety tested for children 3 and over..Not to
be used as a flotation device." Each ball has three picture-
panels.

BEACH BALLS:
1.RONALD, red ball   AVG:$2.00 MINT:$4.50
Scene: RMCD on beach with penguin
and pelican. Seahorse in water.
Seagull and sun in sky.

2.GRIMACE, yellow ball   AVG:$2.00 MINT:$5.00
Scene: Grimace on beach holding
yellow & white umbrella, talks with
puffin (bird), flying overhead is a
Mallard duck. On water is a sailboat
with a gold "M" on the sail.
A yellow fish jumps from the water.

3.BIRDIE, blue ball   AVG:$2.00 MINT:$5.00
Scene;Birdie on the beach
points at a sandcastle flying a
pink flag with a gold "M". She smiles
at a goose with black neck and feet.
On the water is a sailboat. A smiling crab
and a starfish lie on the sand.

CARTON   AVG:$1.50 MINT:$2.75
     "HAVING A WONDERFUL TIME"

"BEACH BALL" HAPPY MEAL (*REGIONAL)   1986
One inflatable beach ball was issued in Florida. It shows a
golden sunlit beach with three palm trees and McDonald's
logo in pink. ball has three picture- panels alternated with
three blue panels.

BIRDIE   AVG:$4.00 MINT:$7.00
Scene: Birdie on yellow sailboat with red sail. "(C) 1985
McDonald's Corporation. Safety tested for children 3 and
over..Not to be used as a flotation device."

"CONSTRUX ACTION BLDG SYSTEM"   HAPPY MEAL   1986
(may have been a test)
Set of four pieces which make a space craft when combined.

COMPLETE SET:
    1.CYLINDER   AVG:$12.00 MINT:$24.00
    2.CANOPY   AVG:$14.00 MINT:$20.00
    3.WING   AVG:$14.00 MINT:$20.00
    4.AXEL   AVG:$11.00 MINT:$18.00

    CARTONS (2):   AVG:$5.50 MINT:$12.50
    1."TOOL TROUBLE"
    2."MARS MISSION"

"LUNCH BOX"   HAPPY MEAL (TESTED)   1986
Embossed with design of a TV picture. Available in three
colors.
1. RED   **AVG:$2.00 MINT:$8.00**
2. GREEN   **AVG:$2.00 MINT:$8.00**
3. BLUE   **AVG:$3.00 MINT:$9.00**

"McDONALD'S CRAYOLA/CRAYON MAGIC" HAPPY MEAL (TEST)   1986
Set of three plastic stencils with Crayola Crayons or
Crayola Markers.

STENCILS:
1.TRIANGLE   AVG:$5.00 MINT:$8.50
Blue: stencils of different sizes,
    circles, check mark and arrows.
Orange marker.

2.CIRCLE   AVG:$4.50 MINT:$7.50
Red: compass, stencils of circles.
Four crayons.

3.RECTANGLE   AVG:$4.50 MINT:$7.50
Red: stencils of squares,triangles,
    squares and hexagons, various edge shapes.
Four fluorescent crayons.

CARTON (like a Crayola box)   AVG:$4.00 MINT:$7.00

LUNCH BOX

BEACH BALL

BEACH BALL - FLORIDA

"HAPPY PAIL"   HAPPY MEAL   MAY
Set of five different pails with handles and sand-sifter
lids. They are decorated with scenes of McDONALDLAND
characters and were accompanied by a red rake or a yellow
shovel. Writing on pails reads; "Safety tested for childres
of all ages / recommended for children age 1 and over / (C)
1986 McDONALD'S CORPORATION / printed in the United States
of America"

PAILS:
1.VACATION   AVG:$3.00   MINT:$5.00
2.TREASURE HUNT   AVG:$4.00   MINT:$6.00

3.PARADE   AVG:$4.00   MINT:$6.00
White pail with red lid and handle.
Scene: McDONALDLAND characters parade.
RMCD plays the drum and leads the parade.
MCD#13-846 FC#8932-252

4.PICNIC   AVG:$3.50   MINT:$6.00
5.BEACH   AVG:$3.00   MINT:$5.00

"PLAY DOH"   HAPPY MEAL   JULY
Set of eight, two-ounce cans of Pla Doh. Was also tested in
1985 in several areas of country.

COLORS: AVG:$3.00   MINT:$5.00
        1.RED
        2.ORANGE
        3.YELLOW
        4.GREEN
        5.BLUE
        6.PURPLE
        7.WHITE
        8.PINK

CARTONS (4):   AVG:$1.50   MINT:$2.00
        1."CIRCUS ANIMALS"
        2."YESTERDAY'S ANIMALS
        3."FARM ANIMALS"
        4."HOUSE PETS"

HAPPY PAILS

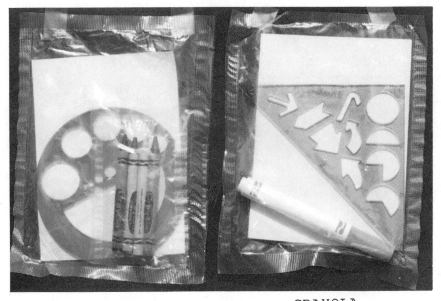 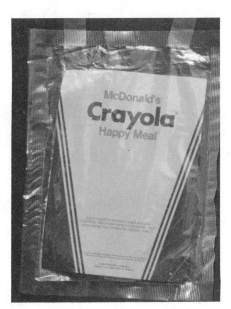

CRAYOLA

"STOMPER 4X4"   HAPPY MEAL   AUGUST
Set of eight cars (size:2.75 X 1.75 X 1.5) with big wheels.
Rubber tires.(Four models Tested in St. Louis in 1985)
Windshields printed "stompers" .Markings on underside read
" STOMPER (R) PATENT PENDING / SCHAPER MFG. CO. /
MINNEAPOLIS, MINN USA /MADE IN HONG KONG".
Since there are eight styles, each with two color
combinations a "full" set would consist of 16 cars.

    1.AMC EAGLE,   NP:$5.00 MIP:$7.50
       Sides, front: "500 HP"
       Sides, doors: "74"
       Sides, back: "EAGLE"
       Cab, top:"74"
       Hood: design of an eagle
       Colors:orange w/ dk. blue, black w/gold

    2.CHEVY S-10 PICKUP   NP:$4.00   MIP:$7.00
       Both sides of hood: "4WD"
       Top of cab and door sides:"S-10"
       Tail gate:"CHEVROLET"
       Colors: Black w/silver, yellow w/black(or yellow
               w/ ppl).

    3.CHEVY VAN   NP:$3.50 MIP:$6.50
       Both sides: "4X4" / " CHEVY" / stripe
       Colors:red w/yellow, yellow w/red

    4.CHEVY BLAZER   NP:$4.00 MIP:$7.00
       Both sides: "BLAZER"
       Top of cab: "4X" (3 times)
       Hood: "4X" (2 times)
       Colors: red w/grey, yellow w/green

    5.DODGE RAM PICKUP   NP:$3.50 MIP:$6.50
       Sides, over front wheels:"RAMPAGE"
       Hood:'2.2"
       Cab top:"4X4"
       Colors:white w/blue, blue w/red

    6.FORD RANGER PICKUP   NP:$4.00 MIP:$7.00
       Sides door:"23"
       Hood: "4/4"
       Tailgate: "FORD"
       Colors: red w/black, orange w/black

    7.JEEP RENEGADE,   NP:$5.00 MIP:$7.50
       Sides: "78 4X4"
       Hood: "RENEGADE 78"
       Tailgate: "JEEP"
       Colors: Maroon w/white, Orange w/yellow

8.TOYOTA TERCEL   NP:$3.50   MIP:$5.50
   Sides: "SR5"
   Hood: "TERCEL" (on gold stripe)
   Above rear window: "TERCEL"
   Colors: blue w/gold, grey w/maroon

UNDER 3 YRS;(plastic wheels)
1.JEEP, orange   NP:$5.00   MIP:$8.00
2.CHEVY VAN, yellow   NP:$5.00   MIP:$8.00

                                   AVG:$2.50   MINT:$3.75
CARTONS (4):
1."JALOPY JUMP"
2."RAMBUNCTIOUS RAMP"
3."QUICKSAND ALLEY"
4."THUNDERBOLT PASS"

"YOUNG ASTRONAUTS"   HAPPY MEAL   SEPTEMBER
Set of four plastic, snap-together space craft models of the
actual vehicles, with decals.

1.APOLLO COMMAND MODULE,   NP:$4.00 MIP:$7.00
2 3/4 inches long. Grey with black band
around base. Four paper stickers on sides:
2 have American flag above words "UNITED STATES".
2 "NASA".

2.SPACE SHUTTLE, ...   NP:$4.25 MIP:$7.50
3 1/2 inches long. White rocket ship,
Paper decals indicate; 3 rockets (in tail),
shuttle nose and window details.
On back: paper American flag.
Underside:"(C) 1986 McDONALD'S CORP /
MONOGRAM MODELS INC"

3.ARGO LAND SHUTTLE,   NP:$4.00 MIP:$7.00
Red, molded plastic details augmented by
paper decals; blue bars on white and
2 "ARGO" labels
Underside: "(C) 1986 McDONALD'S CORP /
MONOGRAM MODELS INC"

4.CIRRUS VTOL,   NP:$4.25 MIP:$7.50
Dark blue.Paper decals; 4 red V on white
label on rockets. Black & white patterned
label at back end. Red paper cutouts:
2 over pilot's area. "CIRRUS".
2 labels on each side. small american flag on back.
Underside: "(C) 1986 McDONALD'S CORP /
MONOGRAM MODELS INC"

UNDER 3 YRS;
1.GRIMACE SMILING SHUTTLE, blue   NP:$4.00 MIP:$7.50
2.FRY GUY AIRPLANE, blue   NP:$4.00 MIP:$7.50

CARTONS (4)   AVG:$4.00 MINT:$6.00
      1.SPACE STATION
      (rest unknown)

"YOUNG ASTRONAUTS"

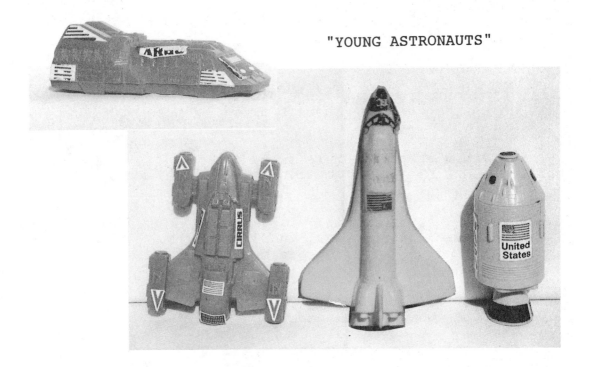

TINOSAURS

"TINOSAURS"   HAPPY MEAL   (REGIONAL*)   SEPTEMBER
(* Regional: St. Louis) Set of eight theme characters. Each
piece reads: (C) AVIVA ENT. INC / TINOSAURS TM / McDONALD'S

1.DINAH   NP:$3.00   MIP:$5.00
Orange dinosaur,green stripe down back.
Pink heart with gold "M" in left arm.

2.LINK, THE ELF   NP:$3.00   MIP:$5.00
Boy creature with pale purple skin,
standing on head. Green jumper.

3.BABY JAD   NP:$3.25   MIP:$5.50
 Light purple creature has large head
with 2 antennae, orange eyes, purple nose.
Purple necklace. A row of purple scales run
from top of head to tip of tail.

4.MERRY BONES   NP:$3.00   MIP:$5.00
Green dinosaur with yellow underside.
Orange spots on each thigh. Big back legs
and tail. Holds a 5-pointed star with "M".

5.GRUMPY SPELL   NP:$3.25   MIP:$5.50
Blue, shaggy creature with pointed ears
and green hands, feet and nose. It opens
the lid of a brown box held between its feet.
"M" on front of box.

6.TIME TRAVELER FERN   NP:$3.00   MIP:$5.00
Girl holds a paint brush in one hand,
balancing a pot of yellow paint in other.
Her green hair is decorated with 2 white bones.
Short orange dress, in points at bottom.

7.TINY   NP:$4.00   MIP:$5.75
Pink dinosaur with petal-like scales
along back ridge. Gold "M" on uplifted
left front foot.

8.KAVE KOLT KOBBY   NP:$4.00   MIP:$5.75
Pink horse creature,with white hooves,
green tipped lion's tail, curly green mane,
green nose and a green stripe on back.

CARTON   AVG:$4.00   MINT:$7.00

"HALLOWEEN"   HAPPY MEAL   OCTOBER
(Same as those tested in the New York area in 1985, smaller
faces) Set of three pumpkin-shaped containers with handles
and perforated lids with round, half-inch holes.

CONTAINERS:
1.McBOO   AVG:$2.00 MINT:$3.75
2.McGOBLIN   AVG:$2.50 MINT:$4.50
3.McPUNK'N   AVG:$2.00 MINT:$3.75

"LITTLE TRAVELERS LEGO BUILDING SETS" HAPPY MEAL NOVEMBER
Set of four building sets.Duplo (R) building sets made in
Switzerland. (note:"Super Traveler" cup in some regions.)

SETS:
1.ROADSTER-A-RED   NP:$4.75 MIP:$8.00
2.TANKER BOAT-B-BLUE   NP:$4.00 MIP:$7.00
3.HELICOPTER-C-YELLOW   NP:$5.00 MIP:$9.00
4.AIRPLANE-D-GREEN   NP:$4.00 MIP:$7.50

UNDER 3 YRS; DUPLO BLOCKS:
1.BIRD, with eye   NP:$6.00 MIP:$10.00
2.BOAT, with sailor   NP:$7.00 MIP:$11.00

CARTONS (4):   AVG:$2.00 MINT:$3.25
    1."WHICH CAME FIRST?"
    2."VACATION"
    3."ANIMAL POWER"
    4."VEHICLE RHYME"

"METRO ZOO" REGIONAL HAPPY MEAL   1986
Region - Miami, Florida. Animal figurines: flamingo,
tiger, chipansee and elephant.

FIGURINES: NP:$8.00 MIP:$15.00

"BEACHCOMBER"   1986
White pails served as containers, blue lids and yellow
shovels .Featured: RMCD, Grimace and Mayor McCheese.

PAILS   AVG:$12.00 MINT:$20.00

3. McPUNK'N   1. McBOO   2. McGOBLIN

AN AMERICAN TAIL

"BERENSTAIN BEARS I"   HAPPY MEAL (TEST)   NOVEMBER
CHRISTMAS THEME.Labels decorated with pine cones & branches.
(Tested in 1986 Evansville, Ind.) Set of four soft figures
with flocked heads with additional piece. MCD#86-130
(C) 1986 McDONALD'S CORPORATION   FC 932-537
(C) 1986 S.&J. Berenstain.

1.SISTER,on SLED   NP:$5.00 MIP:$11.00
2.PAPA, with RED wheelbarrow   NP:$5.00 MIP:$11.00
3.MAMA, in pantsuit, shopping cart NP:$4.00 MIP:$ 9.00
4.BROTHER, scooter   NP:$4.00 MIP:$ 9.00

CARTONS (4):   AVG:$7.00 MINT:$13.50
(cartons may be made into play scenes)
        1. HOME
        2."BEAR COUNTRY SCHOOL"
        3."BARN DANCE TONIGHT"
        4."BEAR COUNTRY GENERAL STORE"

"COLORFORMS PLAYSET" HAPPY MEAL (OPTIONAL)   DECEMBER
5 x 5 inch punch-out paper scenes with sheets of
stickers.Set of five.
(C) COLORFORMS, Ramsey NJ 07466, (C) 1986 McDonald's
Corporation

SET:
1.RMCD   AVG:$2.00 MINT:$3.75
2.GRIMACE   AVG:$2.50 MINT:$4.00
3.BIRDIE   AVG:$3.00 MINT:$5.00
4.PROFESSOR   AVG:$3.00 MINT:$5.00
5.HAMBURGLAR   AVG:$3.50 MINT:$5.50

UNDER 3 YRS;   AVG:$3.00 MINT:$6.00
     (same: larger shapes)

CARTONS (5):   AVG:$1.50 MINT:$2.25
     1."AT THE FARM"
     2."CAMP OUT"
     3."BIRDIE"
     4."BEACH PARTY"
     5."PICNIC"

"AN AMERICAN TAIL"   HAPPY MEAL   DECEMBER
Inspired by the movie adventure story about a mouse
immigrating from Europe to America. Four, 24 page, picture-
story books. The covers have "M-McDonald's" logo in a red
square, front and back. (C) 1986 McDonald's Corporation.

1."FIEVEL'S FRIENDS"   AVG:$1.75 MINT:$2.50
Yellow cover, Fievel and girl mouse.

2."TONY AND FIEVEL"   AVG:$1.75 MINT:$2.50
Blue cover, 2 mice with scissors.

3."FIEVEL AND TIGER"   AVG:$2.00 MINT:$3.00
Violet cover, mouse in bird-cage
on Fat Cat's stomach.

4."FIEVEL'S BOAT TRIP"   AVG:$2.00 MINT:$3.00

CARTONS (2):   AVG:$1.50 MINT:$2.50
     1."MOUSE IN MOON"
     2."SLIPPERY SOLUTIONS"

"GLOTRON SPACE SHIP"   1986
Served as containers, with stickers that glow in the dark.
May have been regional. No further information at present.
     CONTAINERS: AVG:$8.00 MINT:$15.00

HAPPY MEALS 1987

DIRECTORY

```
┌─────────────────────────────────────────────────────────────┐
│        Abbreviations used to describe condition:             │
│        MINT = new, never used or unfolded.                   │
│        AVG  = average condition.                             │
│        NP   = no original package, loose.                    │
│        MIP  = mint in package, in original, sealed           │
│               container.                                     │
└─────────────────────────────────────────────────────────────┘
```

"RUNAWAY ROBOTS"   HAPPY MEAL   (*REGIONAL)   1988
(* Regional- St. Louis. Run again in some regions in 1988)
Set of six small robots with fixed grey tractor treads.
String propelled wheels. Underside reads (C)85 S.COLBURN.

1.BOLT, purple   NP:$4.00 MIP:$5.50
    Yellow face plate and front coil,
    blue under-plate, arms thrust forward.
2.SKULL, dk. blue   NP:$4.00 MIP:$5.50
    Pointed helmet, yellow under-plate
    and front with red bar. Arms straight,
    fingers on tractor treads.
3.JAB, yellow   NP:$4.00 MIP:$5.50
    Tractors are triangular in shape,
    red under-plate, left arm cocked,
    right arm extended in punch position.
4.BEAK, bright blue   NP:$4.00 MIP:$5.50
    Bird-like, yellow hood, arms hunched
    forward, white under-plate.
5.FLAME, red   NP:$4.00 MIP:$5.50
    Profile of sharp teeth, eyes on sides.
    Arms at sides, blue under plate.
6.COIL, green   NP:$4.00 MIP:$5.50
    Snake head, red tongue, yellow eyes,
    cobra-like fins, red under-plate

CARTON;   AVG:$1.75 MINT:$2.75
```

```

"LITTLE ENGINEER"   HAPPY MEAL   FEBRUARY
Set of five train engines with decals and moving wheels.

1.GRIMACE STREAK   AVG:$1.75 MINT:$3.00
     Purple.
2.RONALD RIDER   AVG:$1.75 MINT:$3.00
       Red.
3.FRY GIRLS EXPRESS   AVG:$1.75 MINT:$3.00
       Blue.
4.BIRDIE BRIGHT LITE   AVG:$1.75 MINT:$3.00
       Yellow.
5.FRY GUYS FLYER   AVG:$1.75 MINT:$3.00

UNDER 3 YRS.;(no movable parts):
1. FRY GUY HAPPY CAR   AVG:$2.00 MINT:$4.00
2.GRIMACE HAPPY TAXI   AVG:$2.00 MINT:$4.00

CARTONS (5):   AVG:$2.50 MINT:$4.50
          MCD#86-087   FC#MCDY-932-481
1. BRIDGE
2."ROUNDHOUSE TRAIN GARAGE"
     May be made into a "brick" roundhouse play scene
3. TUNNEL
4. ROUND HOUSE
5."McDONALDLAND STATION"
     May be made into a station house play scene

"POTATO HEAD KIDS"   HAPPY MEAL (REGIONAL*)   FEBRUARY
(* Regional test: Oklahoma) like "McNugget Buddies" with
interchangeable shoes and hats. Set of twelve toys.

```
    1.  LUMPY                    NP:$7.00   MIP:$12.00
    2.  PAT DUMPLING             NP:$8.00   MIP:$14.00
    3.  BIG CHIP                 NP:$8.50   MIP:$14.50
    4.  SMARTY PANTS             NP:$8.50   MIP:$14.50
    5.  DIMPLES                  NP:$9.00   MIP:$15.50
    6.  SPIKE                    NP:$7.00   MIP:$12.00
    7.  POTATO PUFF              NP:$7.50   MIP:$12.50
    8.  TULIP                    NP:$8.50   MIP:$14.50
    9.  SPUD                     NP:$7.00   MIP:$14.00
    10.LOLLY                     NP:$7.00   MIP:$14.00
    11.SLUGGER                   NP:$8.00   MIP:$15.00
    12.SLICK                     NP:$8.00   MIP:$15.00

    CARTON                       AVG:$4.50   MINT:$8.00
```

"CRAYOLA"   HAPPY MEAL   MARCH
(Different from 1986 "Crayola" HAPPY MEAL.) Four sets,
each with a plastic stencil and Crayola crayon or marker.
(C) 1986 McDONALD'S CORPORATION MCD#86-088 FC932-499
Bags are colored to look like Crayola boxes: green and
yellow and included an entry blank for children's drawings
of "What America Means to You / Draw America".

1.HAMBURGLAR stencil   AVG:$2.00   MINT:$3.75
Orange piece shaped like train engine.
Stencils: clover, heart, quarter moon and bell.
Four crayons.

2.BIRDIE stencil   AVG:$2.00   MINT:$3.75
Yellow piece shaped like roadster.
Stencils: arrow, square, triangle and hexagon.
Large orange or green marker.

3.GRIMACE stencil   AVG:$2.00   MINT:$3.75
Stencils: star, circle, ovals etc.
Four fluorescent crayons.

4.RMCD stencil   AVG:$2.00   MINT:$3.75
Red piece shaped like tractor.
Stencils: horse, pig, duck, "R", egg.
Thin blue or red marker.

UNDER 3 YRS;
BAG: AVG:$3.00   MINT:$4.75
Like Crayola Box, white & green.
RMCD driving fire engine.(cardboard)
Stencils: heart, star, cross, "1".
Four crayons

CARTONS (4):   AVG:$1.50   MINT:$3.00
1."ABSENT APPLES"
2."EARLY BIRD"
3."CRAZY FACE"
4."WHACK ON TRACK"

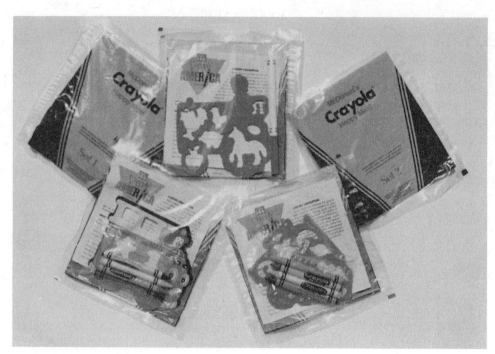

CRAYOLA

KISSYFUR

"KISSY FUR"   HAPPY MEAL (*REGIONAL)   APRIL
(* Regional St. Louis) Set of eight rubber figures, some
with a furry surface. Underside reads:PHIL MENDEZ / Made in
China

1.KISSY FUR   NP:$3.00 MIP:$5.00
Small brown bear, 2 1/4 inches high.
Stands with front paws clasped at chest.
White muzzeled mouth is wide open.
He wears a short-sleeved yellow shirt with a wide red band.

2.GUS   NP:$3.00 MIP:$5.00
Big round,brown bear, 3 inches. standing,
arms thrown wide. Open happy mouth.
He wears a long-sleeved yellow shirt
with red trim. His big white belly shows
beneath the shirt. Blue cap on head.

3.FLOYD   NP:$3.00 MIP:$5.00
Lt. green alligator, 3 inches high,
with blue spots and yellow underside.
He has a tuft of red hair atop his head.
In position of a fast walk; right foot forward.

4.JOLENE   NP:$3.00 MIP:$5.00
Lt. green alligator, 2 1/2 inches high,
with blue spots, yellow underbelly and
a lot of red hair. Her arms are flung
out to the sides.

5.LENNIE   NP:$3.00 MIP:$5.00
Pink, furry pig. seated, feet straight
in front, head turned to look over left
shoulder. "Arms" close to chest. 2 1/4 inches-seated. (*)

6.TOOT   NP:$3.00 MIP:$5.00
2-inch furry beaver, tan with lighter
underbelly. Looking to right, mouth open,
finger of right hand on lower lip.
Left hand behind him. Wide, curved paddle tail.

7.BEEHONIE   NP:$3.00 MIP:$5.00
2 1/2-inch, white furry rabbit.
Yellow tummy, blue eyes. Red-ribboned
ears are 1/2 inch above head. Tail is a round ball.

8.DUANE   NP:$3.00 MIP:$5.00
Smaller pink furry pig. Standing,
left arm forward. Frowning. 2 1/8 inches.
(* items 5 and 8 may be reversed. No info. at this time)

CARTON   AVG:$2.50 MINT:$3.75

"McDONALDLAND BAND"   HAPPY MEAL   APRIL
Set of eight toy plastic musical instruments in various
colors: blue, green, pink, purple, red, orange and yellow.

1.FRY GUY TRUMPET   NP:$2.25 MIP:$3.50

2.HAMBURGLAR WHISTLE   NP:$2.00 MIP:$3.00

3.RONALD HARMONICA   NP:$2.25 MIP:$3.50

4.GRIMACE SAXOPHONE   NP:$2.25 MIP:$3.50

5.RONALD WHISTLE   NP:$2.25 MIP:$3.50
      train whistle

6.RONALD PAN PIPES   NP:$2.00 MIP:$3.00

7.FRY GUY WHISTLE   NP:$2.00 MIP:$3.00
      boat whistle
8.KAZOO   NP:$2.00 MIP:$3.00

UNDER 3 YRS;
(Train whistle and pan pipes safe for under 3 years)

CARTONS (4):   AVG:$1.25 MINT:$2.00
      1."INSTRUMENT RHYME TIME"
      2."SCAVENGER HUNT"
      3."ONE MAN BAND"
      4."BAND LEADER"

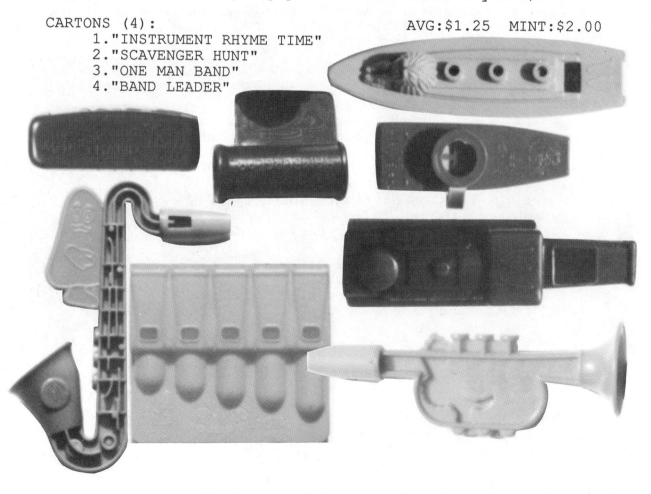

"MUPPET BABIES"   HAPPY MEAL   JUNE

(Same as 1986 test in Savannah, GA.) Figurines, plastic,
soft. Each one has a different toy. (C)1986 McDONALD'S
CORPORATION

1.BABY GONZO   NP:$2.50   MIP:$3.25
     Two pieces; Blue Gonzo
     Green tricycle with red wheels.

2.BABY FOZZIE   NP:$2.50   MIP:$3.25
     Two pieces;Fozzie, yellow suit & hat
     Lt. yellow hobby-horse with wheels.

3.BABY PIGGY   NP:$3.00   MIP:$4.50
     Two pieces;Piggy
     Pink convertible car.

4.BABY KERMIT   NP:$2.50   MIP:$3.25
     Two pieces;Kermit
     Red skateboard.

MUPPET BABIES Continued:

UNDER 3 YRS; (solid)
1.PIGGY   NP:$3.00   MIP:$4.75
     One piece, on roller skates.
2.KERMIT   NP:$3.00   MIP:$4.75
     On roller skates. White shirt, with
     sailor collar, blue shorts and tie.

CARTONS (4):   AVG:$1.00   MINT:$1.50
MCD#86-104   FC#MCDY-932-529
cartons may be made into play scenes;

1."BABY FOZZIE BEAR"
     May be made into a "wooden" horse and armor.
2."BABY GONZO"
     May be made into a horse and chariot.
3."BABY KERMIT"
     Carton made into a hawiian shirt and surf board.
4."BABY MISS PIGGY"
     May be made into a boat which fits over Piggy's car.

"DESIGN-O-SAURS"   HAPPY MEAL (REGIONAL)   JULY
Set of four toys; hard plastic with interchangeable parts.
Embossed lettering reads "Instructions: snap body halves
together/ snap legs into body / insert wing pegs into holes
/ these parts can be switched with other Design-O-Saurs ".

1."RONALD ON TYRANNOSAURUS REX"   AVG:$3.00 MINT:$4.50
Red.

2."GRIMACE ON PTERODACTYL"   AVG:$4.00 MINT:$5.00
Purple.

3."FRY GUY ON BRONTOSAURUS"   AVG:$3.00 MINT:$4.50
Yellow creature with large claws.

4."HAMBURGLAR ON TRICERATOPS"   AVG:$4.00 MINT:$6.00
Orange.

UNDER 3 YRS;
1."GRIMACE HAPPY TAXI"   AVG:$3.00 MINT:$4.50
2."FRY GUY RACER"   AVG:$3.00 MINT:$4.50

CARTON: AVG:$1.25 MINT:$1.75

"BOATS 'N FLOATS"   HAPPY MEAL   AUGUST
Set of four plastic boats, served as container."Safe for
children age 1 and over". Includes decals.
(C)1986 McDONALD'S CORPORATION   MCD#86-102   FC#932-483 "

1.GRIMACE SKI BOAT   AVG:$5.00   MINT:$9.00
9 1/2 inches, purple.

2.FRY KIDS RAFT   AVG:$6.00   MINT:$10.00
8-inch disk, chartreuse green,
3 Fry kids on lid.

3.BIRDIE FLOAT   AVG:$4.00   MINT:$8.00
9 1/2-inch yellow boat,
Birdie on lid reading book.

4.McNUGGET LIFE BOAT   AVG:$5.00   MINT:$9.00
9 1/2-inches, orange,
6 Fry Kids on lid.

"CASTLE MAKER/SAND CASTLE" HAPPY MEAL (*REGIONAL)   SUMMER
(* Regional: Houston, TX) Set of four sand molds, which
served as containers, fit together.

MOLDS:
1.CYLINDRICAL, YELLOW   AVG:$4.00 MINT:$7.00
2.RECTANGLE, RED   AVG:$5.00 MINT:$9.00
3.SQUARE, BLUE   AVG:$4.00 MINT:$6.00
4.DOME, BLUE   AVG:$5.00 MINT:$9.00

"GHOSTBUSTERS"   HAPPY MEAL   SEPTEMBER
Set of five useful implements for school, with movie theme.
(C) 1984 Columbia Pictures Industries Inc. (C) 1987 Columbia
Pictures Television, a division of CPT Holdings, Inc.
(C) 1987 McDONALD'S CORPORATION

1.SLIMER, pencil & topper   AVG:$4.00 MINT:$6.00
White pencil:
"THE REAL GHOSTBUSTERS"TM / (C) 1984 COLUMBIA PICTURES INC.
Topper: laughing green worm-like creature atop a blue
         building (sharpener).

2.STAY PUFT, notepad & eraser   AVG:$3.00 MINT:$6.00

3.CONTAINMENT CHAMBER   AVG:$4.00 MINT:$6.00
clear plastic pencil case.

4.STAY PUFT, pencil sharpener   AVG:$3.00 MINT:$6.00

5.GHOSTBUSTERS,ruler   AVG:$3.00 MINT:$5.00
Six-inch rule at top,
below which are two XOGraph scenes
of the Ghostbusters roping creatures.

UNDER 3 YRS;
(notepad, eraser and ruler safe for under 3 years)

CARTONS (4):   AVG:$1.50 MINT:$2.25
MCD#86-107 FC#MCDY-932-495
1."HEADQUARTERS"
2."HAUNT N' SEEK/PUBLIC LIBRARY"
3."MUSEUM"
4."SCHOOLHOUSE"

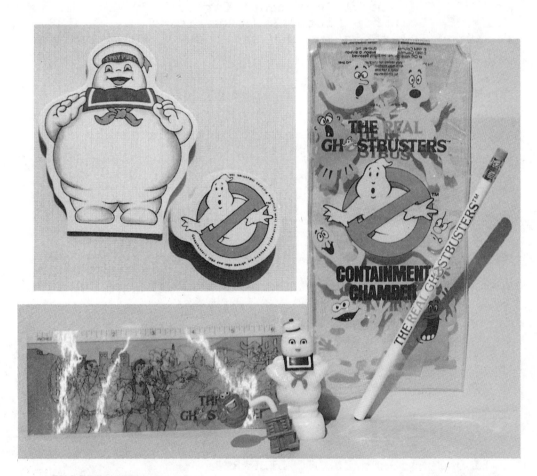

GHOSTBUSTERS

"BERENSTAIN BEARS II"   HAPPY MEAL   OCTOBER
(Tested in 1986 Evansville, Ind. with some differences:
"Christmas" theme, has PAPA with *red* wheelbarrow and SISTER
with *sled*.)
Set of four figures with flocked, movable heads. Each set
has an additional piece. McD#87-007 FC#932-605 (C) 1987
McDONALD'S CORPORATION / (C) 1987 S & J BERENSTAIN.

1.SISTER, wagon   NP:$2.00 MIP:$3.25
Two pieces; Sister in seated position,
wearing a pink jumper and white blouse.
Underside:(C)1986 S & J BERENSTAI /CHINA
     Wagon: red, yellow wheels and handle
Underside;McDONALD'S (R) / CHINA /MBHB-3

2.PAPA, wheelbarrow   NP:$2.00 MIP:$3.25
Two pieces: Papa, standing, wearing
blue overalls, straps with white
buttons.Yellow shirt (square textured).
Underside:(C) 1986 S & J BERENSTAIN/CHINA
       Wheelbarrow: brown, lt. green wheel.
Underside;McDONALD'S (R) / CHINA /MBSC-1

3.BROTHER, scooter   NP:$2.00 MIP:$3.25
Two pieces: Brother, standing, wearing
blue trousers, red long-sleeved shirt.
Underside:(C)1986 S & J BERENSTAIN/CHINA
Scooter:green, yellow handle, red wheels.
Underside (R) McDONALD'S /MADE IN CHINA/S1

4.MAMA, shopping cart   NP:$2.00 MIP:$3.25
Two pieces:Mama: standing, wearing long
light blue dress, white dots and collar.
Underside:(C) 1986 S & J BERENSTAIN/CHINA
          Shopping cart:yellow, red wheels.
Underside (R) McDONALD'S/MADE IN CHINA /T6

UNDER 3 YRS; (soft, no moving parts.) **Heads are not flocked.**

MAMA, same clothing   NP:$3.00 MIP:$4.25
PAPA,   NP:$3.00 MIP:$4.25
Same clothes, head looking left.
Punch-out card: ladder, saw, paint can and hatchet.

CARTONS (4):   AVG:$1.00 MINT:$1.50
(cartons may be made into play scenes)
1."TREE HOUSE"
2."BEAR COUNTRY SCHOOL"
3."BARN DANCE TONIGHT"
4."BEAR COUNTRY GENERAL STORE"

BERENSTAIN BEARS II

"DISNEY FAVORITES"   HAPPY MEAL   NOVEMBER
Set of four "activity" books.

1.CINDERELLA & PRINCE   AVG:$1.75 MINT:$3.50
Paint-with-water book

2.SWORD & STONE   AVG:$1.75 MINT:$3.50

3.LADY AND THE TRAMP   AVG:$1.75 MINT:$3.50
Sticker book

4.DUMBO   AVG:$1.75 MINT:$3.50
Press-out book

CARTONS (2):   AVG:$1.30 MINT:$2.10
1."CINDERELLA & PRINCE"
2."CINDERELLA & GODMOTHER"

"CHANGEABLES"   HAPPY MEAL   (*REGIONAL)   1987
(* Regional: St. Louis) Cleverly constructed miniature
McDONALD'S food packages that turn into "robots" with a few
twists and turns. Set of six. NOTE: Hands and feet are *not*
painted. Shake opens _UP_, not _OUT._

1.CHICKEN McNUGGETS	NP:$1.75	MIP:$3.00
2.QUARTER POUNDER with CHEESE	NP:$2.00	MIP:$3.25
3.FRENCH FRIES	NP:$1.50	MIP:$3.00
4.BIG MAC	NP:$1.50	MIP:$3.25
5.SHAKE	NP:$2.00	MIP:$3.25
6.EGG McMUFFIN	NP:$1.75	MIP:$3.00

CARTON   AVG:$1.00 MINT:$1.75
(Shows various types of changeables)

"GOOD FRIENDS"   HAPPY MEAL   1987
Set of two cartons to be used as needed.(C) 1987 McDONALD'S
CORPORATION MCD#87-056   FC#MCDY-932-601

1."A CLEAN SWEEP"   AVG:$1.00 MINT:$2.00
2."SNAPSHOT SHUFFLE"   AVG:$1.00 MINT:$2.00

"MATCHBOX SUPER GT"   HAPPY MEAL   1987
Sixteen MATCHBOX cars made up this offering. "Off-the-shelf"
cars were provided in a plain plastic envelope with a paper
"disclosure", Cars differed in type with areas of the
country.

CARS   AVG:$8.00 MINT:$12.00
CARTON   **AVG:$3.50 MINT:$7.50**

"HIGH FLYING"   HAPPY MEAL   1987
Set of three kites ,each with a different McDONALDLAND
character.

KITES:
1.HAMBURGLAR   AVG:$12.00 MINT:$20.00
2.RONALD   AVG:$10.00 MINT:$18.00
3.BIRDIE   AVG:$10.00 MINT:$18.00

CARTON   AVG:$8.00 MINT:10.00

"HALLOWEEN"   HAPPY MEAL   OCTOBER
Same as 1986. Set of three pumpkin-shaped containers with
handles and perforated lids with patterns of 1/4 inch holes.

CONTAINERS:
1.McBOO   AVG:$2.00 MINT:$3.75
2.McGOBLIN   AVG:$2.50 MINT:$4.50
3.McPUNK'N   AVG:$2.00 MINT:$3.75

"BIGFOOT"   HAPPY MEAL   1987
This is a confusing issue: According to archive records,
there are four types of Ford trucks in four different
colors. We also find two sizes of plastic wheels. Some cars
are marked with "M (R)" and some are not. It is believed
that this was a problem of supply and demand. "Off-the-
shelf" cars, without the McDonald's Logo, were put into
small plastic bags with a disclosure label which reads:
"This item has been safety tested for children 3 and over.
CAUTION: It may contain small parts and is not intended for
children under 3. / Contents made in CHINA / Printed in Hong
Kong"
Underside marks;"BIGFOOT (R) / CHINA / (#) "
Wheel size: 0.9 inch diameter, snow tire, wide treads &
midrib.
Wheel size: 1.3 inch diameter, narrow treads and midrib.
Note: all are "mag wheels" with silver hubs.
Colors SEEN in body types will be shown.

Body types;
       1.BIGFOOT:
       Sides,door: "BIGFOOT" large solid letters in outline
                   block. Under this "4X4X4" (smaller)
       Sides,back panel by door: white line drawing of truck

       Hood: "POWERED BY FORD". "FORD" is Logo.
       Cab:Top of cab has yellow light-rack with 4 lights
       Tail lights: smooth rectangles, painted red.
       Tailgate: smooth, no details.indented bumper
       Front:small white squares for side and headlights.
             Radiator, grid type, black, 12 sections.
       Bed: black "cover" with FORD Logo and"M (R)".

       2.MS BIGFOOT:
       Like Bigfoot with these differences:
       Double lines of striping curve across front of hood
       and along sides to rear.
       Sides, door: "Ms.Bigfoot" in script. Lettering across
                   door with part of M, extending onto side-
                   panel.
       Hood: FORD Logo
       Cab: yellow light rack has 5 smaller yellow lights.
       Tail lights: curve around corners, 4 sections.
       Tailgate: inset rectangle
       Front:White double headlights
             Radiator, 4 horizontal lines.
       Bed: (same as Bigfoot)

3.SHUTTLE:
  Sides:Lower half of sides in trim color.Right side
        shows 2 doors, left side - 1 door. Centered on
            sides is "BIGFOOT" inside color block.
            Below this:"Shuttle" larger type, italics
  Sides, above back wheel: small Ford Logo.
  Cab & Hood: 3 bands of striping (center band is
            wider) starting at rear cover cab and
            most of hood.
  Tail lights: curve around corners, 4 large sections.
  Back:detailed tail gate, "M (R)" centered on back
        window.
  Front: detailed bumper, white rectangular headlights,
        side-front lights, white, teardrop shaped.
  Radiator: narrow horizotal lines.

4.BRONCO:
  Sides, door to front: band of vertical stripes
            (trim).
  Sides, back panels: "BIGFOOT" in large letters,
            outlined with trim.
  Cab: solid trim color
  Hood:rectangle of trim,broken into stripes and Ford
        Logo
  Tail lights: curve around corner, 3 sections
  Back: indented bumper, "M" centered on back window
  Front:White squares for headlights on front and
        side-front.
  Radiator:horizontal grid, 12 sections.

TYPE: "M (R) ", 0.9 inch diameter tires
COLORS:black, orange, lt. blue and "hot" pink.

    BIGFOOT , lt. blue   AVG:$5.00 MINT:$7.00
    MS. BIGFOOT, hot pink   AVG:$4.50 MINT:$6.50
    SHUTTLE, black   AVG:$4.50 MINT:$6.50
    BRONCO , orange   AVG:$4.50 MINT:$6.50

TYPE: "M (R)", 1.3 inch diameter tires.
COLORS:red, aqua, dark blue, lt. green.

    BIGFOOT , dark blue   AVG:$4.50 MINT:$6.50
    MS. BIGFOOT, aqua   AVG:$4.50 MINT:$6.50
    SHUTTLE,red   AVG:$5.00 MINT:$7.00
    BRONCO , lt. green   AVG:$5.00 MINT:$7.00

TYPE: No "M", 0.9 inch diameter tires.
COLORS:black, orange, lt. b;ue and "hot" pink.

```
        BIGFOOT , lt. blue               AVG:$3.50  MINT:$4.75
        MS. BIGFOOT , hot pink           AVG:$4.00  MINT:$5.00
        SHUTTLE , black                  AVG:$4.00  MINT:$5.00
        BRONCO , orange                  AVG:$5.00  MINT:$7.50
```

TYPE: No "M", 1.3 inch diameter tires.
COLORS:red, dark blue, lt. green, black, aqua.

```
        BIGFOOT , dark blue              AVG:$4.50  MINT:$7.00
        MS. BIGFOOT , aqua               AVG:$4.00  MINT:$6.50
        SHUTTLE ,black, red              AVG:$4.50  MINT:$7.00
        BRONCO , lt. green               AVG:$4.50  MINT:$7.00
```

HAPPY MEALS 1988

DIRECTORY

```
+--------------------------------------------------------+
|          Abbreviations used to describe condition:     |
|          MINT = new, never used or unfolded.           |
|          AVG  = average condition.                     |
|          NP   = no original package, loose.            |
|          MIP  = mint in package, in original, sealed   |
|                 container.                             |
+--------------------------------------------------------+
```

"BLACK HISTORY"   HAPPY MEAL (REGIONAL*)   JANUARY
(* Regional offering- Detroit) Set of two coloring books.

```
1."LITTLE MARTIN JR." Volume I      AVG:$3.50  MINT:$8.00
2."LITTLE MARTIN JR." Volume II     AVG:$3.50  MINT:$8.00
```

"SAILORS"   HAPPY MEAL   JANUARY
Set of four floating toys. (C)1987 McDONALD'S CORPORATION.
Pieces are connected to plastic tree and snap together.

```
1.RONALD AIRBOAT,red                AVG:$4.50  MINT:$5.00
     Four pieces

2.GRIMACE SUB ,purple               AVG:$4.50  MINT:$5.00
     Four pieces

3.FRY KIDS FERRY, green             AVG:$3.00  MINT:$4.50
     Three pieces

4.HAMBURGLAR SAILBOAT, blue         AVG:$3.00  MINT:$4.50
     Three pieces

UNDER 3 YRS;
1.GRIMACE SPEEDBOAT                 AVG:$2.50  MINT:$4.00
2.FRY GUY FLOATER                   AVG:$2.50  MINT:$4.00

CARTONS(4);                         AVG:$1.00  MINT:$3.00
MCD#87-083   FC#MCDY-609
1."SOMETHING FISHY"
2."FRY GUY AFLOAT"
3."ISLAND EYES"
4."HOUSEBOAT"
```

SAILORS

"FROM THE HEART"   HAPPY MEAL   (OPTIONAL*)   FEBRUARY
(* Optional, not in all markets)   Sheets of Valentines.

CARTON: AVG:$1.50 MINT:$3.00

"DUCK TALES I"   HAPPY MEAL   FEBRUARY
Set of four "detective" toys.(C) 1987 Walt Disney Co. (C)
1987 McDONALD'S CORPORATION

```
1.WRIST WALLET DECODER              AVG:$1.75  MINT:$2.75
    Has a secret message compartment,
    blue, logo on lid.
2.MAGNIFYING GLASS                  AVG:$2.00  MINT:$3.00
    With green case.
3.DUCK CODE QUACKER                 AVG:$2.00  MINT:$3.00
    With secret code, orange.
4.TELESCOPE                         AVG:$2.00  MINT:$3.00
    Yellow and blue, logo on side.


UNDER 3 YRS;
1. MAGIC MOTION MAP                 AVG:$3.00  MINT:$4.50

CARTONS (4);                        AVG:$1.25  MINT:$1.75
MCD#87-069  FC#MCDY-607
1."CITY OF GOLD"
    Scene of a lost city
2."WESTWARD DOUGH"
    Scene ofthe "Lost Buckaroo Mine"
3."COOKIE OF FORTUNE"
    Scene in a cookie factory
4."HULA HOOPLA"
    Hawaiian scene
```

"FRAGGLE ROCK"   HAPPY MEAL   MARCH
(tested 1987 in West Virginia) (C)1988 HENSON ASSOCIATES
INC.
(C) 1987 McDONALD'S CORPORATION   MCD#87-016 FC#MCDY-648.
This is a set of four toys featuring the cartoon characters.
It is believed that, except for the "UNDER 3 YRS" toys,
most of these toys were distributed loose, (not Mint-in-
package), and were produced by different vendors, because
there are at least three variations in the statements,
embossed on the underside of the toy. Less than 10% of (OVER
3 yrs) toy finds will be MIP.
Underside reads; (C) HENSON ASSOCIATES INC 1988 / CHINA
Label ident: MCD#87-016   FCMcDY-648. Label has simple, lt.
blue border.

SET 1: GOBO FRAGGLE   NP:$1.50 MIP:$5.00
Car is an orange carrot with large
wheels and a green leafy tail.
Wheel diameter is 1.3 inches.
Positioned along *length* of toy, above button:
"(C) HENSON ASSOCIATES INC / 1988 / CHINA.

SET 2: RED FRAGGLE   NP:$1.50 MIP:$5.00
Car is raddish with green leafy tail.
Underside copyright statement:
Positioned along *length* of toy, above button:
"(C) HENSON ASSOCIATES INC / 1988 / CHINA.

SET 3: MOKEY FRAGGLE   NP:$2.50 MIP:$6.00
Purple eggplant car.

SET 4: WEMBLY & BOOBER FRAGGLE   NP:$2.50 MIP:$6.00
Car is a two-seated green pickle.

UNDER 3 YRS;
1.GOBO   NP:$1.50 MIP:$3.00
One-piece. Orange creature with pink
hair stands on flat green surface, holds
carrot as large as himself.
Underside reads;
"(C) HENSON ASSOCIATES INC 1988 /
MB-KH-1 / CHINA

2.RED   NP:$1.50 MIP:$3.00
One-piece. Orange creature in red shirt,
stands on flat green surface, with left
arm wrapped around large red raddish.
Right arm is flung sideways.

FRAGGLE ROCK - 1988

GOBO FRAGGLE - 1987   GOBO FRAGGLE - 1988
NOTE: Notice difference in wheel size.

CARTONS (4);   AVG:$1.00   MINT:$1.50
1."PARTY PICKS"
2."RADDISHES IN CAVE"
      "What kind of song is Wembly singing?"
3."VEGGIE GAME"
      Carton may be made into underground
      veggie garden play scene.
4."SWIMMING HOLE BLUES"
      Carton may be made into a swimming scene.

"FRAGGLE ROCK"   HAPPY MEAL Tested 1987 in West Virginia.
Fraggle Rock toys, "MINT IN PACKAGE", with very slight
differences from later toys. May have been "tests" or
prototypes of the nationally issued toys. Label border
design leafy, light blue.
Label reads: (C) 1987 McDonald's Corporation / (C) Henson
Associates, Inc. 1987. Label pictures character in car.
Scarce. MCD# 87-106   FC 932-577

"SET 1 GOBO FRAGGLE"   NP:$15.00 MIP:$20.00
"GOBO" with minor differences:
Wheel diameter is 1.15 inches (smaller).
Underside plug is irregular, softer, yellow
plastic "button".
Underside copyright statement:
Positioned along *width* of toy, beside button:
 "(C) HENSON ASSOCIATES INC / 1987".
Other side of button: "CHINA".
Package label reads: MCD#87-106 FC 932-577.

"SET 2 RED FRAGGLE"   NP:$15.00 MIP:$20.00

"SET 3 MOKEY FRAGGLE"   NP:$16.00 MIP:$25.00

"SET 4 WEMBLY & BOOBER FRAGGLE"   NP:$16.00 MIP:$25.00

"FRAGGLE ROCK-DOOZER"   HAPPY MEAL   1988
FRAGGLE ROCK was tested in West Virginia with "DOOZERS"
substituted for set #2 and #4.
(C) Henson AssociatesInc 1987,FRAGGLE ROCK and character
names are trademarks of Henson Associates Inc.
(C) McDonald's Corporation   MCD#87-106   FC 932-577

2. BULLDOOZER AND FRIENDS   NP:$14.00 MIP:$19.00
Green figures with yellow helmets,
tan and yellow boots and gloves,
round red noses. They ride in a tan
bulldozer with black treads and yellow shovel.
Bulldoozer, who sports a flowing mustache,
steers from elevated rear seat. His crew
of two creatures, sit in front on lower seats.
(tractor treads don't move;wheels underneath)

4. COTTERPIN DOOZER AND FRIENDS   NP:$14.00 MIP:$19.00
Green figures with round, red noses
in red helmets, tan and yellow boots
and gloves.. they ride on tan fork-lift
type truck with moveable black wheels and
yellow blades. Cotterpin steers. His 2 friends
are seated on the back, facing outward.

"NEW ARCHIES"   HAPPY MEAL   (REGIONAL*)   SPRING
(* Regional: St. Louis) This is an attractive set of six
comic characters in "Bumper Cars" (C) 1988 McDONALD'S
CORPORATION pieces read; 1977 ACP "THE NEW ARCHIES"

1. REGGIE   NP:$3.00   MIP:$4.75
       Black hair, waving fist.

2. VERONICA   NP:$3.00   MIP:$4.75
       Black hair,yellow & green blouse,
       orange bow on head.

3. ARCHIE   NP:$3.00   MIP:$4.75
       Red-haired boy in red, white and
       blue shirt.

4. BETTY   NP:$3.00   MIP:$4.75
       Yellow hair on top of head,white
       blouse, waving arms.

5. JUGHEAD   NP:$3.00   MIP:$4.75
       Two fingers up,pink hat, purple shirt.

6. MOOSE   NP:$3.00   MIP:$4.75
       Large blond boy,black shirt,arms in air

CARTON   AVG:$1.50 MINT:$2.25

"SEA WORLD OF OHIO" HAPPY MEAL (REGIONAL*)   SPRING
(* Regional - Cleveland) Plastic figurines. The "real"
McDonald's premiums have "(C) 1987 Sea World, Inc. / Made In
China"- ON THE BASE (*Not on side or back*) Average height of
toy is 2 1/2 inches.

1.SHAMU WHALE, Orca   NP:$6.00   MIP:$13.00
White underbelly, black back, tail
and fins. Large white patch over each
white rimmed blue eye. Stands on tail
on flat blue base.Mouth open showing
teeth on lower jaw and pink tongue.

2.DOLLY DOLPHIN, Porpois   NP:$5.50   MIP:$12.00
(Bottle-nose). Pale blue underbelly,
grey back, tail and fins. White eyes
with black centers and eyelashes.
Blue eyelids. On head is wreath of
green leaves, white objects and gold stars.
Stands on tail on a flat blue base.

3.PERRY PENGUIN   NP:$6.00   MIP:$13.00
Stands on two large yellow feet.
White underbelly, black back and flippers
which meet in front. Grey beak.Yellow eyelids.
A long scarf, with wide bands of colors, is
wrapped around his throat.

CARTON   AVG:$3.00   MINT:$6.50

"COSMc! CRAYOLA"   HAPPY MEAL   APRIL
Set of five outline drawings to be colored with Crayola
products. Each bag contains a space scene featuring CosMc!.
"Crayola: the chevron design and the serpentine line are
registered trademarks of Binney & Smith Inc and are used
with permission". (C)1987 Binney & Smith Inc. (C) 1987
McDONALD'S CORPORATION   MCD#87-120   FC#MCDY-658
(colors may vary)

1.CRAYOLAS (4)   NP:$2.00   MIP:$3.50
Blue,copper,red and silver.

2.MARKER   NP:$1.50   MIP:$2.50
Washable ink,(spring green).
connect the dots, CosMc and Grimace
on rocket scooter."Color with CosMc!..."

3.CHALK STICKS, four pastel.   NP:$2.00   MIP:$3.50

4.MARKER   NP:$2.00   MIP:$2.50
Washable drawing marker (black).
CosMc and RMCD in maze.
"What's CosMc thinking?..."

5.PAINT SET   NP:$2.75   MIP:$4.00
Red, blue and yellow paint, with
paintbrush. Drawing has numbered areas
to correspond with paint colors. "Paint by numbers with
CosMc!"..."

UNDER 3 YRS;
1.CRAYONS   NP:$2.00   MIP:$4.00
Two large crayons, "SO BIG",
(orange, purple) with coloring sheet.
Sheet has line drawings on both sides.
Side 1: CosMc in space scene."Color CosMc..."
Side 2: men in space suits, floating.
     "In space there is no gravity."

CARTONS (4);   AVG:$1.50   MINT:$2.25
MCD#87-120   FC#MCDY-643
1."SPACE SCRAMBLE"
2."PLANET ROUNDUP"
3."TOWING TROUBLES"
4."FUZZY SPACE FRIENDS"

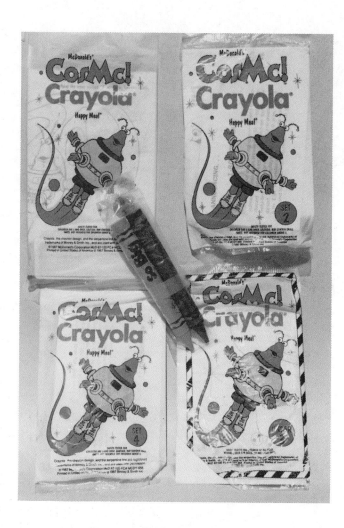

CosMc! CRAYOLA

SUPER SUMMER

"SUPER SUMMER"   HAPPY MEAL   MAY
(Tested 1987 Fresno, CA) Pails were used for containers,
(Other toys in bags) Set of five toys for sand and water
play.

1.BALL, inflatable   AVG:$2.00   MINT:$3.50
      FRY GUYS (bag).

2.SAILBOAT, inflatable   AVG:$2.00   MINT:$3.50
      GRIMACE (bag).

3.PAIL, BIRDIE   AVG:$2.00   MINT:$3.75
      With yellow sifter lid and rake.

4.PAIL, PROFESSOR   AVG:$2.00   MINT:$3.75
      With red sifter lid and shovel.

5.SAND MOLD (bag)   AVG:$2.00   MINT:$4.00

BAG   AVG:$2.00   MINT:$4.00

"BAMBI"   HAPPY MEAL   JULY
Set of four charming characters from the popular DISNEY
movie. Each has movable parts except for the "under 3 yrs"
premium.

1.FLOWER , skunk   NP:$2.00   MIP:$3.50
2.FRIEND OWL , owl   NP:$2.00   MIP:$3.50
3.THUMPER , rabbit   NP:$2.00   MIP:$3.50
4.BAMBI , deer   NP:$3.75   MIP:$5.50

UNDER 3 YRS;
1.BAMBI , with butterfly on tail NP:$5.00   MIP:$8.00
2.BAMBI , (no butterfly)   NP:$7.00   MIP:$10.00
3.THUMPER , rabbit   NP:$5.00   MIP:$8.00

CARTONS (4);   AVG:$1.50   MINT:$2.25
MCD#87-176
1.SPRING
      Bambi with his mother.
2."WHO-OOO'S THERE ?"
      Summer scene.
3."OWL-AWEEN!"
      Fall scene.
4.SNOW SCENE
      Woodland creatures playing in the snow.

"SEA WORLD OF TEXAS I" HAPPY MEAL (*REGIONAL)   SUMMER
(* Regional :TEXAS) Set of four velvet cloth animals. White
cloth label reads: "Sea World / (C) 1988 Sea World, Inc. /
(logo) / All New Materials / Contents: 100% Polyester /
Surface Washable Only / Ohio Permit Reg. #OH13871 / Made In
Korea...(etc)" Average height six inches.

FIGURINES:
1. WHALE, Orca   NP:$3.50 MIP:$5.75
White underbelly, black back, tail,
fins and head with round white spot
over each eye. Mouth is a line of red cord.
Tail is 2-lobed.Black glass eyes.

2. DOLPHIN   NP:$4.00 MIP:$6.00
White underbelly and tail, Grey back,
tail and fins. Tail is split into 2 fins.
Glass eyes are black with blue rims.

3. PENGUIN   NP:$4.00 MIP:$6.00
White belly and underside of flippers.
Black back, flippers and hooded head.
Orange feet and beak. Black glass eyes with tan rims.

4. WALRUS   NP:$3.50 MIP:$5.00
Brown with a fluffy white patch across
nose. Stuffed white tusks at either side
of mouth. Black glass eyes with brown rims.

CARTON   AVG:$8.00 MINT:$14.00
With "bounceback" coupon

BAMBI

FLINTSTONES

"FLINTSTONE KIDS"   HAPPY MEAL   (REGIONAL?)   1988
Set of four action toys with Hannah-Barbera TV cartoon's
Flintstone characters in animal "cars". Embossed on the back
of each seated figurine and beneath the seat of each"car: "
(C) 1988 H.B PROD. INC / CHINA " Wheels are textured to
resemble rough pegged wood.

1.FRED   NP:$3.00   MIP:$4.50
Wears short, orange, sleeveless shirt
with black triangles and pointed hem.
Blue necktie. Black hair.
Car: dark green Alligator with big eyes,
pink mouth and nostrils.

2.WILMA   NP:$3.00   MIP:$4.50
Wears short, white sleeveless shirt
with ruffled neck. Red hair in top-knot,
held with a white band.
Car: purple Dinosaur, large yellow eyes,
head held high.

3.BARNEY   NP:$3.25   MIP:$5.00
In short brown vest, laced in front.
Yellow hair.
Car: green-blue Mastodon with white eyes
and tusks, pink mouth.

4.BETTY   NP:$3.00   MIP:$4.50
Dressed in light blue halter-shirt
held on with a black thong, white shell.
Matching blue bow on top of head.Black hair.
Car: orange Pterodactyl (wings folded),
white eyes and cheeks and large yellow beak.

UNDER 3 YRS;
1.DINO   NP:$4.00   MIP:$6.00
Three inches, soft plastic,
red-violet color.Standing figure,
tail curved up, short front legs drawn up.
Large, pink, duck-like snout. Black spots
and knob atop head. Wears a blue collar
with a yellow tag.

CARTON   AVG:$2.00   MINT:$3.25

"HOT WHEELS"   HAPPY MEAL   (*REGIONAL)   1988
(* Regional : Texas) was run nationally in 1983 with 23
different models. Also tested in 1982. West and East coasts
had some different models. The 12 types listed below have
(C)1988 logo.

1. SILVER STREET BEAST	NP:$7.00	MIP:$12.00
2. RED STREET BEAST	NP:$7.00	MIP:$12.00
3 .WHITE P-911 TURBO	NP:$7.00	MIP:$12.00
4. BLACK P-911 TURBO	NP:$7.00	MIP:$12.00
5. SILVER SPLIT-WINDOW	NP:$8.00	MIP:$14.00
6. BLACK SPLIT-WINDOW	NP:$8.00	MIP:$14.00
7. TURQUOIS '57 T-BIRD	NP:$7.00	MIP:$12.00
8. WHITE '57 T-BIRD	NP:$8.00	MIP:$14.00
9. BLUE 80'S FIREBIRD	NP:$7.00	MIP:$12.00
10.BLACK 80'S FIREBIRD	NP:$7.00	MIP:$12.00
11.SHERRIF PATROL	NP:$7.00	MIP:$12.00
12.RED FIRE CHIEF	NP:$7.00	MIP:$12.00

CARTON   AVG:$5.00   MINT:$8.00

SPORT BALL:
1.BASEBALL   NP:$5.00   MIP:$10.00
     Hard plastic, 3 inches diameter.
2.FOOTBALL   NP:$6.50   MIP:$12.00
     Red and yellow, 5 inches long, soft.
3.BASKETBALL   NP:$8.00   MIP:$13.00
     With basket, soft.
4.TENNIS BALL   NP:$5.00   MIP:$10.00
     Soft.

UNDER 3 YRS;
BASEBALL (same as #1)   NP:$5.00   MIP:$10.00

CARTONS (2);   AVG:$5.50   MINT:$10.25
1."CLEAR THE COURT"
2."MATCH POINTS"

"ON THE GO"   HAPPY MEAL   AUGUST
Lunch bags and boxes. Lunch boxes are green, red and blue
and have decals. Lunch bags are vinyl with velcro closures
at top and are yellow and blue.

LUNCH BAGS: (C) 1988 McDONALD'S CORPORATION MCD#88-052

1.Yellow   AVG:$2.00   MINT:$4.00
    Pictures RMCD juggling.
2.Blue   AVG:$2.00   MINT:$4.00
    GRIMACE painting a green apple.

LUNCH BOXES; (C) 1988 McDONALD'S CORPORATION
    Plastic, 5 inches x 8 inches. The handle is in the
the shape of M-arches and the sides are embossed with
McDONALDLAND characters going to school. Other side:
bulletin board. Sheets of stickers.

1.Green   AVG:$2.00   MINT:$3.50
2.Red   AVG:$2.00   MINT:$3.50

3.Blue   AVG:$3.00   MINT:$4.50

"OLYMPIC SPORTS II"   HAPPY MEAL (OPTIONAL)   SEPTEMBER
(Optional, not used everywhere) Set of six white plastic
medallions with figures in relief and color. "M" in red
square, "1988 TEAM McDONALDLAND" . On the back is a tension
clip. 2 1/8 inches diameter.
Bag reads;"Safety tested for children of all ages.
Recommended for children aged one and over /Made in China ".

MEDALLIONS:
1.RMCD on bicycle.   NP:$2.00 MIP:$3.50
RMCD with hands on blue handlebars.

2.BIRDIE on balance beam.   NP:$2.00 MIP:$3.50
Birdie balancing on right foot,
left foot in air, wings out.

3.CosMc with basketball.   NP:$2.50 MIP:$3.50
Five hands manipulating two basketballs.
Silver body with bluetrim.

4.GRIMACE playing soccer.   NP:$3.00 MIP:$4.00
Kicks a black and white soccer ball

5.FRY GAL on diving board.   NP:$2.00 MIP:$3.50
Yellow Fry Girl stands on diving board.
green shoes, pink stockings and pink bow.

6.HAMBURGLAR running track.   NP:$3.00 MIP:$4.00
Jumps over red hurdle. Red shoes,
gloves and tie. Black cape has yellow lining.

CARTONS (2);   AVG:$1.50 MINT:$2.25
1."HILARIOUS HURDLES"
2."ORDER ON THE COURT"

"ZOO FACE"   HAPPY MEAL (*)   SEPTEMBER
(* Tested 1987 in Evansville) Indiana. Test resulted in
breathing holes being enlarged and elastic string made
heavier. *Test packages have no part number.* The masks are
made of soft plastic and cover the nose. Each package
contains a PAAS Make-up Kit and suggestion for completing
the animal face. Underside of mask reads:"(C) 1987
McDONALD'S CORPORATION." Make-up card reads:" (C) 1988
McDONALD'S CORPORATION   MCD#88-062   FC#MCDY-730"

MASKS:
1-a. TOUCAN   AVG:$2.00   MINT:$3.00
2-a. MONKEY   AVG:$3.00   MINT:$5.00
3-a. TIGER   AVG:$3.00   MINT:$5.00
4-a. ALIGATOR   AVG:$2.00   MINT:$3.00

UNDER 3 YRS;
1. MONKEY   AVG:$4.00   MINT:$6.00
2. TIGER   AVG:$4.00   MINT:$6.00

CARTONS (4);   AVG:$1.00   MINT:$1.75
1.APE HOUSE
2.LION HOUSE
3.BIRD HOUSE
4.REPTILE HOUSE

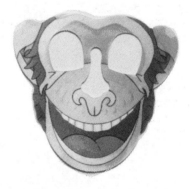

"STORY BOOK MUPPET BABIES"   HAPPY MEAL   OCTOBER
Set of three books, 7 x 7 inches, with library card.

BOOKS:
1."THE LEGEND OF GIMME GULCH"   AVG:$1.75   MINT:$2.25
2."JUST KERMIT AND ME"   AVG:$2.00   MINT:$3.00
3."PIGGY,THE LIVING DOLL"   AVG:$2.00   MINT:$3.00

CARTONS (3);   AVG:$1.00   MINT:$1.50
     1.LIBRARY
     2.NURSERY
     3.PICNIC

"PETER RABBIT"   HAPPY MEAL   (*REGIONAL)   FALL
(* Regional:Eastern Pennsylvania) Set of four books by
Beatrice Potter.

BOOKS:
1."TALE OF SQUIRREL NUTKIN"   AVG:$5.50   MINT:$11.50
2."TALE OF BENJAMIN BUNNY"   AVG:$6.00   MINT:$13.00
3."TALE OF FLOPSY BUNNIES"   AVG:$8.00   MINT:$15.00
4."TALE OF PETER RABBIT"   AVG:$6.50   MINT:$13.00

CARTON   AVG:$6.00   MINT:$12.00

"CRAZY CLINGERS (WALL CRAWLERS)"   1989
This was run internationally. Figurines of plastic which
stick to the wall and creep down. (Further information not
available at this time)

CLINGERS:
1. RMCD , parachute.   ..AVG:$5.00   MINT:$6.50
2. GRIMACE, hot-air balloon.   AVG:$6.00   MINT:$7.00
3. HAMBURGLAR, hang glide.r   AVG:$6.25   MINT:$7.50
4. BIRDIE, with balloons.   ....AVG:$6.00   MINT:$7.00

"DUCK TALES II"   HAPPY MEAL   (*)   1988
(* Test or option in Texas) Set of four toys: character with
vehicle. (C) Disney / (C) 1988 McDonald's

1.UNCLE SCROOGE   NP:$3.00 MIP:$6.00
     Two pieces: Uncle Scrooge.
     Red sports car with yellow wheels and
     radiator. (car = 2.6 inches long)
2.LAUNCHPAD   NP:$3.00 MIP:$6.00
     One piece: figure (duck pilot).
     (Launchpad = 1.8 inches head to waist.
     Orange airplane. Plane's cockpit is
     sealed around figure.
3.WEBBY   NP:$3.00 MIP:$6.00
     Two pieces: (lady duck).
     Blue tricycle with pink wheels.
4.NEPHEWS   NP:$3.00 MIP:$6.00
     One piece: three young ducklings
     in jackets and caps, are firmly attached
     to a yellow ski boat with green hull.
     Duck on left (in green) has left arm out.
     (Ski boat handle projects 1/2 inch.)

UNDER 3 YRS;
1.HUEY   NP:$5.00 MIP:$7.00
     On skates
CARTON   AVG:$2.00 MINT:$3.00

"MOVABLES"   HAPPY MEAL   (*REGIONAL)   1988
Set of six soft, vinyl figurines. marked on back "(C)1988
McDONALD'S CORP / MADE IN CHINA. all but the Fry Girl are
standing with arms straight out from sides.Nice detail in
faces.

1.RMCD   NP:$2.00 MIP:$3.50
    3 3/4 inches. Wears typical costume.
2.HAMBURGLAR   NP:$2.00 MIP:$3.50
    2 3/8 inches. Child-like face version.
    Dots on red tie are hamburgers. Red and
    white sneakers, short black cape,
    yellow lining and hat band.
3.BIRDIE   NP:$2.50 MIP:$4.00
    2 1/2 inches. Pink overalls with legs
    rolled up. Brown braids tied with pink
    ribbons. White goggles and scarf.
4.PROFESSOR   NP:$2.50 MIP:$4.50
    3 inches. Open white lab coat shows
    blue vest. Red, blue and white checked
    trouser. Red bow tie, white shoes.
5.FRY GIRL   NP:$2.50 MIP:$4.50
    2 inches. Pink creature with yellow
    ribbons and yellow and green sneakers
    with pink pom-poms.
6.CAPTAIN CROOK   NP:$2.50 MIP:$4.50
    3 3/8 inches. Red coat with gold
    epaulets and vest. White neck ruffles
    and gloves. "M" on left coat lapel
    Black boots and tricorn hat.

"OLIVER & COMPANY"   HAPPY MEAL   DECEMBER
Set of four finger puppets (one hole in back) soft rubber.
Based on the movie by Walt Disney Pictures. MCD#88-053
FCMCDY-717.   Underside reads; DISNEY / CHINA (C)1988

1.OLIVER   NP:$2.00   MIP:$3.00
Orange,seated kitten.   underside: SL18

2.FRANCIS   NP:$2.00   MIP:$3.00
Tan bulldog, red collar. Underside:P4

3.GEORGETTE   NP:$2.00   MIP:$3.50
White poodle dog, pink ribbon bow
around neck. Underside:P8

4.DODGER   NP:$2.00   MIP:$3.00
Grey and brown terrier dog with black
sun glasses on top of head. Red scarf
around neck. Underside:G9

CARTONS (4);   AVG:$1.00   MINT:$3.00
May be made into city scenery.
MCD#88-053   FC#MCDY-739

1."NOISY NEIGHBORHOOD"
2."FUNNY BONES"
3."TRICKY TRIKE"
4."SHADOW SCRAMBLE"

HAPPY MEALS 1989

DIRECTORY

```
┌──────────────────────────────────────────────────────────┐
│           Abbreviations used to describe condition:        │
│           MINT = new, never used or unfolded.              │
│           AVG  = average condition.                        │
│           NP   = no original package, loose.               │
│           MIP  = mint in package, in original, sealed      │
│                  container.                                │
└──────────────────────────────────────────────────────────┘
```

"McNUGGET BUDDIES"   HAPPY MEAL   JANUARY
Made to celebrate the introduction of McDonald's "Chicken
McNuggets", these ten amusing characters are made of molded
rubber and are equipped with interchangeable belts and hats.
.(C) 1988 McDONALD'S CORPORATION.
    Note: When McNuggets are found without their
accessories in place, it may be difficult to tell them
apart. All have prominent white eyeballs and puffed cheeks
Special differences in faces are described below, as needed.

1."COWPOKE"   NP:$2.50 MIP:$3.50
Accessories: Yellow-dotted, red scarf,
"M" logo. Brown eyes and large brown mustache.
Large, white cowboy hat with a red band.

2."SARGE"   NP:$2.50 MIP:$3.50
Accessories: blue cap, black shade,
white band with gold star. Blue belt
with white buckle, gold "M"
Face: Blue eyes, focused right.
Open lipped smile showing white teeth (3 grooves).

3."CORNY"   NP:$2.50 MIP:$3.50
Accessories: Straw hat with red band
over brown hair WHITE belt holds three
boxes of popcorn, reads "POPCORN".
Face: Eyes look up from center.Mouth open
in laugh showing white upper row of teeth.
Opening below is painted black.

3a."CORNY"   NP:$3.50 MIP:$5.50
Like above but with RED belt.

4."SNORKEL"   NP:$2.50 MIP:$4.25
Accessories: yellow hair, blue visor
and snorkel. Black belt holding a knife
and flash-light, white buckle, gold "M".
Face:Eyes looking right & up.
Mouth: Lips pursed around small black opening.
Groove in upper lip.

5."FIRST CLASS"   NP:$2.50   MIP:$3.50
Accessories: Red postman's hat with
white shade. "FIRST CLASS" in red letters
on yellow hat-band. Brown pouch with white
envelopes , gold "M" .
Face: Eyes look down & left. Pink eyelids
with black lashes. Lips slightly parted
in wide smile which is higher on right side.

6."DRUMMER"   NP:$2.50   MIP:$3.50
Accessories: tall red drum majors hat
with black shade, "M" on front. Yellow hair,
brown belt with red and white drum, drumsticks.
Face: Blue eyes with red lids and black lashes.
Smile: pink lips over a black curved line.

7."SPARKY"   NP:$2.50   MIP:$3.50
Accessories; red fireman's hat has
white shield with gold "M". Tan belt,
holding blue hatchet and red fire-extinguisher.
Face: Eyes focused up & left. A black
line edges wide open eyes (black centers)
Smile is a curved groove, filled with black.

8."ROCKER"   NP:$2.50   MIP:$3.50
Accessories;green star-shaped glasses
over a "beehive" of orange hair. Black
belt holds blue guitar.
Face: Eyes looking right. Eyelids blue
with black lashes. Red lips edge a wide
open (singing) mouth. Opening painted black.

9."VOLLEY"   NP:$2.50   MIP:$4.00
Accessories; red hair held up by white
band, gold "M". Green belt holds blue
pouch with two yellow tennis balls and
a yellow racket.
Face: Dark blue eyes, centered, dark
blue eyelids and black lashes. Small smile,
pink lips slightly parted.

10."BOOMERANG"   NP:$2.50   MIP:$4.00
Accessories: black spanish hat with
green band. Yellow hair. Brown belt has
black buckle with gold "M", yellow
coiled rope and boomerang, brown canteen.
Face: Black lined eyes are blue, centered.
Mouth: off-center, deeply curved, open
laugh. Painted black inside, a pink tongue
shows at the lowest part of the curve.

UNDER 3 YRS;
1."SLUGGER"   NP:$3.00   MIP:$5.00
Accessories;red baseball hat with
yellow shade and "M", over brown
hair. Brown belt with catcher's glove.

2."DAISY"   NP:$3.00   MIP:$5.00
Accessories; yellow hair with
pink bow and white daisy. Pink belt
with lighter pink pouch,"M",
holds brown and white bear.

CARTONS (4);   AVG:$1.00   MINT:$1.50
1."APARTMENTS"
2."GARDENS"
3."BEAUTY SHOP"
4."POST OFFICE"

"RMCD BEDTIME"   HAPPY MEAL (OPTION)   FEBRUARY
Set of four items to be used by children when preparing for
bed.

1.RMCD toothbrush   AVG:$3.00   MINT:$5.00
With sparkle Crest toothpaste

2.Cup, Plastic.   AVG:$1.00   MINT:$2.25

3.RMCD foam washing mitt   AVG:$1.00   MINT:$2.25

4.RMCD Glow-in-the-dark figurine   AVG:$2.00   MINT:$3.00

CARTONS(4);   AVG:$1.00   MINT:$2.00
1."PILLOW FIGHT"
2."FIND THE SLIPPERS"
3."SCAVENGER HUNT"
4."SLUMBER PARTY"

McNUGGETS

RMCD BEDTIME

"MICKEY'S BIRTHDAYLAND"   HAPPY MEAL   MARCH

This set of five toys presents favorite Disney characters in
motorized vehicles(like the 1985 "Fast Mac" cars.
(C)1989 THE WALT DISNEY CO. (C)1988 McDONALD'S CORPORATION
MCD #88-146 FC#MCDY-814

1.DONALD DUCK TRAIN ENGINE   NP:$2.75 MIP:$4.00
     Grey engineer's cap, green steam-engine.
     Underside reads:(C)DISNEY CHINA CW
2.MINNIE MOUSE CONVERTIBLE   NP:$2.75 MIP:$4.00
     Red bow on top of her head, pink
     convertible. Underside reads;(C)DISNEY CHINA YL-8
3.GOOFY JALOPY SPORT COUPE   NP:$2.75 MIP:$4.00
     Blue jeep and wears a red hat.
4.PLUTO'S RUMBLER   NP:$2.75 MIP:$4.00
     Sits in rumble seat of purple coupe.
     Underside reads; (C)DISNEY CHINA HF
5.MICKEY'S ROADSTER   NP:$3.00 MIP:$4.50
     Red convertible.
     Underside reads;(C)DISNEY CHINA V6

UNDER 3 YRS: larger, soft cars.
1.MICKEY'S CONVERTIBLE   NP:$3.50   MIP:$5.00
      Red car, yellow wheels.
2.MINNIE'S CONVERTIBLE   NP:$3.50   MIP:$5.00
      Pink car with tail fins, yellow wheels.
3.DONALD DUCK'S JEEP   NP:$3.50   MIP:$5.00
      Blue and white OR green and red.
4.GOOFY'S CAR   NP:$3.50   MIP:$5.00
      Blue and white OR green and red.

CARTONS (5);   AVG:$1.25   MINT:$2.00
1."PLUTO"
2."MICKEY'S HOLLYWOOD THEATER"
3."MINNIE'S DRESS SHOP"
4."GRANDMA DUCK'S BARN"
5."BIRTHDAYLAND TRAIN STATION"

MICKEY'S BIRTHDAYLAND
      UNDER 3 YRS.

"LITTLE GARDENER"   HAPPY MEAL   APRIL
Set of four gardening tools for children, some included a
packet of seeds. (C)1988 McDONALD'S CORPORATION MCD#88-109
FC#MCDY-784

1.TROWEL, orange, ring-handle.   AVG:$1.50 MINT:$2.25
Embossed design of BIRDIE with basket
of flowers.
Also; packet of Burpee Marigold seeds.

2.PAIL, blue.   AVG:$1.50 MINT:$2.25
With purple lid and handle.
Embossed design of FRY GUYS around side.

3.RAKE, green, ring-handle.   AVG:$1.50 MINT:$2.25
Design of GRIMACE holding carrots.
Also a packet of raddish seeds.

4.WATERING CAN ,yellow and red.   AVG:$2.00 MINT:$3.00
Design of RMCD

UNDER 3 YRS;
1.TROWEL (as above without seeds).   AVG:$1.00 MINT:$2.00

BAGS (4); (#03201)   AVG:$1.00 MINT:$1.50
1."BIRDIE'S BOUQUET"
     Birdie in garden.
2."WHOSE HOSE"
3."GARDEN GOODIES"
4."RADDISH CONTEST"

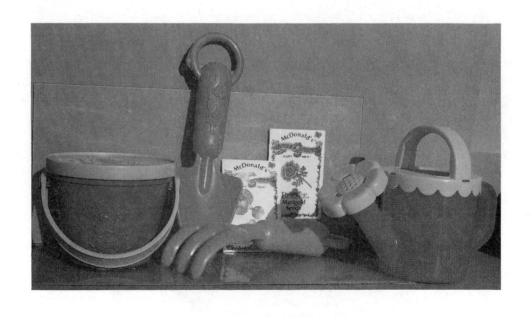

"**McBUNNY**"   HAPPY MEAL (REGIONAL)   SPRING
Set of three plastic pails used as both containers and
premiums. They are decorated with attractive rabbit
faces,and come with perforated lids and yellow, ear-shaped
handles. Undersides read:(C) 1988 McDONALD'S CORPORATION
with "McD" logo.

PAILS:
1."PINKY McBUNNY"   AVG:$3.00   MINT:$5.50
Orange bunny with yellow lid.4/53501

2."WHISKERS McBUNNY"   AVG:$3.50   MINT:$5.75
Green bunny with green lid. 1/53501

3."FLUFFY McBUNNY"   AVG:$3.00   MINT:$5.50
Blue bunny with blue lid. 3/53501

"NEW FOOD CHANGEABLES"   HAPPY MEAL   MAY
These miniature packages of popular McDonald's foods with a
few twist and turns become science fiction type robots.
There are eight in this set. (C) 1988 McDONALD'S CORPORATION
(Some are marked (C) 1987. This set has hands or feet
painted, *whereas the 1987 set does not*, and the *Shake opens
outward*.) MCD#88-161   FC#MCDY-833.

1."QUARTER POUNDER-GALLACTA BURGER"   NP:$1.50 MIP:$2.50
2."HOT CAKES-ROBO CAKES"   NP:$1.50 MIP:$2.50
3."LARGE FRIES-FRY FORCE"   NP:$1.50 MIP:$2.50
4."SHAKE-KRYPTO CUP"   NP:$2.00 MIP:$3.00
5."BIG MAC-MACRO MAC"   NP:$1.50 MIP:$2.50
6."SOFT-SERVE CONE-TURBO CONE"   NP:$1.50 MIP:$2.50
7."CHEESBURGER-C2 CHEESEBURGER"   NP:$1.50 MIP:$2.50
8."SMALL FRIES -FRY-BOT"   NP:$2.00 MIP:$3.00

UNDER 3 YRS;
1. 3-D CUBE   AVG:$3.00 MINT:$5.00
Cleverly constructed cube with three
movable sections which allow the user to
create strange characters from 3-part
pictures of Hamburglar on a balance-beam,
Birdie on roller skates, CosMc! in sneakers
and Grimace, in cowboy hat and boots,
standing on a wooden chest.

CARTONS(4);   AVG:$1.00 MINT:$1.50
MCD#88-161   FC#MCDY-835
1."JEEPERS PEEPERS"
2."TONGUE TIPPERS"
3."LOST IN SPACE"
4."WHO'S THAT?"

"SEA WORLD OF TEXAS II"   HAPPY MEAL (REGIONAL)   SUMMER
Set of three, 6-inch fuzzy, stuffed figurines from Sea World
of Texas (Whale and Dolphin same as 1988), and sun glasses.

FIGURINES: NP:$4.00 MIP:$6.00
1.WHALE , black and white.
2.SEA OTTER ,brown.
3.DOLPHIN ,grey.

SUN GLASSES with animal frames;   AVG:$3.00 MINT:$5.00
1.PENGUIN
2.WHALE

CARTON   AVG:$5.00 MINT:$12.00

NEW FOOD CHANGEABLES

NEW FOOD CHANGEABLES
UNDER 3 YRS.

SEA WORLD OF TEXAS II

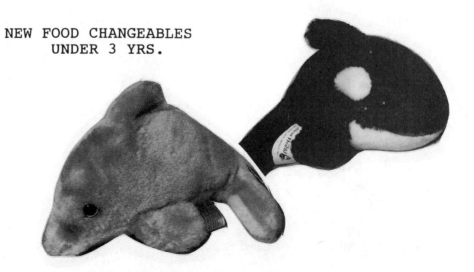

BEACH TOY

"BEACH TOY"   HAPPY MEAL   JUNE
Eight different toys, four are inflatable and four are for
sand moving.(C) 1989 McDONALD'S CORPORATION FC#MCDY-907.
Reissued in 1990 with different bags.

1. Inflatable Catmaran   AVG:$1.25   MINT:$2.50
     FRY GUYS are on the sail. MCD#6035-01
2. Inflatable Beach Ball   AVG:$1.25   MINT:$2.50
     Yellow, Grimace and octopus. MCD#6035-02
3. Inflatable Flying Disc   AVG:$1.00   MIP: $2.00
     RMCD in Hang Glider.   MCD#6035-03
4. Inflatable Sub   AVG:$1.00   MINT:$2.00
     BIRDIE in pink submarine. MCD#6035-04

Sand Pail (2 different scenes):
(C) 1989 McDONALD CORPORATION/PRINTED IN UNITED
STATES OF AMERICA. Embossed on bottom: 53501

5a. RMCD and GRIMACE swimming   AVG:$1.50 MINT:$3.00
     Yellow sifter-lid and handle.
5b. FUNNY FRY FRIENDS playing in sand AVG:$1.50 MINT:$3.00
     Red sifter-lid and handle.
6. Sand Castle Pail   AVG:$1.50 MINT:$3.00

7. Sand Spinner Shovel   AVG:$1.00 MINT:$2.00
     Red with yellow spinner.
     Embossed picture of BIRDIE.
8. Squirting Rake   AVG:$1.00 MINT:$2.00
     Blue and green. Squirts water.
     Embossed picture of BIRDIE.

BAGS (4);   AVG:$1.00 MINT:$1.50
1."FANCY FOOTWORK"
2."SWELL SHELLS"
3."SUBMARINE SURPRISE"
4."REACH THE BEACH"

"McDONALD'S TALKING STORYBOARD" HAPPY MEAL(REGIONAL) SUMMER
Set of four books with casette tapes featuring BONES and
DODO.

SETS:
1."DANGER UNDER THE LAKE"   NP:$4.00   MIP:$7.00
2."AMAZING BIRTHDAY ADVENTURE"   NP:$4.00   MIP:$7.00
3."DINOSAUR BABY BOOM"   NP:$5.00   MIP:$9.00
4."CREATURE IN THE CAVE"   NP:$5.00   MIP:$9.00

BAG;
1.BONES and DODO   AVG:$1.00   MINT:$2.50

"READ ALONG WITH RONALD" HAPPY MEAL (REGIONAL TEST) SUMMER
This offering consisted of cassette tapes with books.

SETS: AVG:$4.00   MINT:$6.00
1."DINOSAUR IN McDONALDLAND"
2."GRIMACE GOES TO SCHOOL"
3."MYSTERY OF MISSING FRENCH FRIES"
4."THE DAY BIRDIE...LEARNED TO FLY"

BAG (RMCD reading)   AVG:$3.00 MINT:$5.00

"MUPPET KIDS"   HAPPY MEAL (REGIONAL)   SUMMER
This regional test was dropped because the Jim Henson Assoc.
retired the "Muppet Kids" idea. The set of four toys
featured the Muppet characters on bikes with moveable
wheels.

1.KERMIT on red bike	NP:$6.00	MIP:$12.00
2.PIGGY on pink bike	NP:$6.00	MIP:$12.00
3.GONZO on yellow bike	NP:$7.50	MIP:$13.00
4.FOZZIE on green bike	NP:$7.50	MIP:$13.00

UNDER 3 YRS:
Storybook:"MUPPET BABIES" same as those offered in 1988

BOOKS:
1. "THE LEGEND OF GIMME GULCH"	AVG:$1.75	MINT:$2.25
2. "JUST KERMIT AND ME"	AVG:$2.00	MINT:$3.00
3. "PIGGY,the living doll"	AVG:$2.00	MINT:$3.00

CARTONS (2);   AVG:$1.00 MINT:$1.50
1."CLUBHOUSE"
2."SCHOOL"

"GARFIELD"   HAPPY MEAL   JUNE
This set of four toys features the ever-popular orange tiger
cat on a variety of vehicles. (C)1988 McDONALD'S CORPORATION
(C)1978 UNITED FEATURE SYNDICATE INC. MCD#88-054 FC#MCDY-828

1."GARFIELD ON SCOOTER"   NP:$1.75 MIP:$2.75
Two pieces: Garfield, purple shorts
and blue tank-top.
     Yellow scooter with purple wheels

2."GARFIELD ON SKATEBOARD"   NP:$1.75 MIP:$2.75
Two pieces: Garfield, white jacket,
pink hat, green knee-guards.
     Pink skateboard, four yellow wheels.
underside reads: CHINA K-6

3."GARFIELD IN 4-WHEELER"   NP:$2.00 MIP:$3.50
Two pieces: Garfield, green safari hat
and jacket.
     Blue 4-wheeler, yellow seat and wheels.

4."GARFIELD AND ODIE.MOTOR SCOOTER" NP:$1.75 MIP:$2.75
Two pieces: Garfield, blue shorts
and pink shirt.
     Red motor scooter with blue wheels.
ODIE in sidecar.
Underside read: "(C)1978,1981 UNITED FEAT
SYND CHINA 826".

UNDER 3 YRS;
1."GARFIELD ON ROLLER SKATES"   NP:$2.50 MIP:$4.00

2."GARFIELD WITH TEDDY BEAR"   NP:$2.50 MIP:$4.00
     ON A SKATEBOARD

CARTONS(4);   **AVG:$4.00 MINT:$8.00**
1."WHAT A GREAT MORNING"
2."I"M A CAT WITH A MISSION"
3."AHH, VACATION!!!"
4."AHH,I THINK.I'VE GOT A NIBBLE"

BAG;(REGIONAL TEST)
1."GARFIELD ON SAFARI"   AVG:$1.25 MINT:$2.00

GARFIELD

"LEGO MOTION"   HAPPY MEAL   AUGUST
The popular LEGO building sets, distributed by McDONALD'S
restaurants. (C) 1989 LEGO Group.This set consists of eight
models with several interlocking peices. Each may be made
into four different models. Made by LEGO Systems A/S DK-
7190 Billund, Denmark

1a."GYRO BIRD"   NP:$3.00 MIP:$6.00
19 pieces. Helicopter, white body,
black rotors and pontoons, red deck.

1b. "TURBO FORCE"   NP:$2.50 MIP:$4.00
10 pieces. Red and yellow car,
yellow spoiler, black wheels and trim.

2a."SWAMP STINGER"   NP:$3.00 MIP:$5.25
16 pieces. Air boat with red
pontoons, blue deck white cab.

2b."LIGHTNING STRIKER"   NP:$3.00 MIP:$5.00
14 pieces. White plane body, blue
trim and wings, red propellor,
red and black wheels.

3a."LAND LASER"   NP:$2.50 MIP:$4.00
13 pieces. White race car body, black
trim, red and black wheels.

3b. "SEA EAGLE"   NP:$3.00 MIP:$5.00
15 pieces. Red and blue sea plane.
Yellow pontoons and propellor.

4a."WIND WHIRLER"   NP:$3.00 MIP:$5.50
17 pieces. Red helicopter, yellow pontoons.

4b."SEA SKIMMER"   NP:$3.00 MIP:$5.50
17 pieces. Air boat with white cabin,
blue and yellow hull, yellow pods,
blue propellor.

UNDER 3 YRS DUPLO BLOCKS;
1."GIDDY THE GATOR"   NP:$3.50 MIP:$5.50
     Six pieces: green and yellow.
2."TUTTLE THE TURTLE"   NP:$3.50 MIP:$5.50
     Six pieces: yellow turtle with blue shell.

CARTONS (4);   AVG:$1.50 MINT:$2.00
1."GAS STATION"
2."TOLL BOOTH"
3."VEHICLE REPAIR"
4."VEHICLE SHOWROOM"

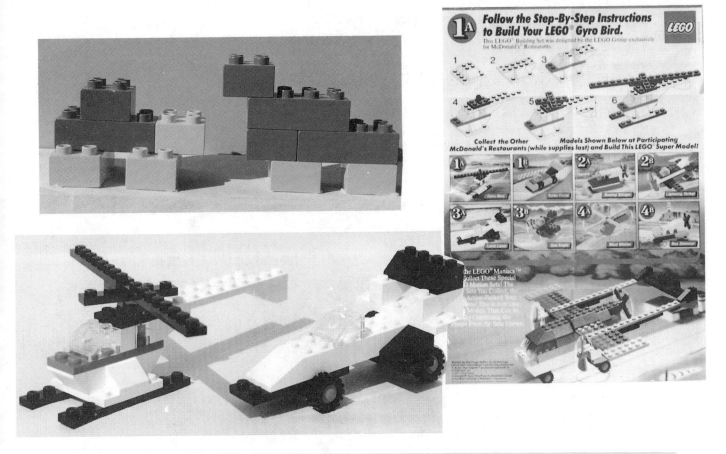

Follow the Step-By-Step Instructions to Build Your LEGO® Gyro Bird.

This LEGO® Building Set was designed by the LEGO Group exclusively for McDonald's Restaurants.

Collect the Other Models Shown Below at Participating **McDonald's Restaurants** (while supplies last) and Build This LEGO® Super Model!

LEGO MOTION

"FUN WITH FOOD"   HAPPY MEAL   (OPTION)   SEPTEMBER
Set of four toys with removable parts and decals.
Fisher-Price / MCD #88-228 FC#MCDY-871.

1.Hamburger guy   NP:$2.50   MIP:$4.00
     Three piece hamburger.

2.French Fry guy   NP:$2.50   MIP:$4.00
     Two piece box of fries.

3.Soft Drink guy   NP:$2.00   MIP:$3.00
     Two piece cup and lid.

4.Chicken McNuggets Guys   NP:$3.00   MIP:$5.50
     Seven pieces; package with 6 McNuggets.

CARTONS (4);   AVG:$1.00   MINT:$2.50
1."MAKING A SPLASH"
2."MOVIE MAKING"
3."3-RING CIRCUS"
4."IN CONCERT"

"RAGGEDY ANN & ANDY" HAPPY MEAL (REGIONAL TEST)   SEPTEMBER
(* Tested in San Francisco, Las Vegas & Hawaii. Released as
an option in 1990. Toys marked with (*) are also listed
under October 1990) (C) 1989 McDONALD'S CORPORATION (C)1989
MacMillian Inc. (See picture 1990)
These favorite storybook characters appear in five sets with
a variety of playground equipment.

1.Raggedy Andy on Slide *   NP:$2.50 MIP:$4.00
     Three pieces: MCD#5078-01
     Andy in blue pants and cap,plaid shirt.
     Yellow slide with red supports.
2.Grouchy Bear on Carousel*   NP:$2.50 MIP:$4.00
     Three pieces: MCD#5078-03
     Panda bear, in white vest, red striped tie.
     Yellow carousel with red supports.
3.Raggedy Ann on Swing*   NP:$2.50 MIP:$4.00
     Three pieces: MCD#5078-02
     ANN, red-dotted blue dress, white apron.
     Yellow swing with red supports.

Rumored to exist:
4.Raggedy Cat on See-saw   NP:$5.50 MIP:$7.00
5.Raggedy Dog on Spin-rider   NP:$5.50 MIP:$7.00

UNDER 3 YRS;
1.Camel with-wrinkled-knees   NP:$2.50 MIP:$4.00

CARTON: made into a schoolhouse.
1.Schoolhouse   AVG:$1.00 MINT:$1.75

HALLOWEEN   HAPPY MEAL   OCTOBER
Set of three plastic pails with handles and perforated lids.
Used as both premium and container.

PUMPKINS:
1."McBOO" yellow jack-o-lantern   AVG:$2.00   MINT:$4.00
2."McGHOST" white ghost   AVG:$3.00   MINT:$5.00
3."McWITCH" green witch   AVG:$2.00   MINT:$4.00

"RESCUE RANGERS"   HAPPY MEAL   NOVEMBER
DISNEY'S "CHIP 'N DALE RESCUE RANGERS" The well known
chipmunk characters appear in four different interchangeable
vehicles.(Gadget-Mobiles)
 (C) 1989 McDONALD'S CORPORATION FC#MCDY-878

1."CHIP'S WHIRLY-CUPTER"   NP:$2.00 MIP:$4.00
     Three pieces: Chip.
     Blue tea cup with red propeller
     and yellow blades.
2."DALE'S ROTOROADSTER"   NP:$2.00 MIP:$3.50
     Two pieces: Dale.
     Yellow measuring cup/roadster
     with orange rotor-blades.
3."GADGET'S RESCUE RACER"   NP:$2.00 MIP:$3.50
     Two pieces: Gadget.
     Pink tennis shoe, blue parasol,
     green rotor blades.
4."MONTEREY JACK'S PROPEL-A-PHONE"   NP:$2.00 MIP:$3.50
     Two pieces: Monterey Jack.
     Green phone, purple rotor,orange blades

UNDER 3 YRS;
1."GADGET ROCKIN' RIDER"   NP:$3.00 MIP:$4.75
     One piece: Gadget in pink teacup,
     blue goggles atop her blond hair.
     Decoration on both sides of car: yellow
     symbol with "RR".marks:"(C) DISNEY / H F / CHINA
2."CHIP'S RACER"   NP:$3.00 MIP:$4.75

CARTONS (4);   AVG:$1.00 MINT:$1.75
1."THE YOLKS ON HIM"
2."FRAMED"
3."ROLLIN' IN DOUGH"
4."WHALE OF A TIME"

"THE LITTLE MERMAID"   HAPPY MEAL   NOVEMBER
Inspired by the delightful WALT DISNEY movie, this set
offers four water play toys. (C) 1989 McDONALD'S CORPORATION
MCD#89-664   FC#MCDY-904

1."FLOUNDER, Ariel's best friend"   NP:$2.00 MIP:$3.00
     Soft rubber squirt-toy.
     Yellow fish with blue fins and stripes.
2."URSULA, the wicked sea witch"   NP:$2.00 MIP:$3.00
     Witch-octopus. Black legs and gown with
     suction cup on back for sticking to tub.
3."PRINCE ERIC..., and SEBASTIAN..."   NP:$3.00 MIP:$5.00
     Two pieces: Prince Eric, in white shirt
     holding red crab.
     Yellow (4 inch) boat.
4."ARIEL,the little mermaid"   NP:$3.00 MIP:$5.00
     Lavender scallop shell and green tail,
     holding a yellow sea horse. (Floats)

CARTONS (4);   AVG:$1.50 MINT:$2.50
1."ARIEL'S GROTTO"
2."SEA GARDEN"
3."URSULA'S DOMAIN"
4."VILLAGE LAGOON"

BAGS (TESTED);   **AVG:$8.00 MINT:$14.00**
1."URSULA'S DOMAIN"
2."VILLAGE LAGOON"

HAPPY MEALS 1990

DIRECTORY

```
+-----------------------------------------------------------+
|           Abbreviations used to describe condition:       |
|           MINT = new, never used or unfolded.             |
|           AVG  = average condition.                       |
|           NP   = no original package, loose.              |
|           MIP  = mint in package, in original, sealed     |
|                  container.                               |
+-----------------------------------------------------------+
```

"FUNNY FRY FRIENDS"   HAPPY MEAL   JANUARY
This is a set of eight colorful and amusing characters. Each
one includes an interchangeable costume piece. Inside each
package was a "McDONALD'S BONUS BOOK" of coupons,
value: " $3.00 in savings".
(C) 1989 McDONALD'S CORPORATION. MCD#89-116 MADE IN CHINA.

1. "HOOPS"   NP:$1.75 MIP:3.00
This 3-inch high, violet creature, with
      blue and white sneakers, holds a brown
      basketball between his knees.
Piece: yellow headband.

2. "ROLLIN' ROCKER"   NP:$2.00 MIP:3.25
Yellow Fry Girl, 2 3/4 inches high,
      with braids, pink roller skates
      and knee-pads.
Piece: pink head-band with radio attached.

3. "MATEY"   NP:$1.50 MIP:2.50
Red with blue shoes and lavender socks.
      2 3/4 inches.
Piece: blue pirate hat with black eye-patch.

4."GADZOOKS"   NP:$1.50 MIP:2.50
Wide-eyed, blue creature, 2 inches.
      It wears two different shoes: a white
      sneaker and an orange, heeled shoe.
Piece:funny face = nose, glasses and a bow tie.

5."TRACKER"   NP:$1.50 MIP:2.50
Blue creature with braids, brown shoes
      and a smiling green snake coiled
      around her ankles. 2 3/4 inches.
Piece: yellow safari hat with attached binoculars.

6."ZZZ'S"   NP:$1.50 MIP:2.25
The 2 1/4 inch high, blue, sleepy-eyed
      creature wears pink bunny slippers.
Piece: a pink polka-dotted white night cap
with a tan teddy bear attached.

7."TOO TALL"   NP:$1.50 MIP:2.50
Standing on stilts which end in big
     yellow bird-feet. 3 1/2 inches tall.
Piece: yellow clown hat with red and
     blue pom-poms and red ball nose.

8."SWEET CUDDLES"   NP:$1.50 MIP:2.75
Wistfull eyed,rosy-red Fry Girl with
     yellow shoes. 2 inches.
Piece: baby bonnet and attached bottle.

UNDER 3 YRS
1."LIL CHIEF"   NP:$2.00 MIP:4.00
     One piece. Orange Guy wearing moccasins
     and a white-feathered indian headband.

2."LIL DARLIN"   NP:$2.00 MIP:4.00
     One piece. Yellow Girl with a tan
     cowboy hat and red boots.

CARTONS (4);
1."COOL DAY AT SCHOOL"   AVG:$1.00 MINT:$1.50
2."SNOWY DAY PLAY"   AVG:$1.00 MINT:$1.50
3."CITY SIGHTS"   AVG:$1.00 MINT:$1.50
4."SKI HOLIDAY"   AVG:$1.00 MINT:$1.50

BERENSTAIN BEARS BOOKS

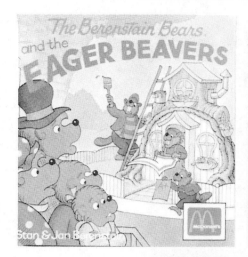
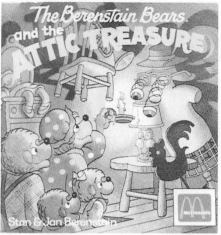

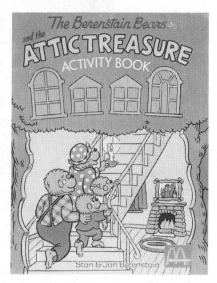

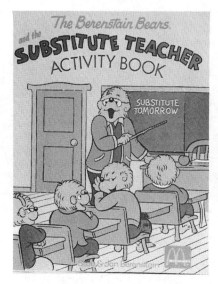
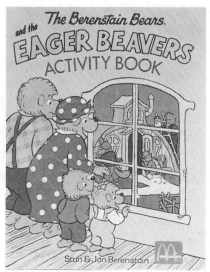

"BERENSTAIN BEARS BOOKS" HAPPY MEAL   JANUARY
Each week, two colorful books were issued.

STORY BOOKS:
THE BERENSTAIN BEARS AND...
1. *"LIFE WITH PAPA"*   AVG:$ .75   MINT:$1.50

2. *"SUBSTITUTE TEACHER"*   AVG:$1.00   MINT:$1.75

3. *"ATTIC TREASURE"*   AVG:$1.00   MINT:$1.75

4. *"EAGER BEAVERS"*   AVG:$ .75   MINT:$1.50

ACTIVITY BOOKS:
THE BERENSTAIN BEARS AND...
5. *"LIFE WITH PAPA"*   AVG:$1.25   MINT:$2.00

6. *"SUBSTITUTE TEACHER "*   AVG:$1.25   MINT:$2.50

7. *"ATTIC TREASURE"*   AVG:$1.75   MINT:$2.25

8. *"EAGER BEAVERS"*   AVG:$1.25   MINT:$2.00

BAGS (Tested in South Bend,Ind.)   AVG:$2.00   MINT:$2.50

CARTONS (4);
1."TEAM WORK"   AVG:$ .75   MINT:$1.25
2."SHARING"   AVG:$ .75   MINT:$1.25
3."WHAT TO DO"   AVG:$ .75   MINT:$1.25
4."THANK GOODNESS"   AVG:$ .75   MINT:$1.25

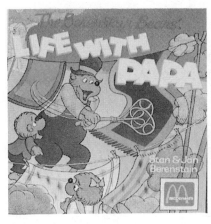
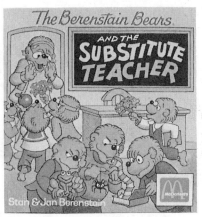

"VALENTINE" HAPPY MEAL   FEBRUARY
Two packages, six cards in each. Pictures of McDONALDLAND
characters on one side, place for address in red ink on the
opposite side. (C) 1989 McDONALD CORPORATIION. These are
"scratch and sniff" cards. scents: chocolate and strawberry.

1. CHOCOLATE   AVG:$3.00 MINT:$5.00

2. STRAWBERRY   AVG:$3.00 MINT:$5.00

CARTON   AVG:$1.25 MINT:$2.00

"McDONALD'S HAPPY MEAL FROM THE HEART"
Carton is attractively designed in red and silver and may be
made into a mailbox for valentines. Games on surface feature
RMCD "PLAY MATCHMAKER", FRY GUYS "LOST AND FOUND
VALENTINE", BIRDIE "A VALENTINE MYSTERY", and GRIMACE
"GRIMACE'S LOVE LETTERS".

"PEANUTS"   HAPPY MEAL   MARCH
Four toys featuring the popular Peanuts characters dressed
for farming.(C) 1989 McDONALD'S CORPORATION MCD#89-117
(FC#MCDXP-293) "Peanuts characters are a property of United
Feature Syndicate, Inc." MADE IN CHINA

1."SNOOPY'S HAY HAULER"   NP:$1.50 MIP:$3.00
Three pieces: (1) SNOOPY in farming
clothes:yellow hat,red scar, blue shoes.
                (2) blue Wheelbarrow with red wheels.
                (3) yellow Haystack with pig.Bird on top.

2."CHARLIE BROWN'S SEED BAG'N'TILLER" NP:$1.50 MIP:$3.00
Three pieces: (1) CHARLIE in orange and
green checked shirt, green pants,purple cap and brown shoes.
                (2) yellow Seed bag.
                (3) orange and blue Tiller.

3."LUCY'S APPLE CART"   NP:$1.50 MIP:$3.25
Three pieces: (1)LUCY in pink dress,
yellow hat and black shoes.
                (2)green Wheelbarrow.
                (3)oranges basket of Tomatoes.

4."LINUS' MILK MOVER"   NP:$1.50 MIP:$3.25
Three pieces: (1)LINUS in purple jumper,
blue shirt, towel, aqua baseball cap.
                (2)grey Milk can, kitten.
                (3)orange Mover,green wheels.

UNDER 3 YRS. All one piece, soft vinyl plastic:
1.SNOOPY   NP:$3.00 MIP:$4.00
     Pulling yellow sack of potatoes. Red hat
     and overalls.
2.CHARLIE BROWN   NP:$3.00 MIP:$4.00
     Green shirt and blue cap, holding
     basket of eggs, topped by yellow chick.

CARTONS (4);
"Peanuts characters (C)1950,52,54,58,60,65,66,71
United Feature Syndicate,Inc.

1."HOEDOWN"   AVG:$1.00 MINT:$1.50
     Outdoor barbecue scene.
2."FIELD DAY"   AVG:$1.00 MINT:$1.50
     Vegetable gerden scene.
3."COUNTY FAIR"   AVG:$1.50 MINT:$2.25
     Scene;Lucy's kissing booth.
4."E-I-E-I-O"   AVG:$1.00 MINT:$1.50
     Carton may be made into a chicken-coop.

PEANUTS

BEACH TOY

"BEACH TOY"   HAPPY MEAL   JUNE
Eight different toys, four are inflatable and four are for
sand moving.(C) 1989 McDONALD'S CORPORATION FC#MCDY-907.
Issued in 1989 with different bags.

INFLATABLES:
1.Inflatable Catmaran   AVG:$1.25 MINT:$2.50
     FRY GUYS are on the sail. MCD#6035-01
2. Inflatable Beach Ball   AVG:$1.25 MINT:$2.50
     Yellow, Grimace and octopus. MCD#6035-02
3. Inflatable Flying Disc   AVG:$1.00 MIP: $2.00
     RMCD in Hang Glider.   MCD#6035-03
4. Inflatable Sub   AVG:$1.00 MINT:$2.00
     BIRDIE in pink submarine. MCD#6035-04

PAILS:
Sand Pail (two different scenes)
(C) 1989 McDONALD CORPORATION/PRINTED IN UNITED
STATES OF AMERICA. Embossed on bottom: 53501

5a. RMCD and GRIMACE swimming   AVG:$1.50 MINT:$3.00
     Yellow sifter-lid and handle.
5b. FUNNY FRY FRIENDS playing in sand AVG:$1.50 MINT:$3.00
     Red sifter-lid and handle.
6. Sand Castle Pail   AVG:$1.50 MINT:$3.00

SAND TOYS:
6. Sand Spinner Shovel   AVG:$1.00 MINT:$2.00
     Red with yellow spinner.
     Embossed picture of BIRDIE.
8.Squirting Rake   AVG:$1.00 MINT:$2.00
     Blue and green. Squirts water.
     Embossed picture of BIRDIE.

BAGS (4) (Pails also served as containers);
1."TREASURE HUNT"   AVG:$1.00 MINT:$1.50
2."HAMBURGLAR"   AVG:$1.00 MINT:$1.50
3."RONALD"   AVG:$1.25 MINT:$1.75
4."GRIMACE"   AVG:$1.25 MINT:$1.75

"CAMP McDONALDLAND"   HAPPY MEAL   JUNE
Set consists of four items of camping gear.

1.CANTEEN   AVG:$1.00 MINT:$1.75
    Blue, with embossed outdoor scene.
    Yellow cap
2.UTENSILS   AVG:$1.50 MINT:$3.00
    Yellow spoon and blue fork, fit inside
    handle of purple knife. Handles of fork
    and spoon are embossed with a pine tree
    design and "CAMP McDONALDLAND (C)1989
    MADE IN USA   MCD#88500
3."BIRDIE CAMPER MESS KIT"   AVG:$1.50 MINT:$3.00
    Pan has detachable orange handle.
4.CUP, red, collapsible   AVG:$1.00 MINT:$2.50
    Red-orange cover embossed with canoeing
    scene and "CAMP McDONALDLAND"   MCD#89-119
    FC#MCDY-941

UNDER 3 YRS;
(same collapsible cup as in item #4)

CARTONS (4):
1.PLAYTIME AT CAMP'   AVG:$1.00 MINT:$2.00
2."AT THE LAKE"   AVG:$1.00 MINT:$2.00
3."NATURE WALK"   AVG:$1.00 MINT:$2.00
4."CAMPING OUT"   AVG:$1.00 MINT:$2.00

BAGS (regional test)(2);
1."TUG OF WAR"   AVG:$ .75 MINT:$1.50
2."NATURE WALK"   AVG:$ .75 MINT:$1.50

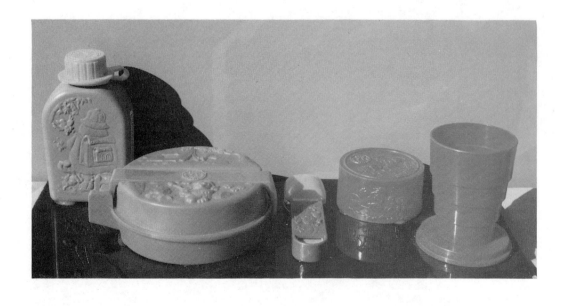

"BARBIE/ HOT WHEELS" HAPPY MEAL   (TEST*)   JULY
(* National test in Savannah, Georgia)
Miniature Barbie Doll figurines or Hot Wheels cars.

1.BARBIE in long pink gown	NP:$8.00	MIP:$14.00
2.BARBIE in black dress	NP:$8.00	MIP:$14.00
3.BARBIE in pink dress	NP:$7.00	MIP:$13.00
4.BARBIE in long white gown	NP:$8.00	MIP:$14.00
5.White CORVETTE Convertible	NP:$8.00	MIP:$14.00
6.Red FERRARI	NP:$10.00	MIP:$15.00
7.Silver PONTIAC Firebird	NP:$10.00	MIP:$15.00
8.Tourquois CHEVY Z-28	NP:$8.00	MIP:$14.00

CARTONS (2);
1.BARBIE at concert /
HOT WHEELS garage   NP:$4.00   MIP:$6.00
2.BARBIE movie star /
HOT WHEELS Road Race   NP:$4.00   MIP:$6.00

I LIKE BIKES" HAPPY MEAL (REGIONAL TEST*)   JULY
(* Northern Illinois,South Carolina) Set of four bike
related toys. Each has mounting clamp and screws. Directions
for attaching to bike are on back of package card.
(C) 1990 McDonald's Corporation MCD #90-052 FC #MCDXP-362.

1.BASKET, RONALD   NP:$12.00 MIP:$19.00
     Three pieces: yellow basket,
     perforated lid (embossed with
     RMCD head) and two fastening straps.

2.FRY GUY'S HORN   NP:$10.00 MIP:$16.00
     Blue horn. Squeeze bulb is orange
     Fry Guy.

3.BIRDIE'S SPINNER   NP:$10.00 MIP:$16.00
     Birdie in red airplane.
     Yellow propeller spins.

4.GRIMACE'S REARVIEW REFLECTOR   NP:$12.00 MIP:$19.00
     Purple Grimace figure holds mirror.

BAGS (2);
1.RMCD, GRIMACE & HAMBURGLAR   AVG:$3.00 MINT:$4.25
2.RMCD   AVG:$2.50 MINT:$3.75

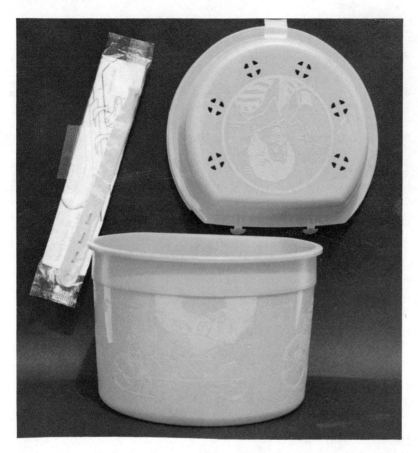

I LIKE BIKES

"JUNGLE BOOK"   HAPPY MEAL   JULY
Four wind-up toys from the WALT DISNEY movie the "Jungle
Book", based on stories by Rudyard Kipling. Underside of
toy reads: "(C) DISNEY / CHINA / (lot number)"
MCD#89-146   (FC#MCDXP-302)

1. "BALOO, the bear"   NP:$1.25 MIP:$3.00
      Grey, 2 3/4 inches high, standing figure
      with left paw extended. Dances in circle.

2. "KING LOUIE, the orangutan"   NP:$1.50 MIP:$3.00
      2 1/2 inches, orange ape."Wind up my
      arm and I flip!"

3. "KAA, the snake"   NP:$1.50 MIP:$3.00
      Olive-green and yellow, 3 inches long.
      Coiled snake has head which moves back
      and forth as he rolls.

4. "SHERE KHAN, the Tiger"   NP:$1.25 MIP:$3.00
      Orange with black stripes, 3 1/8 inches
      long. Pouncing position, rolls forward
      in little "jumps".

UNDER 3 YRS;
1. "JUNIOR, the Elephant"   NP:$3.00 MIP:$5.00
      Grey ,seated, baby elephant. 2 1/2 inches.

2. "MOWGLI"   NP:$3.00 MIP:$5.00
      Boy in a green pot. 2 3/4 inches.

CARTONS (4):

1. "BALOO BEAR"   AVG:$1.00 MINT:$1.50
2. "MOWGLI, the Boy"   AVG:$1.00 MINT:$2.00
      Under the title is a connect-the-dots
      picture. Near top is Mowgli in tree.
3. "KAA SNAKE"   AVG:$1.00 MINT:$1.50
      Under the title is a picture of Mowgli
      wrapped in KAA snake's coils.
4. "KING LOUIE ORANGUTAN"   AVG:$1.00 MINT:$2.00
      Under the title is scene: KING LOUIS
      and MOWGLI. Ancient building ruins.

"SUPER MARIO BROS 3"   AUGUST
Set of four action toys (C)1990 Nintendo of America Inc.
(C)1990 McDONALD'S CORPORATION   MCD#89-234(FC#MCDY-057)

1."MARIO"   NP:$1.00   MIP:$2.00
     Sits on spring-loaded red pedestal
     which pops up when pressed down. Base: YL1-4

2."LUIGI"   NP:$1.00   MIP:$2.00
     Green suit and hat, in white object
     with wheels. Pull-back action. base: OR 55

3."LITTLE GOOMBA"   NP:$1.00   MIP:$2.00
     Mushroom-shaped creature, big brown
     feet. Back flips. Base: A1-7

4."KOOPA PARATROOPA"   NP:$2.00   MIP:$4.00
     Yellow turtle, red shell, white wings.
     (squirt bellows) Hops. Base: FK 41

UNDER 3 YRS.
1."MARIO" squeeze toy   NP:$3.00   MIP:$4.00

CARTONS (4);
1."ISLAND WORLD"   AVG:$1.00   MINT:$2.00
2."SKY LAND"   AVG:$1.00   MINT:$2.50
3."PIPE LAND"   AVG:$1.00   MINT:$2.00
4."DESERT LAND"   AVG:$1.00   MINT:$2.75

"McDONALDLAND DOUGH"   HAPPY MEAL   SEPTEMBER
Ages 2 and over.(C) 1989 McDONALD'S CORPORATION. Cans are 2
inches x 2 7/8 inches. The lid shows the color of the dough
inside. Base of container reads:"Polytainers Ltd. Toronto,
Canada 7 / 734-C.
Modeling compound with plastic molds.Set of eight colors

1.RED WITH RMCD STAR   AVG:$1.50   MINT:$3.00

2.GREEN WITH OCTAGON   AVG:$1.50   MINT:$3.00

3.PURPLE WITH GRIMACE DIAMOND   AVG:$1.50   MINT:$3.00

4.PINK WITH CIRCLE   AVG:$2.00   MINT:$3.50

5.YELLOW WITH RMCD SQUARE   AVG:$1.50   MINT:$3.00

6.BLUE WITH FRY GUY OCTAGON   AVG:$1.50   MINT:$3.00

7.ORANGE WITH GRIMACE TRIANGLE   AVG:$1.50   MINT:$3.00

8.WHITE WITH HEART   AVG:$2.00   MINT:$3.50

CARTONS(4);
(unknown)   AVG:$1.00   MINT:$2.00

"SPORTSBALL"   HAPPY MEAL   (REGIONAL*)   SEPTEMBER
(*Kansas City,Indianapolis)
Set of four balls the size of a tennis ball. Soft vinyl
versions of typical sport balls. Each ball has a white cloth
tag which reads: One side: "(C) 1989 McDONALD'S
CORPORATION". (Other side): "M.B.Sales, Oakbrook, Illinois/
ALL NEW MATERIALS/ CONTENTS:POLYESTER FIBER / MADE IN CHINA
/ REG. NO. PA3344(H.K.) / SURFACE WASHABLE ONLY" . All have
realistic stitching.Safety tested for children of all ages.
NOTE: this was re-issued briefly as a "clean-up" premium in
August, 1991, with these differences:
        Label: no "Oakbrook, Illinois".
        Colors: same, but diffent shades except for football,
        which was brown with yellow laces and logo. Add $2.00
        to each price for 1991 versions.

1.SOCCERBALL   AVG:$2.00   MINT:$5.00
        Stitched red and yellow hexagons.
        In one red hex. is golden ARCHES logo.
2.BASKETBALL   AVG:$2.00   MINT:$5.00
        Brown with black lines.
        Logo: black & white
3.BASEBALL   AVG:$2.00   MINT:$4.00
        White cover printed with red
        stitch lines. Logo: red and blue.
4.FOOTBALL   AVG:$2.00   MINT:$4.50
        Yellow stitched cover, printed
        with red laces. Logo; red and black
        on both sides of ball.

CARTON   AVG:$2.00   MINT:$3.50
        RMCD swinging a golf club at a
        piece of brocolli. (other silly things)
        "McDONALD'S SPORTSBALL HAPPY MEAL".

"McDONALDLAND CRAFT KIT" HAPPY MEAL   (REGIONAL*)   SEPTEMBER
(*optional)

1.HAMBURGLAR PAINT BRUSH & PAINTS   **AVG:$8.00   MINT:$12.50**

2.GRIMACE TAPE MEASURE   **AVG:$6.00   MINT:$10.00**

3.FRY GUY SAFETY SCISSORS   **AVG:$6.00   MINT:$10.00**

4.McDONALD'S TAPE DISPENSER   AVG:$3.00   MINT:$5.00

UNDER 3 YRS;
GRIMACE figurine   NP:$4.00   MIP: $6.00

CARTON   AVG:$2.00   MINT:$3.50

"HAPPY HATS" HAPPY MEAL   (REGIONAL OPTION*)   SEPTEMBER
Container was molded plastic hat.

1. SAFARI HAT. orange, Fry Guys.   AVG:$3.50   MINT:$6.00
2. CONSTRUCTION HAT. yellow, Grimace. AVG:$3.00   MINT:$6.50
3. FIREMAN HAT. red, RMCD.   AVG:$4.50   MINT:$8.00
4. ENTERTAINER HAT. green, Birdie.   AVG:$4.00   MINT:$7.00

"McDONALDLAND CARNIVAL"   HAPPY MEAL (REGIONAL*) SEPTEMBER
(* Florida, Illinois, Ohio, Joplin, Charlestown)
(C)1990 McDONALD'S CORPORATION / MADE IN CHINA. This is an
especially attractive set of four multi-piece toys.

1."RONALD ON CAROUSEL"   NP:$3.50   MIP:$5.00
Two-seated revolving ride.Three pieces:
     (1) RMCD
     (2) green carousel.
     (3) base of the carousel: red and yellow.
     Underside reads:(C)1990
     McDONALD"S CORP / CHINA / AP1-1

2."GRIMACE IN TURN-AROUND"   NP:$4.00   MIP:$6.00
One seated revolving ride. Five pieces:
     (1) Grimace
     (2+3) blue and green base parts.
     (4+5) red crank and yellow seat.

3."BIRDIE ON SWING"   NP:$4.50   MIP:$6.50
BIRDIE on swing. Five pieces:
     (1) Birdie dressed in pink
     (2+3) 2 orange arches
     (4) red swing
     (5) blue base, underside: A1-2.

4."HAMBURGLAR ON FERRIS WHEEL"   NP:$4.50   MIP:$6.50
One-seated Ferris Wheel. Five pieces:
     (1) Hamburglar
     (2) blue crank
     (3+4) orange seat and purple stand.
     (5) yellow base. Underside: VK1-3.

UNDER 3 YRS;
"GRIMACE ON ROCKER"   NP:$5.00   MIP:$7.00
     One piece. Spins when twirled.
     GRIMACE in purple half-sphere,
     decorated with stars.

CARTON   AVG:$2.00   MINT:$3.00
"HAPPY MEAL CARNIVAL".
 McDONALDLAND characters on various rides.

McDONALDLAND CARNIVAL

THE TOM & JERRY BAND

"THE TOM AND JERRY BAND"   HAPPY MEAL (REGIONAL*) SEPTEMBER
(* regional option. tested in LA & S. California)
Set of four characters with interchangeable musical
intsruments.(C) 1989 McDONALD'S CORPORATION / (C) TURNER
ENTERTAINMENT CO.

1."TOM WITH KEYBOARD"   NP:$3.00   MIP:$7.00
Four pieces: (1-3)green keyboard with
two white supports.
          (4) seated grey cat wearing
   a short sleeved yellow jacket and white
   shorts. His hands are in playing position.
   MCD#5089-01.

2."DROOPY WITH MICROPHONE"   NP:$4.00   MIP:$8.00
Three pieces: (1)Droopy (beagle dog)
             (2-3) black microphone
   and stand.   MCD#5089-02

3."JERRY WITH DRUM SET"   NP:$3.00   MIP:$7.00
Two pieces: (1) drum set,large base
     drum with two small side drums .
          (2) Jerry (mouse) standing
   on a large stool.   MCD#5089-03

4."SPIKE WITH BASE"   NP:$4.00   MIP:$8.00
Two pieces;(1) white base fiddle.
          (2) brown,standing bear
     MCD#5089-04

UNDER 3 YRS.
SPIKE   NP:$2.00   MIP:$3.00

BAGS (tested) 2 types;   AVG:$1.00   MINT:$1.75
Smaller: black white red and YELLOW.
Larger: NO yellow.

"MIX EM UP MONSTERS"   HAPPY MEAL (REGIONAL*) SEPTEMBER
(*regional option,tested in 1989 many places including St.
Louis, & Northern California 1990)
There are four toys, each with three interchangeable pieces:
head, body and tail,(pvc plastic). Characters are
trademarks of CURRENT INC. (C) 1988 McDONALD'S CORPORATION.

1."GROPPLE"   NP:$1.25 MIP:$3.00
    Yellow, with two heads and
    a spiked tail.

2."CORKLE"   NP:$1.25 MIP:$3.00
    Blue, serpentine body, yellow
    horned head, pink sides.

3."BLIBBLE"   NP:$1.25 MIP:$3.00
    Green, scales and extended eyes.

4."THUGGER"   NP:$1.25 MIP:$3.00
    Purple, dragon-like, with yellow horn
    and pink fins.

CARTON   AVG:$1.00 MINT:$1.75

"McDRIVE THRU CREW"   HAPPY MEAL (REGIONAL*)   SEPTEMBER
(* regional option)
There are four toys in this set. Each is a popular McD food
in its appropriate container, equipped with wheels.(C) 1990
McDONALD'S CORPORATION

1."HAMBURGER IN CATSUP RACER"   NP:$2.00 MIP:$5.50
     The catsup bottle has wheels and a
     silver engine. A small hamburger sits
     in the driver's seat.On back of car: "McD#1".

2."SHAKE IN MILK CARTON ZOOMER"   NP:$3.25 MIP:$6.00
     A milkshake wearing a blue cap drives
     a milk carton. On back of car: "MSHAK#1".

3."McNUGGET IN EGG ROADSTER"   NP:$3.50 MIP:$6.25
     The McNugget wears a green cap. On the
     back of (egg) car is plate: "McNUGGET".

4."FRIES IN POTATO SPEEDSTER"   NP:$1.75 MIP:$2.50
     Back plate: "IDAHO#1".

CARTON   AVG:$1.00 MINT:$1.75

"FRY BENDERS"   HAPPY MEAL   (REGIONAL*)   SEPTEMBER
(* regional option, tested in Michigan)
This is a flexible yellow stick, made to look like a fry. It
can be shaped into different positions.Each has 2 switchable
parts and are pictured on card in package.   MCD#90-063

1."FROGGY"   NP:$2.50 MIP:$3.50
Scuba diver. Three pieces:
      (1) fry, puffed cheeks, green goggles.
      (2) hands, on purple box with red air tank.
      (3) flippers, big & green on purple box.

2."GRAND SLAM"   NP:$2.50 MIP:$3.50
Baseball player. Three pieces:
      (1) fry, red baseball cap with an "M".
      (2) hands, in blue & white striped box.
          One holds white baseball,
          other in red-brown catcher's mitt.
      (3) feet, in blue & white striped box.
          Big blue sneakers, white soles and socks.

3."ROADIE"   NP:$2.50 MIP:$3.50
Go-Cart. Three pieces:
      (1) fry, pink tongue shows.silver helmet,
          red goggles.
      (2) hands in blue gloves holding silver
          handle-bars. Arms green in green box.
      (3) green cart with purple wheels.

4."FREESTYLE"   NP:$2.00 MIP:$3.00
Roller-skater. Three pieces:
      (1) fry, blue ear-covers and purple cap.
      (2) hands, in white box with music notes
          on a purple band.
      (3) roller-skates on purple box,
          black shoes and silver skates.

UNDER 3 YRS.
"TUNES"   NP:$3.00 MIP:$5.00
      One-piece, small, curved fry on red
      skateboard with yellow wheels. Green
      helmet and gloves. He carries a red
      radio under his right arm.

CARTON   AVG:$1.00 MINT:$1.75

FRY BENDERS

MAC TONIGHT

"MAC TONIGHT"   HAPPY MEAL   (REGIONAL*)   SEPTEMBER
(* regional option,tested St.Louis, Chicago.) Mac is a
quarter moon wearing sunglasses. Set of six travel toys
(C) 1988 McDONALD CORPORATION presents the character on
various vehicles.   MCD#5050-34

1."OFF ROADER"   NP:$2.00   MIP:$3.50
     MAC, in tan suit, green Jeep
     ("M" on hood). Drives with one hand,
     while waving the other.

2."SPORTS CAR"   NP:$2.00   MIP:$3.50
     MAC, in black, waves as he drives
     red convertible ("M" on hood).

3."SURF SKI" (WITH WHEELS)   NP:$2.00   MIP:$4.00
     MAC in green jump suit, rides a yellow
     and white surf ski. Yellow "M" in red
     block on both sides.

3a.SURF SKI"   (WITHOUT WHEELS)   NP:$1.75   MIP:$3.00

4."SCOOTER"   NP:$2.00   MIP:$3.50
     MAC in yellow sweater and blue pants,
     rides a black motor-scooter with
     gold "M" on both sides.

5."MOTORCYCLE"   NP:$2.00   MIP:$3.50
     MAC, yellow jump suit, red motorcycle.

6."AIRPLANE"   NP:$1.75   MIP:$3.00
     MAC, in red sweater, waves from the
     cockpit of a blue and green plane
     with a yellow propellor.

UNDER 3 YRS;
MAC on purple skateboard   NP:$3.00   MIP:$4.00

CARTON;
"ON THE ROAD"   AVG:$1.00   MINT:$1.75
BAG (tested some markets)   AVG:$1.00   MINT:$1.75

"RAGGEDY ANN & ANDY" HAPPY MEAL (REGIONAL*)   SEPTEMBER
(* Regional option, tested in San Francisco, Hawaii, Las
Vegas, Portland.)
The beloved story book characters combine with playground
equipment in a set of four toys. (C) 1989 McDONALD'S
CORPORATION / (C)1989 McMILLAN INC.

1."RAGGEDY ANDY WITH SLIDE"   NP:$3.00 MIP:$4.50
Three pieces:
      (1-2) yellow slide with red supports
      (3) Andy, blue pants and cap,plaid shirt.
                             MCD#5078-01
2."RAGGEDY ANN WITH SWING SET"   NP:$3.00 MIP:$4.50
Three pieces:
      (1-2) yellow swing with red supports
      (3) ANN, red-dotted blue dress, white
             apron.   MCD#5078-02
3."GROUCHY BEAR ON CAROUSEL"   NP:$3.00 MIP:$4.50
Three pieces:
      (1-2) yellow carousel with red supports
      (3) Panda bear, white vest,
             red-striped tie.   MCD#5078-03
4."CAMEL WITH SEE-SAW"   NP:$3.00 MIP:$4.50
Three pieces:
      (1-2) red see-saw with yellow supports
      (3) blue Camel-with-wrinkled-knees
             in red harness.   MCD#5078-04

UNDER 3 YRS.
Camel With Wrinkled Knees   NP;$4.00 MIP:$5.00

CARTON:
"SCHOOLHOUSE"   AVG:$1.00 MINT:$2.00

"TURBO MACS"   HAPPY MEAL   (OPTION)   SEPTEMBER
(REGIONAL / INTERNATIONAL OPTION) Run as regional offerings
in 1988 & 1989. Pull-back cars with larger wheels on the
back and large "M" on front. McDonaldland characters in each
one . Underside of all pieces reads; "(name & number) /
McDONALD'S CORP (C) 1988 / P.C. / CHINA" Set of five.

1.RMCD RACER   NP:$2.00 MIP:$3.00
Red one-seat racing car with
"spoilers" front and back.
Underside: "RONALD McDONALD (R).

2.HAMBURGLAR SPORTS   NP:$2.00 MIP:$3.50
Yellow sports car,raised back fin.
Underside: "HAMBURGLAR (R) / M 6".

3.GRIMACE RACER   NP:$2.00 MIP:$3.00
White racing car with wing-fins,
back and sides.Grimace waves left hand.
Underside: "GRIMACE (R) "

4.BIRDIE SPORTS (*)   NP:$2.00 MIP:$3.00
Pink sports car,Birdie waves
right hand.
Underside: "BIRDIE (R) / M 3 ".

(*)In international markets BIRDIE was replaced by:
5.BIG MAC SPORTS   NP:$3.00 MIP:$4.00
Blue sports car. Underside: "BIG MAC".

UNDER 3 YRS.
RMCD, FORMULA-1   NP:$4.00 MIP:$5.00
Red soft rubber car with painted
yellow wheels,"M" on front. Larger
than above cars. No moving parts.
Underside: RONALD McDONALD (C) 1988 /
McDONALD'S CORP / P C CHINA

CARTON   AVG:$2.00 MINT:$3.00
RONALD IN FORMULA-1 CAR

"DINK THE LITTLE DINOSAUR" HAPPY MEAL (REGIONAL*) SEPTEMBER
(* Regional test - Oklahoma)
Set of six soft plastic dinosaur finger-puppets. Each is
packaged with a diorama of its natural habitat which makes
an attractive play scene when unfolded, and a description of
the dinosaur. (C) 1989 McDONALD'S CORP. (C) 1989 Ruby Spears
Inc.

1.CRUSTY SEA TURTLE   NP:$3.00 MIP:$5.00
     Two shades of green. high domed shell.
     3.3 X 1.6 inches high.

2.AMBER CORYTHAURUS   NP:$3.00 MIP:$5.00
     Orange, sitting creature with a crest
     on its head. 4 inches high.

3."SCAT", COMPSAGNATHUS   NP:$3.00 MIP:$5.00
     Two shades of green, standing alligator
     type creature. Left hand on hip, right
     hand holds up thin tail. 2.6 inches high.

4.SHYLER EDAPHORAURS   NP:$3.00 MIP:$5.00
     Green and yellow, shy little fellow.
     2.3 inches high.

5."FLAPPER", PTERONDON   NP:$3.00 MIP:$5.50
     Brown, bird-like with wings held open.
     Back of head is pointed. 2.5 inches high.

6."DINK", APATASAURUS   NP:$3.00 MIP:$5.00
     Green with yellow chest. Heavy bodied.
     Thick, curved tail. 3.4 inches high.

CARTON   AVG:$1.25 MINT:$1.75

AMBER, WITH DIORAMA

HALLOWEEN   HAPPY MEAL   OCTOBER
Set of three plastic pails, with handles and perforated
lids, to be used for "trick-or-treats". Pails served as
Happy Meal containers.

1. ORANGE DAY-GLO PUMPKIN   AVG:$1.75 MINT:$3.00
2. WHITE,GLOW IN THE DARK, GHOST   AVG:$1.75 MINT:$3.50
3. GREEN DAY-GLO, WITCH   AVG:$1.75 MINT:$3.00

"TALE SPIN" HAPPY MEAL   NOVEMBER-DECEMBER
Fun set of four toys based on a Walt Disney Pictures movie.
Four characters in different types of airplanes with
moveable wheels and propellors. MCD#89-251 (FC#MCDXP-352)

1."KIT'S RACING PLANE"   NP:$2.00 MIP:$3.00
    A bear wearing his cap backwards flies
    a single-wing, blue and orange plane.
2."MOLLY'S BIPLANE"   NP:$2.00 MIP:$3.50
    The biplane is red and yellow and has
    covered wheels. Molly wears a blue
    ribbon by each ear, waves right hand.
3."BALOO'S SEAPLANE"   NP:$2.00 MIP:$3.00
    Baloo Bear gives the "thumbs up" sign
    from the seat of his orange and gold,
    single-wing seaplane with blue pontoons.
    Wheels are on struts. 3-bladed propellors.
4."WILDCAT'S FLYING MACHINE"   NP:$1.75 MIP:$3.00
    Green, rocket-like plane, with four
    wheels and 4-bladed propellor.Wildcat
    wears his hair in pony-tail style under
    an orange cap, turned backwards.
    He waves left hand, steers with right.

UNDER 3 YRS.;
1."BALOO'S SEAPLANE" orange   NP:$3.00 MIP:$4.50
2."WILDCAT'S JET"orange & brown   NP:$3.00 MIP:$4.50

CARTONS (4);   AVG:$1.00 MINT:$2.00
1."HIGHER FOR HIRE"
2."SEA DUCK"
3."PIRATE ISLAND"
4."LOUIE'S"

"RESCUE DOWN UNDER" HAPPY MEAL   NOVEMBER
Set of four toys: shaped like movie cameras, show a strip of
pictures when spindle is turned. MCD#90-081 (FC#MCDXP-388)
(C)Walt Disney Pictures. (Colors vary).

1."WILBUR" the seagull (clear)   NP:$1.50   MIP:$3.00

2."JAKE" kangaroo mouse   (green)   NP:$2.00   MIP:$3.25

3."BERNARD & BIANCA" mice(orange)   NP:$1.50   MIP:$3.00

4."CODY & MARAHUTE" boy (blue)   NP:$2.00   MIP:$3.25

UNDER 3 YRS;
BERNARD   NP:$3.25   MIP:$4.50
Mouse in piece of cheese (rubber).

CARTONS (4);   AVG:$1.00   MINT:$1.50
1.McLEACH / ROPE
2.EAGLE / CLOUDS
3.FIREFLIES
4.FRANK, the lizard.

HAPPY MEALS 1991

DIRECTORY

```
Abbreviations used to describe condition:
MINT = new, never used or unfolded.
AVG  = average condition.
NP   = no original package, loose.
MIP  = mint in package, in original, sealed
         container.
```

"GOOD MORNING" HAPPY MEAL   JANUARY
Set of four Children's grooming aids. MCD#90-080, FC#MCDXP-
375. MADE IN CHINA.

1. RMCD Toothbrush,   NP:$1.50   MIP:$2.75
     Yellow. Simon Marketing Inc.LA
2. RMCD Play Clock,   NP:$1.00   MIP:$2.50
     Red and yellow, movable hands.
     RMCD on clock face.
3. Plastic Drinking Cup,   AVG:$1.25 MINT:$2.50
     12 oz. cup with a coupon:
     value $.25 and a box of fruit juice.
     White cup with scene of RMCD talking
     to woodland animals in a sunny landscape.
4. McDONALDLAND Connectable Comb.   NP:$2.00   MIP:$3.00
     Five combs in five colors,
     featuring McDONALDLAND Characters
     may be joined together as one comb.

UNDER 3 YRS:
Cup with fruit juice   AVG:$1.00 MINT:$1.50

BAG: AVG:$1.00 MINT:$1.50
     White bag, imprinted with
     "McDONALD'S HAPPY MEAL". In outline
     square: RMCD head and "GOOD MORNING".
```

```

TINY TOON ADVENTURES

"TINY TOON Adventures -Flipcars"   HAPPY MEAL   FEBRUARY
(C) 1990 McDONALD'S CORPORATION, TM/(C)WARNER BROS.INC. 1990
MCD#89-083 FC#MCDXP-411. These toys have a different
character and car on each side.

```
1. PLUCKY DUCK,                          NP:$1.75  MIP:$3.00
      PLUCKY DUCK in red boat,
      BABS BUNNY in blue telephone receiver.
2. BUSTER BUNNY,                         NP:$1.75  MIP:$3.00
      BUSTER BUNNY in carrot,
      ELMYRA in orange wagon with grey puppies.
3. GOGO DODO,                            NP:$1.75  MIP:$3.00
      GOGO DODO in bathtub,
      MONTANA MAX in green car.
4. DIZZY DEVIL,                          NP:$1.75  MIP:$3.00
      DIZZY DEVIL in grey amplifier,
      HAMPTON in a Hero Sandwich.


UNDER 3 YRS:
PLUCKY DUCK in a boat,                   NP:$2.25  MIP:$4.00
GOGO DODO in a bathtub ,                 NP:$2.25  MIP:$4.00

CARTON:(4):                              AVG:$1.00  MINT:$1.75
```
1."WACKYLAND"
      All the Tiny Toon characters in strange surroundings.
      At bottom edge, two rabbits look at "wacky map".
2."ACME ACRES"
      Tiny Toon characters riding skateboards down a street
      background scene: "general store - Acme Acres"
3."ACME ACRES FOREST"
      Tiny Toon characters have a tug-of-war across a creek
      trees.
4."ACME LOONIVERSITY"
      With a school in background, the Toonsters are going
      gym class, each carrying a different type of sports
      equipment.

"MUPPET BABIES"   HAPPY MEAL (REGIONAL)   MARCH
There are four toys in this set, which may be snapped
together to make a "train". (C) 1990 McDONALD'S CORPORATION.
/ Muppet Babies and Character names are trademarks of
Henson Associates Inc. /(C) Henson Associates Inc. 1990
Printed in Hong Kong / MADE IN CHINA.

1."BABY KERMIT",   NP:$2.50 MIP:$4.25
       Set consists of three pieces:
soap-box type car. Two red and yellow
pieces, jointed, with snap-on blue wheels
and a red seat.Baby Kermit wears a blue and
white sailor-suit. Embossed on underside of
car is: (C) 1990 McDONALD'S CORP / CHINA / VK3-4 .
Underside of Kermit: HA 1 1990/CHINA/VK2-2 U.

2. "BABY MISS PIGGY",   NP:$2.50 MIP:$4.25
       This two-piece set has red and blue
tricycle with yellow wheels and Baby Piggy
figurine. Baby Piggy wears a pink dress,
gloves, shoes and pink ribbon on her golden
curls. Underside of cycle reads:
(C) 1990 McDONALD'S CORP / CHINA / KY3-2
Underside of Piggy: HA 1 1990/CHINA/ KY1-1.

3. "BABY FOZZIE"   NP:$2.50 MIP:$4.25
   Three pieces: Orange wagon with red
seat, yellow handle, snap-on black wheels.
Baby Fozzie Bear wears yellow jumper,
yellow beanie with a white propellor and
white, purple-dotted bow at neck. Wagon:
(C) 1990 McDONALD'S CORP / CHINA / AG1-1
Underside of Fozzie: MA 1 1990/CHINA/ AG1-4

4. "BABY GONZO'   NP:$2.50 MIP:$4.25
Four pieces. Snap-together airplane,
green body, orange propellor, yellow
wings and pink wheels. Baby Gonzo
wears a red jumper with yellow and white
shoes. Plane:
(C) 1990 McDONALD'S CORP/ CHINA / AG4-1
Underside of Gonzo: MA 1 1990/CHINA/ AG5-2.

UNDER 3: None
BAG   AVG:$ .75 MINT:$1.25
Pictures Muppet Babies racing their
toys down a lane Baby Fozzie waves
finish-flag. Reads: "McDonald's HAPPY
MEAL Featuring Jim Henson's "MUPPET BABIES".

MUPPET BABIES

McDONALDLAND CIRCUS
    PARADE

"McDONALDLAND CIRCUS PARADE' HAPPY MEAL (REGIONAL)   MARCH
This set of four toys,is outstanding for its wit ,color and
quality. Bags read: "This toy has been tested for children
of all ages. It is recommended for children age 1 and above
/ (C) 1989 McDONALD'S CORPORATION / CONTENTS MADE IN CHINA.
PRINTED IN HONG KONG.

1."RINGMASTER RONALD MCDONALD",   NP:$2.75 MIP:$3.75
   Colorful car: blue body, red fenders
and back,yellow wheels and front.M-logo
on back and radiator. RMCD wears yellow
top-hat with red band. As car rolls,
front portion moves, showing Ronald's
big red shoes. His head rocks.MCD#3558-03
Underside: copyright information /HK4.

2."BAREBACK RIDER BIRDIE",   NP:$2.75 MIP:$3.75
   Birdie wears pink Tu-Tu and holds
open pink parasol. Her red braids are
tied with ribbons. She stands on the back
of a white pony. Its red harness, halter
and blanket are spangled with gold stars,
M-logo. As horse rolls, Birdie twirls
around.   MCD#3558-00
Wheel reads: copyright information /MT1-1.

3."ELEPHANT TRAINER FRY GUY",   NP:$2.75 MIP:$3.75
   Grey elephant wears a red head cover
with three gold tassels, and red, fringed
blanket with gold: M-logo on one side.
On its back sits a blue Fry Guy, with a
red-ball nose. His yellow hat topped with
white pom-pom. When toy rolls, Fry Guy
rocks and elephant's trunk moves up and down.
MCD#3558-06
On blanket:copyright information /MT1-2.

4."GRIMACE PLAYING CALLIOPE",   NP:$2.75 MIP:$4.00
   Red drum-major's hat. Grimace rides
in calliope car with yellow pipes and
green wheels, hands (not flippers this time),
over the keyboard. When toy rolls, hands
move up and down as if playing. Gold
M-logo on both sides of car. MCD#3558-09
On his back: copyright information / HK3.

BAG   AVG:$1.00 MINT:$1.50
Colorful bag, designed to be cut and
opened flat presenting a Circus area
and audience. Reads:"McDONALDLAND CIRCUS"

"ALVIN & THE CHIPMUNKS"   HAPPY MEAL (REGIONAL)   MARCH
this set of four: "The Chipmunks (C)1990 Bagdasarian
Productions" / (C)1990 McDONALD'S CORPORATION.

1."ALVIN AND ELECTRIC GUITAR"   NP:$2.50 MIP:$3.75
Two vinyl plastic pieces:
        Alvin in a long shirt with letter "A"
            and a red baseball cap.
        Blue guitar. Pkg card:
            "(C) 1990 Bagdasarian Productions"

2."SIMON WITH VIDEO CAMERA"   NP:$2.50 MIP:$3.75
Two pieces:
        Simon with blue pants and glasses, yellow
            jacket.
        Large purple video camera.Pkg card:
            "(C) 1990 Bagdasarian Productions"

3. "BRITTANY WITH JUKE BOX"   NP:$2.50 MIP:$3.75
Two pieces:
        Brittany, dancing figure ,with yellow
            hair, white blouse and long pink skirt,
            holds micro-phone.
        Green "juke box". Pkg. card:"The Chipettes
        /(C) 1990 Karmen/Ross Productions Inc."

4."THEODORE WITH RAP MACHINE",   NP:$2.50 MIP:$3.75
Two pieces:
        Theodore wears a blue-green gown and bow
            tie, black formal jacket, top hat and pink,
            star-shaped glasses.
        Yellow recording machine. Pkg card:
            "(C) 1990 Bagdasarian Productions"

UNDER 3: None
BAG   AVG:$1.00 MINT:$1.50
White bag with red and gold stars
"McDONALD'S HAPPY MEAL with ALVIN
and the CHIPMUNKS." (pictures of the
Chipmunks, and games. On back:
"LOOK INSIDE FOR YOUR TARGET STORES $2
OFF CHIPMUNK & CHIPETTE CLOTHING
& SHOES COUPON!"

"PIGGSBURG PIGS!"TM   HAPPY MEAL (REGIONAL)   MARCH
Four toys, based on a children's TV cartoon show
"(C) 1990 Fox Children's Network Inc. Contents made
in China /envelopes: Printed in Hong Kong / Safety tested
for Children of all ages / recommended for children age 1
and over.   MCD#3569-00

1."PORTLY AND PIGHEAD ON CYCLE WITH SIDECAR"
                                NP:$2.00 MIP:$3.50
Two happy looking pink pigs. Larger,
drives a watermelon-motorcycle while,
smaller one rides in sidecar. Large pig:
wears green pants, orange shirt, rolled up
sleeves, blue vest and shoes, yellow hair.
Small pig has green cap, worn backwards,
brown hair. One-piece toy with wheels. "TM/
(C) 1990 FOX CHS NET INC/ MADE IN CHINA/ SN1".

2."PIGGY AND QUACKERS ON CRATE RACER"
                                NP:$2.00 MIP:$3.50
Small pig, blue pants, red sweater and
white shoes, steers a brown four-wheeled
crate-racer with one hand while holding
his overlarge blue cap on his head.
Spread across front of the car is a worried
looking white duck. "TM/(C) 1990 FOX CHS
NET INC/ MADE IN CHINA/ OR5".

3."REMBRANDT IN BARNYARD HOT ROD"   NP:$2.00 MIP:$3.50
Car appears to be made of red barn-wood,
with doors and other trim painted white.
Wheels and engine are grey and front of
car has a scowling pig emblem. Pig has
heavy black eyebrows and a "punk" hair style,
wears dark blue jacket and yellow shirt."TM/
(C) 1990 FOX CHS NET INC/ MADE IN CHINA/ SN8".

4."HUFF AND PUFF ON CATAPULT"   NP:$2.00 MIP:$3.50
Wood-like, pale yellow platform with
brown catapult, seating a small, gleeful
wolf. A second, larger wolf is seated
near him with his tail curled up his back.
He waves left hand as he prepares to fire
the weapon. His costume is a green jacket and
blue shirt."TM/(C) 1990 FOX CHS NET INC
 / MADE IN CHINA/ OR6"

BAG   AVG:$1.00 MINT:$1.50
"McDONALD'S (R) HAPPY MEAL PIGGSBURG
PIGS!"

ALVIN & THE CHIPMUNKS

PIGGSBURG PIGS!

GRAVEDALE HIGH

"GRAVEDALE HIGH"   (REGIONAL)   MARCH
Featuring Rick Moranis "Gravedale High" (C) 1991 NBC (C)1991
McDonald Corporation. Marked: "Licensed by HPI / contents
made in China". This group of four toys is based on a
children's TV show produced by the National Broadcasting
Corporation.

1."FRAKENTYKE"   NP:$2.00 MIP:$3.00
Miniature version Frakenstein's Monster.
Green skin, red-lined eyes, orange pants,
black shirt and blue jacket. High forehead
is fringed with black hair. His mouth is open
with pink tongue protruding. When his hands,
which are raised ear-level high, are pushed down,
the tongue juts out another half inch.
MCD#3592-03 Underside: (C) 1991 NBC / MADE IN CHINA / M5 12

2."SID (THE INVISIBLE KID)"   NP:$2.00 MIP:$3.00
Light purple open coffin on a circular
base. Positioned on this, as if worn by
a human,are: baseball cap, sun glasses,
a pair of white gloves, sleevless sweater,
and orange-trimmed, white sneakers. When
the knob on the back is pushed down, the
gloves and shoes move. MCD#3592-06
On back: (C)1991 NBC/MADE IN CHINA / SN.

3."VINNIE STOKER"   NP:$2.00 MIP:$3.00
Orange coffin with bat embossed on lid.
The sides have decoration of bats with
wings spread. When knob at end is turned,
lid revolves revealing a teen-age vampire,
lounging on a bed of earth. His costume is
modern black cycle jacket and boots. His
pocket is a red square with a white #13.
Blue jeans and a red shirt.   MCD#3592-09
On back: (C)1991 NBC/MADE IN CHINA / SV 1

4."CLEOFATRA"   NP:$2.00 MIP:$3.00
One-piece figure with a rounded bottom,
which spins. Figurine is yellow, with
blue skirt, collar and blue bows on
each of two orange braids. She wears
light blue glasses, red lipstick and her
hands are clasped in front. MCD#3592-12
On back: (C)1991 NBC/MADE IN CHINA / OR-6

UNDER 3: Same as set 4.
BAG: AVG:$1.00 MINT:$1.50

"MIGHTY MINI 4 X 4"   (REGIONAL)   MARCH
Small cars mounted over big wheels. 5/8", white spindle (for
winding) projects from side of car. Will climb steep
surfaces. (C)1990 McDONALD'S CORPORATION.
Underside of car: McDONALD'S CORP / MADE IN CHINA.

1."DUNE BUSTER"   NP:$2.00 MIP:$3.50
     Volkswagon-"beetle" type pink car
     with grey trim. MCD#3568-06, ARCHES
     logo on front of roof / IT 05.

2."L'IL CLASSIC"   NP:$2.00 MIP:$3.50
     Yellow, classic Ford Thunderbird
     with grey trim. ARCHES logo on trunk lid.
     MCD#3568-09 / QX 09.

3."CARGO CLIMBER"   NP:$2.00 MIP:$3.50
     Orange van with yellow trim.
     ARCHES logo on roof-spoiler.
     MCD#3568-03 / IT 08.

4. "POCKET PICK-UP"   NP:$2.00 MIP:$3.50
     Red pickup with blue trim.
     ARCHES logo on roof of cab.
     MCD#3568-00 / QX 10.

UNDER 3 YRS:
"POCKET PICK-UP"   NP:$2.00 MIP:$3.50
     Soft, blue vinyl Pick-up with
     yellow trim. Finger hole in base.
     2" X 2" x 1 5/8" high. No moving parts.

CARTON: AVG:$1.00 MINT:$1.50
     Colorful carton: "Hit the Dirt"shows
     desert scenery which may be punched
     out for play scene of hill and gas
     station. Also has a "crossroad" puzzle.

"NATURE'S HELPERS"   HAPPY MEAL   APRIL
Five gardening implements,("M (R)" logo) packaged with
booklet and/or a seed packet from Burpee Company.
(C) 1990 McDonald's Corporation McD#90-158 FC#MCDXP-424.
Theme: "Let's Get Growing America."
Small trees were given away in some states.

1. Double-Digger   AVG:$2.00 MINT:$3.25
    Green, hinged trowels. Cucumber seeds.(No booklet)
2. BIRD FEEDER   AVG:$2.50 MINT:$4.00
    Three peices. Green top, orange
    shaft with suction cup for window.
    Clear plastic seed holder. (no seeds)
    Booklet: "Why Are There Birds?".
3. WATERING CAN   AVG:$1.75 MINT:$2.50
    Two pieces. Blue vessel, yellow
    spout and rim. Green handle.
    Booklet: "Why Are There Flowers?" (no seeds).
4. TERRARIUM   AVG:$3.00 MINT:$5.00
    Two pieces. Green base, clear dome. Seeds: Coleus.
    Booklet: "How Does The World Work?"
5 RAKE   AVG:$1.00 MINT:$2.50
    Yellow. Seeds: Marigolds.
    Booklet: "How Does Your Garden Grow?".
(Under 3 YRS. RAKE, no seeds.)

"McDINO CHANGEABLES"   HAPPY MEAL   JUNE
Set of eight toys, two each week and two different "Under 3
yrs". Cleverly constructed puzzles, models of popular
McDonald's foods which open into comical dinosaur-like
creatures. On the reverse side of the label inside each
package, is shown the method of changing the toy . Some
packages included a coupon book: "McDONALD'S BONUS BOOK /
Over $12.00 in savings / MOM & DAD look inside ".
Toys are marked (C) 1990 McDONALD'S CORP CHINA & (part
number)

WEEK 1:
1.HAPPY MEAL-O-DON   NP:$1.50   MIP:$2.50
Red house-shaped carton with yellow
handle, yellow "M" and white "HAPPY MEAL".
It opens into seated dino with soulful
eyes and a toothy smile. LF 11

2.QUARTER POUNDER WITH CHEESE-O-SAUR   NP:$1.25 MIP:$2.00
Tan bun, tasty-looking brown hamburger
with triangles of yellow melted cheese.
It opens into a standing dino with short
blue-lined legs, a curved blue tail and head.
The large jaw has a serious underbite. LF 9

WEEK 2:
1.McNUGGETS-O-SAURUS   NP:$1.25   MIP:$2.00
The familiar yellow package of CHICKEN
McNUGGETS with McDonald's logo and
"6 pieces", opens into a dino-turtle,
light green. KH.

2.HOTCAKES-O-DACTYL   NP:$1.00   MIP:$2.00
White Hotcakes package : "HOTCAKES" AND
"M-McDONALD'S" logo. It cleverly opens
into a bird-like creature with violet
(striped) tail and head. KH.

WEEK 3:
1.   NP:$1.50   MIP:$2.25
Red large frys package with McDONALD'S
logo in white rectangle becomes a red
creature with curly yellow head, feet
and tail. QX 04.

2.BIG MAC-O-SAURUS REX   NP:$1.00   MIP:$2.00
Three tan buns, two brown 'burgers,
green lettuce and yellow cheese may be
transformed into a creature with orange
head, feet and tail. QX 01.

McDINO CHANGEABLES

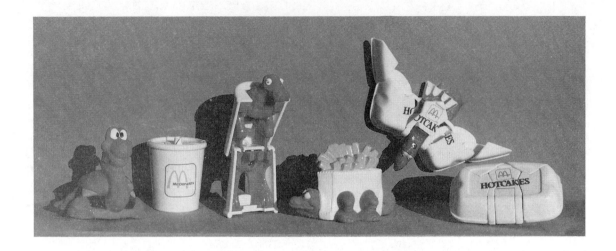

WEEK 4:
1.TRI-SHAKE-ATOPS   NP:$1.50   MIP:$2.50
White milk-shake cup with red-striped
straw projecting from the top, McDONALD'S
logo in rectangle, on the side. It opens
to form a tall, standing, bright-pink
creature with short fore-legs and tail
and a vulture-like head. HF1-4.

2.McDINO CONE   NP:$1.50   MIP:$2.50
Yellow waffle-cone, topped with creamy
white ice cream. Red McDONALD'S logo.
Pushing the bottom of the cone causes
a blue, baby dino to pop up. The bit of
white cone on atop his head suggests he
has just broken through his shell. Blue arms. CW

UNDER 3 YRS: soft 1-piece toys
1.BRONTO CHEESEBURGER   NP:$3.00   MIP:$4.00
The familiar cheeseburger is the body
of a happy orange dino. His long neck
curves back upon his body. Four fat
feet and a tail. Underside: (C) 1990
McDonald's Corp. / Thailand / DN

2.SMALL FRY-CERATOPS   NP:$3.00   MIP:$4.00
White package of small fries with red
"M", is the body for a green lizard-like
dino with a winsome expression. underside:
(C) 1990 McDonald's Corp. / Thailand / DN

BAG: AVG:$0.75   MINT:$1.25
White with designs in yellow,purple,
green.Picture on front features "week 1"
dinosaurs playing.

"101 DALMATIONS" HAPPY MEAL   JULY
Four toys based on the Walt Disney Movie classic -
"101 Dalmations" .(C) 1990 McDonald's Corporation
(C) The Walt Disney Company. McD#90-233 FC#MCDXP-490
The toys all have movable heads and legs.

1. PONGO   NP:$1.25 MIP:$2.50
     Long legged dog, open-mouthed. red collar.

2.LUCKY   NP:$1.00 MIP:$2.00
     Seated puppy holding a bone.

3.THE COLONEL and SERGEANT TIBS   NP:$1.00 MIP:$2.00
     Brown and grey sheep dog, kitten on back.

4.CRUELLA DE VIL   NP:$1.10 MIP:$2.25
     The wicked woman, wearing a full yellow
     coat over a black dress. A puppy's head
     protrudes from pocket. Red gloves and shoes.

CARTONS (4):
1. Roger & Anita   AVG:$0.50 MINT:$1.00
2. Roger at Piano   AVG:$0.75 MINT:$1.10
3. Colonel & puppies, red stairs   AVG:$0.75 MINT:$1.10
4. Barn   AVG:$0.50 MINT:$1.00

"BARBIE/HOT WHEELS"   HAPPY MEAL   AUGUST
Plastic, not poseable, Barbie dolls, packaged with $1.00
coupon for purchase of another doll. Metal, Hot Wheels
cars, are packaged with $2.00 coupon for purchase of a
Jumpbuster(TM) set. (C) 1990 McDonald's Corporation
MCD#90-191
dolls: FC#MCDXP-488, cars:FC#MCDXP-464,(C) 1990 Mattel,Inc.

BARBIE DOLLS:
Underside: "Made for McDonald's / (C) 1991 Mattel Inc.
/ Made in China".

1. "ALL AMERICAN BARBIE"   NP:$1.10 MIP:$3.25
Short-skirted blue jumper, white Rebok
shoes, green grass with pink flowers.
lt. tan skin, yellow hair.

2. "COSTUME BALL BARBIE"   NP:$1.00 MIP:$3.00
Floor length ,frilly, pink gown,
ruffled sleeves. Carries lavender mask
in left hand. Lt. skin, deep yellow hair.

3. "LIGHTS AND LACE BARBIE"   NP:$1.00 MIP:$3.00
Pink dress with -short, ruffled skirt
and long sleeves. Pink mid-calf boots.
Lavendar platform backed by same color star.
Lt. tan skin, yellow hair. Right hand salute.

4. "HAPPY BIRTHDAY BARBIE"   NP:$1.25 MIP:$3.50
Floor length, pink gown with white sash
over right shoulder. Dk. brown skin, black hair.

5. "HAWAIIAN FUN BARBIE"   NP:$1.00 MIP:$3.00
Multi-color bra top, pink sarong skirt,
yellow tote bag over right shoulder.
Feet disappear into mound of sand and
green plants. Lt. yellow hair, lt. tan skin.

6. "WEDDING DAY MIDGE"   NP:$1.00 MIP:$3.00
Floor length white wedding gown and
veil. Pink bouquet. Lt. tan skin, red hair.
UNDER 3 YRS. BARBIE: Used #6, "WEDDING DAY MIDGE"

7. "ICE CAPADES BARBIE"   NP:$1.15 MIP:$3.30
"Ruffled"-skirted short dress, white
ice-skates. White platform backed with blue.
Yellow hair.

8. "MY FIRST BARBIE"   NP:$1.25 MIP:$3.50
Floor length white skirt, purple bodice,
white puffed sleeves. Lt. Brown skin and hair.

HOT WHEELS, "CALIFORNIA CUSTOM":
Underside: MATTEL INC 1979 / HOT WHEELS (R) / MALAYSIA

1. '55 CHEVY   (yellow)   NP:$1.00   MIP:$3.00

2. '63 CORVETTE   (green)   NP:$1.10   MIP:$3.25

3. '57 T-BIRD   (tourquois)   NP:$1.10   MIP:$3.25

4. CAMARO Z-28   NP:$1.20   MIP:$3.50

5. '55 CHEVY   (white)   NP:$1.00   MIP:$3.00

6. '63 CORVETTE   (black)   NP:$1.10   MIP:$3.25

7. '57 T-BIRD   (red)   NP:$1.20   MIP:$3.50

8. CAMARO Z-28   (orange)   NP:$1.00   MIP:$3.00

UNDER 3 YRS. HOT WHEELS:
Yellow wrench and red hammer   NP:$1.50   MIP:$3.75

CARTONS (4):
1. "BARBIE ON STAGE"   AVG:$1.00   MINT:$1.25
May be made into a stage or ticket window.
2. "BARBIE AT HOME"   AVG:$1.10   MINT:$1.50
Home and wedding play scenes.
3. "HOT WHEELS RACERS"   AVG:$1.10   MINT:$1.50
May be made into a car repair garage.
4. "HOT WHEELS CRUISING"   AVG:$1.10   MINT:$1.50
Street scene with ramp.

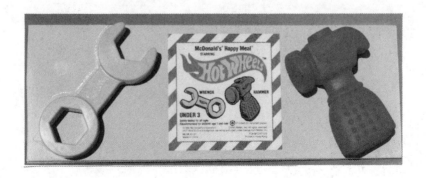

"DISCOVER THE RAIN FOREST"   HAPPY MEAL   SEPTEMBER
Activity type, twenty-page, books. Back page has punch-out
picture of typical rain forest animals.

1. "STICKER SAFARI"   AVG:$1.00   MINT:$2.00
    Animal: Toucan (bird). Stickers
    and activities.

2. "PAINT IT WILD"   AVG:$1.00   MINT:$2.00
    Animal: Tree Frog. Paint and
    activities.

3. "RONALD McDONALD AND THE JEWEL
    OF THE AMAZON KINGDOM"   AVG:$0.75   MINT:$1.75
    Animal: three-toed Sloth. Story.

4. "WONDERS IN THE WILD"   AVG:$1.00   MINT:$2.00
    Animal: Amazon Butterfly. Activities.

BAG   AVG:$0.75   MINT:$

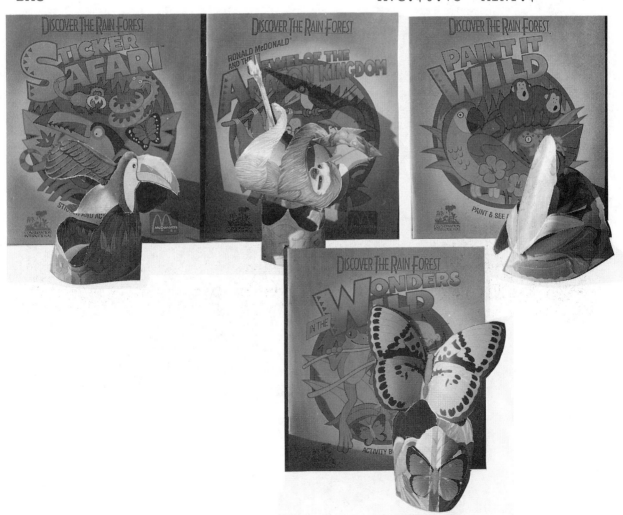

"McDONALDLAND CONNECTIBLES" HAPPY MEAL (REGIONAL)   SEPTEMBER
Appeared very briefly (in California) between the "Rain
Forest" and the Halloween premiums. Set of four toys
which may be connected together. (C) 1991
McDonald's Corporation. Safe for age 1 and over.

1. "Ronald McDonald in a Soap-Box Racer"
      Two pieces, figurine & vehicle.   NP: $1.00   MIP:$2.75

2. "Hamburglar in an Airplane"   NP: $1.00   MIP:$2.75
      Two pieces, figurine & vehicle.

3. "Grimace in a Wagon"   NP: $1.25   MIP:$3.00
      Two pieces. Grimace figurine, open
      mouth shows red tongue.
      Red wagon, Orange, yellow and black trim.

4. "Birdie on a Tricycle'   NP: $1.25   MIP:$3.00
      Two pieces, figurine & vehicle.

BAG   AVG:$0.75   MINT:$1.00

"CRAZY VEHICLES"   HAPPY MEAL (REGIONAL)   SEPTEMBER
Appeared very briefly between the "Rain Forest" and
Halloween premiums. Set of four toys: figurines and snap-
together vehicles. Safe for age 1 and over. (C) 1991
McDonald's Corporation.

1. "RONALD McDONALD BUGGY"   NP:$1.25 MIP:$3.00

2. "HAMBURGLAR TRAIN"   NP:$1.25 MIP:$3.00
Three pieces. Hamburglar figure is
     embedded in cab, showing just head
     and shoulders. Yellow engine with
     purple,blue and orange trim.

3. "GRIMACE CAR"   NP:$1.25 MIP:$3.00
Three pieces. Grimace figure embedded,
     showing head and shoulders. Green
     car with yellow, orange and blue trim.

4. "BIRDIE AIRPLANE"   NP:$1.00 MIP:$2.75
Three pieces. Birdie figure, embedded,
     showing head, shoulders and one wing tip.
     Pink plane with yellow and purple trim.

BAG   AVG:$0.75 MINT:$1.00

"McDONALDLAND HAPPY MEAL"   (REGIONAL)   FALL
McDonaldland characters on snap-together bikes. The label
shows four different toys and how they look connected
together. (No McD-part number.)

RONALD   NP:$2.25 MIP:$3.95
Four pieces. Ronald seated figurine.
     Red vehicle with yellow wheels in three pieces.

GRIMACE   NP:$2.00 MIP:$3.50
Three pieces. Grimace seated figurine,
     with blue cap and blue and white sneakers.
     Blue vehicle with green wheels in two pieces.

HAMBURGLAR   NP:$2.00 MIP:$3.50
Three pieces. Hamburglar seated figure,
     with red gloved, red and white sneakers
     and hamburger-dotted tie.
     Yellow vehicle with red wheels in two pieces.

BIRDIE   NP:$2.00 MIP:$3.50
Three pieces. Birdie seated figure
     in red jumper with pant legs rolled up.
     Pink vehicle with blue wheels in two pieces.

Bag   AVG:$2.00 MINT:$3.50

HALLOWEEN "McBOO BAGS"   HAPPY MEAL   OCTOBER
"GLOW IN THE DARK / VINYL TREAT BAGS"
Three different vinyl bags, beautiful bright colors with
ARCHES- shaped handles. Each shows a figure with arms
outstretched, frontal view on one side and back view on
the other. On both sides is a large ARCHES (R) logo
(without text) in a white circle. (Bag is meal container)

1. WITCH   AVG:$1.00 MINT:$2.00
        Green bag with orange handle. Happy
        young red-haired witch, in blue dress
        and hat. Front: spider in pocket.
        Back: comical cat sits on hat brim.

2. GHOST   AVG:$1.25 MINT:$2.25
        Purple bag with yellow handle. Gleeful
        white ghost, wears a blue "BOO" bow
        around its neck.
        Back: a boisterous blue bat.

3. FRANKEN-KID   AVG:$1.25 MINT:$2.25
        Orange bag with pink handle. Friendly
        young monster with red-freckled green skin,
        red and pink clothing. Back: a pair of rats,
        riding in back pocket, carry a "Trick or Treat" bag.

"FRIENDLY SKIES MEAL"   HAPPY MEAL   NOVEMBER
This McDonald's and UNITED AIRLINES promotion lasted from
October to December, and was available to airline passengers
who requested the Happy meal in advance of the flight.

TOY:
Three inch, white plane with three wheels, red and blue
United Air Lines logo on tail, and stripes along both sides
of plane. Above stripes: "UNITED".
 Underside: embossed text " (C) 1991 McDonald's Corp. (C)
1991 United Air Lines Inc. Plastic bag label is white with
border of yellow stripes and stars. Text: "(C) 1991
McDonald's Corporation / The Friendly Skies (R) is a service
mark of United Airlines / Recommended for children age one
and over". Central design: McDonald's and United Airlines
logos, "Friendly Skies Meal".

Projecting from an opening in top of plane is 1.2 inch high,
     waving, figure (torso). It can be turned four ways.
1. RONALD McDONALD   AVG:$4.50   MINT:$8.00
2. GRIMACE   AVG:$5.00   MINT:$8.50

TRAY LINER   AVG:$2.00   MINT:$3.50
     "HAPPY LANDINGS". Activities.
     MCD#91-145   FC#McDXP-629.
UTENSILS   AVG:$2.00   MINT:$3.00
     Plastic envelope containing: 1 flexible
     straw, 1 towelette, 1 white paper napkin,
     1 red and 1 blue pencil (3 1/4 inches long).

CARTON   AVG:$3.50   MINT:$5.00
     Colorful flat cardboard tray with golden
     ARCHES for handles. Printed with activities,
     puzzles and games.

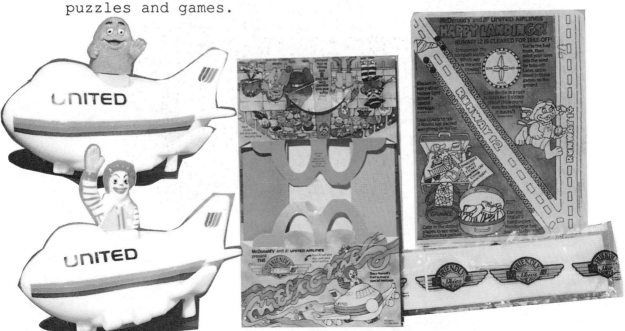

"SUPER LOONEY TUNES"   HAPPY MEAL   NOVEMBER
Warner Bros. Inc. cartoon characters in "Super-Hero"
costumes. Each figure is packaged with a six-page comic
book, and a two-piece, snap-together costume. Figures are
embossed with "TM (C) '91 WBI" and have no movable parts.
Daffy Duck figure is protected by molded plastic shell.

1. TAZ-FLASH   NP:$1.00   MIP:$2.50
Pieces: Tasmanian Devil.
Red *Flash* costume covers all but his face.
      Book: "McDonald's presents LOONEY TUNES
HAPPY MEAL featuring Tasmanian Devil as
TAZ-FLASH". Taz dreams of rescuing his hero, *The Flash*.

2. SUPER BUGS   NP:$1.00   MIP:$2.50
Pieces: Bugs Bunny
Red and blue *Superman* type outfit:
red cape and shorts, blue shirt.
      Book: "McDonald's presents LOONEY TUNES
HAPPY MEAL featuring Bugs Bunny as
SUPER BUGS". Bugs thwarts a carrot-patch robbery.

3. WONDER PIG   NP:$1.25   MIP:$3.00
Pieces: Petunia Pig
Red and blue, *Wonder Woman* costume covers
all but her head.
      Book: "McDonald's presents LOONEY TUNES
HAPPY MEAL featuring Petunia Pig as
WONDER PIG". Petunia makes boys stop telling fibs.

4. BAT DUCK   NP:$1.25   MIP:$3.00
Pieces: Daffy Duck
Blue and grey Batman costume reveals
Daffy's face and legs.
      Book: "McDonald's presents LOONEY TUNES
HAPPY MEAL featuring Daffy Duck as BAT DUCK".
Daffy discovers that he stole his own
piggy-bank while sleep-walking.

UNDER 3 YRS.,   NP:$2.00   MIP:$3.50
Soft, one-piec, BAT DUCK in Bat Car
(dk. blue). Underside marked: "TM &
(C) '91 WBI / Authorized Parody ".
No comic book. Typical Happy Meal label.

BAG   AVG:$0.75 MINT:$1.00
Activities

SUPER LOONEY TUNES

HOOK

"HOOK"   HAPPY MEAL   DECEMBER
Set of four bath-tub toys features characters from the movie
"HOOK"
TM and (C) 1991 Tri-Star Pictures Inc..
(C) 1991 McDonald's Corporation MCD#91-100 FC#MCDXP-588.

1. PETER PAN   NP:$2.00 MINT:$3.50
Three pieces. Man on log raft, holding
     yellow sail. Floats and has wheels.
       On shirt-back: (C) Tri-Star.
Figurine: Peter Pan, green pants, white shirt.
Raft: four "logs", pink.
Sail: yellow, with design of cross over a hook.

2. MERMAID   NP:$2.00 MINT:$2.75
One-piece. Mermaid wind-up toy. Tail
      moves to propell toy over water.
        Floats on back.
Figurine: tail-fin part is movable.
       tail dark blue, hair light blue.
        Body: pink and green. Face: natural.
        Back of hair: "(C) 1991 Tri-Star Pictures
        Inc. (C) 1991 McDonald's Corporation".

3. CAPTAIN HOOK   NP:$2.00 MINT:$2.75
One piece. Captain Hook in a blue boat
      is one piece. Orange sail. Floats.
Figurine: Wears English Tricorn hat trimmed with
gold. Red coat, black hair and boots.

4. RUFIO   NP:$1.75 MINT:$2.50
One-piece. Man on lt. green raft made of
       four barrels, points purple "weapon".
        Squirts water when squeezed. Floats.
Figurine: Man with black hair and short-sleeved
       costume, red trimmed.

CARTONS (4):
1. "PIRATE TOWN"   AVG:$1.00 MINT:$2.00
      Made into treasure chest.
2. "JOLLY ROGER"   AVG:$1.25 MINT:$2.25
      Playscene: part of Hook's ship.
3. "WENDY'S LONDON HOUSE"   AVG:$1.00 MINT:$2.00
      Wendy's windows.
4. "NEVERTREE"   AVG:$1.50 MINT:$2.50
      Playscene: Peter Pan outdoors.

GAMES AND TOYS

Abbreviations used to describe condition:
MINT = new, never used or unfolded.
AVG = average condition.
NP   = no original package, loose.
MIP = mint in package, in original, sealed
        container.

GAMES

BOWLING GAME, 1986   AVG:$3.00   MINT:$9.00
    Six GRIMACE figures, purple

BOWLING GAME, Gobblins, 1982   AVG:$5.00   MINT:$12.00

GIGGLES AND SCREAMS GAME   AVG:$4.00   MINT:$7.75
    paper, Circus World,Florida

GOBBLINS HORSESHOES, 1982   AVG:$3.50   MINT:$7.00

GOLF GAME, 1986 FRY GUY, green   AVG:$3.00   MINT:$6.50

McDONALDLAND HOCKEY, 1982   AVG:$3.50   MINT:$7.00
   FRY KIDS

HAMBURGLAR HOCKEY   AVG:$2.50   MIP:$3.50

MILTON BRADLEY:
    "THE McDONALD'S GAME"   AVG:$18.00 MINT:$40.00
    Board game.

MAYOR McCHEESE BEAD GAME   AVG:$3.00 MINT:$5.50
    Plastic dome, 1 1/2" dia., peg
    with two holes. Ring with two balls.

McDONALD'S SPINNER BASEBALL, 1983 AVG:$3.75 MINT:$6.00
    Green plastic. Four McDland characters.

RONALD BASKETBALL GAME

SPINNER BASEBALL

GOBBLINS HORSESHOES
1982

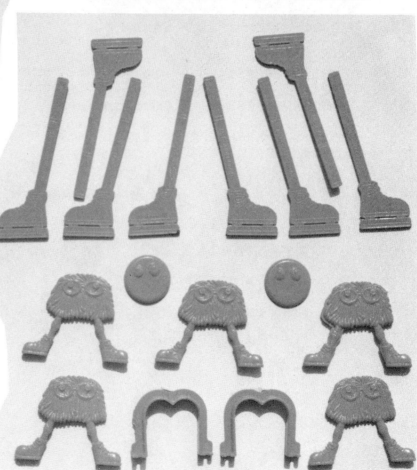

GRIMACE BOWLING GAME

FRY KIDS HOCKEY,1982

PARKER BROTHERS:
"McDONALD PLAYLAND FUNBURST GAME"   AVG:$30.00 MINT:$55.00
        1984 MONOPOLY GAME, paper board.
        Win prizes Gameboard is a playscene.
        Tokens, chips. Carrying handle.

RONALD PADDLE-BALL GAME   AVG:$6.00 MINT:$12.50
        1981, wooden paddle.

RONALD BASKETBALL GAME   AVG:$10.00 MINT:$15.00
        Ball & basket are yellow plastic.
        Ball attached by string.Hold figure
        and try to get ball into basket.

RUBIK'S CUBE   AVG:$6.00 MINT:$9.00
        Printed with names of foods.
        Yellow: ARCHES logo.
        Orange squares: "You Deserve a Break Today".

RUBIK'S CUBE   AVG:$7.00 MINT:$10.00
        Yellow box with ARCHES logo.
        Words on each side, not across
        all squares.
        Green squares: "You Deserve a Break Today."
        White squares: "The World's Community Restaurant."
        Red squares: "McDonald's & You."
        Blue squares: "Q.S.C.&V."
        Orange squares: "Ronald McDonald."
        Yellow squares: McDonald's ARCHES logo.

TIC-TAC-MAC GAME, 1981   AVG:$3.00 MINT:$5.50
Grimace = X, RMCD = O. Yellow base.

PARKER BROS.
"FUNBURST GAME"

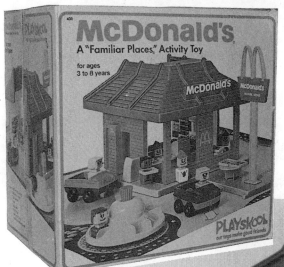

PLAYSKOOL
"FAMILIAR PLACES"

TOYS

BOXED TOYS:

FISCHER-PRICE TOYS:
McDONALD'S "BREAKFAST"   AVG:$4.00   MINT:$7.00

McDONALD'S "CHICKEN McNUGGETS",   AVG:$4.50   MINT:$8.00
     With Crew Uniform. 1988

McDONALD'S "COOKING CENTER"   AVG:$22.00   MINT:$30.00

McDONALD'S "FUN WITH FOOD", 1988   AVG:7.00$ MINT:$12.00
     With Crew Uniform,

McDONALD'S "GARDEN SALAD"   AVG:$4.00   MINT:$6.00

McDONALD'S "HAPPY MEAL"   AVG:$22.00   MINT:$30.00

"McDONALD'S, LITTLE PEOPLE"   AVG:$22.00   MINT:$35.00
     Restaurant

"McDONALD'S PLAYLAND" Board Game   AVG:$22.00   MINT:$35.00

"McDONALD'S SODA FOUNTAIN"   AVG:$18.00   MINT:$27.50

MATTEL:
"Barbie loves McDONALD'S"   AVG:$45.00   MINT:$85.00
  Includes counter and Barbie crew cap.

PLAYSKOOL TOYS:
"FAMILIAR PLACES"   AVG:$25.00   MINT:$37.00

REMCO: "McDONALDLAND"   AVG:$125.00 MINT:$250.00
     Playset train and track, background,
     other pieces. Does not include
     dolls which were sold separately.
     For description of six dolls, see chapter on "DOLLS"

FISHER-PRICE TOYS

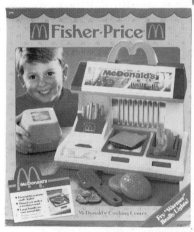

MATTEL
"BARBIE LOVES McDONALD'S"

BARBIE DOLL, CREW UNIFORM   AVG:$5.50   MINT:$12.00
    (C) 1982 McDONALD'S Corporation
    4274-0910. White shoes and cap with
    blue band. Blue dress with blue and
    white striped trim.

BOOMERANG, 1979   AVG:$2.50   MINT:$5.50

FAST MACS, McDonaldland characters,1984
Set of four cars with pull-back action.
    BIG MAC, white   AVG:$3.00   MINT:$6.50
    BIRDIE, pink   AVG:$4.00   MINT:$8.00
    HAMBURGLAR, red   AVG:$3.00   MINT:$6.00
    RMCD JEEP, yellow   AVG:$3.00   MINT:$6.00

FRISBEES:
FLYING RINGS: 6 inch diameter,   AVG:$1.00   MINT:$2.00
    Flexible flying disks, several
    colors. Standing figure of RMCD
    in center. Red, yellow, blue.

FLYER, 6 inch diameter   AVG:$2.00   MINT:$3.50
    RMCD with arms and legs spread.
    Red, yellow, blue.

FLYER, PRO POCKET, flexible, 8 1/4" AVG:$2.25   MINT:$3.24

FRISBEE, 8 inch diameter   AVG:$4.00   MINT:$6.00
    White with RMCD head in center.
    "RONALD McDONALD alternates
    with McDonald's logo, twice.
    Marks: 'McDonald's System Inc. 1980"

FLYER, BIRDIE, 1982   AVG:$5.00   MINT:$7.50

FRISBEE,"WHEN THE U.S...YOU WIN"   AVG:$3.00   MINT:$5.00

FRISBEE, BIG MAC   AVG:$4.00   MINT:$6.00
    Dark yellow with figure of Big
    Mac in center.

M. BRADLEY
"THE McDONALD'S GAME"

FISHER-PRICE
"LITTLE PEOPLE"

FAST MACS

GLIDER,
HUGHES AIRWEST

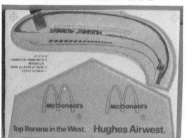

MIGHTY MAC
ROBOT-DOZER

STRING-BLOWER
TOY

GLIDER, Hughes Airwest   AVG:$2.50   MINT:$6.00
     Punch-out plastic foam glider.
     Plane body is yellow banana.
     "Top Bannana in the Wes /Hughes
     Airwest"/ McDONALD'S logo.

HARDWORKING BURGER DUMPTRUCK, 1982   AVG:$4.00   MINT:$7.50
     snap together, orange.

MIGHTY MAC ROBOT DOZER,   AVG:$3.50   MINT:$5.00
     Blue plastic, snap together,
     four pieces: tracks, blades & body.

MIGHTY MAC ROBOT SHUTTLE   AVG:$3.50   MINT:$5.00
     Blue plastic,snap together,
     four pieces.

MAC TONIGHT PIANO, music box   AVG:$17.00 MINT:$27.00
     Plays "Mac The Knife" tune.
     Song book. Keyboard. MCD#88-135
     FC MCDT-219 (C)1988 McDonald's Corporation.

PUPPET, FINGER, 1988   AVG:$1.50   MINT:$2.25
     Fry Guy, Birdie, punch-out cardboard.

PUPPET, FINGERTRONIC   AVG:$10.00 MINT:$3000
     MAC TONIGHT, sponge rubber head
     with finger holes in back. 6 inches,
     in cityscape box. (C) 1988 Suttons
     Happening Inc. Great Neck, NY
     Fingertronic is trademark of Bendy Toys
     Ltd. Ashford, Middlesex, UK. (C) 1988

SOCCER BALLS, CHILDREN'S size 4   AVG:$10.00 MINT:$20.00

SOCCER BALLS, regulation size 5   AVG:$12.00 MINT:$25.00

STRING-BLOWER TOY   AVG:$3.00   MINT:$5.50
     Yellow plastic with red string.
     Figure of RMCD. Blowing makes
     string move.

FRISBEES

MAC TONIGHT PIANO

BASKETBALL

SOCCER BALLS

TIC-TAC-GO SLATES, 1988,   AVG:$3.75   MINT:$5.50
     5" X 3 1/2".

TOP, spinning, 3 1/2" , ARCHES   AVG:$2.00   MINT:$3.00

TOOTLE:, plastic whistle, 1982   AVG:$3.75   MINT:$5.00
     Green, Fry Friend.

TOOTLER: plastic harmonica, 1985   AVG:$2.00   MINT:$3.25
     Green, Grimace in firetruck.

WHISTLES, flexible, 21 inches   AVG:$3.00   MINT:$5.25

WHISTLE: Grimace, purple, 1981   AVG:$2.50   MINT:$3.75

WHISTLE: Goblin, green,   1982   AVG:$2.00   MINT:$3.00

WHISTLE: green, (train) 5 tones   AVG:$2.00   MINT:$3.00
     "McDonald's Express Tooter" 1985

WHISTLE:"Tootlers", plastic:
     GRIMACE, firetruck,1985   AVG:$1.25   MINT:$2.00
     FRY FRIEND, green, 1982   AVG:$1.25   MINT:$2.00

WHISTLE: Spinner   AVG:$1.25   MINT:$2.00
     Red with yellow figure of RMCD, 1990

YO-YO, miniature, 1 1/4" diameter   AVG:$2.50   MINT:$4.00
     Red and Yellow halves. McDonald's
     logo and "safety tested for children
     3 and over".

YO-YO: miniature, red.   AVG:$1.00   MINT:$2.00
     RONALD McDONALD HEAD.

YO-YO, 2 1/4" diameter   AVG:$2.00   MINT:$3.50
     Red and yellow halves. On yellow side
     in red: "Call to Action / Customer
     Satisfaction!" and McDonald's logo.
     On red side, advertising in white, by
     various sponsors.

CHRISTMAS ITEMS

```
┌─────────────────────────────────────────────────┐
│     Abbreviations used to describe condition:     │
│     MINT = new, never used or unfolded            │
│     AVG  = average condition                      │
│     NP   = no original package, loose             │
│     MIP  = mint in package, in original, sealed   │
│            container                              │
└─────────────────────────────────────────────────┘
```

BOOKS:

SANTA CLAUS STORY BOOKS, 1985, from the HAPPY MEAL:
    "SANTA CLAUS, THE MOVIE" Two storybooks published
    by Gosset & Dunlap,(8 X 8 inches) and two
    "activity" books. (See Happy Meals 1985.)
STORY BOOKS:
    1."THE LEGEND OF SANTA CLAUS"   AVG:$3.00   MINT:$5.00
      ISBN# 0-448-18975-5, 24 pages
    2."THE ELVES AT THE TOP OF THE WORLD"
      ISBN# 0-448-18976-3, 24 pages   AVG:$3.00   MINT:$5.00
ACTIVITY BOOKS:
    1."SLEIGHFULL OF SURPRISES"   AVG:$3.50   MINT:$5.50
      activity type book
    2."WORKSHOP OF ACTIVITIES"   AVG:$3.50   MINT:$5.50
      coloring book

DOLLS:

REINDEER, hanging ornament, 1985   AVG:$4.00   MIP:$6.00
    Tan fleece, brown felt antlers.
    Red felt harness. Theme: "*Santa
    Clause, The Movie*" MCD#85-018
    (C) McDonald's Corporation.

"CINDERELLA" movie theme. 1987. Fleece covered figures:
    JACQUE   AVG:$3.50   MIP:$8.00
      Thin mouse, orange jacket.
    GUS   AVG:$3.50   MIP:$8.00
      Fat mouse, green shirt.

MUPPET BABIES, stuffed dolls, 1988:
    (For further detail see the Chapter : DOLLS)
    BABY MISS PIGGY   AVG:$5.75   MINT:$8.00
    BABY KERMIT   AVG:$5.00   MINT:$7.50
    BABY FOZZIE BEAR   AVG:$6.00   MINT:$8.50
```
```

"THE LITTLE MERMAID" movie theme, 1989. Plush ornaments
    SEBASTIAN   AVG:$4.00 MIP:$7.50
        Crab with scarf around its throat.
    FLOUNDER   AVG:$4.00 MIP:$7.50
        Yellow fish with pointed cap.

"RESCUERS DOWN UNDER" movie theme 1990. Fleece covered:
    MISS BIANCA   AVG:$3.50 MIP:$6.50
        Mouse.
    BERNARD   AVG:$3.50 MIP:$6.50
        Mouse.

GARFIELD CHRISTMAS DOLLS from Mexico, 1990:
    (For further detail see the Chapter : DOLLS)
    SANTA GARFIELD   AVG:$4.50 MINT:$10.50
    GARFIELD ELF   AVG:$4.50 MINT:$10.50
    ANGEL GARFIELD   AVG:$5.50 MINT:$11.50
    REINDEER ODIE   AVG:$5.00 MINT:$11.00

FRY GUY AND FRY GIRL, four-inch hanging ornaments
    Soft printed cloth dolls. (See Chapter: DOLLS)
    FRY GUY   AVG:$2.75 MIP:$4.00
    FRY GIRL   AVG:$2.75 MIP:$4.00

GLASSES:

THE NUTCRACKER, set of four glasses issued for the 1990
    Christmas season. (C) 1990 McDonald's Corporation.
    (For further detail see the Chapter: VESSELS)

       1.   AVG:$9.50 MINT:$12.00
        "Marie cried out with delight 'A Nutcracker
        Godfather, he is so beautiful!"
       2.   AVG:$9.50 MINT:$12.00
        "The Nutcracker led the toys to battle against
        the Army of Mice ".
       3.   AVG:$8.00 MINT:$11.00
        "The Sugar Plum Fairy lives here in the Land
        of Sweets" said the Nutcracker.
       4.   AVG:$8.00 MINT:$11.00
        "Marie and the Prince glided across the floor
        in Toyland".

CINDERELLA: GUS & JACQUES

SANTA CLAUSE, THE MOVIE: REINDEER

RESCUERS DOWN UNDER:
BERNARD & BIANCA

LITTLE MERMAID: SEBASTIAN & FLOUNDER

MUSIC BOXES:

"OLIVER AND COMPANY" movie 1988. Wind-up, musical ornaments.
    OLIVER, cat   AVG:$3.50 MIP:$6.50
    DODGER, dog   AVG:$3.50 MIP:$6.50

McDONALD'S RESTAURANT   AVG:$8.00 MIP:$13.50
    2 1/2 X 2 1/2 inches, music-box ornament
    plays "Jingle Bells" and "Silent Night".

STOCKINGS:

PLASTIC CHRISTMAS STOCKING, 1981   AVG:$1.50   MINT:$2.50
        Red. 15 1/2". Clear back. Waving
        RMCD. Top text: "Merry Christmas
        to my Pal" (space to write in name).
        (C)1981 McDonald's System,Inc.

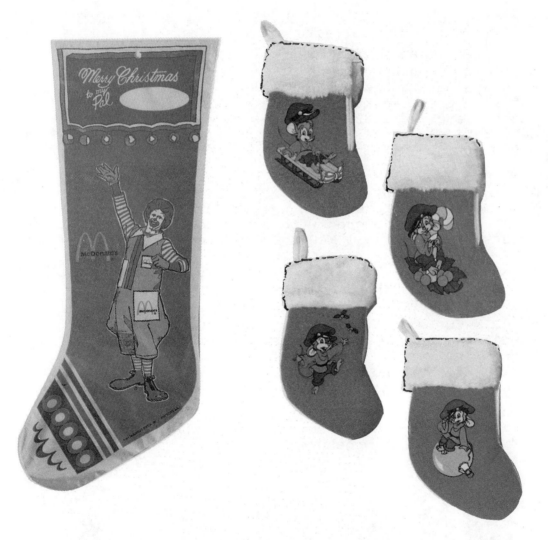

"AN AMERICAN TAIL" movie. 1986. Seven inch long, red
        Christmas stockings with zipper   closing and a white,
        furry band at the top. Appliqued pictures of mouse
        (Fievel).
                1. FIEVEL ON SLED   AVG:$3.50   MIP:$5.50
                2. FIEVEL SEATED ON BALL   AVG:$3.50   MIP:$5.50
                3. FIEVEL DANCING   AVG:$3.50   MIP:$5.50
                4. FIEVEL WITH CANDY-CANE AVG:$3.50   MIP:$5.50

ORNAMENTS, HANGING TYPE:

SATURDAY EVENING POST, 1978   AVG:$8.00 MIP:$15.00
    Design of Christmas carolers:
    two men play violin and trumpet
    while small boy holds book and
    sings. clear plastic. 3.2 inches.
    MCD#4372 AF920-205
    (C) 1978 McDonald's System Inc.

NORMAN ROCKWELL'S TINY TIM, 1979   AVG:$8.50 MIP:$18.00
    Etched glass, in book-like box.

NORMAN ROCKWELL "CHRISTMAS", 1982   AVG:$8.25 MIP:$15.50
    Flat metal, cutout shapes of man
    with axe, boy and dog with newly
    cut Pine tree. Packaged inside
    window-card. (C)1982 McDonald's
    Corporation
    MCD#9470 FC 930-781 (C) CPC 1982

McDONALDLAND FIGURINES, 1991
    Flat metal sculptures with hanging eye. Finished on
    both sides. Each signed with artist's initials: P.F.
    Fine Pewter. (C) 1991 McDonald's Corporation.

    1. RONALD McDONALD   AVG:$10.00 MINT:$18.00
      Reclining figure, head propped
      on right hand, left hand raised.

    2. GRIMACE   AVG:$10.00 MINT:$18.00
      Standing Figure, with boots,
      stocking-hat and neck-scarf.
      Waves right hand.(hands, with
      four fingers each.)

    3. HAMBURGLAR   AVG:$12.00 MINT:$20.00
      Figure (full-length) swings
      from rope. Usual costume

ENESCO TREASURY OF CHRISTMAS ORNAMENTS.
This company makes special christmas ornaments
for McDonald's. They average about three inches
square. Fine details and color.

1. "ONE MILLION HOLIDAY WISHES"   NP:$20.00 MIP:$28.00
1990. Small boy seated on painter's scaffold
eating a 'burger. Other foods are beside him.
The seat hangs from yellow arch trimmed with
Christmas bulbs and a red McDonald's sign.
A can of yellow paint hangs from the seat.

2. "HOLIDAY TREATS"   NP:$17.50 MIP:$20.00
1991. A small boy with crew shirt and cap
behind a red McDonald's counter, writes a
long list for Santa.

3. "McHAPPY HOLIDAYS"   NP:$17.50 MIP:$20.00
1990, 1991. An open BIG MAC box, top trimmed
with a wreath and red stocking. Bottom half
holds a quilt-covered, small boy in a red night
cap, sleeping on a white pillow. He holds a
letter to Santa.

4. "CHRISTMAS KAYAK"   NP:$15.00 MIP:$18.75
1991, 1992. The kayak is a Hot Apple Pie box
and carries a small boy and pkg. of Fries.

5. "T'WAS THE NIGHT BEFORE CHRISTMAS"
1990, 1991, 1992   NP:$15.00 MIP:$20.00
Large red Fry box restaurant. Tan Fries make a
roof. A striped straw is the chimney. From a
window in the side, a brown bear, in a white
crew uniform, holds out a bag of Fries.

6. "HEADING FOR HAPPY HOLIDAYS"
1990, 1991, 1992.   NP:$17.00 MIP:$22.00
Old style McDonald's restaurant with large sign.
Above this, Santa in sleigh with reindeers.

7. "HAPPY MEAL ON WHEELS"   NP:$19.00 MIP:$25.00
1991, 1992, 1993. Happy Meal box on wheels.
Boy in crew cap, holds huge 'burger out from
a side window. Fries protrude from another one.

8. "A QUARTER POUNDER WITH CHEER" NP:$15.00 MIP:$19.50
1991, 1992, 1993. Open Quarter-Pounder box,
trimmed with string of Christmas lights and
wreath. Inside, a crew boy relaxes, reading
newspaper. Sign says: "Christmas Break, Do
Not Disturb."

4. CHRISTMAS KAYAK

5. T'WAS THE NIGHT
   BEFORE CHRISTMAS

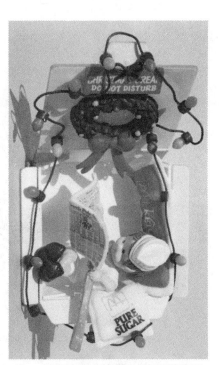

2. HOLIDAY TREATS

8. A QUARTER-POUNDER
   WITH CHEER

ENESCO CHRISTMAS ORNAMENTS

CERAMIC - MUGS

```
ABBREVIATIONS:
MINT = unused condition, no chips or scratches,
       colors bright and even.
AVG =  Average glasses which are faded and in
       poorer condition command lower prices.
```

MUG, white,   3 1/2 inches   AVG:$8.00 MINT:$12.00
     RMCD sitting cross-legged, hands
up by face. On other side is McDonald's
logo in a red square. Underside embossed:
Staffordshire, England / Kilncraft.

MAC TONIGHT,   1988   AVG:$4.00 MINT:$5.00
     Mac with keyboard and microphone.

DELIVERING THE DIFFERENCE   AVG:$12.00 MINT:$15.00
     Dark blue.

The ceramic mugs listed below are offered by GROUP II
COMMUNICATIONS INC. to McDonald's restaurants. They may
be found sometimes at flea markets, thrift shops etc.

SIGNATURE LOGO MUG,   1990   AVG:$3.50   MINT:$ 5.00
    12 oz mug. Decoration: large script
    "McDonald's". Colors: Gold on black
    or cobalt blue, black on grey.

LOGO MUGS,   1990   AVG:$3.50   MINT:$ 5.00
    12 oz mugs like above, but decoration
    is a row of ARCHES logos, around base
    of mug. Colors: Gold on black or
    cobalt blue, black on grey.

RONALD SHOE MUG,   1990   AVG:$3.50   MINT:$4.50
    12 OZ white mug. All-over pattern of
    red clown shoes.

MY MORNING MUG,   1990   AVG:$3.00   MINT:$4.50
    White ironstone mug, 3 3/4 inches
    high. Gold ARCHES with white
    lettering on red rectangle. A
    gold sun with a big smile rises
    at top left. Underneath in gold
    color: "MY MORNING MUG" .

SIGNATURE LOGO TANKARD, 1990   AVG:$4.00   MINT:$5.70
    Like SIGNATURE LOGO mug above,
    but larger: 15oz. Colors: Gold on
    black or cobalt blue, black on grey.

GLASS - GLASSES

MINT =   unused condition, no chips or scratches
         colors bright and even.
AVG =   Average glasses which are faded and in
         poorer condition command lower prices.

McDONALDLAND ACTION SERIES GLASSES, 1977 5 6/8 inches high.
Set of six. McDONALDLAND characters are depicted in a
variety of activities. Base of the glass : Main figure
is in color, the rest of the design is in white line. Black
text below figure: "1977 McDONALDLAND Action Series" and
character name.

RONALD McDONALD leapfrogging Fry Guy into Filet-O-Fish
     lake.

HAMBURGLAR is riding in open railroad car, children are
     driving train engine. Puffs of smoke overhead, in the
     shape of burgers.

GRIMACE bouncing on a pogo-stick, races toward the finish
     line, where children wave a flag

CAPTAIN CROOK. Pulling a plug results in his boat leaking
     and sinking. Children, floating in an inner-tube,
     watch.

BIG MAC. The policeman on roller skates. Blowing his
     whistle, he chases children on a tricycle, pogo-stick
     and scooter. A sign reads "Speed Limit 2 MPH".

MAYOR McCHEESE takes camera pictures of FRY GUYS and
     children. He holds a sign which reads:
     "Say Cheeseburger".

SERIES A:

RONALD McDONALD	AVG:$4.50	MINT:$8.00
HAMBURGLAR	AVG:$5.00	MINT:$9.00
GRIMACE	AVG:$5.00	MINT:$8.00
CAPTAIN CROOK	AVG:$5.00	MINT:$9.00
BIG MAC	AVG:$4.50	MINT:$8.00
MAYOR McCHEESE	AVG:$4.50	MINT:$8.00

McDONALDLAND ACTION SERIES GLASSES, 1977, 6 1/4 inches high.
Set of six. Like the above series but a taller glass. Harder
to find.

SERIES B:

RONALD McDONALD	AVG:$9.00	MINT:$14.00
HAMBURGLAR	AVG:$8.00	MINT:$10.00
GRIMACE	AVG:$10.00	MINT:$15.00
CAPTAIN CROOK	AVG:$8.00	MINT:$10.00
BIG MAC	AVG:$8.00	MINT:$10.00
MAYOR McCHEESE	AVG:$9.00	MINT:$12.00

COLLECTOR SERIES GLASSES. There are at *least* three different versions of this series:

"A" : issued in early 1970's, scarce. 5 1/8 inches high.
      Bright colors. Thick glass.
"B":   issued in mid 1970's, somewhat scarce. 5 5/8 inches
      high. Normal weight glass.
"C" : mid to late 1970's, most common find. 5 6/8 inches
      high. Normal weight glass. Design appears twice around
      the glass.

```
COLLECTOR SERIES  "C", 1977, Indented foot. 5 6/8 inches
Beneath each figure are two rows of black text.
Top row:character's name. Second row: "COLLECTOR SERIES".
```

RONALD McDONALD sits in a cross-legged pose, hands raised
      beside his face: right hand is palm-outward, left hand
      in side view. By left heel:(R), "RONALD MC DONALD (R)".

HAMBURGLAR holds his cape wide open. His face is turned
      toward his left with a broad smile. Yellow cape lining,
      tie, shoes and hat band. By left foot: (R).

GRIMACE stands with flippers open and toes pointing outward.
      Lavendar body, outlined and shaded with darker purple
      dots. Mouth is red, eyes are white with large purple
      dots. "GRIMACE, T.M." By left foot:(R).

CAPTAIN CROOK typical costume and pose. His costume colors
      are mainly black and red: red coat and vest pattern,
      black scarf, hat, boots and dotted trousers."CAPTAIN
      CROOK (R)". By left foot: (R)

BIG MAC, hands spread, quizzical expression. He wears usual
      policeman's uniform: long, blue, belted coat and tiny
      hat perched on his huge head. Black boots. White star
      badge. "BIG MAC TM"" By his left foot (R).

MAYOR McCHEESE in full mayoral attire. Dark blue outlines
      detail and stripes yellow pants. Yellow spats, vest and
      wide hat band. Dark blue sash and hat. Long red coat.
      "MAYOR MC CHEESE (R)". By his left foot: (R).

RONALD McDONALD	AVG:$3.00	MINT:$6.00
HAMBURGLAR	AVG:$3.50	MINT:$6.50
GRIMACE	AVG:$3.00	MINT:$6.00
CAPTAIN CROOK	AVG:$4.00	MINT:$7.50
BIG MAC	AVG:$4.00	MINT:$7.50
BIG MAC	AVG:$4.00	MINT:$7.50
MAYOR McCHEESE	AVG:$4.00	MINT:$7.50

COLLECTOR SERIES

RONALD McDONALD: Varities

GRIMACE: Varities

COLLECTOR SERIES GLASSES "B". 5 6/8 inches.
Differences from the set "C":

RONALD McDONALD. Same, except text is in RED

GRIMACE. Toes point forward. Body is dark blue with black
dots, surface is textured in squares. Mouth and eyes are
white, small dots in eyes. "GRIMACE (R) ". Bottom of glass
shows: Libbey Glass Company mark.

RONALD McDONALD   AVG:$4.50 MINT:$7.50
GRIMACE   AVG:$4.00 MINT:$6.50

COLLECTOR SERIES GLASSES. "A". 5 1/8 inches. Differences
from set "C". Thicker glass, tapers to base. Only one line
of text below characters: their name, followed by (R).

RONALD McDONALD. Same position except that head is tilted
            to right side.Hands are both shown in side view,
               with fingers bent back.

GRIMACE: Dark purple body, toes point forward.

CAPTAIN CROOK: Costume colors are purple and lavendar.

RONALD McDONALD   AVG:$5.50 MINT:$8.00
GRIMACE   AVG:$5.00 MINT:$8.00
CAPTAIN CROOK   AVG:$5.00 MINT:$8.00

COLLECTOR SERIES "D" ?
Another GRIMACE. Dark, rich blue. Shorter glass

GRIMACE   AVG:$9.00 MINT:$12.50

McDONALDLAND ADVENTURE SERIES GLASSES, 1980, 6 1/8 inches.
Set of six. The title of the glass is above the character.
Below, is "McDONALDLAND (R) Adventure Series". On opposite
side: (C) 1980 McDonald's Corporation.

1. "RONALD McDONALD SAVES THE FALLING STAR"
2. "GRIMACE CLIMBS A MOUNTAIN"
3. "HAMBURGLAR HOOKS THE HAMBURGERS"
4. "CAPTAIN CROOK SAILS THE BOUNDING MAIN"
5. "BIG MAC NETS THE HAMBURGLAR"
6. "MAYOR McCHEESE RIDES A RUNAWAY TRAIN"

1. RONALD McDONALD   AVG:$7.00   MINT:$10.50
2. GRIMACE   AVG:$7.00   MINT:$10.50
3. HAMBURGLAR   AVG:$6.00   MINT:$9.00
4. CAPTAIN CROOK   AVG:$6.50   MINT:$10.00
5. BIG MAC   AVG:$6.00   MINT:$9.00
6. MAYOR McCHEESE   AVG:$6.00   MINT:$9.00

PHILADELPHIA EAGLES GLASSES, 1980, 6 inches. Rounded foot.
Set of five. Each glass shows two football players in action
poses. Beside each is his portait inside a football shape.
Black text: "PHILADELPHIA EAGLES", player's signature and
playing position, Arches logo and (C) 1980 McDonald's
CORPORATION"

Randy Logan / Harold Carmichael.   AVG:$6.00   MINT:$9.00
Keith Krepfel / Ron Jaworski   AVG:$6.50   MINT:$9.75
Stan Walters / Tony Franklin   AVG:$6.00   MINT:$9.00
Bill Bergey / John Bunting   AVG:$6.00   MINT:$9.00
Billy Campfield / Wilbert Montgomery AVG:$6.00 MINT:$9.00

MILWAUKEE BREWERS, 1982, 5 5/8 inches. AVG:$3.00 MINT:$5.50

Set of four glasses, each celebrating two members of the
baseball team. Around top is logo: baseball glove & ball
(black & gold), team name and 1982 in blue. Around base band
of ARCHES logo in gold and black. Center: MLBPA (LOGO)
(C)1982 and drawings of baseball players. Photos of two
team members.

1. TED SIMMONS/ROLLIE FINGERS
2. PETE VUCKOVICH/PAUL MOLITOR
3. ROBIN YOUNT/BEN OGILVIE
4. CECIL COOPER/GORMAN THOMAS

McDONALDLAND
ADVENTURE SERIES

SEATTLE SEAHAWKS GLASSES, 1978, 6 inches high. Set of four glasses with indented foot. A pair of blue and green bands circle the base and end with Indian designed eagle heads, facing each other. Above this point is a pyramid of three photos of leading players with their names below them. To the right of this design is a white ARCHES logo. On the left, in white: "SEATTLE SEAHAWKS". Under this is the logo of the NFL, (National Football League Players Association). Under this: "MSA (C)".

1. Carl Ellen,   AVG:$5.00   MINT:$7.00
     Terry Beeson, Autry Beamon.

2. Steve Largent,   AVG:$6.00   MINT:$8.00
     Sherman Smith, David Sims.

3. Jim Zorn,   AVG:$6.00   MINT:$8.00
     Steve Raible, Sam McCullum.

4. Bill Gregory,   AVG:$5.00   MINT:$7.00
     Dennis Boyd, Manu Tuiasosopo.

ATLANTA FALCON GLASSES, 1980,. 5 5/8 inches high. Set of four glasses with indented foot. Around base is a row of white ARCHES logos. Around top, pairs of red and white bands alternate with five red and white stars. A pyramid of three photos of famous players with their names below them. At one side of this design is a picture of a ball-carrier being tackled. Below this: The NFL logo and below this: "MSA (C)". On the other side is a design of a falcon. Below this: "ATLANTA FALCONS". Below this: the DR. PEPPER logo.

1. Jeff Van Note,   AVG:$5.00   MINT:$7.00
     Mike Kenn, William Andrews.

2. Alfred Jackson,   AVG:$7.00   MINT:$9.00
     Al Jenkins, Steve Bartkowski.

3. Joel Williams,   AVG:$6.50   MINT:$8.00
     Buddy Curry, Fulton Kuykendall.

4. Bobby Butler,   AVG:$5.00   MINT:$7.00
     Lynn Cain, R.C.Thielemann.

SEATTLE SEAHAWKS

PHILADELPHIA EAGLES

MILWAUKEE BREWERS

ATLANTA FALCONS

KNOXVILLE WORLD'S FAIR, 1982,   AVG:$6.00   MINT:$9.00

5 1/2 inch, flared. Two different designs around glass.
Below them, a white band with red borders circles glass. On
it in black lettering: "The 1982 World's Fair T.M. / May -
October,1982 / Knoxville, Tennessee / USA " (The "O" in
World is a red globe)

Design 1: White border. Depicts a family in fairground
        setting. Red world (energy symbol) in upper left
        corner.
Design 2: descriptive paragraph, in black, on a white
        background. Title "Energy Turns the World". Below this
        is the paragraph and gold ARCHES logo. Under this in
        red script: "The Coca Cola Company (R) ".

BIG MAC, LANGUAGES GLASS   AVG:$5.50 MINT:$8.50

Six bands of text in three different colors: yellow, red,
black, black yellow, red. And five different languages:
English, German,Italian, Spanish and Greek. On the top band:
the words "BIG MAC" in five different languages, separated
by the ARCHES logo. The other five bands, beginning with the
second from the top (red=English) "Twoallbeefpattiesspecial-
saucelettucecheesepicklesonionsonasesameseedbun".

HOUSTON LIVESTOCK SHOW AND RODEO, 1983. 4 3/4 inches. Heavy.
Set of four glasses. Text: HOUSTON, and logo, COKE logo,
title of glass set, twice around glass, McDonald's logo and
"McDONALD'S (R) COLLECTOR SERIES 1983, SECOND IN A SERIES OF
FOUR, (C)1983 McDONALD CORPORATION." Two different designs on
each glass celebrate types of competitions.

1. SADDLE/BAREBACK BRONC RIDING   AVG:$3.00 MINT:$4.50

2. WOMEN'S BARREL RACING/   AVG:$3.00 MINT:$4.50
   CHUCKWAGON RACES

3. CALF SCRAMBLE/CUTTING HORSE   AVG:$3.00 MINT:$4.50

4. BULL RIDING/STEER WRESTLING   AVG:$3.00 MINT:$4.50

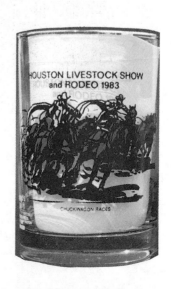

BIG MAC LANGUAGES

MUPPET CHARACTERS GLASSES, 1982, 5 6/8 inches. Set of four,
Around base: ARCHES logo and (C) Henson Associates Inc.1981.

HAPPINESS HOTEL. "The Great Muppet Caper" presents a scene
     of the famous MUPPET characters in a bus.

THE GREAT GONZO. "The Great Muppet Caper" tm. Kermit and
     Fozzie ride in the basket of a hot-air balloon. Gonzo
     hangs by his feet, while photo-graphing a passing bird.
     A banner reads: "Kermit the Frog, Fozzie bear."

THE GREAT MUPPET CAPER. Kermit, Fozzie and other Muppet
     characters riding bikes.

MISS PIGGY. "The Great Muppet Caper" Miss Piggy rides a
     motorcycle through a stained glass window while other
     Muppet characters watch.

HAPPINESS HOTEL.   AVG:$4.00   MINT:$6.00
THE GREAT GONZO.   AVG:$4.50   MINT:$6.50
THE GREAT MUPPET CAPER   AVG:$4.00   MINT:$6.00
MISS PIGGY.   AVG:$4.00   MINT:$6.00

CAMP SNOOPY GLASSES, 1983, Six inches high, Five glasses
    with rounded bottoms. Colorful, active scenes involving
    all the Charlie Brown / Snoopy characters. Each glass
    has a talk-bubble above the main character, which may
    be used as the "title" of the glass. Other identifying
    marks on the glasses: "(C) 1950, 1952, 1958, 1965
    United Feature Syndicate, Inc." / "Camp Snoopy
    Collection" and a golden ARCHES logo.

"RATS! WHY IS HAVING FUN SO MUCH WORK?"
    Charlie Brown struggling to paddle inflated yellow
    boat. Linus and friend pole a raft, Lucy and friend in
    motor-boat. Snoopy snags Charlie's boat with his
    fishing hook.

"THERE'S NO EXCUSE FOR NOT BEING PROPERLY PREPARED".
    Lucy has surrounded herself with the comforts of home,
    chair & table, flowers in vase, radio, while others
    are "roughing it". Kids in sleeping bags, bird in
    tree-tent, Snoopy on tent roof.

"MORNING PEOPLE ARE HARD TO LOVE".
    Snoopy, cosy in his sleeping bag looks up at a bird in
    a tree, blowing trumpet :"BLATT". More birds jump out
    of their tree-tents. Other kids still in sleeping bags.

"THE STRUGGLE FOR SECURITY IS NO PICNIC!"
    Linus yanks his blanket off table, upsetting the food
    set on it.

"CIVILIZATION IS OVERRATED".
    Snoopy frolics on the grass while kids enjoy nature,
    picking flowers and looking at map.

"RATS! WHY.... WORK?"   AVG:$4.00 MINT:$6.00
"THERE'S.PROPERLY PREPARED"   AVG:$4.00 MINT:$6.00
"MORNING PEOPLE...... LOVE"   AVG:$4.00 MINT:$6.00
"THE STRUGGLE..... PICNIC"   AVG:$3.50 MINT:$5.50
"CIVILIZATION IS OVERRATED"   AVG:$3.50 MINT:$5.50

CAMP SNOOPY

THE NUTCRACKER

THE NUTCRACKER.1990. A very attractive set of four glasses
     issued for the Christmas season. At the top and bottom
     edges of glass are white bands bordered with red,
     decorated with green holly leaves and   red berries.
     On one side of the glass is a scene from the *Nutcracker*
     with a quotation from the story in black lettering. On
     the other side is the ARCHES logo inside a red-edged,
     white oval.
     Beneath this:(C) 1990 McDonald's Corporation.

1."Marie   AVG:$9.50 MINT:$12.00

     cried out with delight `A Nutcracker Godfather, he
     is so beautiful!'." Two children: a boy ,in blue,
     with hobby-horse and horn,and Marie, in red,holding
     the Nutcracker.An old man in blue coat with top hat
     and cane. In background: same room with a window.

2. "The Nutcracker   AVG:$9.50 MINT:$12.00

     led the toys to battle against the Army of Mice ".
     Toys and mice, armed with swords, battle. In the
     background is a room with a decorated Christmas
     Tree and Marie (small girl) in a red dress.

3. " The Sugar Plum Fairy   AVG:$8.00 MINT:$11.00

     lives here in the Land of Sweets", said the
     Nutcracker. In the background, is a castle with
     green lawns and candy canes. The fairy, in blue,
     with a red crown and white wings, waves her wand
     in greeting. On a blue river, Marie and the
     Nutcracker, float in a swan-boat.

4. "Marie and the Prince   AVG:$8.00 MINT:$11.00

     glided across the floor in Toyland". Wearing red
     clothing, Marie and the Prince (who was the
     Nutcracker), dance. In the foreground are fairies
     and flowers.

MAC TONIGHT, 1988. Set of four glasses and a storage jar.
      Design: Quarter Moon over a black cityscape.

STORAGE JAR with blue lid.   AVG:$7.00   MINT:$10.00
      Bottom:INDIANA GLASS COMPANY. #4169.

SUPER SIZE glass, 32 oz,   AVG:$6.00   MINT:$9.00
      Tapers to curved foot. 7 inches.

LARGE, 6 3/8 inches, glass   AVG:$5.00   MINT:$8.00
      Underside : DS0100GC (C) 1988
      McDonald's Corporation.

GLASS, 8 oz, 5 1/4 inches   AVG:$6.00   MINT:$9.00

JUICE GLASS, 4 1/8 inches   AVG:$3.00   MINT:$4.75

DAISIES GLASS, 3 1/2 inches   AVG:$3.00   MINT:$5.00

Wide-mouthed glass. Around center of the glass is a band of
yellow and white daisies with red centers. Below this is a
band of linked yellow arches broken only by the ARCHES logo.

JUICE GLASS, 3 5/8 inches   AVG:$3.50   MINT:$5.50

Narrow glass with frosted band around center broken once by
ARCHES logo (clear).

THE DENIM COLLECTION, 6 1/2 inches   AVG:$9.00 MINT:$12.50

Blue and white textured to look like the back of a pair of
denim pants, with two large pockets. Along the upper edge
are brown areas suggesting a tooled leather belt, passed
through belt-loops. Detail and lettering in black: "Enjoy /
Trademark (R) / Coca Cola " logo in white. A red and white
patterned bandana drapes from one "pocket". Under this "The
Denim Collection from McDonald's (R)" The other "pocket" is
printed with red and white daisies.

McDonald's HAWAII. Set of four smoked glasses, 4 inches high
     and 4 inches wide, with heavy bases. Circling glass at
     center is a white-frosted design. At a break in the
     band is the McDonald's logo crossed by "McDonald's
     Hawaii / T.M." / and the design of an outrigger canoe
     with sail unfurled. This set could be purchased in
     Hawaii in a gift box.

1.RACING.   AVG:$10.50 MINT:$12.00

     Five men in each of two long canoes paddle through
     surging waves. Background: sun and island mountains.

2.SURFERS.   AVG:$9.00   MINT:$11.00

     Three men on surf boards, high, rolling waves,
     Sun in background.

3.FISHERMEN.   AVG:$9.00   MINT:$11.00

     Three men. One is close-up, with net over his
     shoulder. Second man gathers in fishing net. Third man
     casts net into foreground, water swirls around his
     legs. Background: two birds, sun and islands.

4.NIGHTFALL.   AVG:$10.50 MINT:$12.00

     Three people on island with coconut palm trees, beckon
     to a group of men in an out-rigger canoe with two
     sails. A long canoe, carrying five men, paddles
     toward them.
     Background: setting sun, island, bird and stars.

DISNEY SERIES. 1989, 5 5/8 inches. Set of four glasses,
Two different designs on glass.
    Design 1: colorful Disneyland scene featuring a popular
Disney character. On each side of main picture is silhouette
of Disneyland buildings.
    Design 2: Descriptive paragraph featuring subject with
a large title above. Below this is ARCHES logo in a red
square. At bottom edge of design: "(C) 1989 McDonald's Corp.
/ (C) 1989 The Walt Disney Company

TOMORROWLAND   AVG:$9.00 MINT:$14.00

    Shows Mickey Mouse in a Rocket Car. Below design:
    "Disneyland" in yellow. Paragraph title: red.

ADVENTURELAND   AVG:$8.00 MINT:$13.00

    Pictures Goofy in Safari hat and shirt. Jungle
    background. Under design "Disneyland" in red-orange.
    Paragraph title is in green.

FANTASYLAND   AVG:$8.00 MINT:$13.00

    Scene: Minnie Mouse riding in a tea-cup. Under design:
    "Disneyland" in blue. Paragraph title: yellow.

CRITTER COUNTRY   AVG:$9.00 MINT:$14.00

    Donald Duck rides log-car down water-way cut into a
    green hill. Under design: "Disneyland" in green.
    Paragraph title: blue.

GLASS - MUGS

OLYMPIC MUGS. 1984, 3 1/2 inches high. Set of four glass
     mugs with handles.
Design one side: five stars in blue,white and red.
Under this:
     (C) 1980 L.A.Olympic Committee TM.
     Five linked blue rings.
     ARCHES logo in gold.
     "Games Of The XXIIIrd Olympiad, Los Angeles 1984 ".
Design on the other side: square, broken into four smaller
     squares with a specific sport depicted in each. The
     design and the accompanying text are a different color
     on each glass.
Text beside design:"(C) 1981 L.A Olympic Committee".
     Below design: "1984 OLYMPICS".

1. RED   AVG:$8.75 MINT:$12.00
     Fencing, Cycling, Ice Skating,
     Equestrian sports.
2. WHITE   AVG:$8.75 MINT:$12.00
     Basketball, Soccer, Baseball,
     Volleyball.
3. BLUE   AVG:$8.75 MINT:$12.00
     Swimming, Kayaking, Sculling,
     Sailing.
4. YELLOW   AVG:$8.75 MINT:$12.00
     WeightLifting, Running,
     Wrestling,Archery.

GARFIELD MUGS. 1987. Set of four , 3 1/2 inch high mugs.
     At lower edge, right of the design, is: "JIM DAVIS"
     (artist / creator of Garfield), the ARCHES logo, and
     (C) 1978 United Feature Syndicate Inc.

1. " I'M EASY TO GET ALONG WITH WHEN THINGS GO MY WAY".
     Garfield paddles a red canoe while Odie, at the other
     end, paddles in the opposite direction.

2. "USE YOUR FRIENDS WISELY ". Garfield rides on a
     skateboard pulled by a panting Odie.

3. " I'M NOT ONE WHO RISES TO THE OCCASION".
     At one end of a See-Saw, Garfield sits, at ground
     level. At the other end, also at ground level, are
     Odie, a cat, a kitten and a teddy bear. This glass
     bears a different inscription: "Garfield characters
     (C) 1978, 1979, 1980 United   Feature Syndicate Inc."

4. " IT'S NOT A PRETTY LIFE BUT SOMEBODY HAS TO LIVE IT".
     Garfield relaxes in a hammock. One end is tied to a
     tree, the other end is held in Odie's mouth while he
     holds a cold drink and fans Garfield.

1.	"I'M EASY..."	AVG:$4.00	MINT:$6.0
2.	"USE YOUR FRIENDS..."	AVG:$4.50	MINT:$6.50
3.	"I'M NOT ONE..."	AVG:$4.50	MINT:$6.50
4.	"IT'S NOT A PRETTY..."	AVG:$4.00	MINT:$6.00

GARFIELD MUG. 3 1/2 inches.   AVG:$3.00 MINT:$6.00
CHECKERBOARD SERIES. "Talk balloons" and a background of squares
in four different colors. Each cup has two different designs.
White ARCHES logo. Marks: JIM DAVIS, Garfield Characters (C) 1978
United Feature Syndicate, Inc.
1. Yellow squares. "The Early Cat Gets The Hot Cake".
2. Blue squares. "I'd Like Mornings If They Started Later"
3. "I've Never Met a Dinner I didn't Like."
4. "I've Never Seen a Sunrise..."

MY MORNING MUG, 3 3/4 inches   AVG:$5.00   MINT:$7.50

White ceramic mug. Gold ARCHES with white lettering on a red
rectangle. A gold sun with a big smile rises at the top left
corner. Underneath, gold color: "MY MORNING MUG".
Available to McDonald's employes.

GOOD MORNING MUG, Milk glass,   AVG:$1.50   MINT:$2.50

3 1/2 inches high with indented foot. Golden ARCHES with
black lettering. On left arch, a smiling, solid orange sun
with a talk balloon: "Good Morning".

MUG, white, 5 1/2 inches   AVG:$8.00   MINT:$15.00

Goblet-like, with stem and foot. white milk glass. Cup area
3 inches diameter. Small McDonald's logo: gold arches, black
text above diagonal band of 3 stripes; colors: yellow,orange
and dk. red. Orange sun rises from right side of ARCHES.

MUG, white, 5 1/2 inches   AVG:$6.00   MINT:$8.50

Goblet-like, with stem and foot. white milk glass. Cup area
= 3 3/8 inches diameter. Large McDonald's logo: gold arches,
black text.

McDONALDLAND ACTION SERIES. Smoked-glass mugs, 4 1/2 inches
   high. Embossed designs which appear twice around the
   mug, show the McDONALDLAND characters in action. Their
   names appear beneath their feet with (R) or "T.M".
   Another (R) close to the figure.
   ARCHES logo on bottom of mug.

RONALD McDONALD   AVG:$6.00   MINT:$9.00
   Throws a football with right arm. Background shows
   goal-posts and stadium wall with flags. "RONALD
   McDONALD (R)".

GRIMACE   AVG:$7.00   MINT:$10.00
   Throws basketball into basket. His position suggests
   that he is airborne. His body is textured with small
   raised dots."GRIMACE T.M."

CAPTAIN CROOK   AVG:$8.000   MINT:$12.00
   Bats a baseball with his sword. Behind him is mesh
   backstop. "CAPTAIN CROOK (R)".

HAMBURGLAR   AVG:$8.00   MINT:$12.00
   With hockey stick and puck. Behind him is goal net.
   (not wearing ice skates).

BIG MAC   AVG:$7.00   MINT:$9.00
MAYOR MC CHEESE   AVG:$7.00   MINT:$9.00

PLASTIC - CUPS

```
MINT =  Bright colors, smooth and even. no chips
        or scratches.
AVG  =  Average, used, slight wear,good color,
        no chips.
```

1. YELLOW PLASTIC CUP,   1970,   AVG:$4.00 MINT:$6.50
5 1/4 inches.
     Standing figure of Ronald McDONALD, arms bent, hands
     held chest high. Large red zipper down front of suit.
     His name is above him in decorative script. Design
     colors: red, blue and tan. Underside of cup:MUTUAL
PLASTICS, LA MIRADA, CALIFORNIA. CD-16-1

2. YELLOW PLASTIC CUP,   1970   AVG:$4.50 MINT:$7.00
5 1/4 inches, indented foot.
     Standing Ronald McDONALD figure, his name above him in
     decorative script. Bottom reads: AMOCO Packaging
Products HD16 5.

3. YELLOW PLASTIC CUP,   1970 5 inches, foot indented 3/8
        inches. Each character's name is placed beside his
foot, in small, black capital letters, with (R). Other side
of cup is ARCHES logo. Beneath it, in large, cursive is:
character's name(R). Underside of cup has same logo, and a
tipi-shaped outline with the word: " Inc".

CAPTAIN CROOK   AVG:$4.00 MINT:$6.00
Standing, left hand on hip,Shoulder-length hair and a long
     mustache. Underside: "Inc / 15"(in Tipi).

RONALD McDONALD   AVG:$4.00 MINT:$6.00
Standing, hands out from sides. Face more realistically
     drawn than most designs. Underside" "Inc"(in Tipi).

4. YELLOW PLASTIC CUP,   1971   AVG:$4.50 MINT:$6.50
5 1/2 inches. indented foot.
     McDONALDLAND characters stiffly posed around cup, in
     primitive type, "stick drawing". Names in blue
     printing: GOBLIN, APPLE PIE TREE, HAMBURGLAR, CAPTAIN
     CROOK, RONALD McDONALD and Mayor McCHEESE.
     Underside reads: AMOCO Packaging Products, HD16 8.

4

3

6

1

5

5. YELLOW PLASTIC HAPPY CUPS, 1977, 4 3/4 inches, indented foot.
Like glass series, McDONALDLAND characters are depicted in a
variety of activities. Colors: red, blue, white and black.
Main figure is in color, the rest of the design is simple
line. Black text below figure: character's name. Reads:
"(C) McDONALDLAND HAPPY CUPS".

RONALD McDONALD   AVG: $4.50   MINT: $8.00
    Leap frogging Fry Guy into
    Filet-O-Fish lake.
HAMBURGLAR   AVG: $5.00   MINT: $9.00
    Rides in open railroad car,
    children drive train engine.
    Puffs of smoke overhead, in the
    shape of hamburgers.
GRIMACE   AVG: $5.00   MINT: $8.00
    Bouncing on a pogo-stick, races
    toward the finish line, where
    children wave a flag.
CAPTAIN CROOK.   AVG: $5.00   MINT: $9.00
    Pulling a plug results in his boat
    leaking and sinking. Children,
    floating in an inner-tube, watch.
BIG MAC.   AVG: $4.50   MINT: $8.00
    Policeman on roller skates, blowing
    his whistle. He chases children on
    a tricycle, pogo-stick and scooter.
    A sign reads: "Speed Limit 2 MPH".
MAYOR McCHEESE   AVG: $4.50   MINT: $8.00
    Takes photographs of FRY GUYS and
    children. He holds a sign which
    reads: "Say Cheeseburger".

6. YELLOW PLASTIC CUP.   1978
   3.7 inch flare with indented foot.
   Background is black line design of APPLE PIE TREES,
   mountains and fence. Figure is in color, name below
   feet.   (C) McDonald's SYSTEM INC. 1978

   1. GRIMACE   AVG: $3.00   MINT: $6.50
       Playing "Tug-of-War" with a pink elephant.   .
   2. RONALD McDONALD   AVG: $4.00   MINT: $5.50
       Jumping a rope held by two apes.
   3. RONALD McDONALD   AVG: $3.00   MINT: $4.75
       Jumping. Right hand in front, left hand back.
   4. CAPTAIN CROOK   AVG: $3.00   MINT: $6.50
       Sitting in boat near a white seal.
       He bounces a ball on tip of sword.

1. CAMP SNOOPY, WHITE PLASTIC 5 1/8 inches. Set of five cups, with indented foot. Like the glass series. Colorful, active scenes involving all the Charlie Brown - Snoopy characters. Each cup has a talk-bubble above the main character, which may be used as the "title" of the cup. Other identifying marks on the cups: (C) 1950, 1952, 1958, 1960, 1966, 1971 United Feature Syndicate, Inc., Camp Snoopy Collection" and a golden ARCHES logo. Underside: SWEETHEART (mfg. co.)

"RATS! WHY IS HAVING FUN SO MUCH WORK?"
    Charlie Brown struggling to paddle inflated yellow boat. Linus and friend pole a raft, Lucy and friend in motor-boat. Snoopy snags Charlie's boat with his fishing hook.

"THERE'S NO EXCUSE FOR NOT BEING PROPERLY PREPARED".
    Lucy has surrounded herself with the comforts of home, chair and table, flowers in vase, radio, while others are "roughing it". Kids in sleeping bags, bird in tree-tent, Snoopy on tent roof.

"MORNING PEOPLE ARE HARD TO LOVE".
    Snoopy, cosy in his sleeping bag looks up at bird in tree, blowing trumpet: "BLATT". More birds jump out of their tree-tents. Other kids still in sleeping bags.

"THE STRUGGLE FOR SECURITY IS NO PICNIC!"
    Linus yanks his blanket off table, upsetting the food set on it.

"CIVILIZATION IS OVERRATED".
    Snoopy frolics on the grass while kids enjoy nature, picking flowers and looking at map.

"RATS!...SO MUCH WORK?"	AVG:$4.00	MINT:$6.00
"THERE'S...PREPARED"	AVG:$4.00	MINT:$6.00
"MORNING PEOPLE... LOVE"	AVG:$4.00	MINT:$6.00
"THE STRUGGLE...PICNIC!"	AVG:$3.50	MINT:$5.50
"CIVILIZATION...OVERRATED"	AVG:$3.50	MINT:$5.50

1. CAMP SNOOPY

3. DUKES OF HAZZARD

2. VALENTINE CUP, WHITE PLASTIC, 1981   AVG:$2.50 MINT:$3.75

Floating hearts. Above GRIMACE, one reads:"BE MY VALENTINE". The heart over HAMBURGLAR reads: "I LOVE YOU". RONALD McDonald's head and right hand are inside a blue heart. Above this heart, in script: "RONALD McDONALD", and beneath: "VALENTINE CUP".
Reads: (C) 1981 McDonald's CORPORATION, MADE IN US

3. HAPPY CUPS, WHITE PLASTIC, 1982, 16 OZ. Set of six cups. TV THEME: "DUKES OF HAZARD". 4.8 inches high. The design shows the head and shoulders of character with name in black text. Above head is "THE DUKES OF HAZZARD" ; below design: "TM & (C) Warner Bros Inc 1982". Alternates twice around cup with golden ARCHES logo,and "McDonald's (R)" in black. Colors used: blue, red, yellow and black.

1.LUKE   AVG:$4.00 MINT:$7.50
    Smiling young man, blue and
    black plaid shirt.
2.BOSS HOGG   AVG:$4.00 MINT:$7.00
    Middle-aged man in white bow-tie,
    shirt,jacket and cowboy hat.
3.SHERIFF ROSCOE   AVG:$4.00 MINT:$7.00
    Man in black cowboy hat and tie,
    blue shirt. Beagle dog.
4.DAISY   AVG:$5.00 MINT:$8.00
    Girl with long brown hair and
    red dress.
5.UNCLE JESSE   AVG:$4.00 MINT:$7.00
    Elderly man with white hair,
    beard and mustache. Blue shirt.
6.BO DUKE   AVG:$4.00 MINT:$7.50
    Blonde young man in white jacket
    over blue shirt.

4. HAPPY BIRTHDAY, WHITE PLASTIC, 1982 AVG:$2.50 MINT:$4.00
5 1/8 inches.
    "HAPPY BIRTHDAY CUP" in white and yellow, outlined in
    red, diagonally slanted. Design begins 7/8 inches from
    bottom of cup. It includes RMCD holding a birthday
    cake, Grimace, Hamburglar and Fry Guys with balloons.

5. RONALD McDONALD HOUSE,   1983   AVG:$2.50   MINT:$3.75
   WHITE PLASTIC, 5 1/8 inches.
        Street of decorative houses and trees. Behind them are
        the figures (from chest-up) of GRIMACE, RMCD and
        HAMBURGLAR. Print on side: (C) 1983 McDonald's Corp.
        TRADEMARKS REG. US PATENT OFFICE PRINTED IN U.S.A.
        Around top in yellow block letters is "RONALD McDONALD
        HOUSE ". Red heart behind the word "HOUSE ".

6. McDonald's FUN CUP,   1983   AVG:$3.00   MINT:$5.50
   WHITE PLASTIC, 5 1/8 inches.
        RMCD,GRIMACE,BIRDIE and FRY GUY on Roller-Coaster. A
        FRY GUY with HAMBURGLAR on Ferris Wheel. Large letters
        around top: "McDonald's FUN CUP". Side reads: (C) 1983
        McDonald's CORP. TRADEMARKS REG. U.S. PATENT OFFICE
        PRINTED IN U.S.A

7. HALLOWEEN CUP.   1983   AVG:$2.00   MINT:$4.00
   WHITE PLASTIC, 5 1/8 inches.
        McDonaldland gang carrying pumpkin pails. Background:
        trees and starry sky with large yellow text "Halloween
        Cup". Legend (vertically beside design): (C)1983
        McDONALD'S CORP. TRADEMARKS REG. U.S.PATENT OFFICE
        PRINTED IN U.S.A.

8. HAPPY BIRTHDAY EXPRESS CUP, 1983   AVG:$2.75   MINT:$3.50
   WHITE PLASTIC, 5 1/8 inches.
        RMCD drives train engine labeled: "HAPPY BIRTHDAY
        EXPRESS". Other open train cars, carry familiar
        McDONALDLAND characters and animals. Overhead,in large
        yellow, smoke- like letters: "HAPPY BIRTHDAY 1". Next
        to this on a small flag are words: "TO YOU ". On side:
        (C) 1983 McDonald's CORP. TRADEMARKS REG. US PATENT
        OFFICE PRINTED IN U.S.A. Underside reads: 26 F16
        SWEETHEART.

9. OLYMPICS, WHITE PLASTIC, 1984   AVG:$3.75   MINT:$5.50
   4.8 inches.
        All white except for 2 1/2" X 3". Design:5 stars, red,
        white and blue. Under this: five black, linked rings,
        all in a white square. Red rectangle with a yellow
        border and yellow ARCHES logo.

11

13

14

7

5   2   6

4   10   8   12

9

10. HAPPY BIRTHDAY TO YOU,   1985   AVG:$2.00   MINT:$3.75
    WHITE PLASTIC, 5 1/4 inches.
            Outer space theme. Pink background, rocket ships and
            space creatures with COSMc! and McDONALDLAND
            characters. RONALD, HAMBURGLAR and GRIMACE ride in
            rocket ships. A Space creature lights birthday candles
            with a ray. (C) 1985 McDonald's CORP. TRADEMARKS REG.
            US PATENT OFFICE PRINTED IN U.S.A. Underside reads :
            SWEETHEART   F16 1.

11. WHITE PLASTIC CUP,   1985,   AVG:$2.00   MINT:$3.00
    3.7 inches height, includes a one-inch indented foot.
            Design of RMCD head, with ARCHES logo is repeated three
            times around cup. (C) 1985 McDonald's CORP.

12. HAPPY BIRTHDAY CUP,   1986   AVG:$2.50   MINT:$3.75
    WHITE PLASTIC, 5 1/8 inches.
            Parading over green landscape are Dinosaurs and
            McDONALDLAND characters. RMCD pulls a wagon carrying
            birthday cake with lighted candles, "M" on the side.
            Bursting from a volcano in background are yellow
            letters on a pink cloud: "HAPPY BIRTHDAY". On a green
            kite: "TO YOU". On side: (C) 1986 McDONALD'S
            CORPORATION. MADE IN U.S.A. / PRINTED IN THE UNITED
            STATES OF AMERICA. Underside of cup : SWEETHEART F16 28

13. WHITE PLASTIC LOGO CUP, 1986, 20 oz.
    Two different manufacturers of same design cup. Logos of
            ARCHES, SPRITE and DIET COKE. Small golden arches run
            in diagonal stripes. McDONALD"S logo in a large red
            square. In red: (C) 1986 McDONALD"S CORP.

    1. Cups Illustrated,Lancaster, TX.   AVG:$2.00   MINT:$3.25
    2. TRI-PLAS INC. CA, NC   AVG:$2.00   MINT:$3.25

14. MAC TONIGHT,   1986   AVG:$2.50   MINT:$3.75
    Black cityscape on blue sky. On red squares:
            ARCHES and COCA COLA logos.
            Made by- Cups Illustrated, Lancaster, TX.

15. INDIANAPOLIS 500 WINNERS, 1986,   AVG:$3.50   MINT:$5.50
    WHITE PLASTIC. 20 oz.
         ARCHES logo and COCA COLA logos in red squares. On one
         side of cup, black text and crossed flag logos. Lists
         years and names of "Indianapolis 500 Winners". Other
         side design: two line drawings of race cars and white
         text on gold rectangle. Text: "Indianapolis 1911 / 75th
         Anniversary / 1986 500-Mile Race."

16. NATIONAL FOOTBALL LEAGUE CUP, 1986, clear plastic.
    Set of four cups. 5 1/4 inches.
         Two famous players of each decade are pictured with a
         brief history of their accomplishments. Between them is
         a design of the Golden Gate Bridge, with the number
         "40" in red. Below this is a scroll reading: " 1946 SF
         1986 ". In an arc above, are the words:"SAN FRANCISCO
         FORTY NINERS". Over this is the year and under it, in
         large red block-letters: "49ers", (year) DECADE. In
         white, around the base is: "(C) MSA 1986", the ARCHES
         logo, NFL, and the National Football League logos.

    1. 49ERS FOURTH DECADE 1980.   AVG:$7.00   MINT:$11.00
       Honors:
    2. 49ERS THIRD DECADE 1970.   AVG:$7.00   MINT:$11.00
       Honors: John Brodie #12 and
       Dave Wilcox #64.
    3. 49ERS SECOND DECADE 1960.   AVG:$7.50   MINT:$11.50
       Honors: Hugh McElhenny #39 and
       Leo Nomellini #73.
    4. 49ERS FIRST DECADE 1950.   AVG:$8.00   MINT:$12.00
       Honors Hardy Brown #33 and
       Joe Perry #34.

17. SAN DIEGO SUPER CUP, 1987   AVG:$2.50   MINT:$3.75
    WHITE PLASTIC. 20 OZ.
         Design at top: "SAN DIEGO / SUPER".
         Scene: Palm tree, blue water with jumping Orca (whale),
         golden Arches against the sky, "CUP" on beach. At right
         side are logos of ARCHES and COCA-COLA, in red squares.
         This design appears twice around the cup. In black, at
         base: "(C) 1987 McDonald's Corporation / Made by
         Louisiana Plastics, Inc.St. Louis, MO.

31   15   18

16

21

19

18. CUP, ASU, 1987,   AVG:$1.50   MINT:$2.75
     WHITE PLASTIC. 20 oz.
          (C) 1987 McDonald's Corporation. Purple and gold bands
          around top and base. ARCHES logo, twice, in base band.
          COCA COLA logo in red square. Logo: "Officially
          Licensed Collegiate Products." Design of devil with
          trident, leaning right elbow on text: "ASU", appears
          twice around cup.

19. IDAHO, THE GREAT GETAWAY   AVG:$2.00   MINT:$3.50
     WHITE PLASTIC. 20 oz.
          Colorful 7 inch cup. Panorama around cup with popular
          features of the state set in frames on background of
          green hills and blue striped sky. "IDAHO...GETAWAY"
          text with silouette of state, appears twice above
          design. At base are logos of McDonald's, Coca-Cola,
          Diet Coke, and Sprite . Legend(C)1987 McDonald's Corp.

20. MINNESOTA TWINS CUP, 1987   AVG:$2.50 MINT:$3.75
     WORLD CHAMPIONSHIP CUP.

21. "HONEY I SHRUNK THE KIDS.", 1988, Movie theme.
     WHITE PLASTIC. Set of three, 20 oz cups.
          Made by Louisiana Plastics Inc. St. Louis, MO.
          Logos of COKE and ARCHES (in red squares.)
          In black: (C) 1988 McDONALD"S Corporation, (C) Buena
     Vista Pictures Distribution Inc.

     1. Tiny kids, on table top with pepper shaker. Large dog.

     2. Tiny kids. Large boy with magnifying glass, looks on as
        one "kid" rides an ant through high grasses.

     3. Two tiny kids, ride a large bee while two others watch
        from a flower large enough to stand on.

     1. TABLE AND DOG   AVG:$1.75   MINT:$2.95
     2. MAGNIFYING GLASS   AVG:$2.00   MINT:$3.25
     3. HONEYBEE RIDE   AVG:$1.74   MINT:$2.95

22. WHITE PLASTIC CUP, 1988   AVG:$1.75 MINT:$2.25
    4 1/4 inches high.
        Wide blue band. Night sky, white clouds ,yellow stars.
        RMCD sits on large star, wearing nightcap. His name is
        on star. Two Fry Guys on clouds. Birdie flys through
        sky. Grimace, in nightcap rides the quarter moon. Small
        black print, bottom edge: (C) 1988 McDonald's
        Corporation. Underside: Louisiana Plastics Inc.
        St.Louis, MO. 12DC 12.

23. OLYMPIC SPORTS CUPS, 1988, 20 OZ. WHITE PLASTIC. 6 3/4 INCH.
    Set of 12.
        Around the bottom is a row of small golden ARCHES.
    Made by Louisiana Plastics Inc. St. Louis,MO. On one side of
    the cup is the McDONALD"S logo in a red square, "USA" and
    five blue rings.
        Above this, in an arc:" 1988 U.S. Olympic Team".
        Each cup names a specific sport, with an informational
    paragraph below. Under this: DIET COKE logo/ (C) 1988
    McDONALD"S Corporation 36-USC-380.
        The other side of the cup pictures athletes performing
    their sport.

    1.   Swimming   AVG:$2.50 MINT:$3.50
    2.   Diving   AVG:$2.50 MINT:$3.50
    3.   Basketball   AVG:$2.50 MINT:$3.50
    4.   Boxing   AVG:$2.75 MINT:$3.75
    5.   Cycling   AVG:$2.75 MINT:$3.75
    6.   Soccer   AVG:$2.50 MINT:$3.50
    7.   Track $ Field, Running   AVG:$2.50 MINT:$3.50
    8.   Track & Field, Hurdles   AVG:$2.75 MINT:$3.75
    9.   Track & Field,High Jump   AVG:$2.50 MINT:$3.50
    10. Gymnastics, Floor Exercises   AVG:$2.50 MINT:$3.50
    11. Gymnastics, Balance Beam   AVG:$2.50 MINT:$3.50
    12. Gymnastics, Rings   AVG:$2.50 MINT:$3.50

24. FOOTBALL CUP, 5.3 inches. Clear plastic, flare type with
        ridged foot. On one side: logos of ARCHES and COKE in
        red squares. Other side: design of football helmet with
        name of team.

    1. Los Angeles RAIDERS   AVG:$1.50 MINT:$2.00
    2. San Diego CHARGERS   AVG:$1.50 MINT:$2.00
    3. San Francisco 49ERS   AVG:$2.00 MINT:$2.50

23

33

24

26

25

25. BALL SPORTS CUP, 1989, 20 oz. Set of four,
WHITE PLASTIC CUPS. 5 1/2 inches
       Ball Sports champions of San Francisco and Oakland,
       California. Designs are in diagonal stripes and each
       cup depicts a different ball sport champion team.

  1. Baseball, Oakland A Athletics. 1989 World Series
     Champions.

  2. Basketball, Golden State Warriors, NBA,
     National Basketball Association.

  3. Baseball, Giants, National League Champions.

  4. Football, San Francisco, Super Bowl Champions.

1. BASEBALL	AVG:$1.75	MINT:$2.75
2. BASKETBALL	AVG:$1.75	MINT:$2.75
3. BASEBALL	AVG:$2.00	MINT:$3.00
4. FOOTBALL	AVG:$1.75	MINT:$2.75

26. CUP, DICK TRACY CUP, 1990, Movie Theme. Set of three.
WHITE PLASTIC. 20 oz.
"Dick Tracy" Characters and Artwork (C) Disney
(C) 1990 McDonald's Corporation. ARCHES logo and COCA
COLA logos in red squares inside a larger white square.
Top of cups read: "DICK TRACY".

  1. DICK TRACY. Framed in a red circle, Dick Tracy talks into
     a wrist radio. Street scene with police station. His
     name is under the circle.

  2. THE KID. The Kid's head in a circle. He wears a red-
     checked cap. Background: cityscape and part of word-
     "HOTEL".

  3. FLATTOP. Flattop's head in circle. Background: cityscape.
     Flattop's picture on a "wanted" poster.

1. DICK TRACY.	AVG:$1.75	MINT:$2.75
2. THE KID.	AVG:$2.00	MINT:$3.00
3. FLATTOP.	AVG:$1.75	MINT:$2.75

"WHO FRAMED ROGER RABBIT?", 1988. Movie Theme. Set of three.
WHITE PLASTIC. 20 oz cups.
Made by two different manufacturers:
        Mfg.A = Louisiana Plastics Inc. St. Louis, MO.
        Mfg.B = The Collectibles, of Canada.
McDonald's and COKE logos in red squares. Around base is a
row of golden ARCHES. (C) 1988 Walt Disney Company and
Amblin Entertainment, (C) 1988 McDonald's Corporation.

Mfg.A = Louisiana Plastics Inc. St. Louis, MO

1. A man, in black formal clothing and a weasel chase Roger.

2. Roger and a man in a yellow car. Roger's wife stands at a
        bus stop marked, "TOON TOWN".

3. Man in yellow car talks to Roger's wife, who sits on
        right fender. Roger stands on other side of car.
        "Hollywood" sign on green background hills

1. THE MAN IN BLACK   AVG:$1.75 MINT:$3.00
2. TOON TOWN   AVG:$1.75 MINT:$3.00
3. HOLLYWOOD   AVG:$2.00 MINT:$3.50

NOTE: For Mfg.B = The Collectibles, of Canada,
        ADD $0.20 TO EACH PRICE .

27. WHITE PLASTIC CUP, 1988   AVG:$1.75   MINT:$2.76
    20 oz.
        Wide red band bordered at top and bottom by narrow gold
        bands. In red bands: "SUPER SIZE", logos of ARCHES,
        SPRITE and DIET COKE. At top: "PLEASE PUT LITTER IN ITS
        PLACE". At base in red: "(C) 1988 McDonald's
        Corporation."

28. GREEN PLASTIC CUP, 20 oz   AVG:$2.75   MINT:$4.00
        Ridged top edge, rim. Design: black
        lines and cursive style "McDonald's" signature.

29. "GOING PLACES CUP"   5 inches   AVG:$1.50   MINT:$2.25

    WHITE PLASTIC CUP. Picture of RMCD driviing white van.
    McDonaldland characters use other modes of travel. Birdie
    in airplane pulls banner with cup name and ARCHES logo.
    Text: (C)1983 McDONALD'S CORP. TRADEMARKS REG.U.S. PATENT
    OFFICEPRINTED IN U.S.A.

30 UNCLE O'GRIMACY CUP   5 inches   AVG:$4.00   MINT:$6.50

    WHITE PLASTIC CUP. Picture of green O'Grimacy T.M.
    Other side: ARCHES logo with black McDONALD'S (R).

31 CUP, JAMMIN JUBILEE, 1990   AVG:$1.00 MINT:$4.50
WHITE PLASTIC. 20 oz.
    (C) 1990 McDonald's Corporation. ARCHES logo and COCA
    COLA logos in red squares set into lt. blue band around
    base. Design full height of cup: basketball and hoop,
    stars, ARCHES logo and text, "Jammin Jubilee". Beneath
    in red text: "1990 McDonald's ALL AMERICAN HIGH SCHOOL
    BASKETBALL GAME".
    Beneath, white text on blue: "MARKET SQUARE ARENA.
    INDIANAPOLIS, INDIANA."

32 CUP, clear plastic   AVG:$2.00 MINT:$3.50
4 inches, flare, indented foot.
    Two designs on cup:Text is dark blue.
    1. McDonald's golden ARCHES logo (R). Under this
       five lines of text giving addresses of restaurants.
    2. Logo of circular red-banded arrows, centered with
       large "R". Text: RIVERSIDE INTERNATIONAL RACEWAY.
       Underside: Chelmsford Mass. U.S.A./79/Comet/T-10

33 CUP, DESERT STORM, 1991   AVG:$3.00 MINT:$4.75
WHITE PLASTIC. 20 oz.
    Striking design of the waving U.S. flag with eagle
    head. Below this is yellow ribbon and bow on black band
    and McDoanld's logo in red square. Around base: USO
    logo on blue, black text: THE PROCEEDS WILL BENEFIT
    LOCAL PROGRAMS FOR MILITARY FAMILIES. Armed Services
    Logo. Around top: in black text: SAN DIEGO SALUTES OUR
    TROOPS, (C)1991 McDONALD'S CORP (vertical).

34 WHITE PLASTIC CUP, 5 1/2 inch flare   AVG:$2.75 MINT:$4.00
    Pictures original style McDonald's restaurant and text:
    "The Oldest Original McDonald's in the World / Downey,
    California / 32 years"

PLASTIC - MUGS

1978   1. MUG, white thermal   AVG:$3.00 MINT:$5.50

Handle, 10 oz, 4 inches high. Arrayed behind the
clear outer wall are the McDONALDLAND characters
and an Apple Pie Tree. Reads:
McDonald's SYSTEM INC. 1978 PRINTED IN USA

1981   2. MUG, yellow   AVG:$4.00 MINT:$6.00

3 3/4 inches, shaped like RONALD McDonald's head
with a handle at the back of the head." Ronald
McDONALD" is lettered in script at base, on both
sides of head. The underside reads: (C) 1981
McDonald's Corporation. Made in U.S.A.

1983   3. MUG, white plastic   AVG:$3.25 MINT:$5.00

Handle: orange, two-finger holes. Shows "old"
version of Hamburglar (torso). He holds out his
cape with both hands. Cape has gold lining and
large inside pocket. Design appears twice on cup.
Opposite the handle is ARCHES logo. At base, in
black: (C) 1983 McDonald's Corp.

1983   4. MUG, white plastic   AVG:$3.50 MINT:$5.50
Handle: orange, two-finger holes. Design: the
McDonaldland gang (heads & shoulders) arrayed
around mug. ARCHES logo is above Fry Kid. Legend
beside handle: "(C)1983 McDonald's Corp. The
names, characters and designs are trademarks owned
by the McDonald's Corporation."

1983   5. MUG AND MATCHING BOWL, White plastic:
          CUP   AVG:$3.50 MINT:$5.00

       Handle: orange, two-finger holes. Shows
RMCD head and torso, arms outstretched around
mug. Black ARCHES logo above each arm.
Made by WHIRLEY Industries Inc.

          BOWL   AVG:$3.00 MINT:$4.00
Same design as cup. 4.8 inches in diameter, 2.2
inches deep.

1984   6.MUG, translucent plastic   AVG:$4.00   MINT:$7.00
                5 1/4 inches. Design: Golden ARCHES logo and
        tiny man with mustache in black tuxedo, top hat
        and "tails". Under this: "MONOPOLY" in red
        rectangle. Large handle, bottom 2 inches sculpted.

1985   7.MUG, white plastic   AVG:$3.00   MINT:$4.75

        Handle: orange, two-finger holes. 2 7/8 inches.
        Underside reads: Whirley Industries Inc. Warren,
        PA. U.S.A./ 13.   McDONALDLAND characters .

1988   8.MUG, MAC TONIGHT.   AVG:$3.00   MINT:$4.50

        Reads: " 20 oz Super Max U.S.A. World's
        Largest Coffee Mug ", "Make It Mac Tonight",
        inside white-outlined rectangle with MAC and
        ARCHES logo. Cobalt blue (dark) cup with
        grooved handle.

1988   9.MUG, MAC TONIGHT.   AVG:$3.00   MINT:$4.50

        5 inches. Reads: "Make It Mac Tonight", White-
        outlined rectangle with MAC and ARCHES logo.
        Cobalt blue (dark) cup with grooved handle.

1985   10.MUG, white plastic   AVG:$2.00   MINT:$3.25

        4 1/4 inches high with handle and indented,
        flared foot. ARCHES logo in gold and black
        appears twice around cup. Underside reads:
        Whirley Industries Inc.Warren.PA. U.S.A. 1985.

1990   11. STYRENE MUG   AVG:$2.00   MINT:$3.25
        10 oz TRAVEL MUG. Red edged, white mug with flared
        (no-tip) foot, red lid. Decoration is McDonald's
        logo:golden arches, black text. (41168).

1990   12. CAPTAIN'S MUG   AVG:$3.50   MINT:$4.75

        12 OZ red mug with white base. Wide angle,
        flared foot with non-skid bottom. (no-spill
        design) McDonald's signature-logo in white.

1   2   12

4   3

15

17   6

14

16

1990   **13.** MUG, white , 32 oz   AVG:$2.00 MINT:$4.00

Decoration:McDonald's logo, gold arches, red text.

1991   **14.** MUG, white plastic   AVG:$2.00 MINT:$3.50

5 inches high. Red lid embossed: "Alladin".
Text around cup: "Receive a Free Coffee Refill
with any $1 Purchase / Food, Folks & Fun /
(C) 1991 McDonald's Corporation"

1991   **15.** MUG, white plastic   AVG:$3.00 MINT:$5.50

6 1/2" high, 3 3/4" wide. Large red handle and
contoured lid. (non-spill type). One-inch high,
indented band around top. Blue stripes on either
side of red band, around base. On one side: large,
black McDonald's logo. Opposite side: Red-banded
circle, enclosing text: OKLAHOMA CITY UNIVERSITY /
BASKETBALL. Inside circle is blue design of oil-
rigs and Indian head-dress. Outside circle blue
text: HOME OF THE NAIA NATIONAL CHAMPIONS / LADY
CHIEFS 1988 / CHIEFS 1991. Underside: THERMO /
Whirley Industries Inc. Warren, PA. U.S.A. / .

1990   **16.** MUG, white   AVG:$4.50 MINT:$6.00

4 inches high. Slanted, red lid. Red handle and
removeable, non-slip base. Outline of state of
Texas with red star and ARCHES logo. Text around
cup: "Refillable only at participating McDONALD'S
with entree purchase thru 9-1-90. (C) 1991
McDonald's Corporation"

        17 "McDonald's & You"   AVG:$ MINT:$
4 inches high, narrow, cylindrical top, wide
flared base, lined with non-slip material. Tan
plastic. Unusual shape handle with round finger
hole. Design in red: ARCHES T.M. with smiling sun
and above text.

SPORT BOTTLES

SPORTS BOTTLES

19XX   SPORTS BOTTLE,   AVG:$2.00   MINT:$3.25

Red and White. "McDonald's" in script.
Underside: Louisiana Plastics Inc.St. Louis MO

1990   SPORTS BOTTLES. Set of four different designs
            Featuring ball sports. Were sold for $1.99 each,
            filled with COCA-COLA or another soft drink.
            Top 3/5ths of bottle has design of sport balls
            on white. Lower portion and screw on lid are in
            bright colors.

   1. TENNIS BALLS, yellow   AVG:$2.00   MINT:$3.25
      Red bottle.

   2. BASKETBALLS, red   AVG:$2.25   MINT:$3.75
      Green bottle.

   3. SOCCER BALLS, blue-wht.   AVG:$2.00   MINT:$3.25
      Yellow bottle.

   4. BASEBALLS, blue-wht.   AVG:$2.25   MINT:$3.75
      Dark blue bottle.

1991   MINUTE MAID, 4.4 inches   AVG:$2.25   MINT:$3.75

"Minute Maid" in band around base. White plastic
and screw cap. Design in red, yellow and purple:
train of open cars with "M" logo on sides.

There are over 5,000 buttons and over 7,000 pins available to the collector at the present time. The following listing is just a sampling from this immense field. Buttons have pin fastenings on the back.

BUTTONS:

(Size unknown)

"LETTUCE AND TOMATO SPECIAL IS NOW MCDLT"	$ 1.50
"ASK HOW TO GET YOUR FREE PAPERMATE.. "	$ 1.25
"TRY NEW SUPER SIZE FRY"	$ 1.50
"MCRIB SANDWICH, TRYIT"	$ 2.00
"I GUARANTEE IT'S FAST"	$ 2.00
"I GUARANTEE IT'S HOT"	$ 2.00
"I GUARANTEE IT'S FRIENDLY"	$ 2.00
"I GUARANTEE IT'S CLEAN"	$ 2.00
"THE NEW EXTRA LARGE FRY"	$ 2.25
"ASK FOR THE LARGE O J"	$ 1.25
"SHOOT FOR THE STARS...."	$ 2.00
"MAKE IT MAC TONIGHT"	$ 2.00

ROUND BUTTON 1 INCH IN DIAMETER: $1.00
"I (red heart) McDonald's (logo)".

ROUND BUTTON 1 1/4 INCHES IN DIAMETER: $15.00
"1985 30th Birthday" over ARCHES in
red square.

ROUND BUTTON 2 1/4 INCHES IN DIAMETER: $1.50
"You're The One, Pardner".

ROUND BUTTONS 3 INCHES IN DIAMETER:
"DO IT" McDonald's ARCHES logo. Red. $2.50

"SPLASH FOR CASH" $3.00

"ORDER UP SUPER SIZES" $2.00

"ASK ME FOR A GAME PIECE / SCRABBLE" $2.50

"NEW MCD.L.T." $5.00

"NEW COUNTRY STYLE McCHICKEN SANDWICH" $2.00

"WELCOME TO AMERICA'S MORNING PLACE" $3.00

"ASK ME...HALLOWEEN GIFT CERTIFICATES" $2.00

"YOUR PIE...RONALD MCDONALD HOUSE" $2.50

"...BERENSTAIN BEARS HAPPY MEALS" $3.00

"GIFT CERTIFICATES AVAILABLE TODAY" (1987) $5.00
     (Cinderella mice).

"FLIGHT MCBLIMP CREW" $4.50

"MAC TONIGHT" $5.00

PHOTO BUTTONS with Ronald mcDonald $3.00

ROUND BUTTON, "MCNUGGET MANIA!" $4.00
Lenticular plastic design: "3-D",
man jumping, 2 positions.

ROUND BUTTONS 3 1/2 INCHES IN DIAMETER:
"GIFT CERTIFICATES AVAILABLE TODAY" (XMAS) $1.50

"2-LITER BOTTLE 49C (Coca Cola) $1.95

Red button: face in lines, eyes $2.25
are "C" & "a" .

Name button: "NSD", McDonald's 22 $1.95

ROUND BUTTONS 4 INCHES IN DIAMETER:
"ALERT...BIG MAC ATTACK..." $3.00

SMILE..."SAY CHEESE-BURGER!" $30.00
Line drawing of counter-man with camera.
Black & white on yellow background. (1960's)

"Fish that catches people" $30.00
"Ask for FILET O'FISH"
Line drawing of fisherman with pole.
Black & yellow on white background. (1960's)
Name button:"HI FRIEND..SO HELP ME". Yellow $2.50

SQUARE BUTTONS, 2.1 INCHES:
"Scrabble Game"   (Group II / Canada) $2.50

"JOIN THE NIGHTHAWKS" $4.00

RECTANGULAR BUTTONS 1.7 X 2.8 INCHES:
"TRY MCRIB" $3.00

"FRESH SALADS" $3.00

"AMERICA'S MEAT & POTATOES(R)" $3.75

"MCDONALD'S ALL STAR RACE TEAM / NASCAR" $5.00

IRREGULAR SHAPED BUTTONS:
2.9 X 3.2 inches:
"91% Fat Free McLEAN DELUXE" $2.75

2.3 X 3.4 inches: $9.00
Three CHICKEN McNUGGETS in fiesta gear.

BUTTONS

PINS:

IRREGULARLY SHAPED PINS:
Pin has irregular outline based on subject.

1.3 inches, Space Shuttle ARCHES on nose and tail. "SPACE CREW".	$4.00
0.9 inches, Snowman, dk. blue hat. On lt. blue scarf:"Seasons Greetings".	$3.00
1.2 inches, "CINDERELLA"	$4.00
1 inch, Garfield and Odie. In large golden ARCH.	$4.75
Medal-shaped, RMCD head, 1986 red & orange,"It's A Good Time....Taste".	$5.25
0.8 inches, white rabbit with egg	$4.75
Ronald McDonald: figure, 1 1/8" stands on white rectangle with name in gold.	$3.50
Ronald McDonald: figure, 1.7" Standing,hands out from side, Red, yellow and gold. Raised ARCHES on pockets. Two fasteners on back.	$5.50
Ronald McDonald House, 0.8", gold text shaped to text, red heart under"House".	$2.95
Ronald McDonald: figure, 1 1/8" stands on white rectangle, name in gold.	$4.75
Ronald McDonald: figure, 1.7" Standing,hands out from side, Red, yellow and gold. Raised ARCHES on pockets. Two fasteners on back.	$3.75
Ronald McDonald House, 0.8", gold text shaped to text, red heart under"House".	$2.95
White, gold edge and text, 1/2" X 6/8" ARCHES above "H U".	$2.50
McDonald's, Spokane, WA scenic: mountain, tower, green land Top shaped around gold ARCHES. 1".	$3.00

Blue and gold. Fish at top right $3.50
with red underside, Text: "Be Better Than
Best GO REDLY" under ARCHES logo.

ARCHES (yellow) shaped. Garfield lower left $3.50
7/8" all over.

Ronald McDonald figure with OLYMPIC flag $5.25
walking figure carries white flag.

GOLDEN GATE BRIDGE under gold ARCHES logo $4.25
red, white and gold. Text: "SAN FRANCISCO"
1" x 0.8".

FRIES (shaped) package full of candles $3.00
1" all-over.

"30" gold pin (shaped)"1955 SAN FRANCISCO $5.00
1985" ARCHES logo on red inside zero.
1" X 1/2".

"Big Mac & Co." (shaped) sculpted foods. $3.00
2" X 2", Shake, fries,and Big Mac,brown table.

Four ARCHES enclose "25" $3.25
silver and grey.

Sillouette : RMCD waving right hand $3.75
(R) by left collar. 1.5" X 1.3".

Shake, Burger, Cone and ARCHES, on $4.00
red area, shaped to fit objects. "TAYLOR".

Mr.Speedee in open red car with sign $4.50
Text on Mr. Speedee: "EXPERT", on sign:
"DRIVE THRU" all-over 0.8".

"THREE BARBERS" (Group II Inc) shaped $4.25
shows three barbers with red-striped pole.
1" X .8".

"GIANTS" (Group II Inc) $4.50
Two football helmets. GIANTS in white
on the blue helmet, Golden ARCHES logo
on the red helmet. 2" X 6/8" .

BUTTONS & PINS   377

ROUND PINS:
Round, 0.9" diameter, hand holding card $2.95
white with details in red and gold.
card is ACE with ARCHES logo in center.

Round, 1" diameter, "TINY TOON ADVENTURES" $3.75
Two rabbits wave from center of circle.

Round, 1 1/2" diameter, Snow White and $5.50
7 Dwarfs. Heads of characters around circle,
ARCHES logo in center.

SQUARE PINS:
Square, blue with silver, 7/8" $3.00
silver ARCHES, white text: "SUPER STAR".

RECTANGULAR PINS:
MAKE IT MAC TONIGHT, white moon (shaped), $4.00
blue rectangle, text in white & yellow.
1" X 1 1/8".

"TOP GUN", lt.blue rectangle $4.00
ARCHES with wings, red plane and text.
0.9 X 0.5 inches.

Red rectangle, OLYMPICS $2.95
Grimace in green sneakers, ARCHES and Olympic
logos. 1" X 1 1/8".

Blue rectangle, WINTER OLYMPICS, 1988 $3.75
BIRDIE on skis. 1.1 X 0.9 inches.

RUSSIAN: colorful doll, ARCHES and "MOSCOW" $5.50
(shaped) 1" X 1/5" .

RUSSIAN: blue with Mosque & ARCHES logo $5.25
blue with red and yellow details.
Text:"MOCKBA" and other. 1.3" x 0.9".

PINS

PORCELAIN PLATES

1991   PLATES, Set of three porcelain plates, 8 3/8 inches in diameter, issued by the *INCLINE GROUP*, authorized by McDonald's Corporation (C)1991. Worldwide edition limited to 25,000 plates.

1. RAY KROC with microphone   AVG:$25.00   MINT:$35.00

2. CAMP NIPPERSINK   AVG:$25.00   MINT:$37.50
    Design made in 1983.

3. RONALD HOLIDAY   AVG:$22.00   MINT:$30.00
    Design made in 1984. Winter scene:
    RMCD on ice skates, children and animals.

PLASTIC PLATES

1977   PLATES, 9 7/8 inches diameter with a 6/8 inch
          yellow border   Inside border is red text:
          "(C) McDonald's System Inc." Set of four.

1. FALL FUN   AVG:$2.50 MINT:$4.50

   "Ronald McDONALD Likes To Have Great Fall Fun
   But Wait   'Till Poor Grimace Sees What He's Done!"
   RMCD jumps into heap of leaves which
   Grimace has raked   together.

2. APRIL SHOWERS   AVG:$3.00 MINT:$4.25

   "Ronald McDONALD Was Watering May Flowers
   But Mayor McCheese Gets Some Cold April Showers! "
   RMCD holds hose, watering Mayor McCheese.

3. SNOWMAN CAPTURE   AVG:$3.50 MINT:$5.00

   "Ronald McDONALD And Hamburglar Share A Big Grin
   When Big Mac Captures A Snowman Twin!"
   Winter scene. RMCD and Hamburglar watch Big Mac
   pull sled "handcuffed" to a snowman. The Snowman
   is dressed to look like Hamburglar.

4. BEACH   AVG:$3.00 MINT:$4.25

   "Ronald McDONALD Saves This Hot Summer Day...While
   Ol' Captain Crook Stays Safely Away!"
   Beach scene. RMCD tries to free hamper from
   the grasp of a hungry octopus.

1985   PLATES, 9 inches diameter. "(C) McDonald's CORP.
            1985" Set of four.

---

1. SAILING   AVG:$4.00   MINT:$6.00
   RMCD and Grimace, red sailboat.

2. SPACE   AVG:$3.50   MINT:$5.50
   RMCD and Birdie, in space helmets,
   rocket ship, strange planet.

3. McDONALDLAND EXPRESS   AVG:$3.50   MINT:$5.50
   RMCD and Grimace in toy train.
   Text on side of car reads: "McDONALDLAND Express".

4. FLYING   AVG:$4.00   MINT:$6.00
   RMCD pilots yellow biplane with
   three goblins (Fry Guys).

1985   PLATE, 7 inch diameter "(C) McDonald's CORP
            1985"

Space theme,   AVG:$4.00   MINT:$7.00

McDONALDLAND characters and rocket ships. In center is
McDonald's restaurant on a rocket-powered platform.

1989   PLATES, "HAMBURGER UNIVERSITY", 9 inches in
         diameter. Each plate has a poem. Set of four.
         Text: in black "(C)1989 McDonald's Corporation.

1. HAMBURGER UNIVERSITY   AVG:$3.00   MINT:$5.50

RMCD stands at front of schoolroom; "student" hamburgers
are seated at desks. Another hamburger peeps into the
window. Text: "Hamburger University".

2. MILKSHAKE LAKE   AVG:$3.00   MINT:$5.50

RMCD and Grimace outdoors. On either side of them are
vanilla cones and chocolate and vanilla sundaes. Milkshakes
float in a three-flavored lake. Text:"Milkshake Lake".

3. THE McNUGGET BAND   AVG:$3.50   MINT:$6.00

RMCD holds a small bandstand in his right hand, where six
Chicken McNuggets play instruments.Text:"The McNugget Band".

4. THE FRENCH FRY GARDEN   AVG:$3.00   MINT:$5.50

RMCD in garden with five Fry Guys. In the garden there are
rows of Fries. Text: "The French Fry Garden".

HAMBURGER UNIVERSITY
Hamburglar knows where a hamburger goes,
To earn their McDonald's Degree.
A place all the Burgers call Hamburger U.
But he calls it Hamburger Me!

MILKSHAKE LAKE
There's a high mountain lake in McDonaldland,
Overflowing with Sundaes and Shakes.
The air is so cool and the clouds are so sweet,
The snow falls in chocolate flakes.

THE McNUGGET BAND
Come one, come all to the Concert Hall,
To hear the McNugget Band.
They fill the air with happy tunes
Throughout McDonaldland.

THE FRENCH FRY GARDEN
There's a garden that grows in McDonaldland,
Beneath the McDonaldland skies.
A garden that grows in neat little rows
A garden of golden-brown fries.

TRAYS

1984   TRAYS, 11 INCH OVAL, OLYMPIC THEME, Metal.
            Raised rim is red, white and blue. Text:
            "Los Angeles 1984 / Games of the XXIII Olympiad"
            Trays have photo of a champion, ARCHES logo and
            Olympic logo (five stars and interlocked rings)
            On underside of tray : "McDonald's Olympic Swim
            Team" and descriptive paragraph on the featured
            sport. Line drawing of swimming pool.
            (C)1984 McDonald's Corporation / (C) 1984
            L.A.OLY.ORG.COM.

1. MALE SWIMMER   AVG:$4.00   MINT:$7.00
2. MALE RELAY RUNNER   AVG:$4.50   MINT:$8.00
3. FEMALE ACROBAT   AVG:$4.00   MINT:$7.00
4. LA MEM. COLOSSEUM   AVG:$6.00   MINT:$9.00

1986   TRAY, rectangular, 10 1/2 X 13 1/2 inches.
            Dark blue metal serving tray with one inch
            raised edge. Charging football players and
            snarling Tiger. Text: "Tigers / Homecoming 86
            Memphis State vs Mississippi State / Liberty Bowl
            Memorial Stadium / October / FM100". McDonald's
            ARCHES logo in red square.

TRAY   AVG:$5.00 MINT:$8.50

19XX   TRAYS, plastic, 10 7/8 X 6 inches, Set of six,
            wedge-shaped. Raised circular area to hold cup is
            embossed with ARCHES logo. Each tray has picture
            of McDONALDLAND character, name below feet. On
            underside of cup area: "(C) Simon Marketing Inc."

1. RONALD McDONALD   AVG:$4.00   MINT:$6.00
2. GRIMACE   AVG:$4.50   MINT:$7.00
3. HAMBURGLAR   AVG:$4.00   MINT:$6.00
4. CAPTAIN CROOK   AVG:$4.50   MINT:$7.00
5. MAYOR McCHEESE   AVG:$4.00   MINT:$6.00
6. BIG MAC   AVG:$4.00   MINT:$6.00

DISPLAYS

Colorful counter DISPLAYS and POINT-OF-PURCHASE or - "P.O.P" displays, are popular collectibles. "P.O.P." displays, refer to all the display items used for one specific promotion, such as: wall posters, hanging and table signs, as well as the counter top DISPLAY of Happy Meal toys. Some displays have moving parts, when electrified.

Early 1970s	"LEGO BUILDING SET HAPPY MEAL" COUNTER DISPLAY	AVG:$225.00	MINT:$375.00

Approximately 16 inches high. Complete figure of Ronald McDONALD with hand raised. Made with lego blocks.

1987	"LITTLE ENGINEER"	AVG:$60.00	MINT:$85.00
	"CRAYOLA"	AVG:$35.00	MINT:$50.00
	"McDONALDLAND BAND"	AVG:$45.00	MINT:$75.00
	"MUPPET BABIES"	AVG:$60.00	MINT:$90.00
	"BERENSTAIN BEARS"	AVG:$45.00	MINT:$85.00
	"HALLOWEEN TRICKS"	AVG:$40.00	MINT:$60.00
	"DISNEY FAVORITES"	AVG:$85.00	MINT:$125.00
	"MATCHBOX SUPER GT"	AVG:$100.00	MINT:$175.00
	"HIGH FLYING"(kites)	AVG:$60.00	MINT:$90.00
	"BIGFOOT"	AVG:$60.00	MINT:$90.00
1988	"DUCK TALES I"	AVG:$45.00	MINT:$65.00
	"COSMc! CRAYOLA"	AVG:$35.00	MINT:$60.00
	"ON THE GO"	AVG:$35.00	MINT:$60.00
	"ZOO FACE"	AVG:$40.00	MINT:$65.00
	"STORY BOOK MUPPET..."	AVG:$55.00	MINT:$75.00
	"OLIVER & COMPANY"	AVG:$45.00	MINT:$70.00
1989	"McNUGGET BUDDIES"	AVG:$55.00	MINT:$85.00
	"BEDTIME"	AVG:$40.00	MINT:$60.00
	"LITTLE GARDENER"	AVG:$40.00	MINT:$60.00
	"NEW FOOD CHANGEABLES"	AVG:$40.00	MINT:$60.00
	"GARFIELD"	AVG:$55.00	MINT:$85.00
	"LEGO MOTION"	AVG:$40.00	MINT:$60.00
	"RESCUE RANGERS"	AVG:$45.00	MINT:$75.00
	"THE LITTLE MERMAID"	AVG:$75.00	MINT:$90.00

DISPLAYS

1990			
	"FUNNY FRY FRIENDS"	AVG:$50.00	MINT:$75.00
	"BERENSTAIN BEARS BOOKS"	AVG:$35.00	MINT:$48.00
	"PEANUTS"	AVG:$40.00	MINT:$65.00
	"BEACH TOY"	AVG:$35.00	MINT:$48.00
	"CAMP McDONALDLAND"	AVG:$40.00	MINT:$65.00
	"JUNGLE BOOK"	AVG:$45.00	MINT:$75.00
	"SUPER MARIO BROS 3"	AVG:$40.00	MINT:$65.00
	"McDONALDLAND DOUGH"	AVG:$40.00	MINT:$65.00
	"RESCUERS DOWN UNDER"	AVG:$45.00	MINT:$70.00

1991			
	"GOOD MORNING"	AVG:$50.00	MINT:$75.00
	"TINY TOON ADVENTURES"	AVG:$50.00	MINT:$75.00
	"NATURE'S HELPERS"	AVG:$50.00	MINT:$75.00
	"CARNIVAL"	AVG:$75.00	MINT:$95.00
	"101 DALMATIONS"	AVG:$75.00	MINT:$90.00
	"BARBIE/HOT WHEELS"	AVG:$150.00	MINT:$225.00

DISPLAYS WITH MOVING PARTS

"MICKEY'S BIRTHDAYLAND"   AVG:$90.00   MINT:$150.00
Platform holding toys
revolves.

"BAMBI"   AVG:$90.00   MINT:$150.00
   Platform holding toys
   revolves.

"TALE SPIN"   AVG:$75.00   MINT:$125.00
Airplane propellers turn.

"McDINO CHANGEABLES"   AVG:$60.00   MINT:$95.00
Lenticular background
panel moves, alternating
between two different views of toys.

"P.O.P." DISPLAYS: above displays, plus hangers and signs.
                        ADD: 20% to display price.

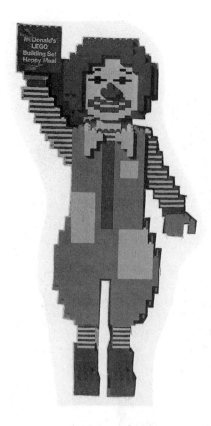

DISPLAYS

DISPLAYS

TRANSLITES

Translites are plastic panels, backed with lights, used above the counter and in outdoor menu displays, to advertise foods and Happy Meals. They are available in two sizes: 22 X 22 inches and 14 X 14 inches.

Some panels are made in "3-D", or *lenticular plastic*, (the lamination of two different scenes on "ridged" plastic layers, so that the picture seems to move as the viewpoint changes). This type is nearly twice as thick as the normal translite because it is backed with clear plexiglass.

NATIONAL HAPPY MEAL TRANSLITES   22 X 22 INCHES

1978	"KEEP.... EYES ON FRIES"	AVG:$20.00	MINT:$28.00
1979	"SPACE ALIENS"	AVG:$22.00	MINT:$38.00
1983	"GET TODAY'S TOY" (McDONALDLAND Junction Happy meal)	AVG:$20.00	MINT:$28.00
1986	"OLD McDonald's FARM"	AVG:$22.00	MINT:$32.00
	"AIRPORT"	AVG:$23.00	MINT:$34.00
	"SKYBUSTERS"	AVG:$23.00	MINT:$34.00
	"STOMPER MINI 4 x 4'S" Design of car and lettering is raised 1"	AVG:$25.00	MINT:$37.00
	"HAPPY PAIL"	AVG:$20.00	MINT:$28.00
1987	"LITTLE ENGINEER"	AVG:$22.00	MINT:$28.00
	"CRAYOLA"	AVG:$20.00	MINT:$25.00
	"McDONALDLAND BAND"	AVG:$22.00	MINT:$28.00
	"MUPPET BABIES"	AVG:$22.00	MINT:$28.00
	"BERENSTAIN BEARS"	AVG:$22.00	MINT:$32.00
	"HALLOWEEN TRICKS"	AVG:$20.00	MINT:$30.00
	"DISNEY FAVORITES"	AVG:$24.00	MINT:$35.00
	"MATCHBOX SUPER GT"	AVG:$22.00	MINT:$32.00
	"HIGH FLYING"(kites)	AVG:$19.00	MINT:$27.00
	"BIGFOOT"	AVG:$20.00	MINT:$28.00

NATIONAL HAPPY MEAL TRANSLITES   22 X 22 INCHES

1988   "DUCK TALES I"   AVG:$15.00   MINT:$19.00
            "COSMc! CRAYOLA"   AVG:$12.00   MINT:$17.00
            "BAMBI"   AVG:$18.00   MINT:$25.00
            "ON THE GO"   AVG:$12.00   MINT:$17.00
            "ZOO FACE"   AVG:$12.00   MINT:$17.00
            "MAC TONIGHT"   AVG:$15.00   MINT:$20.00
            (floating keyboard, McD
            sign on left)
            "STORY BOOK MUPPET BABIES" AVG:$13.00   MINT:$18.00
            "OLIVER & COMPANY"   AVG:$15.00   MINT:$19.00

1989   "McNUGGET BUDDIES"   AVG:$12.00   MINT:$17.00
            "BEDTIME"   AVG:$15.00   MINT:$19.00
            "MICKEY'S BIRTHDAYLAND"   AVG:$18.00   MINT:$24.00
            "LITTLE GARDENER"   AVG:$12.00   MINT:$17.00
            "NEW FOOD CHANGEABLES"   AVG:$12.00   MINT:$17.00
            "GARFIELD"   AVG:$15.00   MINT:$26.00
            "LEGO MOTION"   AVG:$12.00   MINT:$17.00
            "RESCUE RANGERS"   AVG:$13.00   MINT:$18.00
            "THE LITTLE MERMAID"   AVG:$15.00   MINT:$22.00

1990   "FUNNY FRY FRIENDS"   AVG:$15.00   MINT:$22.00
            "BERENSTAIN BEARS BOOKS"   AVG:$16.00   MINT:$22.00
            "FROM THE HEART"   AVG:$14.00   MINT:$19.00
            "PEANUTS"   AVG:$14.00   MINT:$20.00
            "BEACH TOY"   AVG:$12.00   MINT:$19.00
            "CAMP McDONALDLAND"   AVG:$16.00   MINT:$22.00
            "JUNGLE BOOK"   AVG:$14.00   MINT:$20.00
            "SUPER MARIO BROS 3"   AVG:$12.00   MINT:$18.00
            "McDONALDLAND DOUGH"   AVG:$12.00   MINT:$18.00
            "HALLOWEEN"(pails)   AVG:$12.00   MINT:$18.00
            "TALE SPIN"   AVG:$14.00   MINT:$20.00
            "RESCUERS DOWN UNDER"   AVG:$14.00   MINT:$19.00
      "LET'S GET GROWING AMERICA"   AVG:$12.00   MINT:$18.00

NATIONAL HAPPY MEAL TRANSLITES   22 X 22 INCHES

1991   "GOOD MORNING"   AVG:$14.00   MINT:$18.00
            "TINY TOON ADVENTURES"   AVG:$18.00   MINT:$24.00
            "McDINO CHANGEABLES"   AVG:$13.00   MINT:$17.00
            "NATURE'S HELPERS"   AVG:$14.00   MINT:$18.00
            "CARNIVAL"   AVG:$18.00   MINT:$23.00
            "101 DALMATIONS"   AVG:$18.00   MINT:$24.00
            "BARBIE/HOT WHEELS"   AVG:$20.00   MINT:$30.00
            "RAIN FOREST"   AVG:$14.00   MINT:$18.00
            "HALLOWEEN" (MCBOO BAGS)   AVG:$14.00   MINT:$18.00
            "SUPER LOONEY TUNES"   AVG:$15.00   MINT:$20.00
            "HOOK", Peter Pan   AVG:$15.00   MINT:$20.00

LENTICULAR (3-D) TRANSLITES   22 X 22 INCHES

1987   "MAC TONIGHT"   AVG:$20.00   MINT:$29.00
            (floating keyboard,
            McD sign on right)
            "MAC TONIGHT"   AVG:$20.00   MINT:$29.00
            (seated at piano,
            wide red frame)
1990   "JUNGLE BOOK"   AVG:$18.00   MINT:$26.00
1991   "TINY TOONS ADVENTURE"   AVG:$17.00   MINT:$25.00

MISCELLANEOUS TRANSLITES   22 X 22 INCHES

1988   "PLAY SCRABBLE"   AVG:$12.00   MINT:$17.00

1986   "FOOD, FOLKS, FUN"   AVG:$12.00   MINT:$17.00

1990   "DICK TRACY CRIMESTOPPER" AVG:$15.00   MINT:$20.00
            "GIFT CERTIFICATES"(Xmas) AVG:$14.00   MINT:$19.00
            "SUPER MARIO GAME WATCHES" AVG:$14.00   MINT:$19.00
            "FREE ORNAMENTS"   AVG:$15.00   MINT:$20.00
            (from Little Mermaid,
            Christmas)
            "SPORTS BOTTLES"   AVG:$14.00   MINT:$19.00
            "McMILLIONS ON NBC"   AVG:$14.00   MINT:$19.00
            "WHO WILL WIN?"   AVG:$15.00   MINT:$20.00
              Super Bowl XXIV
            "BLAST BACK WITH MAC"   AVG:$13.00   MINT:$17.00

1991   "INDIANA JONES"   AVG:$12.00   MINT:$16.00
            "GIFT CERTIFICATES"   AVG:$10.00   MINT:$15.00

McDonald's FOOD TRANSLITES   22 X 22 INCHES

1987	"CHICKEN McNUGGETS SHANGHAI"	AVG:$10.00	MINT:$15.00
	"DELICIOUS DOUBLE FEATURES"	AVG:$12.00	MINT:$16.00
	"VALUE PACK"	AVG:$10.00	MINT:$15.00
1988	"SUPER SUMMER SIZE"	AVG:$10.00	MINT:$15.00
	"KRAFT DRESSING...SALAD"	AVG:$12.00	MINT:$16.00
1989	"CHICKEN McNUGGET FIESTA"	AVG:$12.00	MINT:$16.00
1990	"WESTERN OMLETTE McMUFFIN"	AVG:$12.00	MINT:$16.00
1991	"COKE FLOAT"	AVG:$13.00	MINT:$17.00

TRANSLITES

NATIONAL HAPPY MEAL TRANSLITES   14 X 14 INCHES

1986	"OLD McDonald's FARM"	AVG:$15.00	MINT:$20.00
	"AIRPORT"	AVG:$15.00	MINT:$20.00
	"SKYBUSTERS"	AVG:$13.00	MINT:$18.00
	"STOMPER MINI 4 x 4'S"	AVG:$15.00	MINT:$20.00
	"HAPPY PAIL"	AVG:$12.00	MINT:$16.00

1987	"LITTLE ENGINEER"	AVG:$12.00	MINT:$16.00
	"CRAYOLA"	AVG:$12.00	MINT:$16.00
	"McDONALDLAND BAND"	AVG:$13.00	MINT:$18.00
	"MUPPET BABIES"	AVG:$12.00	MINT:$16.00
	"BERENSTAIN BEARS"	AVG:$12.00	MINT:$16.00
	"HALLOWEEN TRICKS"	AVG:$14.00	MINT:$19.00
	"DISNEY FAVORITES"	AVG:$13.00	MINT:$18.00
	"MATCHBOX SUPER GT"	AVG:$13.00	MINT:$18.00
	"HIGH FLYING"(kites)	AVG:$13.00	MINT:$18.00
	"BIGFOOT"	AVG:$15.00	MINT:$20.00

1988	"DUCK TALES I"	AVG:$12.00	MINT:$15.00
	"COSMc! CRAYOLA"	AVG:$12.00	MINT:$15.00
	"BAMBI"	AVG:$15.00	MINT:$19.00
	"ON THE GO"	AVG:$10.00	MINT:$13.00
	"ZOO FACE"	AVG:$12.00	MINT:$15.00
	"STORY BOOK MUPPET BABIES"	AVG:$12.00	MINT:$15.00
	"OLIVER & COMPANY"	AVG:$13.00	MINT:$16.00

1989	"McNUGGET BUDDIES"	AVG:$10.00	MINT:$14.00
	"BEDTIME"	AVG:$10.00	MINT:$14.00
	"MICKEY'S BIRTHDAYLAND"	AVG:$18.00	MINT:$22.00
	"LITTLE GARDENER"	AVG:$13.00	MINT:$18.00
	"NEW FOOD CHANGEABLES"	AVG:$13.00	MINT:$18.00
	"GARFIELD"	AVG:$13.00	MINT:$18.00
	"LEGO MOTION"	AVG:$12.00	MINT:$15.00
	"RESCUE RANGERS"	AVG:$13.00	MINT:$16.00
	"THE LITTLE MERMAID"	AVG:$17.00	MINT:$20.00

NATIONAL HAPPY MEAL TRANSLITES   14 X 14 INCHES


```
1990        "FUNNY FRY FRIENDS"          AVG:$12.00  MINT:$16.00
            "BERENSTAIN BEARS BOOKS"     AVG:$12.00  MINT:$16.00
            "FROM THE HEART"             AVG:$10.00  MINT:$14.00
            "PEANUTS"                    AVG:$13.00  MINT:$16.00
            "BEACH TOY"                  AVG:$10.00  MINT:$14.00
            "CAMP McDONALDLAND"          AVG:$10.00  MINT:$14.00
            "JUNGLE BOOK"                AVG:$13.00  MINT:$16.00
            "SUPER MARIO BROS 3"         AVG:$10.00  MINT:$14.00
            "McDONALDLAND DOUGH"         AVG:$ 9.00  MINT:$12.00
            "HALLOWEEN" (pails)          AVG:$10.00  MINT:$14.00
            "TALE SPIN"                  AVG:$14.00  MINT:$18.00
            "RESCUERS DOWN UNDER"        AVG:$10.00  MINT:$15.00
```


NATIONAL HAPPY MEAL TRANSLITES   14 X 14 INCHES


```
1991        "GOOD MORNING"               AVG:$17.00  MINT:$20.00
            "TINY TOON ADVENTURES"       AVG:$16.00  MINT:$20.00
            "McDINO CHANGEABLES"         AVG:$15.00  MINT:$19.00
            "NATURE'S HELPERS"           AVG:$15.00  MINT:$19.00
            "CARNIVAL"                   AVG:$17.00  MINT:$20.00
            "101 DALMATIONS"             AVG:$19.00  MINT:$22.00
            "BARBIE/HOT WHEELS"          AVG:$19.00  MINT:$22.00
            "RAIN FOREST"                AVG:$15.00  MINT:$18.00
            "HALLOWEEN" (MCBOO BAGS)     AVG:$15.00  MINT:$18.00
            "SUPER LOONEY TUNES"         AVG:$15.00  MINT:$18.00
            "HOOK"                       AVG:$15.00  MINT:$18.00
```


McDonald's FOOD TRANSLITES   14 X 14 INCHES

```
1987   "CHICKEN McNUGGETS SHANGHAI"  AVG:$13.00  MINT:$17.00
       "DELICIOUS DOUBLE FEATURES"   AVG:$12.00  MINT:$16.00
         "VALUE PACK"                AVG:$11.00  MINT:$13.00
1988     "SUPER SUMMER SIZE"         AVG:$12.00  MINT:$16.00
         "KRAFT DRESSING...SALAD"    AVG:$10.00  MINT:$14.00
1989     "CHICKEN McNUGGET FIESTA"   AVG:$10.00  MINT:$14.00
1990     "BLAST BACK WITH MAC"       AVG:$12.00  MINT:$16.00
       "WESTERN OMLETTE McMUFFIN"    AVG:$10.00  MINT:$14.00
1991     "COKE FLOAT"                AVG:$10.00  MINT:$14.00
```

TRANSLITES

MISCELLANEOUS

DIRECTORY

MISCELLANEOUS DIRECTORY CONTINUED:

```
Abbreviations used to describe condition:
MINT = new, never used or unfolded.
AVG  = average condition.
NP   = no original package, loose.
MIP  = mint in package, in original, sealed
         container.
```

BAG, travel   AVG:$12.00 MINT:$25.00
    Man's, calf color, lined vinyl
    embossed ARCHES logo in square.
    Mfg. BEARSE, Chicago, Ill and
    Newburgh, NY.

BANK: Grimace,   AVG:$10.00 MINT:$14.00
    9 inches high, ceramic, purple
    (49051 Group II)

BANK: Ronald McDonald   AVG:$10.00 MINT:$14.00
    Seated, cross-legged, right
    hand raised. 7 1/2 inches high.
    Hand painted.

BANK: Singing Wastebasket   AVG:$3.50 MINT:$8.00
    5 1/8 inches high, white plastic,
    yellow top with coin slot.

BELT: leather (1975)   AVG:$12.50 MINT:$20.00
    Adult size. tooled with ARCHES
logo and slogan: "Twoallbeefpatties..."
etc. Heavy bronze belt buckle sculpted
as a Big Mac. Inside:(C) 1975 McDonald's
Systems Inc / limited edition.

BIB: white plastic, disposable   AVG:$2.50 MINT:$4.00
    MC0006. Design: RMCD waving.

BIB: plastic, disposable   AVG:$2.50 MINT:$4.00
    MC0001. Design like RMCD shirt
    front: collar, zipper.

BIB: vinyl, disposable   AVG:$0.25 MINT:$0.50
    RMCD feeding teddy bear in blue
    high-chair.

BIB: TIME TO EAT   AVG:$3.00 MINT: $4:00
    Large, padded bib.

GRIMACE BANK

RONALD McDONALD BANK

BIB

BIB

TIME TO EAT

LEATHER BAG & BELT

BOOKS

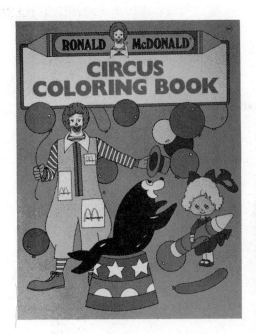

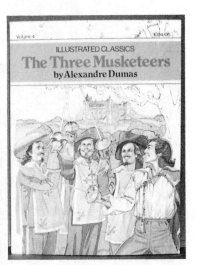

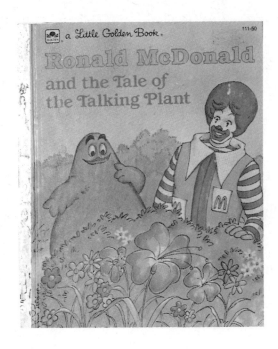

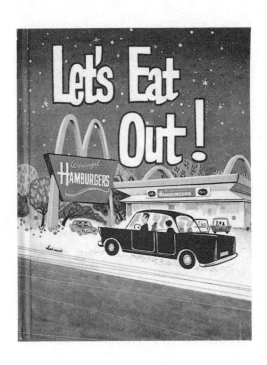

BOOK: *LET'S EAT OUT!*   AVG:$130.00   MINT:**$150.00**
By John Jones.
(C)1965 MELMONT PUBLISHERS, INC. CHICAGO.
9" x7 1/4" . Children's book about looking
fora place to eat. Celebrates McDonald's
tenth birthday. 14 pages.

BOOK: Classics Series. 5 1/2" X 4 1/4".
Tie-in with McDonald's PBS Television series
"Once upon a Classic". Copyright (C) 1977
I. WALDMAN & SON, INC.
3. Vol.3 *"Black Beauty"*   AVG:$3.50   MINT:$5.75
4. Vol.4 *"The Three Musketeers"*   AVG:$3.50   MINT:$5.75

BOOK: *Little Golden Book*   AVG:$3.50   MINT:$6.00
"Ronald McDONALD and the Tale of the
Talking Plant". Cover shows RMCD and
Grimace in garden.(C)1984 by John Albano.

BOOK: Circus coloring   49950   AVG:$1.00   MINT:$2.00

BOOK: Birthday, activity   (1983)   AVG:$3.50   MINT:$5.00

BOOK: Activity, dot-to-dot   49951   AVG:$1.00   MINT:$2.00

BOOK: Activity, Magic Maze   49952   AVG:$1.00   MINT:$2.00

BOOK: Activity,"Family Fun For All"   AVG:$2.00   MINT:$3.00
     1978, 8 pages. 5 1/2" X 8 1/2",
     travelers Funbook.

BOOKS: *McDonald's Super Bowl*, 1977, History
of the Super Bowl:
     Volume 1. Super Bowls I - IV   AVG:$3.50   MINT:$5.50
     Volume 2. Super Bowls V - VIII   AVG:$4.00   MINT:$6.00
     Volume 3. Super Bowls IX - XI   AVG:$4.00   MINT:$6.00

BOOKMARKERS:(1978) McDland characters AVG:$2.50   MINT:$3.00

BOX, for toys   AVG:$8.00   MINT:$15.00
Cardboard, used for birthday parties
in stores. Made to look like McDonald's
Restaurants. (Approx. 13" X 8" X 12").

BRACELETS: (1979)   AVG:$4.00   MINT:$4.50
McDONALDLAND characters and (name).

BRACELET, CHARM, gold chain   AVG:$4.00   MINT:$8.00
     (for Charms, see: JEWELRY)

McDonald's

POSTCARDS

CALENDAR: coloring, "Olympic Games"   AVG:$3.50   MINT:$5.00
     1984

CALENDAR: coloring, "DINO Fun Facts"   AVG:$2.00   MINT:$4.00
     1991

CARDS: Playing, 2 decks/box   AVG:$2.00   MINT:$3.50
     McDonald's logo, yellow and brown.

CARD: Greeting, Mother"s Day (1979)   AVG:$2.50   MINT:$5.50
CARD: Greeting, Birthday   AVG:$2.00   MINT:$3.00
"Hooray for the birthday Boy".
Ronald McDONALD, Ambassador Cards
(Hallmark) 100B 168K.

CARD: Greeting, Birthday   AVG:$2.00   MINT:$3.00
"A Birthday Badge from McDONALDLAND".
McDONALDLAND characters, raised design.
Ambassador Cards. 150B 146J.

CARD: Postal (1978) "The Whole Gang"   AVG:$3.00   MINT:$5.50
Drawn McDLand Characters. White "McDonald's".

CARD: Postal (1985)   AVG:$3.00   MINT:$5.00
McDonald's Riverboat-St. Louis.

CARD: Postal (1987) "The Whole Gang"   AVG:$3.00   MINT:$5.00
Photographed McDLand Characters. ARCHES logo.

CARD: Postal (1989)   AVG:$3.00   MINT:$5.00
McDonald's Des Plaines Museum.

CARD: Postal, Barstow Station   AVG:$3.00   MINT:$5.00
Barstow, California

CARD: Postal, World's Largest McD's   AVG:3.00$ MINT:$5.00
Vinita, Oklahoma.

CARD: Postal, Belvidere Oasis   AVG:$3.00   MINT:$5.00
Built over highway. Belvidere, Illinois.

CARD: Postal MC0020 "Your Pal" RMCD   AVG:$3.00   MINT:$5.00
Picture of RMCD in McDONALDLAND

CARD: Postal, "Oldest McDonald's.."   AVG:$3.00   MINT:$5.50
Large size card, picturing
"The Oldest McDonald's In The World,
Downey, California"

FOOTBALL CARDS, Sets of cards with ARCHES logo in upper left corner. Upper right corner shows team's helmet. In "Scratch-Off" band at bottom of card: "PLAY TO WIN" and McDonald's logo. Above this: NFL logos and player's name. Center of card shows player in action. 1986.

ALL STAR TEAM, 30 Cards   AVG:$7.00 MINT:$12.00

Complete set is 24 cards: AVG:$8.00 MINT:$15.00
CLEVELAND BROWNS
DALLAS COWBOYS
DETROIT LIONS
GREEN BAY PACKERS
HOUSTON OILERS
NEW ENGLAND PATRIOTS
SEATTLE SEAHAWKS
TAMPA BAY BUCCANEERS
WASHINGTON REDSKINS

Complete set is 24 cards. Each set was issued in four colors (borders and scratch-off band); blue, gold, green and black.

ATLANTA FALCONS:
    Black Set:.................... AVG:$125.00 MINT:$240.00
    Blue Set:.................... AVG:$22.00 MINT:$55.00
    Gold Set:.................... AVG:$22.00 MINT:$55.00
    Green Set:.................... AVG:$10.00 MINT:$18.00

BUFFALO BILLS
    Black Set:.................... AVG:$15.00 MINT:$35.00
    Blue Set:.................... AVG:$90.00 MINT:$160.00
    Gold Set:.................... AVG:$12.00 MINT:$30.00
    Green Set:.................... AVG:$12.00 MINT:$30.00

CHICAGO BEARS
    Black Set:.................... AVG:$6.00   MINT:$12.00
    Blue Set:.................... AVG:$10.00 MINT:$20.00
    Gold Set:.................... AVG:$6.00   MINT:$12.00
    Green Set:.................... AVG:$6.00   MINT:$12.00

CINCINNNATI BENGALS
    Black Set:.................... AVG:$9.00   MINT:$18.00
    Blue Set:.................... AVG:$19.00 MINT:$37.00
    Gold Set:.................... AVG:$9.00   MINT:$18.00
    Green Set:.................... AVG:$9.00   MINT:$18.00

DENVER BRONCOS
    Black Set:.................... AVG:$10.00   MINT:$18.00
    Blue Set:.................... AVG:$18.00   MINT:$45.00
    Gold Set:.................... AVG:$10.00   MINT:$18.00
    Green Set:.................... AVG:$10.00   MINT:$18.00

INDIANAPOLIS COLTS
    Black Set:.................... AVG:$20.00   MINT:$40.00
    Blue Set:.................... AVG:$50.00   MINT:$100.00
    Gold Set:.................... AVG:$12.00   MINT:$20.00
    Green Set:.................... AVG:$12.00   MINT:$20.00

KANSAS CITY CHIEFS
    Black Set:.................... AVG:$20.00   MINT:$30.00
    Blue Set:.................... AVG:$15.00   MINT:$40.00
    Gold Set:.................... AVG:$20.00   MINT:$30.00
    Green Set:.................... AVG:$12.00   MINT:$20.00

LOS ANGELES RAIDERS
    Black Set:.................... AVG:$12.00   MINT:$25.00
    Blue Set:.................... AVG:$15.00   MINT:$29.00
    Gold Set:.................... AVG:$8.00   MINT:$14.00
    Green Set:.................... AVG:$8.00   MINT:$14.00

LOS ANGELES RAMS
    Black Set:.................... AVG:$8.00   MINT:$14.00
    Blue Set:.................... AVG:$12.00   MINT:$20.00
    Gold Set:.................... AVG:$8.00   MINT:$14.00
    Green Set:.................... AVG:$8.00   MINT:$14.00

MIAMI DOLPHINS
    Black Set:.................... AVG:$10.00   MINT:$20.00
    Blue Set:.................... AVG:$15.00   MINT:$40.00
    Gold Set:.................... AVG:$10.00   MINT:$20.00
    Green Set:.................... AVG:$10.00   MINT:$20.00

MINNESOTA VIKINGS
    Black Set:.................... AVG:$18.00   MINT:$30.00
    Blue Set:.................... AVG:$30.00   MINT:$50.00
    Gold Set:.................... AVG:$15.00   MINT:$25.00
    Green Set:.................... AVG:$12.00   MINT:$20.00

NEW ORLEANS SAINTS
    Black Set:.................... AVG:$20.00   MINT:$30.00
    Blue Set:.................... AVG:$75.00   MINT:$125.00
    Gold Set:.................... AVG:$20.00   MINT:$30.00
    Green Set:.................... AVG:$20.00   MINT:$30.00

NEW YORK GIANTS
    Black Set:..................... AVG:$8.00   MINT:$15.00
    Blue Set:..................... AVG:$9.00   MINT:$20.00
    Gold Set:..................... AVG:$7.00   MINT:$13.00
    Green Set:..................... AVG:$7.00   MINT:$13.00

NEW YORK JETS
    Black Set:..................... AVG:$80.00   MINT:$130.00
    Blue Set:..................... AVG:$80.00   MINT:$130.00
    Gold Set:..................... AVG:$18.00   MINT:$35.00
    Green Set:..................... AVG:$18.00   MINT:$35.00

PHILADELPHIA EAGLES
    Black Set:..................... AVG:$12.00   MINT:$18.00
    Blue Set:..................... AVG:$45.00   MINT:$80.00
    Gold Set:..................... AVG:$9.00   MINT:$15.00
    Green Set:..................... AVG:$9.00   MINT:$15.00

PITTSBURGH STEELERS
    Black Set:..................... AVG:$22.00   MINT:$50.00
    Blue Set:..................... AVG:$30.00   MINT:$75.00
    Gold Set:..................... AVG:$12.00   MINT:$28.00
    Green Set:..................... AVG:$12.00   MINT:$28.00

SAN DIEGO CHARGERS
    Black Set:..................... AVG:$12.00   MINT:$28.00
    Blue Set:..................... AVG:$18.00   MINT:$35.00
    Gold Set:..................... AVG:$10.00   MINT:$20.00
    Green Set:..................... AVG:$10.00   MINT:$20.00

SAN FRANCISCO 49ERS
    Black Set:..................... AVG:$8.00   MINT:$14.00
    Blue Set:..................... AVG:$12.00   MINT:$20.00
    Gold Set:..................... AVG:$8.00   MINT:$14.00
    Green Set:..................... AVG:$8.00   MINT:$14.00

ST. LOUIS CARDINALS
    Black Set:..................... AVG:$6.00   MINT:$10.00
    Blue Set:..................... AVG:$8.00   MINT:$15.00
    Gold Set:..................... AVG:$6.00   MINT:$10.00
    Green Set:..................... AVG:$6.00   MINT:$10.00

NASCAR. McDONALD'S ALL-STAR RACE TEAM

"McDonald's ALL-STAR RACE TEAM" CARDS. NASCAR. Set of 32 cards in clear, plastic box. Two cards invite the holder to "Join Cluc Maxx". (on back). The face of this card is black with logos and text: "The 1991 Limited Edition McDonald's-MAXX Collector Series." Printed in Canada. The other 30 cards have pictures of noted drivers on front and data concerning them on the back. Cards are bordered in black, yellow and red, and have special logo in upper right corner.

Cards:
1. Dale Earnhardt	AVG:$1.90	MINT:$2.75
2. Mark Martin	AVG:$0.80	MINT:$1.00
3. Geoff Bodine	AVG:$1.40	MINT:$1.85
4. Bill Elliott	AVG:$1.75	MINT:$2.40
5. Morgan Shepherd	AVG:$0.80	MINT:$1.00
6. Rusty Wallace	AVG:$0.80	MINT:$1.50
7. Ricky Rudd	AVG:$0.85	MINT:$1.25
8. Alan Kulwicki	AVG:$0.80	MINT:$1.00
9. Ernie Irvan	AVG:$0.75	MINT:$1.00
10. Ken Schrader	AVG:$0.75	MINT:$1.00
11. Kyle Petty	AVG:$0.85	MINT:$1.25
12. Brett Bodine	AVG:$0.80	MINT:$1.00
13. Davey Allison	AVG:$0.90	MINT:$1.50
14. Sterling Marlin	AVG:$0.50	MINT:$1.00
15. Terry Labonte	AVG:$1.25	MINT:$1.75
16. Michael Waltrip	AVG:$0.75	MINT:$1.00
17. Harry Gant	AVG:$0.85	MINT:$1.25
18. Derrike Cope	AVG:$0.85	MINT:$1.00
19. Bobby Hillin	AVG:$0.85	MINT:$1.00
20. Darrell Waltrip	AVG:$1.50	MINT:$2.25
21. Dave Marcis	AVG:$1.00	MINT:$1.60
22. Dick Trickle	AVG:$0.50	MINT:$1.00
23. Rick Wilson	AVG:$0.50	MINT:$1.00
24. Jimmy Spencer	AVG:$0.50	MINT:$1.00
25. Dale Jarrett	AVG:$0.50	MINT:$1.00
26. Richard Petty	AVG:$2.00	MINT:$3.25
27. Rick Mast	AVG:$0.50	MINT:$1.00
28. Hut Stricklin	AVG:$0.50	MINT:$1.00
29. Jimmy Means	AVG:$0.75	MINT:$1.00
30. Picturing three drivers	AVG:$1.25	MINT:$2.75

"The 1991 McDonald's All-Star Race Team"

CLOCK: wall, RMCD   AVG:$40.00   MINT:$75.00
Seated with left hand raised,
clock in stomach. Quartz movement,
battery powered. 13 1/4 X 16 inches
(04729 Group II).

CLOCK: WALL, Hamburglar   AVG:$25.00   MINT 60.00
Jumping figure, clock numbers and
hands on torso. Pendulum, battery
powered.   (43323 Group II)

CLOCK: wall, Pocket Watch   AVG:$25.00   MINT:$ 45.00
15 1/4 X 11 1/4 inches, RMCD on
face. Quartz movement, battery
powered.(00120 Group II).

CLOCK: alarm, wind-up type   AVG:$45.00   MINT:$65.00
Handle on top, red case, metal
round-shaped "ringer" between two
silver bells. 7/10 inch brass feet.
Diameter= 4.1 inches.
Back:"ROBERTSHAW CONTROLS / LUXtime
division Lebanon ,Tenn. USA." Face has
picture: seated RMCD with raised hand.

CLOCK: alarm, wind-up type   AVG:$35.00   MINT:$50.00
Handle on top, red case, metal
bell-shaped "ringer" between two
red bells. 1/2 inch brass feet.
Diameter= 4.1 inches.
Back:"Pat#3678679, (US) 1217647,
(UK)2031131". Face has picture of
seated RMCD with raised right hand.

CLOCK: alarm, wind-up type   AVG:$27.50   MINT:$45.00
Handle on top, red case, metal
hammer-shaped "ringer" between two
silver bells. 1 inch "silver" feet.
Diameter= 4.7 inches. Face has
picture of RMCD, head tilted to
right side, with hands together.

COIN: Fiesta   AVG:$6.00   MINT:$9.00
In package: coin and card with map
and flags of South America. 1988
McDonald's CORP. McNugget Fiesta.

```
COLORING THINGS:
     CARDS (1977)                    AVG:$3.00    MIP:$4.00
     STAND-UPS, 3 diff (1978)        AVG:$4.00    MINT:$5.00
     COLORING BOARDS                 AVG:$2.50    MINT:$3.50
     CALENDARS                       AVG:$4.00    MINT:$5.00
     PAINT WITH WATER  (1978)        AVG:$4.75    MINT:$6.00
2.6 x 3.9 INCHES, with paper easel


COOKIE CUTTERS:                      AVG:$2.50    MINT:$4.25
     Mcdonaldland characters, in various colors.


COMB: handle is McDONALDLAND figure,
made for several years in several
colors: red-orange, orange, yellow, pink,
green and purple. 1980, 1981, 1983, 1985,1988

1980 RMCD                            AVG:$2.00    MINT:$2.75
     GRIMACE                         AVG:$1.50    MINT:$2.00
     CAPTAIN CROOK                   AVG:$1.50    MINT:$2.00
1981 FRY GUY                         AVG:$1.25    MINT:$1.75
     HAMBURGLAR                      AVG:$1.25    MINT:$1.75
1983 COBINED FIGURES                 AVG:$2.00    MINT:$3.25
1985 GRIMACE GROOMER                 AVG:$1.50    MINT:$2.25
     VROOMER GROOMER (RMCD)          AVG:$2.00    MINT:$3.00
1988 RMCD                            AVG:$1.00    MINT:$1.50
     FRY GUY                         AVG:$1.00    MINT:$1.50
```

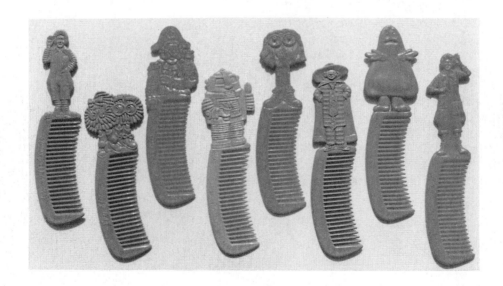

CUP HOLDER: for 32 oz cup   AVG:$2.50   MINT:$3.75
Red. Hangs form dashboard.
"Super Size Coca Cola".

FIGURE, advertising, six foot   AVG:$150.00 MINT:$275.00
Plastic figure of RMCD, waving. White
conical metal stand.

FIGURE, Balloon blowing   AVG:$150.00 MINT:$225.00
Head of RMCD. Fits over air tank.
Balloons are filled through valve in mouth.

GOLF BALLS: ARCHES logo   AVG:$2.00   MINT:$3.00

GOLF TEES: yellow   AVG:$3.00   MINT:$4.75
Set of four in white matchbook-like
folder. Yellow button inside with logo.

GROWTH CHART: Magic castle   AVG:$2.00   MINT:$3.50
In paper envelope package,
showing McDONALDLAND characters
riding on a green dinosaur. Inside is
growth chart, picturing them in
castle tower windows. 4 6/8 inches wide.
Height to 4 feet. Full color.

GROWTH CHART: Ronald McDonald   AVG:$1.75   MINT:$2.50
Pictures RMCD with chart. 3 1/2 inches
wide. Height to 5ft. (C)McDonald's Corp. 1981

HARMONICA: "Tooter" (1985)   AVG:$3.00   MINT:$3.50

ALARM CLOCKS

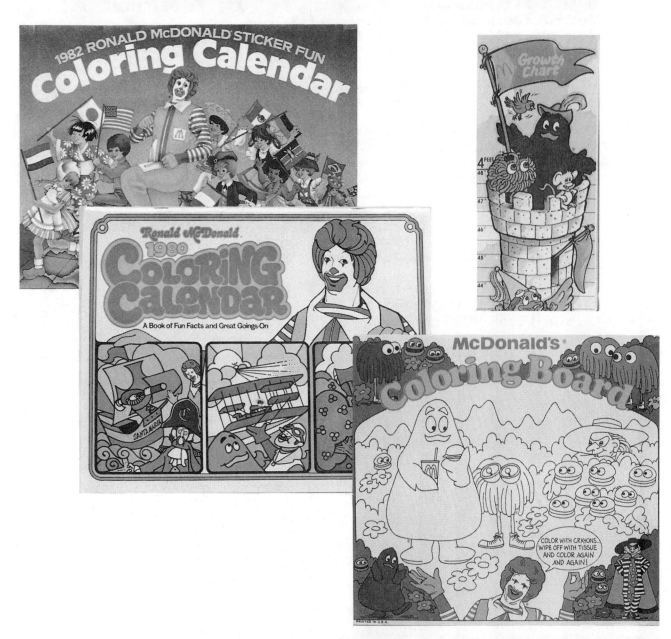

HAT: I'M "SPEEDEE"   AVG:$7.00   MINT:$12.00
Mesh top.(old).Blue band on bottom
edge Both sides shows picture of Mr.
Speedee in chef's hat carrying sign
with above slogan.
Text, red, "McDonald's.

HAT: Brown banded paper hat   AVG:$6.00   MINT:$9.50
Mesh top. McD logo. "Cellucap" (old).

HAT: Dk. Blue banded paper hat   AVG:$6.00   MINT:$8.00
Mesh top. McD logo."Cellucap" (old).

HAT: paper. RMCD "Happy Hat"   AVG:$4.50   MINT:$7.00
White counter hat, design of text,
RMCD,yellow stars.

HAT: baseball type, Olympic   AVG:$4.00   MINT:$5.50
Back half is blue mesh, red eyeshade,
white front with applique of "SAM"
the Olympic eagle, holding a torch.
He wears a red, white & blue top-hat.
Inside label: "Sam the Olympic Eagle /
(C) 1980 LAOOC "

HAT: OLYMPIC SAM, Baseball type.   AVG:$4.00   MINT:$9.00
White front, red shade, blue mesh
back, red button on top. Applique
of Sam, the Olympic Eagle holding
the torch. Olympic and ARCHES logos.

HAT: OLYMPIC, Baseball type.   AVG:$4.00   MINT:$7.50
White front, red shade with blue
border, red mesh back. Blue button
on top. Applique of Olympic and ARCHES logos.

**HAT: CREW HAT, McDONALD'S   AVG:$3.00   MINT:$5.00
Maroon with gold trim and logo.**

**HAT: MAC TONIGHT, Baseball type.   AVG:$4.00   MINT:$7.50
Blue. Design of Mac Tonight on front.**

JEWELRY, Bracelet Charm   AVG:$3.50   MINT:$7.00
RMCD standing holding kite in
left hand, 1 1/2" high.

JEWELRY, Bracelet Charm   AVG:$3.00   MINT:$6.00
RMCD riding old fashioned
3-wheel bike. 1.3" high.

JEWELRY, Bracelet Charm   AVG:$3.00   MINT:$6.00
Gold metal, package of fries.
Logo on front. 0.8" high.

DINO LIFT-PADS

MR. SPEEDEE, 1960'S

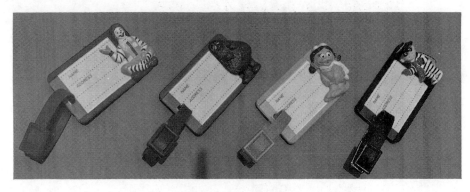

LUGGAGE TAGS

JEWELRY, Bracelet Charm, 0.8"   AVG:$5.00   MINT:$15.00
Gold metal, ARCHES on "V"
(five years), one diamond. 10Karat.

JEWELRY, Bracelet Charm, 0.8"   AVG:$15.00   MINT:$30.00
Gold metal, ARCHES on "X"
(ten years), two diamonds. 10 Karat.

KEYRING: "The Bare Necessities"   AVG:$2.00   MINT:$3.50

KEYRING: "Cinderella"   AVG:$2.00   MINT:$3.50

KEYRING: TRI-RING Key Fob, 1990   AVG:$3.00   MINT:$7.50
Triangular shape, from Owner/Operator
Convention, Las Vegas, NV. May 1990.

KEYRING: Leather Fob   AVG:$7.00   MINT:$10.50
Embossed design of restaurant on
metal disk.

LICENSE PLATE: "Powered By (name)" AVG:$2.00   MINT:$3.50

LICENSE PLATE REFLECTOR FRAME   AVG:$5.00   MINT:$8.00
Full size. Arches logo, "McDonald's".

LIFT-PAD: RMCD Magic pad (1976)   AVG:$2.50   MINT:$3.50

LIFT-PAD: DINO, (Dinosaurs)   AVG:$3.00   MINT:$5.00
On back of cards are pictures of
two dinosaurs with descriptions.
On front: McDONALDLAND characters.

LIFT-PAD: 1985   AVG:$2.25   MINT:$4.00
    McDonald's Magic Tablet.

LIFT-PAD: 1986   AVG:$1.95   MINT:$3.00
McDONALDLAND Magic, rub a pencil
over the pages.

LITTER BAG: plastic   AVG:$2.00   MINT:$3.75
McDonald's System Inc 1978.
"You, You're The One".

LUGGAGE TAG: AVG:$3.00   MINT:$4.00
    McDONALDLAND characters.

LUNCH BOX: PLAYSCHOOL   AVG:$4.00   MINT:$7.50
Shaped like a McDonald's restaurant.
Peaked roof ends in handles which pull
apart to open the box. 7 X 6 inches. #431

LUNCH BOX: Box with thermos   AVG:$20.00 MINT:$ 45.00
"Sheriff of Cactus County" 1982.

LUNCH BOX: McDONALDLAND   AVG:$10.00   MINT:$12.50
(C)1987 McDONALD'S CORPORATION.
Back half of box colored: red, yellow
purple or blue. Large decal covers
front, white half. Different for each box.

LUNCH BOX: McDONALD'S   AVG:$10.00   MINT:$12.50
Solid color box, large logo embossed
on front. Whirley Industries Inc.
Red, yellow, green and blue.

MAC TONIGHT, plastic head   AVG:$5.00   MINT:$8.00
Large head of quarter moon. 1988
     by"FUNDEX".

MAGAZINE: Fun Times children's magazine,
averages 8 pages, stories and activities.
     1980   Cover: RMCD at   AVG:$5.00   MINT:$7.00
             chalkboard: "2+5= ".
     1981   Cover: RMCD on stilts   AVG:$3.50   MINT:$5.50
             making strange footprints.
     1988   "Around the World With   AVG:$3.00   MINT:$5.00
             Ronald McDONALD".
     1989   "Camping With Garfield"   AVG:$3.00   MINT:$5.00
     1990   "Animal Friends From   AVG:$3.00   MINT:$5.00
             Around the World".
     1990   "4 Colorful Seasons"   AVG:$3.00   MINT:$4.50
             Calendar.

MAGAZINE: Olympics   AVG:$3.00   MINT:$5.00
1984, informational. "McDonald's
Salutes the Games of the XXIIIrd Olympiad".

MAGAZINE: TIME, SEPT. 17, 1973   AVG:$12.00 MINT:$30.00
Cover features drawing of Hamburger
in the sky above a McDonald's Restaurant.
"The Hamburger Empire".(pg.84-92)

SHERIFF OF CACTUS COUNTY,
LUNCH BOX & THERMOS

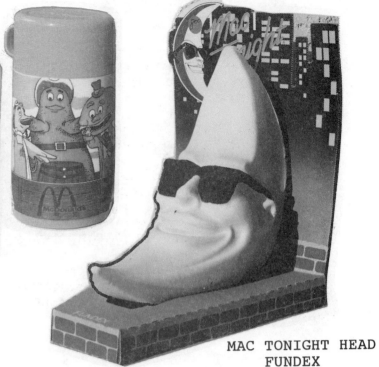

MAC TONIGHT HEAD
FUNDEX

PLAYSKOOL LUNCH BOX

1987 LUNCH BOXES

NATIONAL GEOGRAPHIC MAGAZINE

TIME MAGAZINE

FUN TIMES MAGAZINE

MAGAZINE: NATIONAL GEOGRAPHIC   AVG:$4.50   MINT:$9.00
DECEMBER 1988, VOL. 174, NO. 6.
Featured McDonald's. Holographic picture
of McDonald's Restaurant on back cover.

MAGNETS: Refrigerator (set of 3)   AVG:$2.00 MINT:$3.50
Two-inch square 1985. space scenes:
1. Blue-bordered,RMCD in rocket car.
2. Orange-border,Grimace in red airplane.
3. Hamburglar on burger-rocket.

MAGNETS: Refrigerator (Set of two)   AVG:$1.50 MINT:$2.00
From Las Vegas, food with ARCHES logo:
1. Egg McMuffin/Chicken salad Oriental.
2. McChicken Sandwich/Chicken McNugget.

MAP: RMCD / MOON   AVG:$5.00   MINT:$12.00
Ronald McDonald (TM) cartoons of the
old-style clown with space, moon and
sport facts. RMCD Map,of Outer Space
is on one side and the Official Rand
McNally Map of the Moon is on the
other side. 24 3/4" X 15" .
Copyright (C) 1969 by Rand McNalley Company.

MOLD: POPSICLE. RMCD   AVG:$2.50 MINT:$5.00

MUSIC BOX: McDonald's Restaurant   AVG:$9.00 MIP:$15.00
4 x 3.5 inches. separate piece:
McDonald's sign on post. When door is
opened, the "Good Taste" song plays.

ORNAMENT, window type.Plastic (looks
like stained glass).Tab reads "PEEL HERE".
Average size: 3 1/2 inches.
1. RMCD with Fry and 'burgers   AVG:$1.00   MINT:$1.75
2. HAMBURGLAR with two Frys   AVG:$1.25   MINT:$2.00
3. CAPTAIN CROOK   AVG:$1.25   MINT:$2.00
      with boat and two Frys.

PAPER, WRAPPING: Happy Times   AVG:$5.00   MINT:$7.00
PATCH: iron-on type   AVG:$1.75   MINT:$2.50
Pocket shaped. 1981
RMCD holding Fry Guys.

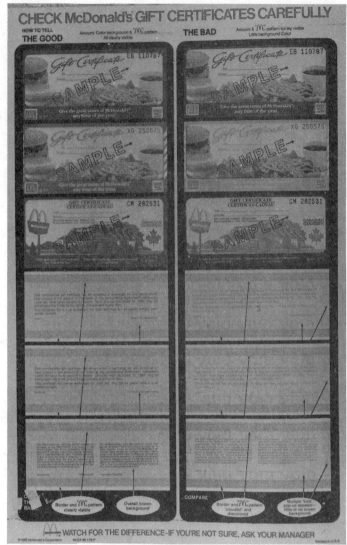

COUNTER POSTER

WINDOW POSTER

PENCIL CASE

PITCHER

McDONALD'S RESTAURANT
MUSIC BOX

WINDOW ORNAMENTS

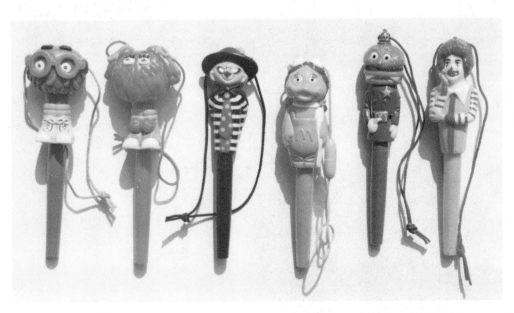

PEN TOPPERS: McDONALDLAND CHARACTERS

PEN TOPPERS: with pen.
Average: 2.7 inches. Fits over pen
of same color. Hanging cord through head.

1. RMCD Red and yellow.   AVG:$2.50   MINT:$6.00
   Resting cheek on right hand,
   elbow propped by left hand.
2. HAMBURGLAR. Black and white   AVG:$2.50   MINT:$6.00
   (red tie). Arms hidden by cape.
3. BIRDIE. Pink and yellow.   AVG:$3.00   MINT:$8.00
   Wings at sides
4. BIG MAC. Blue, Hands down.   AVG:$3.00   MINT:$7.00
5. FRY GUY. Green, wears glasses. AVG:$2.50 MINT:$6.00
6. FRY GIRL. Pink. Yellow ribbons. AVG:$3.00 MINT:$7.00

PENCIL with Button   AVG:$3.00   MINT:$5.00
     Papermate "giveaway", 3 inch
     button:Free Papermate Advancer
     Pencil". Various colors.

PENCILS   AVG:$1.00   MINT:$1.75

PENCIL CASE: notebook insert   AVG:$1.25   MINT:$2.00
White plastic, 5 1/2" X 10".
Figures of RMCD and red Fry Guy.
Text at top in black script:
"Ronald McDonald", at base in red:
"PENCIL CASE".

PENCIL SHARPENER: RMCD   AVG:$2.50   MINT:$3.50
Head & torso. (C) 1983 McDonald's
Corporation.

PICTURE: transparent, window   AVG:$3.00   MINT:$4.00

PITCHER: plastic, 1978   AVG:$7.00   MINT:$9.00
Handle sculpted for easy grip.
White handle, yellow lid. Picture:
RMCD pouring into Grimace's glass.
(C) 1978 McDonald's System Inc./
MCDONALD'S 38824 / Williams Industries.

PLACEMATS: laminated plastic, 10 x 16 inches
1. Scene: United States map   AVG:$1.75   MINT:$3.00
McDONALDLAND characters on other side,
2. RMCD and friends   AVG:$1.75   MINT:$3.00
in hot-air balloon over a McDonald's Restaurant.

POSTERS: St. Louis Cardinals (3)   AVG:$3.00   MINT:$5.50

POSTERS: Detroit Pistons   (3)   AVG:$3.00   MINT:$5.50

POSTERS: Oklahoma Sooners   AVG:$3.00   MINT:$5.50

POSTER: " New Kids On The Block"   AVG:$2.50   MINT:$3.50

POSTER: RMCD painting a fence (1970)   AVG:$3.00   MINT:$4.00

POSTER: theater," Little Mermaid"   AVG:$3.50   MINT:$5.00

POSTER; window, Halloween, (1984)   AVG:$1.75   MINT:$3.00
Safety rules on back. McD #11129
FC 931-496

POSTER: Mac Tonight (1988) (4X)   AVG:$3.50   MINT:$5.00

POSTER: McDONALDLAND (197X)   AVG:$5.00   MINT:$8.00
      early years,Grimace has 4 arms.

POSTER, Counter   AVG:$4.00   MINT:$7.00
Comparing counterfeit Gift
Certificates with genuine.

POSTER, window, 1989   AVG:$3.50   MINT:$5.00
Roger Rabbit poster, showing that
"HAPPY HALLOWEEN CERTIFICATES HERE"
were being given for "Trick or Treat."
.
PRINT: watercolor style   AVG:$5.00   MINT:$10.00
McDonald's Campus Office Bldg.
Nov. 1988, 34 1/2 X 20 1/4"

PUPPET: "Fingertronic"   AVG:$8.00   MIP:$11.00
      Mac Tonight head, 1988

PUZZLE: jigsaw   AVG:$4.00   MINT:$8.50
100 pieces, 12 X 15 1/2 inches.
Made by WHITMAN / 4605-42.
"THE AMAZING RONALD McDONALD". RMCD
on stage,performing a magic hat trick.

MOON MAP

TRAYLINER (4)

LITTER BAG

PAPER, WRAPPING
"HAPPY TIMES"

RADIO: MR. SPEEDEE, 1985
AVG:$45.00 MINT:$65.00

Shaped like a soft-drink can. White
plastic, tuning and volume wheels on
sides. Speaker (Aluminnum grill) on top.
Base unscrews to replace battery and
repair. Design, in red and blue, appears
twice around can. Mr. Speedee, in chef's
hat carries sign, text: "Custom Built
HAMBURGERS". Above him "McDonald's" .
Below him: "COAST TO COAST" in blue
band around base. Below volume wheel,
in red: "1955-1985".

FRENCH FRY RADIO   BIG MAC RADIO

RADIO: French Fry   AVG:$25.00   MINT:$45.00
Replica of Large Fry box with golden
fries. AM/FM radio. Antenna and black
vinyl carrying strap. 8-rayed star-
pattern of holes for speaker. on back:
two knobs. 1977. (Bottom: Copyright
McDonald's System 1977 / made in Hong Kong)
Was still being sold in 1990.

RADIO: Big Mac box   AVG:$45.00   MINT:$75.00
Red box, "Big Mac" on top, sides:
yellow logo, controls on bottom.
General Electric. 3.9" X 3.8" X 2.7".

RATTLE: baby   AVG:$5.00   MINT:$7.00
Handle is ARCHES, RMCD, Hamburglar
and Birdie.

RAZOR: Gillette   AVG:$2.00   MIP:$5.00
Gillette minitrac. "We'll change
the way you look at breakfast" .1986

RECORD: "THE NIGHT BEFORE CHRISTMAS"
Poem read by Ronald McDonald.   AVG:$5.50   MINT:$10.50
 Mfg.CBS records 1972.

RECORD: "MENU MUSIC CHANT"   AVG:$4.00   MINT:$8.00
Mfg. MCA RECORDS (c)1981.

RECORD: RMCD DISCOVERY SERIES   AVG:$4.25   MINT:$8.50
"SHARE A SONG FROM YOUR HEART"
and "FRIENDS". Ronald McDonald
& Friends. Mfg. (C)1980 Casablanca
Record and Film Works, Inc.

RECORD: "Menu Song"   AVG:$3.00   MINT:$6.00
33 1/3 RPM record, attached to
large picture of juke-box. Was special
promotion in newspaper. (C) 1988
"Play McDonald's $1,000,000 Menu Song"

RECORD: ALPHABET   AVG:$3.00   MINT:$6.00
Talking storybook. Book and record.
Mfg. KID STUFF Records.
Dist. I.J.E. Distributing.

RAZOR, GILLETTE

RECORDS

RINGS: McDONALDLAND characters outlined
with raised areas on plastic panels
affixed to open bands of the same material.
Average size of panel: 1 3/4 inches.
Several types, some have contrasting
paint on raised outlines.

1. GRIMACE, purple disk, red paint   AVG:$1.50   MINT:$2.00
2. HAMBURGLAR, yellow disk,blk. paint   AVG:$1.50   MINT:$2.00
2a.HAMBURGLAR, yellow shape   AVG:$1.50   MINT:$2.00
3. BIG MAC, yellow disk, blk. paint   AVG:$1.50   MINT:$2.00
4. UNCLE O'GRIMACY, grn. disk,blk. pt.   AVG:$1.50   MINT:$2.00

RING: Pumpkin, orange   AVG:$1.50   MINT:$2.00

RING: "Happy Haloween"   AVG:$4.00   MINT:$6.50
(1979) Wiggle Ring RMCD, McBoo ghost.

RINGS:"Wiggle" XOGraph pictures   AVG:$8.00   MINT:$10.00
Two different scenes depending on
view point, set into large flat frame
of dark blue plastic.
    1. RMCD diving into water
    2. RMCD juggling
    3. RMCD flying in hamburger
    4. RMCD jumping rope

RINGS:"Wiggle" XOGraph pictures   AVG:$8.00   MINT:$10.00
Two different scenes depending on
view point, set into dark blue
plastic ring. *No frame shows at top or bottom.*

RING: Heart shaped, RMCD LG. head   AVG:$4.00   MINT:$5.50
White plastic, red rim and design. 1979

RING: SANTA CLAUS   AVG:$0.75   MINT:$1.50
White plastic, shaped to head.
Red paint on raised areas. 1 1/2in.

RINGS: Lt. Blue (1985)   AVG:$2.00   MINT:$4.50
    Friendship Spaceship
    McDonald's 500 smile racer

RING: Blow Horn, RMCD   AVG:$3.00   MINT:$5.50

RING: Grimace "Wind Twirler"   AVG:$2.50   MINT:$4.00

WIGGLE RINGS

500 SMILE RACER RING   FRIENDSHIP SPACESHIP RING

SUPER STICKER SQUARES

SMILE KIT

RULER: 6" Big Mac   AVG:$3.00   MINT:$3.50

RULER: 12" "McMetrics"   AVG:$3.00   MINT:$4.00

RULER: "Ruler Coaster"   AVG:$2.00   MINT:$3.00
White, McDONALDLAND characters in
roller-coaster. Centimeters:inches,
and conversion chart.

RULER: "Fun Ruler",   AVG:$2.00   MINT:$3.00
(like "Ruler Coaster") McDONALDLAND
characters with pencils, doing tricks.

SCARF: McNugget Fiesta.   AVG:$4.00   MINT:$7.00
     1988. Purple or yellow.

SCISSORS: 1982 RMCD, yellow plastic   AVG:$1.00   MINT:$1.50

SHIRT: 1990, white "T",   AVG:$5.00   MINT:$10.00
imprinted with picture of Quarter-pounder
"burger, ARCHES logo and slogan
"Fremont, California / Home of McDonald's
Quarter-Pounder / 20th Anniversary 1971-1991 /
The World Famous Taste That Started here."
On back: "Fremont is Fantastic."

SMILE KIT: AVG:$2.50   MINT:$4.00
Kit contains: wall mountable cup,
toothbrush holder and small white
plastic cup (2.9") with waving RMCD.

SPEEDEE, MR. Old McDonald's logo.
See: HAT, also serving paper materials
with "SPEEDEE" logo.
FRIES BAG, white   AVG:$2.00   MINT:$4.00
BAG, #3, white   AVG:$1.50   MINT:$3.00

SPONGES: Average size: 5 inches.
"Tickle Feather", red & yellow   AVG:$1.50   MINT:$2.00
Grimace, shaped, brown   AVG:$1.50   MINT:$2.00
Grimace "Carwash", purple, 4"   AVG:$1.50   MINT:$2.00

STICKERS: Fun Set (1988)   AVG:$1.50   MINT:$2.00

STICKERS:"Dress Up McNuggets"(1988) AVG:$1.50   MINT:$2.00

STICKERS: "Super Sticker" squares   AVG:$4.00   MINT:$4.50
Nine scenes, over 100 reusable
stickers, 1985.

SUNGLASSES

TRAY LINERS

"We couldn't do it without you!"

STICKER: puffy, Roger Rabbit   AVG:$2.50   MINT:$4.00
(C) Touchstone Pictures and Amblin
Entertainment. Came with a Halloween
gift certificate book with eleven
coupons. 1989

STICKER, HARD PLASTIC. Same type as
on rings but with adhesive strip on backs.
Average size 1 1/2 inches.
1. RMCD head, red on white plastic   AVG:$0.75   MINT:$1.25
2. Big Mac, blue on yellow plastic   AVG:$0.50   MINT:$1.00
3. Hamburglar, blackon yellow   AVG:$0.50   MINT:$1.00
4. Cap't Crook, green on yellow   AVG:$0.75   MINT:$1.25

SUNGLASSES: plastic   AVG:$3.50   MINT:$4.50
Several colors: a McDONALDLAND
character featured in center.

SUNGLASSES: AVG:$2.50   MINT:$5.50
Adult. 49ERs logo

TELEPHONE: RMCD   AVG:$75.00   MINT:$125.00
Nine-inch standing figure of RMCD
on white base. Front of base:
"Ronald McDONALD".
Touch-tone buttons on back.

TELEPHONE

```
TOPS: flip-flop                        AVG:$1.00    MINT:$2.00
RMCD and Grimace pictured on inside,
top flips from one side to the other.
(04793 Group II).


TOTE BAG: white vinyl,                 AVG:$2.50    MINT:$5.00
White vinyl, thick drawstring.
Scene: RMCD & sailboat.


TRAY LINER,
1."We Couldn't do it Without You!"     AVG:$1.00    MINT:$2.00
2. Breakfast Nutritional Analysis      AVG:$1.00    MINT:$2.00
3."A Sunny Good Morning To You",1981   AVG:$2.00    MINT:$3.00
4."VOTE FOR ME"                        AVG:$2.00    MINT:$4.00


UTENSILS: plastic forks, spoons        AVG:$3.00    MINT:$4.00
The ends are shaped and embossed
with McDONALDLAND characters.
Colors: yellow, green. 1988

FORK      RMCD                         AVG:$2.50    MINT:$4.00
          GRIMACE                      AVG:$2.00    MINT:$3.00
          RMCD IN CAR                  AVG:$2.50    MINT:$3.25
          FRY GUY ON ELEPHANT          AVG:$2.00    MINT:$3.00
SPOON     RMCD IN CAR                  AVG:$2.50    MINT:$3.25
          GRIMACE                      AVG:$2.00    MINT:$3.00
          FRY GUY ON ELEPHANT          AVG:$2.25    MINT:$3.00
          GRIMACE ON CAR               AVG:$1.75    MINT:$3.00
          FRY GUY ON BEAR              AVG:$2.00    MINT:$3.25
```

VALENTINES: 1974   AVG:$20.00   MINT:$33.00
        Four card sheets, 3 sets.

VALENTINES:"Design a Valentine" 1979 AVG:$2.50   MINT:$3.50

VIDEO TAPES: "Muppet Baby"   AVG:$8.00   MINT:$12.00
     "THE DAILY MUPPET'
     "SNOW WHITE AND THE 7 MUPPETS"
     "THE GREAT MUPPET CARTOON SHOW"

VIDEO TAPE: McTREASURE ISLAND   AVG:$5.00   MINT:$12.00

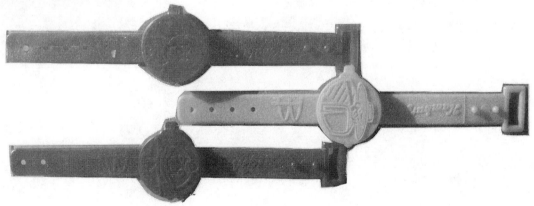

WALLETS: wrist, plastic   AVG:$1.50   MINT:$2.00
Several colors. McDONALDLAND
characters embossed on lid.

WASTEBASKET: Mac Tonight   AVG:$12.00 MINT:$20.00
Full size, metal. black with design
of Mac Tonight seated at piano.
"Make It Mac Tonight". 1988

WATCH: Ronald McDONALD   AVG:$4.00   MINT:$9.00
Digital, plastic, numbers in black
around rim.

WATCH: digital, ARCHES   AVG:$3.50   MINT:$5.00

WATCH: digital, "SPORT WATCH"   AVG:$5.00   MIP:$8.00
Black dial with ARCHES,black numbers
around rim. Colors: orange, green, white.

WATCH: digital, RMCD House   AVG:$7.00   MIP:$10.00
"Official Ronald McDONALD watch /
thank you for supporting Ronald
McDonaldhouse." On card with COCA-COLA
logo. Face: RMCD holding rectangle where
time appears. colors:black, red. (C) 1984

WATCH: digital,with lid   AVG:$13.00 MINT:$15.00
RMCD face on lid, opens to reveal
watch. White plastic.
"Ronald McDONALD" in red.

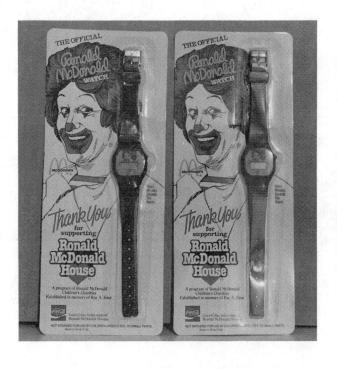

HAPPY MEALS 1977 CHECK LIST
FUN TO GO:_____
CARTONS (7):
_____1. 20,000 FILET-O-FISH
_____2. PROFESSOR IN HIS
          LABORATORY
_____3. 2002 HAMBURGERS
_____4. McMOBILE
_____5. McDONALD'S
          BREAKFAST
_____6. BIG BURGER COUNTRY
_____7. MAZE CRAZE/
          PLANET OF PICKLES

STRAWS:_____
_____1. RONALD McDONALD
_____2. HAMBURGLAR
_____3. BIG MAC
_____4. CAPTAIN CROOK

JOKE BOOKS:_____
by local children.
_____1.
_____2.
_____3.
_____4.

CARTONS:_____
" ROUND TOPS"
_____1. WHAT'S WRONG HERE?
_____2. RAINING CATS & DOGS
_____3. RONALD McD &
          MAYOR McCHEESE

WRIST WALLET:_____
_____1. RONALD McDONALD
_____2. HAMBURGLAR
_____3. BIG MAC
_____4. CAPTAIN CROOK

RINGS:_____
_____1. RONALD McDONALD
_____2. HAMBURGLAR
_____3. BIG MAC
_____4. CAPTAIN CROOK
_____5. GRIMACE

MAGIC TRICKS:_____
_____1. FAVORITE FRIENDS
          CARD TRICK
_____2. VANISHING
          HAMBURGER
_____3. THE FAKE SHAKE
_____4. THE BURGLED
HAMBURGER

PAPER STENCIL:_____
_____1. RONALD McDONALD
_____2. HAMBURGLAR

MAKE FUNNY FACES_____
_____

STICKERS:_____
_____1. RMCD: "RIDE SAFELY"
_____2. HAMBURGLAR:
          "LIGHTS ON FOR
SAFETY"
_____3. BIG MAC: "OBEY ALL
          RULES OF THE ROAD"
_____4. CAPTAIN CROOK:
          "DON'T TAILGATE"

"FORTUNE BURGER"_____
_____

COLOR CARD_____
_____

PUNKIN' MAKINS:_____
_____1. GRIMACE
_____2. HAMBURGLAR
_____3. GOBLIN

PAPER, MAZE & PUZZLE CARDS:
_____1. MCDONALD'S MAZE &
          PUZZLE
_____2. RACE TO
          MCDONALDLAND
_____3. POUR-UM GAME
_____4. MATCH GAME

HAPPY MEALS 1978 CHECK LIST

McDONALDLAND PENCIL PUPPETS

_____

_____

McDONALDLAND PRESS-ONS_____

UNCLE O'GRIMACY RINGS_____

RONALD MAGIC PADS_____

SUNDAE SMILE SKIMMER_____

CARTONS:
_____1. MAKE A FACE
_____2. JINGLE JAMBOREE
_____3. WEIRD CREATURES

FOUR JOKE BOOKS_____

JIGSAW PUZZLES:_____
_____1. PROFESSOR AND
          GRIMACE
_____2. CAPTAIN CROOK
          AND BIG MAC.

McDONALDLAND RUB-OFFS_____

RING-AROUND-RONALD_____

COLOR YOUR OWN
XMAS ORNAMENT_____

BIKE REFLECTORS:_____
_____1. RONALD McDONALD
_____2. HAMBURGLAR
_____3. BIG MAC
_____4. CAPTAIN CROOK

BAG: Halloween_____

SPINNING TOPS_____

STICKER, "KIDS DAY"_____

MYSTERY PUZZLE:
white cardboard_____

COMIC BOOKS:_____
_____RONALD McDONALD AND
        THE FRIES FARMERS.
_____RONALD McDONALD in
        THE DISAPPEARING ACT.

FINGER PUPPETS:_____
_____1. HAMBURGLAR
_____2. BIG MAC

McDONALDLAND
PAINT-WITH-WATER_____

McDONALDLAND
COLORING STAND-UPS_____

GAME CARDS:_____
_____SILLY METRICS
        TRADING CARD
_____RACE TO McDONALDLAND
_____McDONALDLAND
        PAIR-UM GAME
_____McDONALDLAND MATCH
        GAME
_____PUNCH OUT CARD,
        MAKE-A-SCULPTURE

FAVORITE FRIENDS
MAGIC TRICK_____

HAPPY MEALS 1979 CHECK LIST

LION CIRCUS:_____
_____1. LION
_____2. ELEPHANT
_____3. HIPPOPOTAMUS
_____4. BEAR
CARTON:_____

SKYSCRAPERS_____

WHAT IS IT ?:_____
_____1. OWL
_____2. BEAR
_____3. BABOON
_____4. HORNED SNAKE
_____5. SKUNK
_____6. SQUIRREL
CARTON _____

ANIMAL RIDDLES:_____
_____1. CONDOR
_____2. SNAIL
_____3. TURTLE
_____4. MOUSE
_____5. ANTEATER
_____6. ALLIGATOR
_____7. COW
_____8. DINOSAUR
CARTON:_____

McDONALDLAND CHARACTERS:____
_____1. RONALD McDONALD
_____2. HAMBURGLAR

SMART DUCK_____
CARTON_____

MINI-FLEXI:_____
_____1. COSMOBIL
_____2. FANDANGO
_____3. PLANET SCOUT
_____4. HAIRY HUSTLER
_____5. DATSUN
_____6. HI-TAILER
_____7. BAJA BUGGY
_____8. BEACH HOPPER

McDONALDLAND COMIC BOOKS____

McDONALDLAND Lift-ups:_____
_____MaYOR WORD GUESS
_____RONALD MAZE
_____PROFESSOR DOT GAME
_____BIG MAC TIC-TAC-TOE

CIRCUS WAGON:_____
_____1. CLOWN
_____2. HORSE
_____3. APE
_____4. POODLE DOG
CARTONS (6):

SPACE ALIENS:_____
_____1.GILL FACE
_____2.TREE TRUNK MONSTER
_____3.LIZARD MAN
_____4.VAMPIRE BAT
_____5.WINGED AMPHIBIAN
_____6.HORNED CYCLOPS
_____7.INSECTMAN
_____8.VEINED CRANIUM

MISCELLANEOUS ITEMS:_____
_____O'GRIMACY INFLATABLES
_____McDONALDLAND YOYO
_____SKIMMER RINGS,
          SUNDAE SMILE SAUCER
_____FRENCH FRY RINGS
_____RONALD STYRO-GLIDER
_____FRENCH FRY FLUTES,
          SPINNING TOPS
_____SILLY SIDE SHOW,
          PUNCH OUT CARD
_____FISHIN' FUN WITH
          CAPTAIN CROOK

SPACE RAIDERS:_____
_____1.POINTED EARS, DARD
_____2.ALIEN, ZAMA
_____3.ALIEN, HORTA
_____4.ROUND HEAD, DRAK
_____5.FLYING SAUCER,
          LYRA 4
_____6.ROCKET, KRYOO 5
_____7.ROCKET, CETI-3
_____8.ROCKET, ALTAIR 2
CARTONS (6):

STAR TREK:_____
VIDEO COMMUNICATOR
WITH STRIP:
_____1.*"STAR TREK STARS"*
_____2.*"A PILL SWALLOWS*
          THE ENTERPRISE"
_____3.*"TIME AND TIME AND*
          TIME AGAIN"
_____4.*"VOTEC'S FREEDOM"*
_____5.*"STARLIGHT STAR*
FRIGHT"*

STARFLEET GAME _____
DECALS:
_____1.MR. SPOCK
_____2. LT. MIA
_____3.
_____4.
BRACELET:NAVIGATION _____
RING: SPACE
_____1. CAPTAIN KIRK
_____2. SPOCK
_____3. STARTREK INSIGNIA
_____4. ENTERPRISE

CARTONS
_____1.TRANSPORTER ROOM
_____2.KLINGONS
_____3.THE BRIDGE, planets
_____4.UNITED FEDERATION
          OF PLANETS
_____5.SPACESUIT
_____6.BRIDGE, alien

HAPPY MEALS 1980 CHECK LIST

DALLAS COWBOYS SUPER BOX___
baseball cards_____
_____1.CHUCK HOWLEY /
          DON PERKINS
_____2.DON MEREDITH /
          BOB LILLY
_____3.ROGER STAUGACH /
          W.GARRISON

"LOOK-LOOK BOOKS":_____
_____1. ANIMALS THAT FLY
_____2. ANIMALS OF THE SEA
_____3. CATS IN THE WILD
_____4. THE BIGGEST ANIMALS

UNDERSEA:_____
DIENER FIGURES:
_____1.SEAL
_____2.DOLPHIN
_____3.TIGER SHARK
_____4.HAMMERHEAD SHARK
_____5.SEA TURTLE
_____6.PENGUIN
_____7.WHALE
_____8.WHALE SHARK
_____9.WALRUS
_____10.CROCODILE
_____11.GREAT WHITE SHARK
CARTONS:5

JUNGLE SAFARI:_____
ANIMAL FIGURINES:
_____1. ELEPHANT
_____2. TIGER
_____3. HIPPOPOTAMUS
_____4. RHINOCEROS
_____5. LION
_____6. ALLIGATOR
_____7. GORILLA
CARTONS (4):

HAPPY MEALS 1981 CHECK LIST

OLD WEST:_____
FIGURINES:
_____1.FRONTIERSMAN
_____2.LADY
_____3.INDIAN
_____4.SHERIFF
_____5.MAN

CARTONS (6):
_____1.BLACKSMITH SHOP
_____2.HOTEL
_____3.SHERIFF'S OFFICE
_____4.GENERAL STORE
_____5.MUSIC HALL
_____6.TRAIN DEPOT

THE ADVENTURES OF
RONALD McDONALD:_____
CARTONS (6):
_____1.MIDNIGHT AT
       McDONALD'S
_____2.END OF RAINBOW
_____3.WHO'S GOBLIN UP
       THE FRIES
_____4.THE BIG HUNT
_____5.CHEESEBURGER EXPRESS
_____6.RODEO COWBOY

GOING PLACES:_____
CARTONS (6):
_____1.AIRPLANE
_____2.GREY ELEPHANT
_____3.PADDLE WHEELER
_____4.DUNE BUGGY
_____5.FIRE ENGINE
_____6.STEAM ENGINE

3-D HAPPY MEAL:_____
CARTONS (4):
_____1.BUGSVILLE/HUNGRY
       FUNNIES
_____2.CLOWNISH CAPERS/
       HIGH JINX
_____3.LAUGHING STOCK/
       LOCO MOTION
_____4.SPACE FOLLIES/
       GURGLE GAGS

DINOSAUR DAYS:_____
DINOSAUR FIGURES:
_____1.DIMETRODON
_____2.STEGOSAURUS
_____3.TYRANNOSAURUS
_____4.TRICERATOPS
_____5.ANKYLOSAURUS
_____6.PTERANODON

XOGRAPHS:
_____1.MASTODONS
_____2.STEGOSAURUS
_____3.TRICERATOPS
_____4.BRONTOSAURUS
_____5.SABER-TOOTHED TIGER
_____6.TYRANNOSAURUS REX
CARTONS (6):

HAPPY MEALS 1982 CHECK LIST

SPACESHIP_____
_____SPACESHIPS

GOING PLACES:_____
CARTONS (6):
_____1. DUNE BUGGY
_____2. STEAM ENGINE
_____3. AIRPLANE
_____4. GREY ELEPHANT
_____5. PADDLE WHEELER
_____6. FIRE ENGINE

GIGGLES AND GAMES:_____
CARTONS:
_____1.CHASE
_____2.MONSTER
_____3.OUTER SPACE
_____4.BUMPER CAR
_____5.SUNKEN TREASURE
_____6.ROAD RALLY

"AIRPLANE", CARTONS:_____

"SKYBUSTERS"
_____1.UNITED DC-10
_____2.MIG-21
_____3.MIRAGE F1
_____4.TORNADO
_____5.PHANTOM F4E
_____6.SKYHAWK AAF
CARTON _____

DUKES OF HAZZARD:_____
CARS:
_____1.CADILLAC
_____2.GENERAL LEE CAR
_____3.JEEP
_____4.SHERIFF CAR
_____5.PICKUP
HAPPY CUPS:
_____1.LUKE DUKE
_____2.BOSS HOGG
_____3.SHERIFF ROSCOE
_____4.DAISY DUKE
_____5.UNCLE JESSE
_____6.BO DUKE

McDONALDLAND EXPRESS:_____
_____1.RONALD McDONALD
        ENGINE
_____2.COACH
_____3.FREIGHT CAR
_____4.CABOOSE

LITTLE GOLDEN BOOKS:_____
_____1."MONSTER AT THE END
        OF THE BOOK"
_____2."COUNTRY MOUSE AND
        CITY MOUSE"
_____3."TOM AND JERRY'S
        PARTY"
_____4."POKY LITTLE PUPPY"
_____5."BENJI,FASTEST DOG
        IN THE WEST"
CARTON_____

PLAYMOBILE:_____
_____1.SHERIFF
_____2.INDIAN
_____3.HORSE & SADDLE
_____4.UMBRELLA GIRL
_____5.FARMER
CARTONS   _____
_____1.BARN
_____2.LOG CABIN
_____3.SCHOOLHOUSE
_____4.TRADING POST

HOT WHEELS:_____

_____1126 STUTZ BLACKHAWK
_____1130 TRICAR X-8
_____1132 3 WINDOW '34,
           "HI RAKERS"
_____1136 SPLIT WINDOW
           '63, gold
_____1694 TURISMO, red
_____1697 MINITREK,
           camper, white
_____1698 CADILLAC SEVILLE
_____2013 '57 T-BIRD
_____2019 SHERIFF PATROL,
           "Sheriff 701"
_____2021 RACE BAIT 308
_____2022 BAJA BREAKER,
           camper,orange
_____3250 FIREBIRD
           FUNNY CAR, red
_____3255 DATSUN 200 SX
_____3257 FRONT RUNNING
           FAIRMONT
_____3259 JEEP CJ7, brown
_____3260 LAND LORD,
           orange
_____3261 MERCEDES 380
           SEL, silver
_____3362 CHEVY CITATION,
           brown
_____3364 DIXIE CHALLENGER
_____5180 PORSCHE 928,
           Turbo
_____9037 MALIBU GRAND
           PRIX, black
_____9241 CORVETTE
           STINGRAY, red
_____9647 '56 HI-TAIL
           HAULER

HAPPY MEALS 1983 CHECK LIST

McDONALDLAND JUNCTION:_____
_____1.RMCD ENGINE
_____2.HAMBURGER PATCH
         FLAT CAR
_____3.BIRDIE PARLOR CAR
_____4.GRIMACE CABOOSE
CARTONS (6)
_____1.TOWN HALL
_____2.STATION
_____3.TRAIN TUNNEL
_____4.POST OFFICE
_____5.ENGINE BARN
_____6.SIGNAL TOWER

ASTROSNIKS I:_____
_____1.SPORT,WITH FOOTBALL
_____2.ROBO THE ROBOT
_____3.SCOUT WITH FLAG
_____4.THIRSTY WITH DRINK
_____5.ICE SKATER
_____6.ASTRALIA, WITH CONE
_____7.LASER
_____8.SNIKAPOTAMUS
CARTONS (4)

SHIP SHAPE I:_____
_____1.HAMBURGLAR JET
         SPLASHDASHER
_____2.GRIMACE TUBBY
TUBBER
_____3.CAPTAIN CROOK
         RUB-A-DUB SUB
_____4.RMCD RIVERBOAT

CIRCUS:_____
_____1.STRONG GONG
_____2.ACROBATIC RONALD
_____3.MCD FUN HOUSE
MIRROR
_____4.FRENCH FRY FALLER
PUNCH-OUT SHEETS;
_____5.CIRCUS BACKDROP I
_____6.CIRCUS BACKDROP II
_____7.PUPPET SHOW
BACKDROP
_____8.FUN HOUSE BACKDROP
CARTONS (6):

WINTER WORLDS
Hanging ornaments:_____
_____1.RMCD
_____2.GRIMACE
_____3.HAMBURGLAR
_____4.BIRDIE
_____5.MAYOR McCHEESE
CARTONS (5)

MYSTERY:_____
_____1.UNPREDICT-A-BALL
_____2.RONALD DETECTIVE
        KIT
_____3.MAGIC BALL
_____4.MAGNI FINDER
CARTONS (6):

HAPPY MEALS 1984 CHECK LIST

GOOD SPORTS:_____
_____1.RMCD
_____2.BIRDIE
_____3.GRIMACE
_____4.MAYOR McCHEESE
_____5.SAM OLYMPIC EAGLE
_____6. HAMBURGLAR
CARTONS (4)
_____1.SKI JUMP
_____2.SLED RUN
_____3.GYMNASTICS
_____4.BASKETBALL

OLYMPIC SPORTS
Puzzles:_____
_____1. WINNING GOAL
_____2. BIGGEST SPLASH
_____3. HELP THEM ROW
_____4. SMILES AHEAD
_____5. UNDER THE WIRE
CARTONS (5):
_____1. BOATS AFLOAT
_____2. IN THE SWIM
_____3. MAKING TRACKS
_____4. JUST FOR KICKS
_____5. PEDAL POWER

HAPPY PAIL
Olympic themes:_____
_____1.CYCLING
_____2.TRACK & FIELD
_____3.OLYMPIC GAMES
_____4.SWIMMING

ASTROSNIKS II:_____
_____1.DRILL
_____2.COMMANDER
_____3.RACING
_____4.COPTER
_____5.SKI
_____6.PERFIDO
CARTONS (2):

SCHOOL DAYS:_____
PENCILS:
_____RMCD
_____HAMBURGLAR
_____GRIMACE
ERASERS:
_____RMCD
_____HAMBURGLAR
_____GRIMACE
_____BIRDIE
_____CAPTAIN CROOK
RULER_____
PENCIL SHARPENERS:
_____RMCD

LEGO BUILDING SET:_____
_____1.TRUCK
_____2.SHIP
_____3.HELICOPTER
_____4.AIRPLANE
UNDER 3 YRS:
_____1.ANIMAL
_____2.BUILDING
CARTONS (4):

HAPPY HOLIDAYS:_____
_____1.STICKER SHEET,HOUSE
_____2.STICKER SHEET,TRAIN
CARTONS (2):
_____1.GIFT TAG
_____2.ORNAMENT

BEACH BALL
Olympic themes:_____
_____1. BIRDIE
_____2. RMCD
_____3. GRIMACE

HAPPY MEALS 1985 CHECK LIST

PLAY DOH:_____
_____1.RED
_____2.ORANGE
_____3.YELLOW
_____4.GREEN
_____5.BLUE
_____6.PURPLE
_____7.WHITE
_____8.PINK
CARTON_____

DAY AND NIGHT
Cartons:_____
_____1.WHO'S AFRAID OF
         THE DARK?
_____2.ALL STAR SUNDAY

ON THE GO:_____
_____1.DECAL TRANSFER
_____2."STOP AND GO" BEAD
         GAME
_____3."STOP LIGHT" SHAPE
         BEAD GAME
_____4."SLATE-BOARD
RONALD" LIFT-PAD
_____5."SLATE-BOARD
         HAMBURGLAR" LIFT-PAD
CARTONS (4)

CRAZY CREATURES:_____
_____1. CUBE, 6 holes
_____2. BALL, 6 holes
_____3. FLAT CIRCLE,
         10 holes
_____4. PENTA JOINT
CARTONS (4):

MAGIC SHOW, Tricks:_____
_____1.DISAPPEARING
         HAMBURGER PATCH
_____2.MAGIC STRING PULL
_____3.MAGIC TABLET
_____4.MAGIC PICTURE
CARTONS (4):

STICKER CLUB
Stickers:_____
_____1. 12 STICKERS,
          McDONALDLAND
characters
_____2. 5 SCRATCH & SNIFF
          STICKERS,RMCD,
          GRIMACE,
          HAMBURGLAR, BIRDIE
& FRY GUY
_____3. 6 REFLECTOR
STICKERS,
          McDONALDLAND
          characters
_____4. ACTION STICKERS,
          RMCD, HAMBURGLAR,
          BIRDIE & PROFESSOR
_____5. 2 PUFFY STICKERS,
          RMCD & GRIMACE
CARTONS (4):

SHIP SHAPE:_____
_____1.HAMBURGLAR JET
          SPLASHDASHER
_____2.GRIMACE TUBBY
          TUBBER
_____3.CAPTAIN CROOK
          RUB-A-DUB SUB
_____4.RMCD RIVERBOAT
UNDER 3 YRS;
_____1.GRIMACE TUB TOY,
          purple
_____2.FRY GUY & FRIENDS
          TUB TOY

COMMANDRONS:_____
_____1. VELOCITOR (TM)
_____1a.COMIC BOOK:*"Dawn
of the Commandrons"*
_____2. MOTRON (TM)
_____2a.COMIC BOOK:
          "Robo Mania"
_____3. SOLARDYN (TM)
_____3a.COMIC BOOK:
          "The Copy-Bots"
_____4.COMMANDER MAGNA(TM)
_____4a.COMIC BOOK:
          "Airborne"

MY LITTLE PONY /
TRANSFORMERS:_____
TRANSFORMERS
_____1.BUMBLEBEE
_____2.GEARS
_____3.CLIFF JUMPER
_____4.BRAWN

PONY CHARMS
_____1.MEDLEY
_____2.APPLEJACK
_____3.SKYFLIER
_____4.LIKETY SPLIT
_____5.FLUTTERBYE
_____6.CHERRIES JUBILEE

PICTURE PERFECT_____
_____CARTON; RONALD
                QUICK DRAW

E.T., POSTERS:_____
_____1. BOY AND E.T. ON A
          FLYING BIKE
_____2. BOY AND E.T.
TOUCHING FINGERS
_____3. E.T. WITH RADIO
_____4. E.T. RAISING HAND
CARTONS (2):

MUSIC:_____
_____1.GREEN LABEL
_____2.YELLOW LABEL
_____3.PURPLE LABEL
_____4.BLUE LABEL
CARTONS (4):

POPOIDS:_____
_____SET 1, CYLINDER
_____SET 2, CUBE
_____SET 3, SPHERE
_____SET 4, TRIANGLE
CARTONS (4):

STOMPER MINI I:_____
_____1. JEEP RENEGADE,
           white & maroon
_____2. CHEVY S-10, yellow
_____3. CHEVY S-10,
           silver & black
_____4. DODGE RAMPAGE
           maroon & blue
CARTON_____

HALLOWEEN:_____
_____ JACK-O-LANTERN

ASTROSNIKS III:_____
_____1. COMMANDER
_____2. ROBO THE ROBOT
_____3. SCOUT WITH FLAG
_____4. PERFIDO
_____5. ASTRALIA
_____6. LASER
_____7. SNIKAPOTAMUS
_____8. BOY WITH CONE
_____9. PYRAMIDO
_____10.ASTROSNIK WITH RADIO
_____11.ASTROSNIK ON ROCKET
_____12.RACING
_____13.COPTER
_____14.GALAXO

SANTA CLAUS, THE MOVIE
Books:_____
_____*"THE LEGEND OF
           SANTA CLAUS"*
_____*"THE ELVES AT THE TOP
           OF THE WORLD"*
_____*"SLEIGHFULL OF
       SURPRISES"*
_____*"WORKSHOP OF
           ACTIVITIES"*
CARTONS (2):

FEELING GOOD:_____
_____1. TOOTHBRUSH, RMCD
_____1a.TOOTHBRUSH,
           HAMBURGLAR
_____2. SOAP DISH, GRIMACE
_____3. SPONGE, FRY GUY
_____4. MIRROR, BIRDIE
_____5. COMB,
           CAPTAIN CROOK
UNDER 3 YRS;
_____1.GRIMACE TUB TOY,
         purple
_____2.FRY GUY TUB TOY,
         yellow
CARTONS (4):

HAPPY MEALS 1986 CHECK LIST

AIRPORT:_____
_____1. FRY GUY FLYER
_____2. BIG MAC 'COPTER
_____2a.FRY GUY
"HELLO'COPTER"
_____3. RMCD SEA PLANE
_____4. GRIMACE ACE
_____5. BIRDIE BLAZER

UNDER 3 YRS
_____1. GRIMACE SMILING
SHUTTLE
_____2. FRY GUY FRIENDLY
FLYER
CARTONS (4):

OLD McDONALD'S FARM:_____
_____1.FARMER
_____2.WIFE
_____3.COW
_____4.ROOSTER
_____5.PIG
_____6.SHEEP
CARTONS (2):
_____1.BARN
_____2.HOUSE

THE STORY OF TEXAS:_____
_____1.TEXAS I
_____2.TEXAS II
_____3.TEXAS III
CARTON_____

BEACH BALL:_____
_____1.RONALD, red ball
_____2.GRIMACE, yellow
ball
_____3.BIRDIE, blue ball
CARTON:
_____ HAVING A WONDERFUL
TIME

CONSTRUX ACTION
BLDG SYSTEM :_____
_____1.CYLINDER
_____2.CANOPY
_____3.WING
_____4.AXEL
CARTONS (2):
_____1. TOOL TROUBLE
_____2. MARS MISSION

LUNCH BOX:_____
_____RED
_____GREEN
_____BLUE

McDONALD'S CRAYOLA
CRAYON MAGIC:_____
STENCILS:
_____1.TRIANGLE
_____2.CIRCLE
_____3.RECTANGLE
CARTON

HAPPY PAIL:_____
_____1.VACATION
_____2.TREASURE HUNT
_____3.PARADE
_____4.PICNIC
_____5.BEACH

YOUNG ASTRONAUTS:_____
_____1.APOLLO COMMAND
            MODULE
_____2.SPACE SHUTTLE
_____3.ARGO LAND SHUTTLE
_____4.CIRRUS VTOL
UNDER 3 YRS:
_____1.GRIMACE SMILING
            SHUTTLE
_____2.FRY GUY AIRPLANE
            blue
CARTONS (4):
_____1.SPACE STATION

PLAY DOH:_____
_____1.RED
_____2.ORANGE
_____3.YELLOW
_____4.GREEN
_____5.BLUE
_____6.PURPLE
_____7.WHITE
_____8.PINK
CARTONS (4):
_____1.CIRCUS ANIMALS
_____2.YESTERDAY'S
          ANIMALS
_____3.FARM ANIMALS
_____4.HOUSE PETS

STOMPER 4X4:_____
_____1.AMC EAGLE
_____2.CHEVY S-10 PICKUP
_____3.CHEVY VAN
_____4.CHEVY BLAZER
_____5.DODGE RAM PICKUP
_____6.FORD RANGER PICKUP
_____7.JEEP RENEGADE
_____8.TOYOTA TERCEL

UNDER 3 YRS:
_____1.ORANGE JEEP
_____2.YELLOW CHEVY VAN
_____3.RED CHEVY BLAZER
_____4.BLUE TOYOTA TERCEL

CARTONS (4):

TINOSAURS:_____
_____1.DINAH
_____2.LINK, THE ELF
_____3.BABY JAD
_____4.MERRY BONES
_____5.GRUMPY SPELL
_____6.TIME TRAVELER FERN
_____7.TINY
_____8.KAVE KOLT KOBBY
CARTON_____

LITTLE TRAVELERS
LEGO BUILDING SETS":_____
_____1.ROADSTER-A-RED
_____2.TANKER BOAT-B-BLUE
_____3.HELICOPTER-C-YELLOW
_____4.AIRPLANE-D-GREEN
UNDER 3 YRS; DUPLO BLOCKS:
_____1.BIRD, with eye
_____2.BOAT, with sailor
CARTONS (4):
_____1. WHICH CAME FIRST?
_____2. VACATION
_____3. ANIMAL POWER
_____4. VEHICLE RHYME

METRO ZOO_____
FLORIDA, FIGURINES

BEACHCOMBER, PAILS_____

BERENSTAIN BEARS I
CHRISTMAS VERSION:_____
_____1.SISTER,on SLED
_____2.PAPA, with RED
          wheelbarrow
_____3.MAMA, shopping cart
_____4.BROTHER, scooter

UNDER 3 YRS: (soft.)
_____1.MAMA
_____2.PAPA

CARTONS (4):

HALLOWEEN, PAILS:_____
_____1.McBOO
_____2.McGOBLIN
_____3.McPUNK'N

AN AMERICAN TAIL
Books:_____
_____1.FIEVEL'S FRIENDS
_____2.TONY AND FIEVEL
_____3.FIEVEL AND TIGER
_____4.FIEVEL'S BOAT TRIP
CARTONS (2):

COLORFORMS PLAYSET:_____
_____1.RMCD
_____2.GRIMACE
_____3.BIRDIE
_____4.PROFESSOR
_____5.HAMBURGLAR
CARTONS (5):

GLOTRON SPACE SHIP_____
CONTAINERS

HAPPY MEALS 1987 CHECK LIST

RUNAWAY ROBOTS:_____
_____1.BOLT, purple
_____2.SKULL, dk. blue
_____3.JAB, yellow
_____4.BEAK, bright blue
_____5.FLAME, red
_____6.COIL, green
CARTON_____

CRAYOLA:_____
_____1.HAMBURGLAR stencil
_____2.BIRDIE stencil
_____3.GRIMACE stencil
_____4.RMCD stencil
UNDER 3 YRS:
_____BAG & STENCIL: RMCD
          driving fire engine.
CARTONS (4):

LITTLE ENGINEER:_____
_____1.GRIMACE STREAK
_____2.RONALD RIDER
_____3.FRY GIRLS EXPRESS
_____4.BIRDIE BRIGHT LITE
_____5.FRY GUYS FLYER

UNDER 3 YRS.:
_____1. FRY GUY HAPPY CAR
_____2.GRIMACE HAPPY TAXI
CARTONS (5):

POTATO HEAD KIDS:_____
_____1. LUMPY
_____2. PAT DUMPLING
_____3. BIG CHIP
_____4. SMARTY PANTS
_____5. DIMPLES
_____6. SPIKE
_____7. POTATO PUFF
_____8. TULIP
_____9. SPUD
_____10.LOLLY
_____11.SLUGGER
_____12.SLICK
CARTON_____

KISSY FUR:_____
_____1.KISSY FUR
_____2.GUS
_____3.FLOYD
_____4.JOLENE
_____5.LENNIE
_____6.TOOT
_____7.BEEHONIE
_____8.DUANE
CARTON_____

MUPPET BABIES:_____
_____1.BABY GONZO
_____2.BABY FOZZIE
_____3.BABY PIGGY
_____4.BABY KERMIT
UNDER 3 YRS:
_____1.PIGGY
_____2.KERMIT
CARTONS (4):

McDONALDLAND BAND:_____
_____1.FRY GUY TRUMPET
_____2.HAMBURGLAR WHISTLE
_____3.RONALD HARMONICA
_____4.GRIMACE SAXOPHONE
_____5.RONALD WHISTLE
_____6.RONALD PAN PIPES
_____7.FRY GUY WHISTLE
_____8.KAZOO
CARTONS (4):

DESIGN-O-SAURS:_____
_____1.RONALD ON
          TYRANNOSAURUS REX
_____2.GRIMACE ON
          PTERODACTYL
_____3.FRY GUY ON
          BRONTOSAURUS
_____4.HAMBURGLAR ON
          TRICERATOPS
UNDER 3 YRS:
_____1.GRIMACE HAPPY TAXI
_____2.FRY GUY RACER
CARTON_____

BOATS 'N FLOATS:_____
_____1.GRIMACE SKI BOAT
_____2.FRY KIDS RAFT
_____3.BIRDIE FLOAT
_____4.McNUGGET LIFE BOAT

CASTLE MAKER/SAND CASTLE
Molds:_____
_____1.CYLINDRICAL, YELLOW
_____2.RECTANGLE, RED
_____3.SQUARE, BLUE
_____4.DOME, BLUE

GHOSTBUSTERS_____
_____1.SLIMER,
          pencil & topper
_____2.STAY PUFT,pad &
          eraser
_____3.CONTAINMENT CHAMBER
          plastic pencil case
_____4.STAY PUFT,sharpener
_____5.GHOSTBUSTERS,ruler
CARTONS (4):

BERENSTAIN BEARS II:_____
_____1.SISTER, wagon
_____2.PAPA, wheelbarrow
_____3.BROTHER, scooter
_____4.MAMA, shopping cart

UNDER 3 YRS: (soft.1 piece)
_____1.MAMA
_____2.PAPA

CARTONS (4):

HALLOWEEN,
3 Pumpkins:_____
_____1.SMILE
_____2.FROWN
_____3.SURPRISE

DISNEY FAVORITES
Activity books:_____
_____1.*CINDERELLA & PRINCE*
_____2.*SWORD & STONE*
_____3.*LADY AND THE TRAMP*
_____4.*DUMBO*
CARTONS (2):

CHANGEABLES:_____
Hands & Feet - not Painted.
_____1.CHICKEN McNUGGETS
_____2.QUARTER POUNDER
          with CHEESE
_____3.FRENCH FRIES
_____4.BIG MAC
_____5.SHAKE, *opens UP.*
_____6.EGG McMUFFIN
CARTON_____

GOOD FRIENDS:_____
Cartons:
_____1. A CLEAN SWEEP
_____2. SNAPSHOT SHUFFLE

MATCHBOX SUPER
16 Matchbox Cars_____

HIGH FLYING
Kites:
_____1.HAMBURGLAR
_____2.RONALD
_____3.BIRDIE
_____4. (?)
CARTON_____

BIGFOOT, WITH "M":_____
0.9" tires
COLORS:black,orange,
lt. blue and "hot" pink.
_____BIGFOOT
_____MS. BIGFOOT
_____SHUTTLE
_____BRONCO

1.3" tires.
COLORS:red, aqua,
dark blue, lt. green.
_____BIGFOOT
_____MS. BIGFOOT
_____SHUTTLE
_____BRONCO

BIGFOOT, WITHOUT "M":_____
0.9" tires
COLORS:black, orange,
lt. blue and "hot" pink.
_____BIGFOOT
_____MS. BIGFOOT
_____SHUTTLE
_____BRONCO

1.3" tires.
COLORS:red, dark blue,
lt. green, black, aqua.
_____BIGFOOT
_____MS. BIGFOOT
_____SHUTTLE
_____BRONCO

HAPPY MEALS 1988 CHECK LIST

BLACK HISTORY:_____
Coloring books:
"*LITTLE MARTIN JR.*"
_____1. Volume I
_____2. Volume II

SAILORS:_____
Four floating toys
_____1.RONALD AIRBOAT,red
_____2.GRIMACE SUB ,purple
_____3.FRY KIDS FERRY,grn.
_____4.HAMBURGLAR SAILBOAT
UNDER 3 YRS:
_____1.GRIMACE SPEEDBOAT
_____2.FRY GUY FLOATER
CARTONS(4):

FROM THE HEART:_____
_____Sheets of Valentines
CARTON_____

DUCK TALES I:_____
_____1.WRIST WALLET
            DECODER
_____2.MAGNIFYING GLASS
_____3.DUCK CODE QUACKER
_____4.TELESCOPE

UNDER 3 YRS:
_____1. MAGIC MOTION MAP
CARTONS (4):

SEA WORLD OF OHIO:_____
_____1.SHAMU WHALE
_____2.DOLLY DOLPHIN
_____3.PERRY PENGUIN
CARTON_____

FRAGGLE ROCK:_____
_____1.GOBO IN HIS CARROT
_____2.RED IN HER RADDISH
_____3.MOKEY
            IN HER EGGPLANT
_____4.WEMBLY & BOOBER
            IN A PICKLE
UNDER 3 YRS:
_____1.GOBO
_____2.RED
CARTONS (4):
_____1.PARTY PICKS
_____2.RADDISHES IN CAVE
_____3.VEGGIE GAME
_____4.SWIMMING HOLE
            BLUES

FRAGGLE ROCK-DOOZER:_____
_____2.BULLDOOZER
_____4.COTTERPIN DOOZER

NEW ARCHIES:_____
_____1.REGGIE
_____2.VERONICA
_____3.ARCHIE
_____4.BETTY
_____5.JUGHEAD
_____6.MOOSE
CARTON_____

SPORT BALL:_____
_____1.BASEBALL, 3".
            Hard plastic.
_____2.FOOTBALL, 5".
            Red & Yellow, soft.
_____3.BASKETBALL, soft.
            With basket.
_____4.TENNIS BALL, soft.
UNDER 3 YRS:
_____BASEBALL (same as #1)
CARTONS (2):
_____1. CLEAR THE COURT
_____2. MATCH POINTS

COSMc! CRAYOLA:_____
_____1.CRAYOLAS (4)
_____2.MARKER
_____3.CHALK STICKS (4)
_____4.MARKER
_____5.PAINT SET

UNDER 3 YRS:
_____1.CRAYONS

CARTONS (4):

SUPER SUMMER:_____
_____1.BALL, inflatable
_____2.SAILBOAT,inflatable
_____3.PAIL, BIRDIE
_____4.PAIL, PROFESSOR
_____5.SAND MOLD (bag)
BAG_____

BAMBI:_____
_____1.FLOWER , skunk
_____2.FRIEND OWL , owl
_____3.THUMPER , rabbit
_____4.BAMBI , deer

UNDER 3 YRS:
_____1.BAMBI, butterfly.
_____2.BAMBI (No b'fly.)
_____3.THUMPER , rabbit

CARTONS (4):
_____1.SPRING,
_____2. WHO-OOO'S THERE ?
_____3. OWL-AWEEN! ,
_____4.SNOW SCENE,

DUCK TALES II:_____
_____1.UNCLE SCROOGE
_____2.LAUNCHPAD
_____3.WEBBY
_____4.NEPHEWS
UNDER 3 YRS:
_____1.HUEY
CARTON _____

SEA WORLD OF TEXAS I:_____
_____1.WHALE
_____2.DOLPHIN
_____3.PENGUIN
_____4.WALRUS
CARTON_____

FLINTSTONE KIDS:_____
_____1.FRED
_____2.WILMA
_____3.BARNEY
_____4.BETTY
UNDER 3 YRS:
_____1.DINO
CARTON_____

HOT WHEELS:_____
_____1.SILVER STREET BEAST
_____2.RED STREET BEAST
_____3 WHITE P-911 TURBO
_____4.BLACK P-911 TURBO
_____5.SILVER SPLIT-WINDOW
_____6.BLACK SPLIT-WINDOW
_____7.TURQUOIS '57 T-BIRD
_____8.WHITE '57 T-BIRD
_____9.BLUE 80'S FIREBIRD
_____10.BLK 80'S FIREBIRD
_____11.SHERRIF PATROL
_____12.RED FIRE CHIEF
CARTON_____

ON THE GO:_____
LUNCH BAGS:
_____1.Yellow
_____2.Blue
LUNCH BOXES:(school scenes)
_____1.Green
_____2.Red
_____3.Blue

MOVEABLES, Figurines:_____
_____1.RMCD
_____2.HAMBURGLAR
_____3.BIRDIE
_____4.PROFESSOR
_____5.FRY GIRL
_____6.CAPTAIN CROOK

OLYMPIC SPORTS II:_____
MEDALLIONS:
_____1.RMCD on bicycle
_____2.BIRDIE,balance beam
_____3.CosMc, basketball
_____4.GRIMACE, soccer
_____5.FRY GAL, diving
_____6.HAMBURGLAR, running
CARTONS (2):

ZOO FACE, MASKS:_____
_____1-a. TOUCAN
_____2-a. MONKEY
_____3-a. TIGER
_____4-a. ALIGATOR
UNDER 3 YRS:
_____1. MONKEY
_____2. TIGER
CARTONS (4):

STORY BOOK MUPPET BABIES
BOOKS:_____
_____1."THE LEGEND OF
          GIMME GULCH"
_____2."JUST KERMIT AND
ME"
_____3."PIGGY, THE LIVING
DOLL"
CARTONS (3):

"PETER RABBIT" BOOKS:_____
_____1."TALE OF SQUIRREL
          NUTKIN"
_____2."TALE OF BENJAMIN
          BUNNY"
_____3."TALE OF FLOPSY
             BUNNIES"
_____4."TALE OF PETER
          RABBIT"
CARTON _____

CRAZY CLINGERS:_____
(WALL CRAWLERS)
_____1. RMCD , parachute.
_____2. GRIMACE,
            Hot-air balloon.
_____3. HAMBURGLAR,
            Hang glider.
_____4. BIRDIE,
            With balloons.

OLIVER & COMPANY:_____
_____1.OLIVER
_____2.FRANCIS
_____3.GEORGETTE
_____4.DODGER
CARTONS (4):
_____1.NOISY NEIGHBORHOOD
_____2.FUNNY BONES
_____3.TRICKY TRIKE
_____4.SHADOW SCRAMBLE

HAPPY MEALS 1989 CHECK LIST

McNUGGET BUDDIES:_____
_____ 1. COWPOKE
_____ 2. SARGE
_____3. CORNY, White Belt
_____3a.CORNEY, Red Belt
_____4. SNORKEL
_____5. FIRST CLASS
_____6. DRUMMER
_____7. SPARKY
_____8. ROCKER
_____ 9. VOLLEY
_____10. BOOMERANG
UNDER 3 YRS:
_____1. SLUGGER
_____2. DAISY
CARTONS (4):

RMCD BEDTIME:_____
_____1.RMCD TOOTHBRUSH.
_____2.PLASTIC CUP
_____3.RMCD BLUE MITT.
_____4.RMCD GLOW-FIGURINE
CARTONS(4)

LITTLE GARDENER:_____
_____1.TROWEL , orange.
_____2.PAIL, blue.
_____3.RAKE, green.
_____4.WATERING CAN

UNDER 3 YRS:
_____1.TROWEL
BAGS (4):

EARSAN, PAILS:_____
With lids & handles.
_____1. PINKY McBUNNY
_____2. WHISKERS McBUNNY
_____3. FLUFFY McBUNNY

MICKEY'S BIRTHDAYLAND:_____
_____1.DONALD DUCK,
         TRAIN ENGINE
_____2.MINNIE MOUSE
         CONVERTIBLE
_____3.GOOFY JALOPY
         SPORT COUPE
_____4.PLUTO'S RUMBLER
_____5.MICKEY'S ROADSTER

UNDER 3 YRS:
_____1.MICKEY'S CONVERT.
_____2.MINNIE'S CONVERT.
_____3.DONALD DUCK'S JEEP
_____4.GOOFY'S CAR
CARTONS (5):

BEACH TOY:_____
Inflatable toys (4):
_____1.CATAMARAN
_____2.BEACH BALL
_____3.FLYING DISC
_____4.SUBMARINE

Sand Pails(3):
_____1. Castle Mold
_____2. RMCD & GRIMACE
_____3. FRY GUYS

Sand Toys (2):
_____1. Spinner Shovel
_____2. Squirting Rake
BAGS (4):

HALLOWEEN, Pumpkin Pails:__
_____1. McBOO yellow
        jack-o-lantern
_____2. McGHOST, white ghost
_____3. McWITCH, green witch

NEW FOOD CHANGEABLE:_____
Hands or Feet are painted.
_____1. QUARTER POUNDER
          GALLACTA BURGER
_____2. HOT CAKES
          ROBO CAKES
_____3. LARGE FRIES
          FRY FORCE
_____4. SHAKE-KRYPTO CUP
          Opens OUT.
_____5. BIG MAC-MACRO MAC
_____6. SOFT-SERVE CONE
          TURBO CONE
_____7. CHEESBURGER
          C2 CHEESEBURGER
_____8. SMALL FRIES
          FRY-BOT

UNDER 3 YRS:
_____1. 3-D CUBE
CARTONS(4):

READ ALONG WITH RONALD:_____
Cassette tapes with books:
_____1. *"DINOSAUR
          IN McDONALDLAND"*
_____2. *"GRIMACE GOES TO
          SCHOOL"*
_____3. *"MYSTERY OF THE
          MISSING FRENCH FRIES"*
_____4. *"THE DAY BIRDIE...
          LEARNED TO FLY"*
BAG, RMCD reading_____

THE LITTLE MERMAID:_____
_____1. FLOUNDER
_____2. URSULA,WITCH
_____3. PRINCE ERIC & CRAB
_____4. ARIEL,MERMAID
CARTONS (4)
BAGS (TESTED)

McDONALD'S
TALKING STORYBOARD:_____
Books with casette tapes:
_____1. *DANGER UNDER
          THE LAKE*
_____2. *AMAZING BIRTHDAY
          ADVENTURE*
_____3. *DINOSAUR BABY BOOM*
_____4. *CREATURE
          IN THE CAVE*
BAG:
_____1. BONES and DODO

MUPPET KIDS:_____
_____1. KERMIT, red bike
_____2. PIGGY, pink bike
_____3. GONZO, yellow bike
_____4. FOZZIE, green bike
MUPPET BABIES BOOKS:
_____1. *THE LEGEND OF
          GIMME GULCH*
_____2. *JUST KERMIT AND ME*
_____3. *PIGGY, THE LIVING
DOLL*
CARTONS (2)

SEA WORLD OF TEXAS II:_____
6" fuzzy, plastic figurines
FIGURINES:
_____1. WHALE , blk & wht.
_____2. SEA OTTER, brown.
_____3. DOLPHIN, grey
SUNGLASSES
With animal frames:
_____1. PENGUIN
_____2. WHALE
CARTON_____

GARFIELD:_____
_____1.GARFIELD, SCOOTER
_____2.GARFIELD,SKATEBOARD
_____3.GARFIELD, 4-WHEELER
_____4.GARFIELD AND ODIE
          ON MOTOR SCOOTER

UNDER 3 YRS:
_____1.GARFIELD
         ROLLER SKATES
_____2.GARFIELD WITH
         TEDDY BEAR
CARTONS(4):
BAG(TEST)

"FUN WITH FOOD":_____
_____1.HAMBURGER GUY
_____2.FRENCH FRY GUY
_____3.SOFT DRINK GUY
_____4.CHICKEN MCNUGGET
CARTONS (4):
_____1.MAKING A SPLASH
_____2.MOVIE MAKING
_____3.3-RING CIRCUS
_____4.IN CONCERT

RESCUE RANGERS:_____
_____1.CHIP'S WHIRLY-CUPTER
_____2.DALE'S ROTOROADSTER
_____3.GADGET'S RESCUE RACER
_____4.MONTEREY JACK'S
         PROPEL-A-PHONE
UNDER 3 YRS:
_____1.GADGET ROCKIN' RIDER
_____2.CHIP'S RACER
CARTONS (4):

RAGGEDY ANN & ANDY:_____
_____1.RAGGEDY ANDY
          ON SLIDE
_____2.GROUCHY BEAR
          ON CAROUSEL
_____3.RAGGEDY ANN
          ON SWING
_____4.CAMEL WITH WRINKLED
          KNEES ON SEE-SAW

Rumored to have been made:
____RAGGEDY CAT ON SEE-SAW
____RAGGEDY DOG, SPIN-RIDER
UNDER 3 YRS:
_____CAMEL, WRINKLE-KNEES
CARTON:

"LEGO MOTION":_____
_____1a.GYRO BIRD
_____1b.TURBO FORCE
_____2a.SWAMP STINGER
_____2b.LIGHTNING STRIKER
_____3a.LAND LASER
_____3b.SEA EAGLE
_____4a.WIND WHIRLER
_____4b.SEA SKIMMER

UNDER 3 YRS
DUPLO BLOCKS:
_____1.GIDDY THE GATOR
_____2.TUTTLE THE TURTLE
CARTONS (4):

HAPPY MEALS 1990 CHECK LIST

FUNNY FRY FRIENDS:_____
_____1. HOOPS
_____2. ROLLIN' ROCKER
_____3. MATEY
_____4. GADZOOKS
_____5. TRACKER
_____6. ZZZ'S
_____7. TOO TALL
_____8. SWEET CUDDLES

UNDER 3 YRS:
_____1. LIL CHIEF
_____2. LIL DARLIN
CARTONS (4):

BERENSTAIN BEARS BOOKS:_____
STORY BOOKS:
_____1. *"LIFE WITH PAPA"*
_____2. *"SUBSTITUTE*
TEACHER"
_____3. *"ATTIC TREASURE"*
_____4. *"EAGER BEAVERS"*

ACTIVITY BOOKS:
_____5. *"LIFE WITH PAPA"*
_____6. *"SUBSTITUTE TEACHER*
_____7. *"ATTIC TREASURE"*
_____8. *"EAGER BEAVERS"*

BAGS (Test)_____
CARTONS:

VALENTINE
scratch and sniff cards:___
_____1. CHOCOLATE
_____2. STRAWBERRY
CARTON_____

"PEANUTS":_____
_____1. SNOOPY'S HAY HAULER
_____2. CHARLIE BROWN'S
            SEED BAG'N'TILLER
_____3. LUCY'S APPLE CART
_____4. LINUS' MILK MOVER

UNDER 3 YRS:
_____1. SNOOPY
_____2. CHARLIE BROWN
CARTONS:

BEACH TOY:_____
INFLATABLES:
_____1. CATMARAN
_____2. BEACH BALL
_____3. FLYING DISC
_____4. SUBMARINE

SAND PAILS:
_____1. RMCD AND GRIMACE
_____2. FUNNY FRY FRIENDS
_____3. SAND CASTLE PAIL

UTENSILS:
_____6. SAND SPINNER SHOVEL
_____8. SQUIRTING RAKE
BAGS:

"BARBIE/ HOT WHEELS":_____
BARBIE FIGURINES:
_____1. BARBIE, pink gown
_____2. BARBIE, black dress
_____3. BARBIE, pink dress
_____4. BARBIE, white gown

HOT WHEELS:
_____5. Wht. CORVETTE Cnvrt
_____6. Red FERRARI
_____7. Slvr. PONTIAC FRBRD
_____8. Tourq. CHEVY Z-28
CARTONS (2):

CAMP McDONALDLAND:_____
_____1. CANTEEN
_____2. UTENSILS
_____3. BIRDIE CAMPER
        MESS KIT
_____4. CUP, collapsible
CARTONS (4):
BAGS (test):

JUNGLE BOOK:_____
_____1. BALOO, bear
_____2. KING LOUIE, ape
_____3. KAA, snake
_____4. SHERE KHAN, tiger

UNDER 3 YRS:
_____1. JUNIOR , Elephant
_____2. MOWGLI ,boy in pot
CARTONS (4):

I LIKE BIKES:_____
_____1.BASKET, RONALD
_____2.SQUEEZE HORN,
        FRY GUY
_____3.BIRDIE SPINNER
_____4.MIRROR, GRIMACE
BAGS:

SUPER MARIO BROS 3:_____
_____1. MARIO
_____2. LUIGI
_____3. LITTLE GOOMBA
_____4. KOOPA PARATROOPA
UNDER 3 YRS.:
_____1. MARIO squeeze toy
CARTONS:

McDONALDLAND DOUGH :_____
_____1.Red with RMCD star
_____2.Green with octagon
_____3.Purple with GRIMACE
        diamond
_____4.Pink with circle
_____5.Yellow with RMCD
        square
_____6.Blue with Fry Guy
        octagon
_____7.Orange with GRIMACE
        triangle
_____8.White with heart
CARTONS:

SPORTSBALL:_____
Soft, stitched, vinyl balls
_____1.SOCCERBALL, red and
        yellow hexagons.
_____2.BASKETBALL, Brown.
        black lines.
_____3.BASEBALL, White.
        red stitching.
_____4.FOOTBALL, yellow.
        red laces.
CARTON_____

McDONALDLAND CARNIVAL:_____
_____1.RONALD ON CAROUSEL
_____2.GRIMACE IN
        TURN-AROUND
_____3.BIRDIE ON SWING
_____4.HAMBURGLAR
        ON FERRIS WHEEL
UNDER 3 YRS:
_____ GRIMACE ON ROCKER
CARTON_____

McDONALDLAND CRAFT KIT:_____
_____1.HAMBURGLAR PAINT
        BRUSH & PAINTS
_____2.GRIMACE TAPE
MEASURE
_____3.FRY GUY SCISSORS
_____4.McDONALD'S
        TAPE DISPENSER
UNDER 3 YRS:
_____ GRIMACE FIGURINE
CARTON_____

HAPPY HATS:_____
_____1.SAFARI HAT. orange,
        Fry Guys.
_____2.CONSTRUCTION HAT.
          yellow, Grimace.
_____3.FIREMAN HAT. red,
          RMCD.
_____4.ENTERTAINER HAT.
          green, Birdie.

MIX EM UP MONSTERS:_____
_____1. GROPPLE
_____2. CORKLE
_____3. BLIBBLE
_____4. THUGGER
CARTON_____

THE TOM AND JERRY BAND:_____
_____1.TOM WITH KEYBOARD
_____2.DROOPY & MICROPHONE
_____3.JERRY WITH DRUM SET
_____4.SPIKE WITH BASE
UNDER 3 YRS:
_____SPIKE
BAGS:
_____smaller;blk, wht, red
        and YELLOW
_____larger ; NO yellow

McDRIVE THRU CREW:_____
_____1. HAMBURGER
          IN CATSUP RACER
_____2. SHAKE IN
          MILK CARTON ZOOMER
_____3. McNUGGET IN
          EGG ROADSTER
_____4. FRIES IN
          POTATO SPEEDSTER
CARTON_____

FRY BENDERS:_____
_____1. FROGGY
_____2. GRAND SLAM
_____3. ROADIE
_____4. FREESTYLE
UNDER 3 YRS
_____ TUNES
CARTON_____

MAC TONIGHT:_____
_____1. OFF ROADER
_____2. SPORTS CAR
_____3. SURF SKI
_____4. SCOOTER
_____5. MOTORCYCLE
_____6. AIRPLANE
UNDER 3 YRS:
_____ MAC, purple
skateboard
CARTON:

RAGGEDY ANN & ANDY":_____
_____1. RAGGEDY ANDY
          WITH SLIDE
_____2. RAGGEDY ANN
          WITH SWING SET
_____3. GROUCHY BEAR
          ON CAROUSEL
_____4. CAMEL WITH SEE-SAW
UNDER 3 YRS:
_____CAMEL, WRINKLED KNEES
CARTON:
_____ SCHOOLHOUSE

TURBO MACS:_____
_____1.RMCD RACER
_____2.HAMBURGLAR SPORTS
_____3.GRIMACE RACER
_____4.BIRDIE SPORTS
_____4a.BIG MAC SPORTS
UNDER 3 YRS:
_____1.RMCD, FORMULA-1
CARTON:

DINK THE LITTLE DINOSAUR:
_____1.CRUSTY SEA TURTLE
_____2.AMBER CORYTHAURUS
_____3.SCAT,
          COMPSAGNATHUS
_____4.SHYLER EDAPHORAURS
_____5.FLAPPER, PTERONDON
_____6. DINK, APATASAURUS
CARTON_____

HALLOWEEN, Pumpkin Pails:__
_____1.ORANGE JACK-O-LANTERN
        "Day-glo"
_____2.WHITE GHOST
        glows-in-the-dark.
_____3.GREEN WITCH,
        "Day-glo"

TALESPIN:_____
_____1.KIT'S RACING PLANE
_____2.MOLLY'S BIPLANE
_____3.BALOO'S SEAPLANE
_____4.WILDCAT'S
          FLYING MACHINE
UNDER 3 YRS:
_____1.BALOO'S SEAPLANE
_____2.WILDCAT'S JET
CART0NS:

RESCUE DOWN UNDER:_____
Movie cameras.
_____1. WILBUR , seagull
_____2. JAKE , kangaroo
_____3. BERNARD & BIANCA
          mice
_____4. CODY & MARAHUTE
          boy
UNDER 3 YRS:
_____1.BERNARD
          mouse in cheese
CARTONS:

HAPPY MEALS 1991 CHECK LIST

GOOD MORNING:_____
_____1. RMCD TOOTHBRUSH
_____2. RMCD PLAY CLOCK
_____3. PLASTIC CUP
_____4. MCDONALDLAND
          CONNECTABLE COMB.
UNDER 3 YRS:
_____CUP WITH FRUIT JUICE
BAG_____

TINY TOON ADVENTURES:_____
_____1. PLUCKY DUCK
_____2. BUSTER BUNNY
_____3. GOGO DODO
_____4. DIZZY DEVIL
UNDER 3 YRS:
_____1. PLUCKY DUCK
_____2. GOGO DODO
CARTONS:
_____1. WACKYLAND
_____2. ACME ACRES
_____3. ACME ACRES FOREST
_____4. ACME LOONIVERSITY

MCDLAND CIRCUS PARADE_____
_____1. RONALD MCDONALD
          RINGMASTER
_____2. BIRDIE
          BAREBACK RIDER
_____3. FRY GUY
          ELEPHANT TRAINER
_____4. GRIMACE
          PLAYING CALLIOPE
BAG_____

MUPPET BABIES:_____
_____1. BABY KERMIT
_____2. BABY MISS PIGGY
_____3. BABY FOZZIE
_____4. BABY GONZO'
BAG_____

GRAVEDALE HIGH:_____
_____1.FRAKENTYKE
_____2.SID (INVISIBLE KID)
_____3.VINNIE STOKER
_____4.CLEOFATRA
BAG:_____

ALVIN & THE CHIPMUNKS:_____
_____1.ALVIN AND
         ELECTRIC GUITAR
_____2.SIMON WITH
         VIDEO CAMERA
_____3.BRITTANY WITH
         JUKE BOX
_____4.THEODORE WITH
         RAP MACHINE
BAG_____

PIGGSBURG PIGS! TM:_____
_____1. PORTLY AND PIGHEAD
       ON CYCLE WITH SIDECAR
_____2. PIGGY AND QUACKERS
          ON CRATE RACER
_____3. REMBRANDT IN
          BARNYARD HOT ROD
_____4. HUFF AND PUFF
          ON CATAPULT
BAG_____

MIGHTY MINI 4 X 4:_____
_____1.DUNE BUSTER
_____2.MIGHTY MINI
         4X4 L'IL CLASSIC
_____3.MIGHTY MINI
         4X4 CARGO CLIMBER
_____4.POCKET PICKUP
CARTON_____

MCDINO CHANGEABLES:_____
_____HAPPY MEAL-O-DON
_____QUARTER POUNDER
         WITH CHEESE-O-SAUR
_____MCNUGGETS-O-SAURUS
_____HOTCAKES-O-DACTYL
_____FRY-CERATOPS
_____BIG MAC-O-SAURUS REX
_____TRI-SHAKE-ATOPS
_____MCDINO CONE
UNDER 3 YRS:
_____BRONTO CHEESEBURGER
_____SMALL FRY-CERATOPS
BAG_____

HALLOWEEN "MCBOO BAGS"
_____WITCH
_____GHOST
_____FRANKENTYKE

101 DALMATIONS:_____
_____1.PONGO
_____2.LUCKY
_____3.THE COLONEL
          AND SERGEANT TIBS
_____4.CRUELLA DE VIL
CARTONS:
_____1.ROGER & ANITA
_____2.ROGER AT PIANO
_____3.COLONEL & PUPPIES
_____4.BARN

BARBIE/HOT WHEELS:_____
BARBIE DOLLS:
_____ALL AMERICAN BARBIE
_____COSTUME BALL BARBIE
_____LIGHTS & LACE BARBIE
_____HAPPY BRTHDAY BARBIE
_____HAWAIIAN FUN BARBIE
_____WEDDING DAY MIDGE
_____ICE CAPADES BARBIE
_____MY FIRST BARBIE

HOT WHEELS:
_____'55 CHEVY
_____'63 CORVETTE
_____'57 T-BIRD
_____CAMARO Z-28
_____'55 CHEVY
_____'63 CORVETTE
_____'57 T-BIRD
_____CAMARO Z-28

UNDER 3 YRS. HOT WHEELS:
_____YEL. WRENCH,RED HAMMER
CARTONS (4):
_____1. BARBIE ON STAGE
_____2. BARBIE AT HOME
_____3. HOT WHLS. RACERS
_____4. HOT WHLS. CRUISING

DISCOVER THE RAIN FOREST:
_____STICKER SAFARI
_____PAINT IT WILD
_____RONALD MCDONALD...
       .AMAZON KINGDOM
_____WONDERS IN THE WILD
BAG_____

MCDLAND "CONNECTIBLES"
_____RONALD MCDONALD
      IN A SOAP-BOX RACER
_____HAMBURGLAR
      IN AN AIRPLANE
_____GRIMACE
      IN A WAGON
_____BIRDIE ON A TRICYCLE
BAG_____

CRAZY VEHICLES:_____
_____RONALD MCDONALD BUGGY
_____HAMBURGLAR TRAIN
_____GRIMACE CAR
_____BIRDIE AIRPLANE
BAG_____

McDONALDLAND HAPPY MEAL_____
Connectable bikes.
_____RONALD
_____GRIMACE
_____HAMBURGLAR
_____BIRDIE
Bag_____

FRIENDLY SKIES MEAL:_____
UNITED AIRLINES
_____RMCD in Airliner
_____GRIMACE in Airliner
_____TRAY LINER
_____UTENSILS
CARTON_____

SUPER LOONEY TUNES:_____
_____TAZ-FLASH
_____SUPER BUGS
_____WONDER PIG
_____BAT DUCK
UNDER 3 YRS:
_____BAT DUCK .
BAG_____

HOOK:_____
Bathtub toys:
_____PETER PAN on raft.
_____MERMAID, wind up.
_____CAPTAIN HOOK in boat.
_____RUFIO squirt toy.
CARTONS:
_____ PIRATE TOWN
_____ JOLLY ROGER
_____ WENDY'S LONDON HOUSE
_____ NEVERTREE

GLOSSARY:

Abbreviations used to describe condition:
MINT =   New, never used, unfolded or unpackaged
AVG =   Average condition.
NP   =   Not or Never Packaged; loose.
MIP =   Mint-in-package. In original, sealed container.

Abbreviations used to save space:
RMCD   =   RONALD McDONALD
McDLAND = McDONALDLAND

CONTRIBUTORS:

LYLE & JEANIE ANDERSON
    "COLLECTIBLES"
MORGAN HILL, CALIFORNIA

RESOURCES:

"HAPPY MEALS LISTING"
MCDONALD'S ARCHIVES
DEPARTMENT 159
2010 EAST HIGGINS ROAD
ELK GROVE, ILLINOIS 60007
(PLEASE SEND LARGE SASE.)

"THE MCDONALD'S COLLECTOR
    CLUB" (NEWSLETTER)
    C/O   JIM WOLFE
    2315 ROSS DRIVE
    STOW, OHIO 44224
    (ANNUAL CONVENTION:
     APRIL 11, 1992)

"COLLECTING TIPS
    NEWSLETTER"
 Tips for collecting
McDonald's Restaurant
    Memorabilia
MEREDITH WILLIAMS,EDITOR
    P.O. BOX 633
  JOPLIN, MO 64802
$19.75/yr 12 issues

"THE ILLUSTRATED GUIDE
TO McDONALD'S HAPPY MEAL
  BOXES, PREMIUMS AND
    PROMOTIONS."
    JOYCE LOSONSKY
7506 SUMMER LEAVE LANE
  COLUMBIA, MD 21046
$6.95 plus $2.00 Shipping

"COLLECTOR GLASS NEWS"
Quarterly   Publication
BOX 308, Slippery Rock,
     PA 16507
  $10.00 per year

INDEX: